SMASH SMASH SMASH

—•—

The True Story of Kai the Hitchhiker

Philip Fairbanks

Smash, Smash, Smash:
The True Story of Kai the Hitchhiker

Printed in the United States of America

Library of Congress Cataloging-in-Publication Data

DEDICATION

Dedicated to my grandmother Norene Dougan and my best friend Darrah Simpson-Walters. Wish they were here to see it.

Also dedicated to all survivors of assault and trauma and to all those wrongfully imprisoned, and to everyone who seeks justice, or to right some wrong.

TABLE OF CONTENTS

LIST OF ILLUSTRATIONS

FOREWORD

BY ALISSA FLECK

When I first met Phil, he was already swept up in investigating Houston, Texas-based accused conman, Lucky Srinivasan, and his roster of lackeys, whose alleged racketeering exploits had cost his victims more than just their life savings. In 2016, finding himself in a pit of financial ruin thanks to his own part in his father's ill-conceived exploits spanning many decades, Lucky's son Jeremy Raju Srinivasan murdered his wife and two young children in cold blood before turning the gun on himself.

I was solicited to assist in investigating this story by one of Phil's more persistent sources, a source who thought the story was too big for one man to take on alone. One man, that is, who was recently paralyzed below the neck during a massage-gone-terribly-wrong. Yes, when I met Phil, he was fighting to expose injustices despite having just sustained a life-threatening injury himself, while living abroad.

If it sounds like the ultimate underdog story, I think that's because Phil doesn't mess around with any other kind. Phil convinced me our source, who was no Erin Brockovich in his demeanor nor delivery, had a story worth hearing. The idea of an imperfect "victim" – or maybe even an unhinged whistleblower – is a consistent theme in the stories Phil brings to the light. He has a keen ability – and the patience – as an interviewer, to toggle between different interpersonal styles, to be vulnerable himself, to help put interviewees at ease to tell their stories. He has also honed that hard-fought skill for a journalist of putting down a boundary when that is what's required. Hard-fought, in part, because journalism is by nature a job you take home with you, one where you walk at times a nearly imperceptible line between therapist and investigator.

In *Smash, Smash, Smash*, Phil has found a perfectly imperfect subject – a sort of folk antihero who was spit out by society after his viral fifteen minutes had run their course. A man with no past and no last name can become a vessel for all our wildest projections. Being an effective journalist means understanding that when you get to know a "victim" or "survivor" you must also shed all your expectations of what that person could or should be.

You must neither glorify that person as a saint, nor cast aspersions about how they wound up in that position. Reality is far too complicated for such reductions. Being human is far too complicated. Most stories don't wrap up nicely in the end. And it takes a special kind of human to tell these stories and also remain human.

Why more mainstream outlets didn't seem inclined to take up the fight for Kai, and the damaging way Kai's story was presented in the media, are explored throughout Phil's book. Kai is a male survivor of alleged sexual assault, and that's something we haven't been comfortable addressing as a society, which is to our own detriment. Kai was also living unhoused and struggling with mental illness, which made him an unsympathetic figure compared to the survivors who tend to get mainstream news coverage. But Kai matters and how we tell his story matters. And there are a lot more Kais out there, falling victim to the system.

Journalism today is a constant anxious hum. There's little reward for slowing down, eschewing scoops, pursuing narrow obsessions and seeking deep, lingering truths. It's not a lucrative nor glamorous career. The payoff is only in knowing the story you tell is as close to the truth as truth comes, and you, the closest thing there is to a guide to it. And hopefully someone who has suffered will breathe a little easier, but even that is a complicated ask.

Phil is not the kind of journalist who files a story and gets on with his life. That passion and integrity shine through in this book, and generally in the way Phil makes you care about the people he's covering.

I've seen Phil stand up to the bullies intimidating his sources without a second thought to his own safety. This is in a media climate where the editor of *Vanity Fair* can awake to find a decapitated cat's head outside his apartment, payback for the sin of covering Jeffrey Epstein. I've seen Phil pull from a seemingly bottomless pool of compassion toward society's down and out, when it would be easier to adopt a disillusioned cynicism. He is a true champion for the underdog, even when the underdog is a pain in the ass.

Most people shrugged off Kai the Hitchhiker, they were happy to let him be a colorful viral moment and then they were happy to file him away as irredeemably troubled. But in Kai I think Phil sees a kindred spirit of sorts, another damaged idealist whose freedom he'll, without a second thought – even whilst paralyzed from the neck down and wheelchair-bound – sacrifice some of his own to fight for. The way Kai, without a second thought, grabbed a hatchet and repeatedly smashed it into Jett McBride's head when McBride grabbed a woman off the street and violently assaulted her. It's about the principle of the fight. The gut instinct that someone else's need perfectly matches your drive to stand up for them. Old-school journalists might accuse Phil of getting too attached, too emotional. However, Kai's story ends, I'm heartened to know there are journalists like Phil out there continuing to fight through their journalistic acts for better human understanding and connection between us all. When I read this book, as with so many things Phil has written, I feel that I am in good hands, being carefully guided to the truth.

INTRODUCTION

BY WENDY S. PAINTING

In his latest book, Philip Fairbanks wields a wealth of laboriously earned evidence and detail, the product of five years of research, to tell a harrowing and heartbreaking tale nobody (until him) deemed worthy of telling, and some would rather remain untold.

The story is that of Caleb McGillivary, aka Kai The Hitchhiker, who most were content to let remain a caricature. An internet meme. A joke.

To tell this story, Fairbanks, out of necessity, attempts and often succeeds in sorting sensationalism from surety and countering rumor with reality. When unable to do so, it is only because of missing information resulting from the sloppy destruction of evidence and the refusal of certain people with crucial information to speak about the case, an investigatory dilemma with which I am all too familiar.

In his characteristically engaging style and with a dexterous balance of compassion, curiosity, and analysis, the author walks the reader through a hellish nightmare; one that Kai was born into and in which he continues to exist.

Fair warning: this nightmare is populated by more than a few sick, twisted fuckers; villains that diabolically devour and discard the most vulnerable among us. Only to do it again. And again. And again. Smash. Smash. Smash.

This is not only a story about Kai, however. It is also about broader and just as troubling systemic problems plaguing our culture and institutions of social control.

Fairbanks methodically peels back, one gruesome layer at a time, the calloused coating that shields the reality of a criminal justice system rotten to its core.

His meticulously and doggedly researched and stunningly well-documented account exposes the long reach and abounding depth of institutionalized fuckery – abuse, distortions, lies, and omissions – startling conflicts of interest – corruption – the very sort of sanctioned shenanigans that, in a larger sense, allowed, protected and even nurtured the type of familial fuckery faced by his subject, Kai, who, confronted by all of this never really had much of a chance, neither as a child or as an adult.

At the book's conclusion, Fairbanks challenges certain squeamish individuals who stealthily inhabit and, in some cases, actually helped construct the scaffolding of the labyrinthian hellscape he guides us through to "bring it on." To put up or shut up. No slouch, Fairbanks answers his own call and brings it, and it is horrific, an ouroboros of trauma from start to finish.

But in this bringing, numerous questions are raised, not only about the fairness of Kai's criminal trial and its outcome but also those surrounding sexual consent and who society permits the status of victim...and who it does not, and about sprawling abuses in a much wider system.

In doing so, Fairbanks renders a memed man real, wiping the clown paint off his subject's face to reveal the portrait of an actual person whose story is much deeper than anyone might imagine. A person whose story is worth telling.

The author does not pussyfoot around the empathy he has for his subject. Nor should he. In his humanization of Kai, the so-called Hatchet Wielding Hitchhiker, internet sensation cum societies' easily disposable trash, Fairbanks does what so many journalists, internet experts, attorneys, social workers, clergy members, and guardians (whether socially or self-appointed) of all that is proper should have done from the beginning. Their jobs.

AUTHOR'S NOTE

It's been about five years since my first article about Caleb McGillivary was published in *The Inquisitr*. Not long after that, I conducted a series of telephone interviews. I was taken aback by how implausible the inherent corruption was: evident in multiple conflicts of interest; and an apparent cover-up during the investigation, that was allowed to go practically un-challenged from the prosecutor's mouth to the media. All that ugliness nakedly on display surely should have attracted a frenzy of media interest.

Over the years, a sickening realization came to mind. As far as reporters covering the case, I seem to be one of the "experts" if not "an authority." Certainly, one of the few, if not only, journalists who took the time to check Kai's claims and allegations against the evidence at hand.

It might be kind of nice being a leading authority on some benign subject. Rare arthropods, maybe? I could dig being a foremost authority on some obscure Flemish Renaissance-era painter's oeuvre, for sure. The gravity of the situation can be almost overwhelming, though, when your expertise is on a subject about which a human life hangs in the balance.

So, you can imagine my mixed feelings when a production company known for prestige projects approached me with the idea of using some of my work in a film for one of the "Big 3" streaming companies.

I was flattered, of course. Probably the first in a wave of emotions to come up. The thought that Kai's words, from calls I'd recorded, might achieve a bit of immortality. Even better, the prospect that the film could make a difference. Something like *The Thin Blue Line*, one of the most important and influential works in the entirety of the corpus of "True Crime." Like Truman Capote's *In Cold Blood*, it is a work that somehow manages to both define and transcend the boundaries of "True Crime."

After a few rounds of emails, a call was set up. Everyone I had dealt with was pleasant and nice, but I couldn't shake the feeling I was being purposefully put at ease. For what reasons I couldn't tell. Hell, I couldn't even tell if I was just being paranoid because of my close connection to the story. Admittedly compounded by the investment of time, work, and emotional energy I'd put into it for some years. They understood that I might be quite attached to the story (specifically to the "materials" they wished me to license for their use). And of course, the more I thought about it, the more worried I was about the misrepresentation of my work or Kai himself and the case.

And to be honest, attached is not the right word for this case, or for another case I've been working on for the past few years. The second involved a decades-long running fraud ring connected to multiple murders.

I finally managed to get some interest from journalist Alissa Fleck (*Newsweek, SF Gate, Houston Chronicle, Huffington Post, Adweek,* and others).

Apart from her, I'd struggled to get any other reporters or outlets to even take a look. That or being ghosted after some initial interest is shown. The situation is similar to the work of Justine Barron, another noteworthy journalist who pursues cases wherever they lead. Whether or not the major papers are interested in doing due diligence themselves. For whatever reason, there are incredibly important stories that are suppressed, sometimes for years. Just look at how Harvey Weinstein, Jeffrey Epstein, Peter Nygard, and others managed to float along all those years.

With Kai's case and that of the Texas-based Ponzi ring, I've spent years researching and tracking down the truth. In the hopes of holding it to the light. I also got to know the living, breathing humans that exist at the other end of the story. Many of my biggest stories are the smallest ones. For me, success is exposing some injustice or imbalance. Some wrong to be righted.

For instance, the honor student nearly expelled over doctor-recommended CBD oil being mistaken for THC oil by an ignorant school administration. The case of a young man selling the herbal plant medicine kratom in Tennessee. A story I covered that would be a turning point in the war for kratom legality in the state. Shortly after the case, the attorney general expressed a formal opinion that the plant was not included in a blanket synthetic drug ban. The couple arrested with kratom in their car. Initially charged with distributing heroin. Their life and small business thrown into disarray as a result. These are stories no one else was telling, or at least not in totality.

In each of those above cases, an eventual positive outcome would be achieved. Even if the only thing I was able to do was to provide some hope to victims of outrageous fortune. To make sure their stories were heard. The result was something I could—and do— take seriously. Something I take pride in. It's rewarding to have achieved success (by Emerson's standards anyway) by having made someone breathe a little easier, having made their life a little less hard for the day.

In Kai's case, the stakes are too high. Not to mention the evidence of corruption is so ample and readily available to just leave it be.

So yes, I suppose that at the very least you could say I was a little "attached" to the story. In my first email back to the production company, I pointed out that I was the sole, or nearly only, source of several salient points of information about the case. That these claims were backed up by evidence released in discovery: crime scene photos, investigative notes, and interviews.

They too had read the entirety of the available transcripts, they told me. However, they warned me, that they wouldn't be "focusing" on the trial or the investigation.

That would be a totally different documentary, they said. My dream of an Errol Morris-style hit film freeing an innocent man were, if not dashed at this point, precariously hanging by a thread like a loose tooth spinning, barely affixed to the gum.

So here it was. My Catch-22. My very own Faustian bargain. And though it has been quite a while since I've read Goethe, I almost certainly recall there being no section on freeing one's soul from the grips of Mephistopheles come in the guise of a documentary materials release form. I knew I had no place to tell them what should or should not be in the documentary. That would be, not only in bad taste but a violation of journalistic ethics on my part. That said, I made it clear I would gladly sign over usage rights if they could make sure to include at least a handful of those major facts that point to the cover-up and, dare I say it, yes, a conspiracy that had taken place.

It was then made plain and simple to me. The best possible way to get that information, Kai's side of the story, on the books for them would be to let him speak. Kai had declined involvement with the documentary before they spoke to me, however, and they only used people "directly related" to stories in their documentaries which counted me out.

As it turns out, my fears of potentially making a deal with the devil were unfounded. A producer at the company informed me just as they were going into post-production that they were using other material "to lay out Kai's defense." Despite my precautions and concerns, I would be lying if I said I wasn't disappointed after hoping that a tangential connection to a major documentary and my name in the credits might help me get this story the attention it deserves.

No worries, though. The interviews that were licensed for and would have appeared in the documentary were transcribed and will be available online. Links to the recordings on YouTube will be there as well as links to all relevant files, court documents, crime scene photos, and more both in cloud storage and at bit.ly/kaidocs and philfairbanks.com.

Kai is at the center of the book, but at the same time the book is about how his case is just one of many examples. That's the scary part. If his case was some crazy exception that'd be awful still; but what's so chilling is we know about this case only because he was mistaken for someone who wasn't well known. Galfy wanted a vagrant, somebody who could be used and discarded, someone with no ties; he chose wrong but even so, they were able to do this.

Now imagine if you don't have worldwide press coverage of your story.

CHAPTER 1

TWO FATEFUL RIDES

It was a chilly but humid day in Fresno, February 1st, 2013.[1] Between the time the frigid, overcast skies broke with sunlight until the day would turn to cold, foggy night several lives would be forever changed. It was the day that Jett Simmons McBride picked up a young "homefree" hitchhiker. It was the day that Rayshawn Neely would be nearly crippled.[2] And it was the day that Caleb McGillivary,* better known as "Kai the Hatchet-Wielding Hitchhiker" would become a folk hero to millions across the world.[3]

Kai earned his "hatchet-wielding hitchhiker" moniker during that first ride that brought him to the attention of the internet at large. Kai had been picked up by Jett Simmons McBride, a 6-foot-4, nearly 300-pound, 54-year-old man who boasted to Kai about raping a 14-year-old girl in the Virgin Islands[4] just before the chaos he would unleash on that fateful Fresno day. McBride also loudly bragged that he was, in fact, Jesus Christ reincarnated.

---

* Kai's legal name is Caleb McGillivary, but some court documents and newspaper stories have his name improperly listed as "McGillvary."

As a result, he reasoned, he could do anything he wanted. As if to prove his point, he took a sharp turn towards some Pacific Gas & Electric employees doing roadwork outside.[5]

"He's like, well I've come to realize I'm Jesus Christ and I can get away with anything I want to. Watch this, and there's a whole crew of construction people in front of me and most of them jumped aside and one pinned underneath," Kai explained in the interview that initially made him a star.

"He said 'I am God. I am Jesus. I was sent here to take all the [racial slurs] to heaven,'"[6] Nick Starkey, one of the PG&E workers on the scene claimed. Neely said he never heard the racial slurs, but something about being the victim of attempted vehicular homicide tends to do a number on one's memory and focus.

McBride pinned Rayshawn Neely against a vehicle at which point, Kai jumped out to help. McBride also attacked a woman on the scene. Kai shared in his memorable interview how he feared McBride might seriously harm her if he didn't spring into action. The woman on the scene confirmed that Kai had indeed saved her. As Kai put it, without his fortunate appearance at the scene there would have been "hella lot more bodies."[7]

With Rayshawn dangerously pinned by McBride's vehicle, Tanya Baker, who was at the scene attempted to help him. At this point, McBride turned on her as well.[8]

"Like a guy that big can snap a woman's neck like a pencil stick," Kai explained why he sprung into action. "So I fucking ran up behind him with a hatchet—smash, smash, suh-mash!"[9]

The interview with Jessob Reisbeck made an instant star out of Kai.

Something about the heroic encounter, Kai's character, and his message of redemption resonated within the public consciousness. "Before I say anything else, I want to say no matter what you've done, you deserve respect, even if you make mistakes. You're lovable and it doesn't matter your looks, skills, or age, or size or anything. You're worthwhile... no one can take that away from you."[10]

February 7, 2013, Jessob Reisbeck caught back up with who he described as a "world-class hero." Reisbeck, who continues to keep in touch with Kai "found him after 5 or 6 days" to conduct a follow-up interview.

Kai's cheeky humor shined through with portions sounding like an Abbott and Costello bit: "What have you been up to since?" "About 6 foot," Kai replied. He also admitted he didn't like the idea of a "stereotypical normal life." That meant, in part, no 9 to 5 job or smartphone to weigh him down.

"Are you aware what you've become?" Reisbeck asked. "I've seen it." As for his thoughts on the outpouring of support from all over the country even worldwide, Kai's response was simply: "Shock and awe." Asked if he was happy about the exciting new world he'd accidentally entered, his reply was simply, "I'd prefer if I was American, but yeah."

Jessob asked if there was anything else Kai would like to say to "all of your fans right now, because you do have them around the world." Kai spurned the hero worship. Instead, he offered another simple, heartfelt message to the many who idolized him since the selfless act. "I do not own you, I do not have you, please do not be obsessed. Thank you, love, respect, I value you."[11]

Within 48 hours of the KMPH interview being released and subsequently going viral, Kai was a household name earning accolades and mentions in media worldwide. *Philadelphia* magazine called Kai "the hero millennials need" in a February 8th article from 2013.[12]

In the next few days, his star would continue to rise as he was featured in Autotune the News.[13] Kai also released a cover of the song "Wagon Wheel."[14] An IndieGogo page[15] was also set up to get him a new surfboard. The *Philly* magazine piece marks Kai as emblematic of the millennial generation, especially following the economic upheaval of the 2008 housing bubble which resulted in severe inflation, higher cost of living, and a recession we still haven't truly escaped.

Just under three weeks out, Kai had his first day in court, perhaps foreshadowing what was to come in just about three months. He had just appeared on "Jimmy Kimmel Live"[16] and would now be stealing the show during the preliminary hearing against Jett McBride. Despite some of the urban myths surrounding this story, Kai did not kill McBride. McBride had told his wife that Kai was the "coolest son-of-a-bitch" he had ever met. Even expressing a desire to "adopt" the homefree hitchhiker. And spurious claims that Kai may have made up the story of underage rape in the Virgin Islands were refuted by McBride himself admitting the act to police on the scene. Kai's court appearance inspired laughter and spawned headlines further cementing his place as a beloved character to so many.[17]

But by the time Jett Simmons McBride was tried in California, Kai was unable to appear.[18] The lack of one of the primary witnesses in attendance likely altered the disposition of the case according to Scott Baly, McBride's defense attorney. By January 2014, McBride was found guilty on some, but not all charges. The most serious charges, that of attempted murder, would not go through and even the charges he was found guilty of only resulted in psychiatric confinement for a maximum of 9 years. He was sent up to the famous Atascadero State Hospital rather than prison. Atascadero had been home for a time to the likes of serial killers like Tex Watson, Ed Kemper, and Roy Norris among others.

"I won't say whether it hurt or helped, it affected everything," Baly told the press.[19] Admitting that he had hoped for acquittal on all charges. "I think there's mixed emotions for all of us. I mean certainly, I think the moment not guilty on count one was read there was relief; it was followed shortly by a guilty reading on count two and count three so there's a different feeling on those charges."

What we can tell for certain, however, is that if not stopped McBride would have almost certainly wreaked far more havoc. According to the case text of the McBride court proceedings, Jett Simmons McBride was laboring under the delusion that he had uncovered a secret terrorist plot that would target the Super Bowl.[20]

At this point, Jett McBride packed his bags to head down to New Orleans for the Super Bowl where he was convinced a bombing would occur. McBride destroyed his phone and tossed the broken remnants of it in a parking lot and some bushes to evade being tracked by the CIA, FBI, and Department of Defense who he was convinced were following his every step.

Before reaching his destination, McBride started noticing that he was being passed by white utility trucks. These were no ordinary trucks, McBride was convinced. They were, to his mind, evidence of the Illuminati following him, on his trail. Intent on killing him. Quite disturbed mentally at this point, McBride stopped in Bakersfield staying the night at the illustrious Vagabond Inn, a motel where he watched television and had some Scotch to wind down. The next day he got back on the road, then picked up a soon-to-be-famous hitchhiker he saw near the on-ramp to northbound State Route 99 not far from the Vagabond.[21]

The hitchhiker introduced himself as Kai and asked McBride if he was heading as far as Fresno. McBride told him that he would be heading through the area on his way to Tacoma. While staying in Bakersfield, he had received messages from his nephew and Donna, his wife, who he was supposed to pick up at the airport. This unexpected intrusion from reality slightly changed his unhinged "attempt at heroism" at the Super Bowl in New Orleans.[22]

It was once they made it into Fresno's Tower District that Kai offered to pick up some cannabis. Jett McBride handed him $40 after which Kai disappeared into a convenience store, shortly after emerging with a bag of weed and some rolling papers.[23] Kai rolled the joint as McBride, who was unfamiliar with Fresno, began to drive. McBride describes having a "deep" conversation with Kai and eventually extended his hand to the young hitch-hiker, leaning over to hug him. "Depressed and distraught" is how he's described in the court transcript.[24]

The grown man also began crying over his wife. From this point on, it becomes obvious that the story has been doctored somewhat to make McBride look better. Even though it was admitted that McBride began believing that white utility trucks were agents of the Illuminati, it was McGillivary who supposedly said the electrical workers were planting bombs. Of course, it's quite likely that this was a narrative cooked up by McBride's attorney, Scott Baly. Considering Kai wouldn't be able to defend himself or offer his eye-witness testimony, it was possible to try and pin more blame on him to alleviate the well-earned scorn directed at the alleged rapist with his racist slurs and dangerously unhinged conspiracy theories.

Despite the reported flurry of racial slurs aimed toward Neely and other minorities at the scene, McBride's defense claimed that he was "trying to heal Neely."[25] The defense claims, contrary to what witnesses on the scene have claimed,[26] that McBride "at no time" made any racial statements or used "racial epithets."

Neely's reported response to McBride attempting to "heal" the serious and potentially life-threatening injury he was responsible for was something to the tune of, "Get this fucker off of me."[27] This, once again, ripped straight from McBride's trial transcript.

The big bear of a man described the flurry of activity, the desperate attempt to put his rampage to a halt. He "thought he was dying" as he felt a knee on his back, someone grabbing his neck, someone pushing him to the ground, a boot in his face. All he claims to recall is saying, "Get off of me."

Around this time, for whatever reason, McBride began to disrobe. He was now convinced he was not only "filled with the Holy Spirit" and an incarnation of Jesus Christ. He was also playing the role of "witness to the end times" (as per Revelations, the two witnesses who would be killed, stripped, and left in the streets for three and a half days).

If the people attacking him, or rather, attempting to slow or stop his assault, in the real world, were to kill him then "they were going to have to drag his body through the street, naked." Now McBride has decided he's not just a witness to the end times, Jesus, and filled with the Holy Spirit. He's also the prophet Enoch. A direct ancestor of Jesus Christ.

McBride, once he had conferred with defense to set the stories straight for the trial, would have little positive to say about Kai. This despite the fact he had earlier referred to him as the "coolest son-of-a-bitch" he had ever met. He had gone from telling his wife Donna that he wanted to adopt Kai to changing his story to Kai being the one jerking the wheel so the vehicle would crush Neely after Donna reported to him how Kai had explained McBride's stated aim was to "clean all the n****rs out."

McBride would eventually admit that it was not Kai who had twisted the wheel to pin Neely but did deny that his attack had anything to do with his race. Neely was, McBride claimed, Illuminati. The disorganized thinking of a schizophrenic or person in the throes of a psychotic break is hard to follow.

Perhaps the racial element and the delusion regarding white utility vehicles being secret Illuminati spies were conflated in McBride's muddled head.

Chicago's *ABC7 Action News* spoke with some of the victims of McBride's rampage. Most expressed a hope to fully recover from their injuries and put the whole nightmare behind them, though at least one expressed concern, hoping that McBride wouldn't find himself released without consequences for his brutal actions.[28]

One popular misconception that has entered Kai the Hitchhiker lore is that Kai killed the deranged, attempted murderer rather than subduing him with the flat end of his hatchet. It probably didn't help that during the Jimmy Kimmel appearance, the host jokingly thanked Kai for not killing him. Stephen Colbert, currently the host of *The Tonight Show*, was starring in *The Colbert Report* on Comedy Central at the time. On the show, Colbert covers the Kai the Hitchhiker story, joking that he has "highway prejudice of my own: against axe-wielding hitchhikers."[29]

The story played into an already existing urban myth regarding the mythical ax or hatchet or knife-wielding serial killer hitchhiker. The Union County prosecutor and associate of the alleged rapist Joseph Galfy[30] promoted severely damaging disinformation. That, perhaps, Kai was some nefarious serial killer utilizing the highways as his hunting ground.[31] That same prosecutor, by the way, incidentally or coincidentally stepped down, after 11 years, the same day Kai was arrested.[32] Perfect timing if you'd rather not have your recusal on the record.

Within the first few days of the event, Kai was an instant folk hero. He was "a mixture of Bill and Ted and The Big Lebowski" according to UK's *Daily Mail*. He "seems by turns free-spirited, proud and warm-hearted."[33] *Philly* magazine called him the encapsulation of the millennial generation.

Something truly resonated with people due to his character and philosophy. Something that made him instantly lovable to so many. He had listed his location as Eureka, California[34] where he had been locked up in jail for four days in December. Shortly after the excitement, according to social media posts, he had been "sleeping in a hay field off the 199 in Lathrop."[35]

Humboldt, California's *North Coast Journal* also covered the story, hinting at a possible future appearance on *Jimmy Kimmel Live* in their original coverage. The author, Andrew Goff, also noted that after seeing Kai he realized he recognized him. In the article there he shows some pictures from a day he had run into and photographed Kai in Humboldt.[36]

Part of what attracted a certain type of person to Kai and his story was his philosophy. As *Philly* magazine pointed out he seemed to embody the character of a particular stoner stereotype, or perhaps even archetype, the carefree but socially concerned toker. Facebook posts like the following were certainly responsible in part for that:

"now, you! and me! and everyone! and everytwo! and everythree...! no more borders! pleasin to the eye! destroy the prisons and hunt down the NSOR! ninja training with vets on the street! [M]IA crooked cops! Free Haiti! Free all black lands!! Bring down the House of Wettin and share the wealth of those rothschild/bilderberg/whoever 'rich' peeps with those who actually LABOR for it! REPOST IF YOU LIKE!!! SAY ITS FROM ME!!!"[37]

If he'd been a different sort of person, Kai could have easily turned the buzz into something akin to a modern-day Beatlemania. Offers were pouring in from Hollywood and elsewhere,[38] but Kai seemed more interested in maintaining his way of life. It was a lifestyle many would not choose, but for those who do choose it, it offers a sort of freedom that reality TV bucks can't buy.

Perhaps another thing that added to the mystique was the fact that Kai kept so much to himself, declining to share a full name or age. Not especially surprising. Having crossed the border without papers, Kai feared being hassled as an "illegal immigrant." Despite the 1794 Jay Treaty allowing Indigenous Americans to travel freely between Canada and the United States,[39] we, sadly, live in the world we do. You can have your rights all day long, but they won't do much good until you prove those rights with the help of a lawyer.

"Do you have a last name," Reisbeck asked, in the famous viral footage. Laughing, Kai replied, "No, bro. I don't have anything." Not dissuaded, the itinerant Fresno reporter asks Kai his age. "I can't call it," he simply replied. SophosLabs security blog noted on February 5th how Kai was much more circumspect than people they'd attempted to "social engineer" into handing over personal details.[40]

In the days after Kai's on-the-scene interview, he managed to get back in touch with Reisbeck to record another exclusive. Here, Kai opened up a bit more about his past. Institutionalized due to an abusive home life. A survivor of molestation, and other serious traumas. Through all this, or perhaps even in part because of this, Kai developed a positive attitude and concern, and empathy for others.

Reisbeck admitted in the interview at one point that, "much of his past is darker and more gut-wrenching than you can imagine. Stuff that we can't put on air." Perhaps one of the reasons why I identify with Kai. I too am a survivor of trauma. Diagnosed with PTSD, I know from experience that awful events can open up someone's empathy, and make them aware of how a positive attitude can be a literal life-saver in the hardest of times.

Regarding the sudden shower of various deals, offers, and opportunities, Kai simply answered, "I'm just gonna be Kai any way it goes. Obviously, I was put in a situation for a reason. I would hope, I do hope, that people don't become obsessed with this because there's still so much more that we can do."

A savvy mover and shaker could have easily parlayed the viral fame into lasting prosperity, but Kai was more interested in staying on the path he had already started down. This interview also had Kai revealing the fact that he was trilingual as well as a musician and practitioner of meditation.

"Oooohm, vibration bro, you know. It's being a part of everything."

Kai describes being raised "by the TV" as a latchkey kid in the 90s. "Wandering around with no support, no one around to help me out. And there's a lot of bad stuff that happened," Kai explains to KMPH why he doesn't share personal details with strangers. Kai explains feeling "trapped" and wanting to run away at a young age. "All these scars are healed, but they're still scars," Kai tells Jessob Reisbeck. For those who deal with such emotional scars, this is a concept that may be all too familiar.

The initial interview by Reisbeck brought Kai to attention, but from there *Mediaite* claims responsibility for helping the story go viral through one of their posts by Meenal Vamburkar[41] Then, of course, the auto-tuned version of portions of Kai's interview by YouTuber Schmoyoho spread the acclaim even further.[42]

The YouTube channel What's Trending announced that the Auto-Tune the News segment featuring Kai the Hitchhiker was the top video on the YouTube for the day.[43] Another popular video from KMPH released just days after the incident has Kai singing a sort of punk and ska-flavored original tune reminiscent of Sublime, entitled "Movement." The track was recorded for a segment by Jessob Reisbeck in a music store in Northern California where Kai would pick up a very different type of "ax" for the road. The kind with six strings in place of a sharp edge.[44]

Reisbeck was clearly impressed by Kai's heroics as well as the inner strength, the maturity beyond his years that sometimes comes with having to grow up too fast on your own. "He's kind of like a superhero," Reisbeck noted. "He's impossible to get a hold of because he has no phone and he's this mysterious guy, but he has this hero status."[45]

As for what it was like coming to terms with his newfound fame, when Jessob Reisbeck ran into Kai not far from the scene of the tragic incident that brought him into the public eye, Kai made it clear he was still processing the sudden exposure. Despite the flash of glitz and promise of fame, Reisbeck felt that Kai was fundamentally unchanged where it matters. "He's just doing the exact same thing he's always done. Living a homefree life, as he calls it. He's living the same homefree life that he's always lived, man."

Reisbeck told *Mashable* how a producer with *Keeping Up With the Kardashians* even got in touch with him in the hopes he could spread the word to Kai. In the *Mashable* piece, Reisbeck explains how he came to be entwined in the Kai the Hitchhiker saga.

It all started with a report heard over the police scanner. Someone had crashed into a utility worker. What's more, there was now a homeless man with a hatchet going after the man who had wrecked into the utility worker, Rayshawn Neely. Trusting his journalistic instincts, Reisbeck skipped the sports shoot he had planned and instead left the studio with a crew from KMPH to check out the situation in person.

While interviewing bystanders, a woman who had been attacked by McBride points out Kai. "There's the hero right there who saved my life." Reisbeck got the first interview and the first follow-up, but once Kai had finished his segment with KMPH, the reporter scrum approached. Reisbeck recalled Kai merely lifted his hands and replied, "No comment, bro."

Segments from the initial interview earned him mentions on ESPN host Jim Rome's show, and the E! program *The Soup*. He was all across the internet and social media.[46] And of course, there were the memes. Kai was not just a hero. He was likable and relatable. He was fit to be memed. He was of course much more than just a meme as many who were captivated by him and his story would be quick to point out.

Christian Worzalla from Wisconsin helped run the Kai of Dogtown fan page on Facebook. "There's people that see him as just another meme—'Hey, look at this guy. Crazy personality. Haha. Look at him,'" Worzalla tells *Mashable*. "Then you have the other group that really sees Kai as who he is and who they want him to be. His personality. That's what's garnered the most interest and support for him."[47]

Even in the early days of "Kai fever" there were painfully off-base think pieces circulating that, like Colbert and Kimmel's humor, could potentially feed into negative tropes. *Unreality Magazine* published a piece in the early days, around February 13th, positing "How Kai the Hatchet Hitchhiker Proves We Would Embrace a Real-Life Dexter." In the article proper it exclaims at one point in all caps how Kai "BEAT HIM [Jett McBride] TO DEATH WITH A HATCHET."[48] The article goes on to say this is "like if Antoine Dodson had shot the guy in the face who trying [sic] to rape his sister."

The article questions why "we're making a national hero of someone who killed someone else, vigilante style." It's a perfect example of how the smallest misunderstanding in the presentation of a story can affect people's perception. Kai was never "famous for hacking someone to death with a hatchet" because that never happened. The persistence of this bit of nonsense is very telling and explains why things like prosecutor Theodore Romankow's insistence that Kai might be some super-secret serial killer were pushed by the state.

The author of the piece, who in his bio brags about appearances in *Forbes*, *IGN*, and other publications as well as a segment for *The Colbert Report*, at least takes the time to "update" the story:

"Update: I've been hearing about this story for two weeks now, and never once did I figure out that the guy Kai attacked didn't actually die. I just heard 'hatchet to the head,' and drew my own conclusions. I suppose that negates nearly all of what I say here in this post, but feel free to read anyway."

I mean, at least he admits that pretty much everything he said has been negated. When discovering the major premise of one's article is completely fallacious, however, I'd probably just retract it rather than add a few short sentences explaining why the story's very foundation is completely off base.

Meanwhile, those who actually saw the events going down had a different feeling about Kai altogether. International Brotherhood of Electrical Workers, the union that Rayshawn Neely, the PG&E worker whose leg was crushed by McBride, belonged to, had planned an all-expense paid surfing weekend trip to go with the new wetsuit and board he received from Jimmy Kimmel.[49]

"We decided to do something to honor Kai. Since he loves surfing so much, we wanted to give him a surfing weekend. All expenses paid by the Union," Chris Habecker, the executive board secretary of IBEW said. The union was offering him travel and meal expenses, two nights at the Del Mar

Hotel in San Diego plus a bit of spending money to get him by in the Bay area.

"We had to do something to recognize him," Habecker told KMPH, the news network that first discovered Kai on the scene of the incident just over a couple of weeks earlier. "His act of heroism, courage, and what he did, touched all of us."

They also hoped to have Neely reunite with Kai during the trip.

"We have so many members that we represent, they put their lives on the line every day. It goes to your heart what happened. That somebody, intentionally, went after one of our members, and this man, stepped up and saved his life."

Seven of Neely's coworkers were also honored for heroism under fire and were nominated for the National Life Saving award. The February 26th story notes that "the home free hitchhiking lifestyle is unpredictable" so they couldn't be sure he would be able to accept the offer of the free trip. In about two and a half months, much more drifted out of the control of Kai and his supporters.

After all, it would be under a season, just over a dozen weeks that would pass between the first and second fateful thumbed rides Kai would hitch.

Kai testified at the preliminary hearing for Jett McBride, but due to his arrest was unable to attend the trial itself. The jury was only offered the preliminary hearing testimony. McBride's attorney attempted to use the arrest "to impeach McGillivary's credibility." The prosecutor moved to keep the arrest and indictment from the jury due to their irrelevance to the case at hand.

"This case gained some notoriety, and it was for the reason we did the [juror] questionnaires, [...] in large part, because of the colorfulness of Mr. McGillivary. That was plainly on display in the photographs that the Defense attached to their points and authorities in this case.

"But the difficulty is that while attempting to focus attention on the colorfulness of this witness, it seems to detract from what is at issue in this case, and that is, the events earlier this year... allegedly involving Mr. McBride. This case is not about Kai, the hitchhiker, basically. It's not. It is not about whether that individual, Mr. McGillivary, was raped and for that reason killed another individual in New Jersey, as has been portrayed in the media. And all of these things, [...] if the Court were to allow reference to Mr. McGillivary's arrest in May of 2013, all of these issues would be placed in front of the jury. What happened, why did it happen, involving someone who is not really the focus of the events alleged here."

"So the Court is going to preclude either side from mentioning the arrest of Mr. McGillivary in May of 2013. It is clear to the Court that the arrest, which came [...] months after Mr. McGillivary's testimony at the preliminary hearing in this case, is not relevant as to his credibility at the time of his testimony in this case. Because the arrest came so long after the testimony there is no likelihood that Mr. McGillivary was motivated by any attempt to gain leniency or to gain favor by testifying untruthfully at the preliminary hearing here. And that is the basis for allowing prior convictions or misconduct to be allowed ... to impeach an individual during the course of the proceeding is to show that this person is not to be believed based upon their past experience, prior experiences to that witness's taking the witness stand. We just don't have this here."[50]

The Defense had hoped to include clips from the media coverage of the case, to showcase the "colorful" nature of Kai's testimony, in the hopes of making him less credible to jurors. The testimony did showcase Kai's unique personality. While being sworn in, he made sure to clarify that in swearing it was to: "God being Sophia, yes."

When asked about the packaging of the marijuana he had purchased in the Tower District, Kai explains the bag was, "Plastic, made out of dinosaurs." When asked he clarified, "It is plastic. It was made out of dinosaurs, fossil fuels."[51]

When asked if he shared the joint he rolled with the defendant, Kai's answer was exacting: "I suppose that's a matter of perception. You could say he shared the joint with me." It may seem like a bit of semantic quibbling, but, isn't that a large part of what the practice of law is?

Pressed further regarding whether the joint was passed back and forth, Kai further clarified: "The joint shared itself with us."

The Court decided that the verbal testimony was enough to establish Kai's demeanor and attitude toward testifying without the need for "visual aids."[52]

McBride's defense team attempted to exclude testimony related to Jett's admission that he raped a 14-year-old girl in the Virgin Islands. This was mentioned in Kai's testimony at the preliminary hearing and McBride admitted it to law enforcement on the scene. The prosecutor argued that this information was vital to explaining Kai's actions, "particularly why he struck defendant with the hatchet."[53]

Due to the potential of doctor testimony related to McBride's "state of mind" at the time of the attack entering the record, the probative value of the pre-attack confession was ruled admissible. Prosecution and defense also wrangled over the admissibility of McBride yelling out "88" while in the hospital. 88 has been used as a code to reference the 8th letter of the alphabet, HH standing for "Heil Hitler."

The defense argued that the number had some mystical import unrelated to the meaning that gang officers had assumed. McBride had referenced Hitler's birthday on his calendar as well, which made things a bit more confusing especially taken alongside the attacker spontaneously asking a nurse if she "was a Jew."[54]

Regardless of the full circumstances of McBride's state of mind, he would be tried and found not guilty on the most serious of the charges, the attempted murder charge. He was found guilty of the other two, but courts ruled him insane. He was sentenced to Atascadero State Hospital for the Criminally Insane.

McBride began his stint in a psychiatric care facility right around 8 months from the time of the event which might have made him a murderer had Kai not been on the scene. I have found no recent news related to McBride, but judging from the maximum 9 years sentence,[55] if he has not reoffended while incarcerated he has likely already been released. Let us hope that this will be the last violent event from Jett McBride. Ed Kemper, for instance, was released from Atascadero before becoming the "Co-ed Killer."[56]

Kai spent years in solitary confinement during pretrial detention. A clear violation of his right to a speedy trial.[57] McBride, on the other hand, didn't spend a day in prison for his actions.

Kai ended up on the East Coast. Another twist of fate conspired to lead inexorably to a night of horror in Clark, New Jersey. Shane Dixon Kavanaugh wrote on May 16th, just after the arrest, how he had gone "from a folk hero to alleged murderer overnight."[58] Untold in that article, was how Kai nearly averted the injury of assault, the insult of injustice. The night before the assault, he had reached out to Kavanaugh about crashing on his couch.

Kavanaugh had reached out to him on Facebook back in February around the time the interview with Reisbeck had gone viral. He hadn't heard anything back for nearly three months. Then he received a call.

He told Kavanaugh he'd been through Brooklyn for a few days with a friend and had just gotten into Newport, Rhode Island. "Sadly, her landlord is being a total dick and she's getting kicked out her house! Hey, you wouldn't happen to have a couch I could crash on for a few days?"

Kavanaugh invited Kai over and he told me he smoked a joint with him. His girlfriend and roommate were uncomfortable with the idea of a stranger crashing on the couch, so he left.

Though Kai had no real plan as to how long he would stay in Brooklyn, Kavanaugh still decided to mull it over with his fiancee and their roommate who, he attests, thought he was "bonkers" for even considering it. Without having even gotten to know him personally, Kavanaugh counted himself "lucky" that he was unable to convince his partner and their roommate.

"He might have spent that night at my place," Kavanaugh exclaims, milking the one phone call with Kai at a time when he was fairly desperate to find a place to stay for the night while he was in New Jersey. "Now, he probably wouldn't have killed me, based on what he claims happened at Galfy's house."

Kavanaugh would, however, later write a far more positive piece about Kai in 2016 at *Vocativ*.[59] Probably one of the last bits of major media coverage before my reporting in 2017 at *Inquisitr*. Kavanaugh's article was in the minority that breaks from acting as unofficial stenographers for the prosecution.

The missed connections there on the east coast led to that fateful night that changed everything. A night that spun Kai into a miserable, Kafkaesque nightmare. Subject to a kangaroo court and a good ol' boy network to put Prince Albert's friends from the Cleveland Street Scandal to shame.[60]

Another example of the kind of irresponsible, misleading reporting regarding this case, Kavanaugh, perhaps jokingly, notes that there was no word whether Galfy, the alleged rapist who died with his own semen and unidentifed blood on his penis[61] was killed with a hatchet. He even ties up the piece with another pithy line, responding to Kai's post about his fear that he'd been drugged and raped, "Depends — do I have my hatchet, or not?"

"He's one of the most intelligent people I've met, one of the most bizarre humans I've ever come in contact with and will ever come in contact with, but he can do the craziest thing and then the most good-hearted thing after," Reisbeck told *NJ Advance Media* after the arrest.

"It just breaks my heart to think about how it ended up," he said.[62]

Kai had come "straight outta dogtown, skateboarding, surfing it up"[63] to find himself faced with incredible opportunity. The world opening before him effortlessly.

"He could have had anything," Reisbeck said, "in any way, shape or form. He had everyone loving him, and unfortunately things didn't end up like that. And it just sucks."

While at Jimmy Kimmel's show, he stayed at the Roosevelt in Hollywood. Reisbeck noted how he took off the bag he brought with him, containing everything he owned. Right down to the sleeping bag he used on the road. "I'm staying in this hotel, someone needs this more than I do."[64]

It was May 11, 2013, that Kai happened across a wealthy and well-connected

New Jersey lawyer in Times Square, New York.[65] Kai had already been trying to make it towards New Jersey, so when offered a ride he gladly accepted. It's quite possible that Joseph Galfy was unaware of Kai's renown. It's likely that if he was seeking prey, he would have chosen someone more expendable. Perhaps someone like the "vagrant" Galfy's former Chief of Police brother mentioned in his interview with police in Union County.[66]

Reisbeck, who has kept in touch with Kai over the years had heard him share stories from childhood and his youth involving sexual assault and abuse. "Kai has a very deep anger and passion for predators and people who prey on and abuse others."

What at first seemed like so many other chance meetings with people who had seen Kai online would become an absolute nightmare that wouldn't let up for years to come. A nightmare that persists to this day.

CHAPTER 2

BRIEF HISTORIES: SURFING, HITCHHIKING AND NEW JERSEY CORRUPTION

Before we get back to Kai's story, it may be helpful to go back in time a bit. To fully understand Kai's position, we will be taking a detour to explore a brief history of surfing and hitchhiking subcultures as well as a quick survey of New Jersey's culture of corruption.

If you're not familiar with surfing history, it may come as some surprise that the origins date back to pre-colonial, Indigenous culture. The genesis of surfing in western culture begins in the late 18th century. It was in 1778 Hawaii that Captain James Cook observed the practice.[1] Surfing as a part of the indigenous way of life was lucky to survive the influence of European colonization. Drew Kampion writes that "the Polynesian relationship to the sea was beyond European comprehension. To the islanders, the ocean meant life and joy and freedom. But by 1900, disease, religion, and a new plantation work ethic had all but exterminated Hawaiian culture and the ancient sport of surfing."

Surfing got a bad rap from the Europeans who felt it was "immoral and wrong." Ironically, it was European conceptions of spirituality that resulted in much of this friction. To the Austronesian inhabitants of the Pacific Islands, surfing was an important part of their religious experience. But to the colonizers surfing represented "nakedness, sexuality, [...] shameless exuberance, informality, ignorant joy, and freedom" which they found upsetting.[2]

Surfing did survive, though the practice, culture, and makeup of surfers changed drastically and for much of the 20th century, the surfing subculture was stigmatized. Sociologist Stephen Wayne Hull studied the surfing subculture in Santa Cruz, California.[3] The subculture had its own lingo, symbols, norms, values, specialized media and other elements that separate it from other sports creating a distinct subculture.

Surfing subculture was often associated with rebellion. The use of the term "radical" by surfers is somewhat apt considering surfing's role in early rock and roll from Misirlou to Jan and Dean, the Ventures and Surfaris, the Beach Boys[4] and beyond. The surfer was seen by some as a ne'erdowell "often sleeping in cars and on beaches, saving every possible cent for necessities."[5] Surfing subculture's roots, according to historian Jon Stratton, become apparent in the period following World War II.[6] Incidentally, this was also one of the golden ages for hitchhiking.[7]

The idea of the surfer as a "societal dropout" was already a common trope even before the introduction of characters like Spiccoli[8] from *Fast Times at Ridgemont High* or Bill S. Preston and Theodore Logan from *Bill and Ted's Excellent Adventure*. Even the Teenage Mutant Ninja Turtles played off the idea of the pizza loving, outsider enamored with surf culture and lingo.[9] Again part of the conflict lies in the juxtaposition of Protestant work ethic with a lifestyle considered unproductive.

Destigmatizing the subculture has come slowly but surely. In part due to the commodification of the culture as well as mainstreaming of professional surfing as a sport. This type of arc is not unfamiliar in subcultures. Consider the punk movement: once the nonconformist style of punk proved marketable it began to infiltrate mainstream society. Surfing clothing lines like Ocean Pacific, Quicksilver, and Pacific Sun played an important role in the commodification of what was once an outsider experience.[10]

The surfer was seen as an outcast by many throughout the 20th century. The surfer eschewed respectability and responsibility for a potentially dangerous leisure activity that was often associated with "long haired rebels that were impartial to work or a career."[11] Straight-laced society wasn't ready for the "mythical surfer lifestyle: the freedom and joy of movement, the living out of an automobile, and the roaming, in the case of surfers, from surf break to surf break, even from country to country."[12]

The Z Boys were skateboarders and surfers who put Dogtown on the map. In order to catch a crest in Dogtown "outsiders had to earn their way in."[13] In theory, this initiation of sorts acclimated the neophyte or journeyman surfer into the ways of the subculture.

Despite surfing becoming more mainstream and acceptable, there are still stereotypes related to surfers that affect the way they are perceived by many. Micah Peasley was another surfer gone viral. Known simply as the "surfer dude" or "get pitted" guy, Peasley's exuberant description of catching a wave garnered millions of views.[14]

Peasley described in his interview with Daniel Tosh on Comedy Central that people had assumed he wasn't very bright, based on the language he used. He admitted to leaning into the "dumb surfer" stereotype.

Another world we need to understand before we go on is that of the hitchhiker. Hitchhiking began as a quintessentially American practice in the 1920s. In the 20s there were very few automobiles on the road and most were owned by rural farmers. A new class of traveler appeared along with the horseless carriage. They were primarily white males interested in recreation and adventure on the open road.[15] Hitchhiking became a popular way to travel to and from vacation spots. New York and Florida were common routes.

Even in the very early years of hitchhiking some decried the practice as potentially dangerous, both to those hitching rides and those picking up hitchers. The beginning of the fears of hitchhiking's impact on society related more so to the idea of "prospective social and moral dangers."[16] In 1926, the New York Girl's Service League took it upon themselves to warn young women of the dangers of picking up rides from strangers. Hitchhiking was a "special problem" and "true ladies" did not take part.[17]

Franklin D. Roosevelt's New Deal resulting in the creation of our system of highways was another important historical point in the evolution of hitchhiking[18] and the perception of hitchhikers. The difficulties of the Depression made hitching a ride more common and accepted. On the one hand, you have authors like Samuel Zeidman in 1937 positioning hitchhikers as hardy stock that admire "hard work" and "free-enterprise capitalism."

"To the hitchhiker himself there is one final word. Hold your head high – not arrogantly but proudly. The road develops characteristics in you which are requisites for entrance into business and professional life. […] [I]f you are impatient, it teaches you to wait. If you have a temper, it gives you a placid nature. If you are selfish, it teaches you to be generous. If you are impetuous, it forces you to think."[19] On the other hand, there was a growing distrust of "tramps" and "hobos" which would extend to Okies looking for work.[20] They were often seen as "taking jobs" from locals. Despite all this in 1938, 43% of Americans were willing to offer rides to someone with a thumb out.[21]

Flannery O'Connor's *Wise Blood* is a seminal text of the Southern Gothic tradition. At the same time, it is also an important foundational text in the punk rock world.[22] Hazel Motes, the antihero and protagonist, makes it clear how his identity and freedom are inextricably tied to his ability to stay mobile: "Nobody with a good car needs to worry about nothin', do you understand? Nobody with a good car needs to be justified."

By the 1950's Jack Kerouac's *On the Road*, "arguably the seminal text for rock rebellion," would further position the automobile as vital to "self-expression and escape."[23] Unsurprisingly car culture, like surfing culture, would play a role in the seed of rock and roll rebellion that would be planted in the early 50s and germinate fully into the flower of youth rebellion by the 1960s. Underground Komix artists such as Big Daddy Roth and Von Dutch[24] and filmmakers like Kenneth Anger[25] would further stress the importance of automobility to the rebellious ethos that continued to develop in the post-war period.

By the 80s, that world of youthful rebellion seemed to have metastasized into unbridled consumerism. Ronald Reagan was a hitchhiker in his youth. At the time of his presidency, his tale of hitching a ride to get a job in a radio station was hailed as a "true American story."[26] Somewhat ironic considering the once common form of mobility had lost the veneer of romanticism that surrounded it for the first few decades of the 20th century. By the 80s there was a common perception of the hitchhiker as an "unsavory individual."[27]

These days, hitchhiking, as well as picking up hitchhikers, is viewed as a potentially dodgy endeavor. Much had changed since the 1930s and 40s when hitchhiking was as common as it was necessary.[28] And once again there is a definite correlation between the necessity of hitchhiking and its societal acceptance. During WWII the most common type of hitchhiker you might run into was an enlisted man.[29]

Things had changed vastly from the 1930s when historian and hitchhiker John Schlebecker pointed out that "the vast, indeed overwhelming majority of hitchhikers appear to have been law-abiding." It had even strayed quite a long way since the 1970s when one writer noted: "You never have to drive very far to find a hitchhiker."[30]

In Jack Reid's *Roadside Americans*, it's pointed out that car ownership and crime rates don't seem to be what's primarily pushing the fear of hitchhiking. Increased numbers of automobiles on the road did affect the makeup of the hitchhiker as well as thinning out their herds through the 50s, but in between Kerouac and rock and roll culture, this would soon change. Once again, just as with the surfing subculture, the identification of hitchhikers with civil rights, youth rebellion and rock and roll would color how they were perceived by society at large.[31]

It did however result in fewer hitchhikers as well as affecting the type of hitchhikers that one would find on the road.

Hitchhiking was viewed as a sort of freedom. It was counterculture lifestyle in practice. From this time on, the perception of the dangers of hitchhiking would steadily increase despite the actual dangers inherent for those thumbing and those picking up not altering all that much.[32]

By the late 70s and 80s, a waning counterculture combined with the rise of "law and order politics" would culminate in the Reagan, Bush, and Clinton years.[33] Hitching was seen as equivalent to risky behavior such as promiscuity and drug use. There was a definite connection between fear of hitchhikers and fears of societal downfall and decay. Added to this, a new era of homelessness was on the rise in the 80s[34] due to various issues such as the closing of state mental institutions.[35]

Government agencies such as the FBI, state and local governments, state troopers, and police departments as well as new laws and regulations also played a part.[36] In some cases, blatant propaganda was employed in an attempt to clear the roads of ride-hoppers. Certain hitchhikers managed to retain some respectability and were less likely targeted by police, meanwhile vagrants, women, and minorities were more likely to be hassled by law enforcement.

In Canada, where Kai is from, there has been a good deal of discourse related to Indigenous mobility and how that impacts hitchhiking trends and potential dangers. Due to a large number of missing and murdered Indigenous women "constraining Indigenous mobility is a preoccupation of the province of British Columbia."[37]

Especially tragic are the unsolved crimes of the "Highway of Tears."[*38] As with the situation in the mid-20th century, the Protestant work ethic was often considered tied to self-determination and means, including mobility. It's not self-evident, initially perhaps, how morality and mobility are intertwined in many minds, but the case of missing and murdered Indigenous women in Canada exposes part of this dark underbelly.

Kai belongs to multiple marginalized groups, as a survivor of multiple sexual assaults, Indigenous, an "illegal immigrant," and a hitchhiker. Sadly, this social marginalization can lead to apathy where empathy could be more productive. The idea that there are "wasted lives" versus those with "no productive purpose within society" who are simply "chaos to be managed" results in an internal triage for some when hearing tragic stories before sparing any concern or care.[39]

This leads to what is called "willing victim" construction. A most insidious

---

*   Highway 16 in Northwestern British Columbia.

form of victim-blaming mentality. By simply stigmatizing hitchhiking, society puts the onus and responsibility for what happens to the hitchhiker on themselves (rather than their would-be attacker). By believing that certain people by nature of their "bad/irresponsible behavior" put themselves in a situation that led to them being abused, assaulted, or murdered, society attempts to assuage its guilt regarding any complicity. As a result, it's not at all surprising why so many serial killers have singled out marginalized groups such as sex workers, the indigent, or other vulnerable groups to cull from.[40]

Ironically, the history of New Jersey's corruption is somewhat rooted in the corruption of its neighboring state of New York. One of the foundations of this corruption that spread through both states was the infamous Tammany Hall political machine. Tammany Hall[41] had existed as a force to be reckoned with since the early 1800s but grew to great power following the Civil War when William Marcy "Boss" Tweed and "The Ring," his political cabal ran New York city politics employing graft[*] and other corrupt practices.[42]

The Tammany Hall machine managed to last well into the 20th century. But it was far from the sole genesis of New Jersey's culture of corruption.[43] Tammany machine politics was tightly tied to the saloons[44] of New York and the competitiveness of elections occasionally turned into all-out street brawls.[45]

Ballot box stuffing and other brazen forms of election fraud were a cornerstone of the Tammany system. Once the infamous Boss Tweed took hold of Tammany Hall, open graft and election fraud were joined by protection rackets and payoff schemes.[46] It's a credit to the success of Tweed's system

---

[*]   Graft is a type of political corruption that may involve bribery, extortion, nepotism, and many of the types of practices mentioned by Professor Mario Garcia as indicators of organized crime, many of which we see time and again in Union County.

that you can still see many of the same practices occurring to this day in New Jersey.

Just last year, Princeton's *Journal of Public & International Affairs* published "How New Jersey Political Parties Rig the Ballot." The paper is frank in explaining that "New Jersey has a robust Democratic machine" and that "machine politics are the real power."[47] This is not to say there is no corruption in the state's Republican party. The indictment of multiple close political allies of former governor and affirmed reformer Chris Christie would certainly suggest otherwise,[48] but in general it's the Democratic party's political machines[49] such as the influential Norcross machine[50] that play the largest role.

Speaking of Princeton, it was that New Jersey Ivy League institution that was responsible for what is commonly called the "Princeton Oligarchy Study"[51] which shows that against the outsized influence of big money donors, especially in the wake of the Citizens United ruling[52] a single person's vote has a "near-zero" impact on the outcome of our electoral politics. So it seems very little has changed since the days of the old smoke-filled rooms in back halls of saloons. Political bosses are still buying and selling favor in the open and profiting off the backs of the taxpayer's hard-earned dollars.

As far as saloons go, alcohol is another monumental factor in what created the conditions in which the petri dish of corruption could thrive. Alcohol, sex, and gambling were the trifecta that made these vice centers tick. The Tenderloin section of New York City had earned a reputation for depravity. Sex workers, some as young as 12 were forced into servicing customers just to survive.[53] An attempt was made to clean up the area.

The problem here is that when "Satan's Circus" was brushed aside after years of police protection rackets and shakedowns, the sinful center would migrate to New Jersey's north shore: specifically, the Atlantic Highlands.[54]

Again, the reformers would attempt to throw a monkey wrench in the popular capital of vice for the region.

Now it was time for New Jersey to be swept clean. Reformer candidate James A. Bradley aimed to do just that. Bradley, a wealthy industrial magnate, even handed out brushes from his New York City brush factory to symbolize the plan to sweep the state clean.[55] Bradley was far from the first or the last "reformer" candidate in New Jersey with the two latest governors of the state, Democrat Phil Murphy and Republican Chris Christie branding themselves as such.

Bradley was vehemently opposed to the gambling industry that had drawn tourists from New York City and elsewhere for years. When Bradley succeeded at making gambling illegal; Long Branch's popular tourist trap the Monmouth Racetrack[56] was no longer a draw. As a result, the area was swiftly gentrified.

Conditions would continue to decline with the introduction of alcohol prohibition. Once again, we see well-meaning reformers unintentionally making things worse in an attempt to squelch sin. Only succeeding in creating new outlets for said sin to thrive. The impact of prohibition and its influence in creating a powerful system of organized crime is imperative to understanding corruption in the area.

One of the important characters in New Jersey corruption history, and an important figure in boss politics is Frank Hague. Hague served at the helm of Jersey City as mayor for 30 years. Hague was one of many "reformer candidates" whose interests strayed far from true reform. Utilizing the "clean" image of a man who wasn't a womanizer or drunkard assisted him in this. Hague also led the Tammannee Club, a political machine obviously inspired by the Tammany Hall machine in New York City. It was a time when magnates were running rampant and railroads, utility companies and robber barons of all stripes managed to keep lawmakers in their back pockets.

New Jersey Democrat leader James R. Nugent attempted to expose this seemingly contradictory effect. He published a report noting the correlation between prohibition and crime.[57] It wasn't enough to save the country from the disastrous amendment that led to the rise of various crime families that would have an enormous and deadly impact on crime, business, politics, and other facets of life.

Benjamin Franklin once referred to New Jersey as a beer barrel or "keg tapped at both ends."[58] He was referring to the state's placement between the important ports of Philadelphia and New York City, but the phrase almost seems to foreshadow the rise of bootlegger culture in the Atlantic Highlands.

By the 1920s things had swiftly devolved into chaos. In Chicago, a mayor and 24 others were indicted for corruption that sprung from Prohibition and the organized crime that it helped create. Mayors under indictment would become a common occurrence in New Jersey for years to come. Meanwhile, in Morris County, authorities expose a county prosecutor's culpability in accepting bribes to keep the liquor flowing. In Edgewater, the mayor, chief of police, and two police detectives are busted. In New York, a police sergeant along with eight others is found guilty of conspiracy to commit criminal acts.[59] In all of these cases, the root cause is circumventing the prohibition of alcohol.

By the time the failed experiment in keeping Americans dry and sober was scrapped the damage was already done. Multiple influential crime families had already become not just established but enshrined. The logistics of running alcohol from Canada[60] throughout the country helped ensure that these crime families no longer had turf of a few street corners or a city.

They had gone national, international in some cases.

In 1931, infamous mobster Charles "Lucky" Luciano wanted to take care of some inconvenient competition.[61] Irving Wexler, better known as Waxey Gordon,[62] is immortalized alongside Enoch "Nucky" Johnson in the HBO series *Boardwalk Empire*.[63] Enoch "Nucky" Johnson, the New Jersey political boss in Atlantic City is, in addition to being the head of a political machine known as Nucky Johnson's Organization, the model for the fictional Boardwalk character Nucky Thompson.

Waxey, a Philly crime boss and bootlegger, was operating out of Union County's own Elizabeth, New Jersey. As for exactly what went down at the Elizabeth-Carteret Hotel, no one living is certain but by the end of the day, two of Gordon's bootleg business partners had been assassinated. Many historians speculate it was none other than Meyer Lansky, the gangster that Hyman Roth from *The Godfather*[64] is modeled after, who perpetrated the hit. Gordon and Lansky already had a longstanding beef going back years.

Illustrating how these crime networks don't operate in a vacuum as well as the danger they pose to our political process, Luciano managed to take down Gordon quasi-legally. Luciano managed to obtain documents that implicated Gordon in tax fraud. At this point, Jake Lansky, Meyer's brother, made sure that Thomas Dewey, assistant attorney for New York received all the relevant details.[65]

New Jersey had a large immigrant population, many of them hailing from Italy. Italian Americans in New Jersey were often reticent to cooperate with police in the early 1900s. The established WASP constituency often took this as a sign of the newly Americanized immigrants being part of a criminal element. A less racist explanation however is one that also holds true to this day. Immigrants were often treated poorly and chose to seek justice within their own communities.[66] Often the police were little more than enforcers of the corrupt system. A situation that is for the most part unchanged. Eventually, the recent arrivals would find themselves in a system with its own series of protection rackets.

Late nineteenth century until World War II, Atlantic City was a seat of racketeering, gambling, prostitution, and Prohibition-era speakeasies.[67] Municipal officials even jailed Prohibition agents in the 1920s. This led to a Justice Department official calling the town "the most corrupt city in America."[68]

In 1976, citizens of the state of New Jersey voted to grant Atlantic City sole right to legal gambling. This came along with a pinkie promise that the mob would absolutely not be running the whole shebang. The extent of port-related corruption in New Jersey would lead to a bi-state compact creating a commission meant to oversee waterfront corruption and mafia connections. Just recently, the state of New York had to take the rare step of seeking an injunction from the Supreme Court to keep the commission intact, much to New Jersey's dismay.[69] (Much more on the Union County connection later, in the chapter On the Waterfront.)

Adding legalized gambling to the mix somehow didn't magically erase the culture of graft, kickbacks, and backroom dealmaking. Two more mayors would be chased from office in the 80s. Michael Matthews, caught after being heard on tape bragging about his ties to Philly crime boss Nicodemo "Little Nicky" Scarfo (ties between the Philly mob and New Jersey municipal corruption are long and storied) and Phil Leonetti.[70]

"Greed got the best of me," Matthews would say after his perp walk, but one local businessman claimed that maxim might as well "be the logo of the whole town."[71]

Hugh Addonizio, former mayor of Newark, was elected with Mafia help.[72] Feds would eventually convict him and several other local officials of extortion. Sharpe James, another Newark mayor from 1986 to 2006, had his finger in the till until it sent him to prison. As with Matthews, several of his staff and administration followed along behind him.[73]

"They should tie a yellow ribbon around City Hall," one prosecutor said at the time, "and designate it a crime scene."[74]

Then there's the ABSCAM investigation. It all started with a shell company run by "fake Arab sheikhs."[75] This front was used to bribe local and federal officials. One of the officials caught up was Camden Mayor Angelo Errichetti who tried to sell casino licenses in Atlantic City.[76] I spoke with retired FBI agent Myron Fuller about ABSCAM, one of the most jaw-dropping examples of municipal corruption in the contemporary era. Beginning in July 1977 and running until January 1980, Fuller says the FBI "did not hesitate" at the chance to seek out connections between white collar crime and public corruption.

Initially, the operation intended to "penetrate the criminal relationship between sophisticated White-Collar Crime con men and members of the Five Families of Organized Crime in the New York Metropolitan area." Fuller was already aware that both conmen and members of the Gambino family had already taken over Iverson Cycle Company in Queens.

That's how it began anyway. By the end, various New Jersey local and state government officials, multiple congressmen, and a senator were embroiled in the sting operation after attempting to trade on their public offices. Granting contracts, graft, bribery, rubbing elbows with mobsters, this is a tradition that was still alive and well in 1980. And lives on to this day.

And unlike Las Vegas, what happens in New Jersey doesn't always stay there. The corruption was far-reaching. Canada, the United Kingdom, and Switzerland were also "in the mix" according to Fuller.[77]

ABSCAM was one of the most well-known FBI operations netting public officials in New Jersey, (and just one of many connecting New Jersey politicians to the Philly mob).[78] The sting connected these crooked public servants to various forms of corruption, but dozens of other less publicized cases also exist. The operation centered around a non-existent Arab sheikh with loads of oil money to throw around. This phony sheikh purportedly wanted to invest in Atlantic City among other things. Though the sheikh was fake, the $3.2 million in cash[79] was very real. The cases highlighted here, of course, are just samples. There are a multitude of similar stories. And though time passes and fashions change, some things tend to stay the same.

As of 1980, the *Washington Post* wrote hopefully of an end of the era of such shenanigans. The article admitted the long string of trials throughout the 70s was a sign of massive, far-reaching corruption but the fact that trials were occurring "proved that New Jersey was cleaning itself up." The article praised a new era on the way, rather than the "same old story of corrupt, boss-dominated politics." Besides, Hudson County was now one of the "last bastions of political boss rule in the nation." As we will see later, boss politics in New Jersey and machine corruption are far from being just a relic of the pre-ABSCAM era.

Author Hannah Arendt wrote *The Banality of Evil* about how the most horrifically evil acts can be, at times, rather unassuming, even boring.[80] Case in point, Nazi officials argued they were "just following orders." Sometimes the most heinous acts arise from disappointingly mundane motives. The beauty of a good ol' boy system is you don't need some top-down "conspiracy." There's no need for illuminati robes and secret, underground bases. Just get enough greedy, power-hungry sociopaths in positions of power and naturally, a hierarchy arises and certain covert concessions and unwritten agreements will emerge of their own accord.

Any time a police officer agrees to withhold certain information or highlight irrelevant information so they can build a case for a prosecutor, you have two people agreeing to take part in a criminal act. The very definition of a conspiracy. And they happen all the time.

After going over numerous cases of political corruption past and present, I propose a new term, a possible corollary to this concept: the unoriginality of corruption. Because as we will see, the classics never really go out of style. The same goes for means of defrauding the public and subverting the best interests of the people.

CHAPTER 3

THE CHURCH & THE FAMILY

For some, the lucky ones, a sense of respite and peace can be found amidst the most difficult of circumstances by taking refuge in family and church. As seen with The Family cult (formerly known as Children of God) and the United Church of Canada (who are responsible for numerous instances of physical, psychological, and sexual abuse of kidnapped indigenous children); the church and The Family are the last places one would want to seek shelter. To really understand Kai's case, you need to know about Kai, the human. To do that, we need to look at his history and some formative moments in his life. That will take place in the next chapter, mostly in his own words with some additional material from Tony Cantu, one of the first people Kai met when he crossed the border for his trip into the US back in the early 2010s.

In movies about trials, there's often a last-minute revelation entered into evidence. In reality, that pretty much never happens. There is a protocol for introducing evidence and you can't introduce evidence without the prosecution or defense knowing in advance. That said, this was research for a book, not a trial, though obviously I've done my fair share (and then some) of reading through court filings, motions, other documents and transcripts. But it very much felt like the kind of a 3rd act bombshell moment that set me back at least two weeks as I was nearing completion of the first draft.

It all started when, in a letter to Kai, I mentioned a recent discovery related to "The Family," a racist secret society that had long infiltrated the Elizabeth Police Department in Union County. I found Reverend Michael Granzen's book *Breaking The Plate Glass Window*,[1] almost by chance. I was doing research for the section on abuse in the Union County carceral system. I'd been trying to find more evidence of police, corrections officers, and inmates in Union County referencing the so-called "code of silence."

This code of silence at first glance seems like a rental rate Omerta, inmates who run up against it find themselves violently beaten with no help and even law enforcement and correctional officers who go up against that thin blue line end up regretting it. As Newark Police Department whistleblower Samuel Clark pointed out, you're honestly better off being a dirty cop than the cop trying to clean things up, and the potential consequences, he explained, can be lethal.[2] If you're familiar with investigative journalist Justine Barron's work on the Sean Suiter case, you should be aware that exposing dirty cops can be deadly.[3]

The code of silence research led to the case of Sgt. John Guslavage in Elizabeth, New Jersey. He attempted to get justice by way of the CEPA. Clark noted that despite the best efforts of CEPA there are many ways around the protections purportedly conferred by the statute. When I saw Guslavage's mention in Dr. Granzen's excellent book, released May of 2022, things started to get very interesting. "The Family" sounded eerily similar to the "Lords of Discipline" secret society within the Newark PD which, like "The Family," operated more like a street gang than the Fraternal Order of Police.

Police gangs, of course, are nothing new. Recently, the *New Yorker* reported on what they called a "shadow government" within the LA County Sheriff's Department.[4] This isn't even the first time that LASD gangs have risen to prominence. In 2000 the Department of Justice finally ruled that LAPD was liable for RICO investigation which, as *LA Times* reported was meant to get to the bottom of "who's the real gang."[5] This was in response to events going back at least to the early 1990s. This Union County-based police gang with secret society overtones resulted in a surprising and unexpected last-minute discovery.

A letter I wrote to Kai telling him about "The Family" jogged his memory about some of his childhood trauma. I saw the first line of his letter regarding "The Family" being the "weird fundamentalist cult" his mother Shirley Stromberg was under the sway of during her time in California. Before even finishing the letter, I started to type up my response.

There are multiple cults with the same name. For instance, the Australia-based cult that Julian Assange's father was a member of that was also known for horrific acts of child abuse. It also went by the name "The Family."[6] I had to be sure, so I was going to ask if he ever heard terms like "flirty fishing." Was the leader called David "Moses" Berg? Did he ever see anything that looked like religious comics but that often-had disturbing sexual themes, occasionally involving children?

After that, I realized I was getting ahead of myself a bit and went ahead and finished his letter which answered my questions, fairly well confirming that this was that "The Family" cult:

"The Family? That's the same name of the fundamentalist Christian cult my birth mother went to California to join when she was in her twenties. I remember seeing what looked like "Chick Tracts" laying around as a kid, but there was a leader guy named David something-or-other."

Hippie offshoot of Christianity that arose during the "Jesus Freaks" era in the late 60s and 70s? Check. Creepy comics reminiscent of religious tracts by cartoonist Jack Chick? Check. Led by a prolific pervert and pedophile named David? Check, check and check. I got chills. I've researched the Children of God (later rebranded as The Family or The Family International) for decades and have a section on them in my book about institutional pedophilia.

To people who are unfamiliar with institutional pedophilia and abuse of children done under the guise of religion; the stories Kai has shared with me may seem outlandish, and unbelievable. Sadly, they mirror so many stories I've heard from survivors of The Family and other cults and even those abused in mainstream religious organizations such as the United Church of Canada that Gilbert McGillivary was connected to (which has its own weighty baggage we will explore shortly).

Six weeks after Waco, The Family finally broke "years of virtual silence;" by inviting reporters and religious scholars to visit the commune in La Habra Heights in an attempt to rehabilitate their image.[7] Despite numerous investigations worldwide into massive and widespread abuses within the cult, Berg died a free man. Those who survived the group's abuse still live with the memories. Rose McGowan has also opened up about abuse at the hands of The Family.[8] She, River and Joaquin Phoenix are probably some of the most famous survivors of the cult.

When asked if there was anything he felt he did too early in life, River admitted "having sex" was the main regret. The interviewer asked how old he was.[9] Four years old, he replied. Many other victims of The Family's abuse committed suicide, while several others succumbed to overdoses.[10]

Then there was Berg's wife, Karen Zerby. Not only was Zerby's son Ricky Rodriguez molested as a child but it was filmed and used as a manual for the

Family's child brides and their "Law of Love doctrine."[11] Another example of their child pornography operation masquerading as religious materials is the mention of "kiddy viddy shows" as they're called internally. These are referred to in some of the extant pamphlets published by Berg and his disciples.[12]

New York Times reported on a literal child abuse manual published by the cult: "The toddler Ricky is described or else pictured as watching intercourse and orgies, fondling his nanny's breasts and having his genitals fondled."[13]

Zerby also wrote material for The Family. In one communique regarding "intimacy" with Jesus, the lines between spiritual intimacy and sexual intimacy are clearly blurred. This is disturbing enough before you realize that Zerby's target audience was 14-16-year olds:

"You cannot comprehend how complete you have made Me feel now that we are one, now that we are lovers and we revel in the bed of passion and intimacy. Each time you kiss My lips and look deeply into My eyes and share your heart and express your love and your desire for Me, each time you reach out to Me and hold Me and want Me, each time you fuck Me and receive My penis and fuck My golden rod and drink in My golden seeds, it fills My heart with joy until I feel I could almost burst!"[14]

The *BBC* spoke with Verity Carter, one of many victims of The Family. She was sexually abused from the age of 4 years old by her father and other members of the cult. Verity explained how Berg's "Law of Love" doctrine resulted in normalizing the rape of children as young as two or three years old within the abusive cult. In addition to the sexual abuse, Verity describes being beaten and whipped in stories that mirror some of what I've heard from Kai. It was "hell on earth" she explains.[15]

The Family was raided on multiple continents, but for whatever reason

they generally managed to slip away. Rumors of sexual blackmail and insin-
uating themselves into government similar to the Unification church (colloquially known as the "Moonies") could be one reason. Professor Ruth
Wangerin of City University of New York suspects they may also be some
sort of "Cointelpro-sponsored" organization which would also be a possible
explanation. Additionally, the children of the cult, abused though they were,
were taught to lie to "systemites" (anyone who didn't abide by the twisted
perversion of religion promulgated by David "Moses" Berg).[16]

The Guardian reported on how The Family had been the target of disturbing allegations going all the way back to the early 1970s, though the
behavior almost certainly dates back to the 1960s when Berg's "Teens for
Christ" group attempted to garner a following of hippie runaways. The New
York Attorney General's Office report[17] related to Berg's proclivity for pedophilia, incest,* and child rape as a means to "increase the tribe," the FBI and
even Interpol probed the elusive and abusive sex cult. These investigations
all evaporated in 1994 with the death of Berg, despite the group's continued
existence. Karen Zerby (who still acts as "spiritual and administrative co-director of The Family International") walks free to this day.[18]

Kai shared with me a bit about his experience with the cult's "brainwashing techniques" and how they affected his memories of the events. He also
shared how isolation, a classic cult tactic also brought up by The Family
survivor Verity Carter, exacerbated the situation:

> "For instance, the cult my birth mother joined near Bellis did
> what amounts to stage hypnotism EVERY DAY to my birth
> siblings. They surrounded them while chanting gibberish in
> 'tongues'; swayed back and forth until they were entranced;

---

* Berg is accused by his own daughters and granddaughters as well as others of child abuse and
rape.

commanded them to surrender to "the spirit"; then slapped them in the forehead so they fell backwards into the waiting arms of the cult leaders.

While "slain in the spirit" like this, the cult leaders would "pray" (more like "prey") over them, but the prayers were actually hypnotic commands that rewrote history and created a cult "persona" in their minds that made them easier to control. They did that to me for awhile too, but Red Deer was a city of about 50,000 at the time, so I could run away sometimes.

They moved to Bellis when I went to social services, which has a population of about 100. In the middle of nowhere. Totally isolated. That's where the brainwashing took a whole new dimension."

As bad as it was for children raised within the group, they were convinced from an early age that things could only get worse if they attempted to appeal to authorities or outsiders. All in addition to the physical and sexual violence visited upon them,

Verity Carter describes her experience:

"When I was 10, I secretly hoped I'd be taken away. By then I'd already tried running away and killing myself. I thought it couldn't be worse in the outside world.

But I didn't dare tell an outsider the truth. I was told that if I did, my siblings would be taken to separate homes and suffer a life of abuse and even untimely death. My parents would be arrested and I'd never see them again.

When I finally escaped the cult at 15, I was told my younger sisters would be smuggled abroad to live with the worst abuser if I told anyone about my life in the cult."[19]

Shirley's connection to The Family was the source of a great deal of early trauma, but Gilbert McGillivary also has ties to a church with a rather shady past. The United Church was formed in 1925 by the merger of two large Canadian denominations, the Methodists and the Presbyterians, as well as the much smaller Congregationalists. During the social and cultural upheaval of the 1960s, The United Church of Canada attempted to be progressive and keep up with the times. They dropped the church's opposition to premarital sex and even lobbied the federal government to legalize abortion, reversing their traditional moralistic stances on sex.

On the one hand, the church was praised for being one of the more progressive denominations. They attempted to stay relevant and adhere to the stated ministry of Jesus Christ by helping others and attending to their needs. On the other hand, the church's involvement in the residential schools and the massive institutional abuse over decades belied the purported progressive stance.

The initial apology from the United Church of Canada in 1986 was, to put it kindly, fairly weak:

"We tried to make you be like us and in so doing we helped to destroy the vision that made you what you were."[20]

In 1988 a second apology was made:

"We pray that you will hear the sincerity of our words today and that you will witness the living out of our apology in our actions in the future."[21]

The UCC apologized and acknowledged their shameful part in the dark history of Canadian residential schools. They also pointed out that since 2008 they had "actively engaged in the Truth and Reconciliation Commission of Canada (TRC),*" The United Church of Canada ran 15 residential schools between 1849 and 1969. Around 7% of the 80,000 total residential school students grew up in a UCC facility. They attempted to apologize while still working against survivors of abuse at the hands of the UCC and its staff (including indigenous staff in some cases).[22]

Dr. Philip Gardner in his Ph.D. thesis at the University of Toronto wrote about church sexuality in the "age of Aquarius." Gardner also delved into the "sex problem" that arose within the church with changing attitudes amid the cultural and sexual revolutions of the 1960s. Gardner also references the "tensions" that arose in Chatham, a city in Southwestern Ontario. The Chatham church had a clergyman removed due to what was considered at the time "radical" notions, especially concerning sexuality.[23]

This wouldn't be the last time that Chatham was the center of a sex scandal embroiling the United Church of Canada. In 2008, former minister Robert James Duthie was found not guilty on charges of sexual assault. Two years later, the survivor of seven years of abuse beginning at age twelve (identified as "Jim") initiated a civil case against the United Church.[24]

"I went through hell and back when it came to criminal court," Jim said, of the day he walked out of the courthouse after watching Justice Terrence Patterson find Duthie not guilty.

"One aspect Jim's case highlights is a criminal justice system that has become so stringent with its rules of admissibility and its threshold of

---

* The TRC was founded to raise awareness about the history of the Indian Residential Schools and their painful, lasting legacy.

reasonable doubt," Rob Talach, of Ledroit Beckett Litigation Lawyers, said.

"There was all kinds of reality to Duthie's life—other victims, other incidents, run-ins, temporary reporting of Jim after the abuse to church officials—all that didn't get before the (criminal) court," Talach said.[25]

In an article from 2000 in *Maclean's* magazine, Patricia Treble, and Jane O'Hara wrote about the residential school scandal. They mention George Gordon First Nation, a school in Saskatchewan. It was there that Lorne Pratt attempted suicide at age 12 "[so he could] escape the constant sexual abuse he had suffered over a five-year period."

Around 100,000 indigenous children were stripped of their families, their language, and their culture, forcefully placed in these "schools." Some were even operated by predators who took advantage of the fact that there was no family involvement. Nowhere for the children to seek help. Molestation and beatings as accompaniment to cultural genocide are no way to live.

Sadly, it wasn't even just the white administrators who took part in the abuses. In multiple cases, Indigenous staff at these schools were responsible for beating, taunting, or raping children meant to be under their care. In short, First Nations or White, many adults were involved in stealing their native language, their local folkways passed down for generations, and most tragically... their innocence.

The abuse ran the gamut from emotional to physical to sexual. There were children burned with cigarettes. Some punched in the ear so hard they went deaf. On top of this, the schools were sorely underfunded exacerbating all the other issues. By the mid-1990s litigation began. Suddenly, thousands of individual plaintiffs appeared in addition to multiple class-action suits suing the federal government "and in some cases, the Roman Catholic, United, Anglican and Presbyterian churches."[26]

Regardless the denomination of these religious schools responsible for "institutionalizing abuse," what angers many survivors the most is that so many of their abusers are still walking free. We're talking about massive institutional pedophilia that was unimpeded for decades, perpetrated and perpetuated by the very people who were charged with protecting these children.

The cases are too numerous to go into each one individually, one however involves "Mr. Starr." William Starr spent 1968 to 1984 engaging in an "unimpeded 16-year run of pedophilia at Gordon by enticing impoverished boys into having sex, then buying their silence with money, arcade games and clothes." Starr took some boys with him on a trip to Regina, leaving them alone in his car while he gambled until 2 am. After he was done getting his betting fix taken care of, he felt the urge to sate other desires. Starr took the boys to a motel where he raped them. He was found guilty of abusing multiple children for years.[27] For this, he received a four-and-a-half-year prison sentence. For perspective, that's about how long Kai spent in solitary awaiting a trial date.

"The thing about abuse is that it keeps coming back," Jim said, growing agitated as he recalled his experiences. "Now I'm trembling. I get anxiety attacks. I don't feel like going out anywhere."[28]

In 1996, the year the last school closed, a government-appointed commission concluded that thousands of aboriginal students died in horrid conditions at the residential schools. Thousands more were physically and sexually abused. All as a result of attempts by the churches and the government to "elevate the savages,"[29] according to the report.

95% of claims involve sexual and physical abuse according to Cindy Clegg, spokeswoman for the school's resolution office. An article from 2002 in the *Washington Post* reported that the UCC had 750,000 members and had currently settled 60 of the 600 current claims.[29]

Despite the apology, that didn't stop the UCC from appealing a ruling that found it "jointly liable for the sexual abuse of students at a native residential school." Not surprisingly, survivors who suffered years of physical, psychological, and sexual abuse at the hands of UCC staff at the school were not pleased.[30]

Willy Blackwater suffered years of abuse at the hands of the UCC residential school. "I think it's totally disgusting," he told the *Toronto Globe and Mail*. "The officials who are appealing weren't raped."[31]

Kai told me personally about his experiences related to the child abuse cult but also wanted to make sure to set some things clear. Here and in the next chapter I'll leave it to Kai to explain in his own words:

> Hey, you asked about the United Church, and I think there's more than enough graphic detail about what they did in the Indian Residential Schools out there. Google "Truth and Reconciliation Commission." Gilbert likes to play the victim, but he was like a capo at the concentration camps: the priests let him have his pick of the younger boys and girls as long as he snitched on the kids who were speaking their Native language or teaching each other the Native beliefs. Although its widely publicized that the priests made the kids line up and fondled each of their genitals in some creepy ceremony, it's not as well-known that some of the older kids were made into capos and abused the younger kids. Gil was one of those. He said that the priests got the kids aroused so they could "steal their sexual energy"; but he's such a hypocrite because that's what he and Lenora did when they watched soft-core porn and "cuddled" with me.

Speaking of "Family"-inspired practices, PLEASE make a distinction between my maternal grandparents and Shirley. My maternal grandad and grandma were regular Canadian Baptists. My grandad was a pastor at Gull Lake Bible Camp for decades, and never once abused any of the hundreds of children in his care. He and his wife were and are upstanding, morally excellent people who regularly help those in need. My birth mother Shirley idolized the Hell's Angels and ran away to California on her motorbike when she was in her early twenties. That's where she joined The Family. My maternal grandparents never hesitated to call her out for her abusive behavior towards children, so she severely limited their ability to contact me. They strongly disapproved of her brand of "Christianity"; and repeatedly warned her that the harmful practices she picked up from the Family would come back to haunt her. They told me she changed a lot after she got back from California but wouldn't elaborate other than that I "should find my own way and examine scripture for myself."

Although she's mostly gone underground with her Family practices nowadays, she does insidious things like naming her dogs "Penis"; "Bolles"; and "Spunky"; so that her neighbors hear her calling their names at night in some perverse flirty fishing ritual. She does weird head games like deadpanning the question to people in a church meet and greet, "what does penny and bollah mean in French?" (it means penis and balls, the names of her dogs). Her husband works for the Canadian Government, so they know damn well what those names mean in French (Canada is bilingual, so government employees are required to speak both languages). But she gets off on acting indignant and surprised when the French parishioners tell her, then laughing at them later when she's at home. Did I mention she's a trained actor/clown too? She ACTUALLY went to clown college (there's actually a college for clowns).

CHAPTER 4

ON THE ROAD: THE EARLY YEARS

To truly understand this story, we need to understand Kai's childhood, youth, and what led him to his homefree lifestyle. Much has been made of Kai's being "institutionalized" at a young age. What some don't understand is that being a victim of child abuse and neglect is not a judgment of the abused child. No one knows Kai's story better than he does, so I can think of no better way to shine a light on his formative experiences than letting him tell his story in his own words.

—•—

I was born on September 3, 1988. Both of my birth parents were in a fundamentalist Christian cult. They locked me in a room deadbolted from the outside and regularly beat me with broom handles. I woke up screaming from night terrors regularly, and for doing so I was beaten and thrown in freezing cold showers until hypothermic and unable to scream. My birth parents admitted that I was sexually abused at a very young age, but no one will tell me by who.

My birth parents split when I was 4; they had separated at least a dozen times before then. Shirley and Gil both got off on the attention they received from other people for being the "super-parents" of a "problem child." For example, Shirley hit me upside the head right before we walked into a funeral gathering so that I'd start screaming and acting angry: just so she could be seen quelling my "tantrum." Gil abused Shirley until she had fits of rage, then incited her to take it out on me: so he could be seen pretending to "rescue" me from her. Their behavior has a technical name: "Munchausen-by-proxy Syndrome," which is when a caregiver induces an injury in a child to benefit from the sympathies of others.

Author: In the most severe cases of Munchausen by proxy (MBPS) children have been killed by parents or caretakers. One especially horrific case is that of Marybeth Tinning who killed multiple of her children. Doctors initially believed the early childhood deaths were due to a genetic condition. That is, until she adopted a son who also died from a mysterious fall.

Munchausen by proxy is also called factitious disorder imposed on another (FDIA). Victims tend to be under the care of the person who gains pleasure from "nursing back to health" a person who without their meddling would be healthy in the first place. MBPS survivors have been fed poison or kept ill by a variety of means, occasionally ending in death. In at least a few cases, multiple children were killed by parents with MBPS.1

It was more than just neglect and psychological abuse, however. As Jessob Reisbeck has pointed out, it's understandable why Kai would have a strong visceral reaction to predators due to his personal experiences as a child and teenager dealing with parents shaped by The Family cult and the United Church of Canada's abusive residential school program. He has however asked me to make sure it's understood that his grandparents were not party to the abuse he experienced at the hands of both Shirley Stromberg and Gilbert McGillivary. Shirley's indoctrination into the Children of God/The Family cult occurred when she left home in her

twenties for California which was a hotbed of Family recruiting all through-
out the 60s, 70s, and 80s. He tells me that Shirley also had a fascination with
the Hell's Angels, though she was never officially associated with the biker gang.

Gil took me with him when he left Shirley. He let his girlfriend Lenora move in. At home, she either ignored me, used "tickle fights" as a pretext to molest me, or went into fits of apoplectic rage and tried to kill me using knives or her bare hands. The cops were called on her at least 20 times that I can remember, usually by me, after I barricaded myself in a room to escape her attacks. I once wrestled the knife from her, when I was 7, and cut up her favorite couch with it. At the after-school care where she worked, she transformed into a different person... like Jekyll and Hyde. Gil started fucking her when she was 11 and he was 22.

They put soft-porn on the TV when I was 6 and "cuddled" with me; then coached me to have sex with the girls from my elementary school. Gil was trying to use me to lure them over to my house, but I was always trying to spend as much time as possible away from Gil and Lenora, so I stayed at my friends' houses whenever possible.

Starting when I was 6, every day I'd run away after school and spend as much time away from "home" as I could. When they had a particularly vicious day with me, they'd take me to an amusement park or someplace fun the next day and take pictures of me laughing and having fun. I didn't know at the time that those pictures were to show the social workers that "see, everything's OK, he's happy here." I wasn't. I used to run away to comic book stores to read comic books and wish I was one of the heroes. The comic book store people were really nice to let a 6-year-old paw up their comics like that. I formed my ideas of what a man should be like from Peter Parker and Wolverine and Archie Andrews. Gil and Lenora couldn't match my persistence, so after awhile they stopped trying to catch me when I ran away, and I got free rein of Edmonton.

Gil and Shirley had a custody battle going on over me, and they both used me as a weapon against the other. I would go on week-long "visits" to Shirley and Ross's, and they would beat me and keep me confined while trying to brainwash me back into their branch of the cult. Gil and Lenora gave me sabotage manuals to read and incentivized me with junk food and video games for things like flushing a roll of toilet paper down the toilet to flood Shirley's house or letting the air out of their tires. During this time, I found supportive, loving women who saw a runaway urchin and compassionately invited me to their homes for tea or a family meal. This sort of community Surrogate-Mother-behavior is almost an institution in Western Canada, and there's even a "Block Parent" program that sponsors it. I never knew how lucky I was to live in Western Canada. I just thought that most women besides Shirley and Lenora were angelic, loving beings.

Author: One of the things I find most impressive about Kai, perhaps more so than his willingness to put his own personal safety at risk to help others, is his ability to stay positive and maintain decency despite the horrific and traumatic past visited upon him.

When I was 9 1/2, Gil lost the custody battle. Shirley and Ross apprehended me with Social Services, and I lost all my runaway friends. Shirley and Ross made me throw away all my "devil music" and "secular books" (i.e. comics) and beat me, and confined me any time I ran away. I was hyper-sexualized ever since 5 years of age, so Shirley stood outside my door to listen for me masturbating, then threw open the door and dragged me out of bed with my dick in my hand to strap me. The ministers in her cult advised her to use a rubber strap instead of broom handles so it wouldn't leave evidence (i.e. caning bruises). She dropped me out of public school after I told a teacher about the abuse and the cult. She knew how to talk to psychologists and social workers from the custody battle and had a lot of connections in social services from it. So she talked her way out of any consequences for her child abuse.

After awhile, strapping me wasn't enough. She degraded me by making me give her foot rubs. The foot rubs began to have massage oil, then became shoulder rubs, then full massages with a vibrator and everything. Any time I made friends in the neighborhood, she found a reason to ruin my friendships with stories of how bad I was as a child; then beat me and told me I was unworthy of those friends and needed to beg for Jesus' forgiveness; then made me give her a full massage, starting with her feet.

When I was 11, I went to a Christian Youth Conference, and made a bunch of female friends. When I got back, I stole a phone from the Victory Christian Fellowship kitchen and used a basement line at Shirley and Ross's house to call my friends. Shirley was lurking on the phone upstairs listening in, and she interrupted us to call my friends whores and threaten to call their parents. She beat me, then called two ministers from her cult to exorcise "the daughter of Satan" from me. After they left, she made me give her a full massage and held me in an armchair repeating "it's OK to feel sexually attracted to your mother." I called social services that night and told them I was being abused.

When the social worker asked to speak to Shirley, she told her *I* was the abuser and had "behavioral problems." They came to apprehend me, but she talked them into letting the minister of her cult keep me at his house. Her cult had brainwashed me into being stupidly honest; but she had a decade of experience in talking to social workers and psychologists, so she lulled them into complacency while Ross drove my two siblings to another province to evade apprehension. The minister of her cult kept trying to "exorcise the daughter of Satan" from me and make me freak out; so that the social workers could see evidence of the "behavioral problems" Shirley and Ross claimed I had. Meanwhile, they coached my siblings on what to say to the investigators in Alberta, over the phone from B.C. Ross professionally trains actors to historically re-enact events for the Canadian Government, and Shirley is a trained clown/actor and practically a psychologist, so I really had no chance against them. Social services bought their story, and I got sent to a group home where I was expected to attend hypno- and group-therapy and admit to "my problem behavior"; and "make amends to my family."

As much as that "therapy" chafed on me, Ross and Shirley had to keep up their act around the social workers, and the group home staff was full of open-minded college students who taught me how the world actually is and how to succeed in it. I got my so-called "devil music" back with interest, and was allowed to read my "secular books" and have friends that weren't in the cult. My siblings weren't so lucky. They moved with Ross and Shirley to a farm in the middle of nowhere, surrounded by about a hundred fundamentalist Christian cult members, who "preyed in tongues" and brainwashed them for years.

My foster dad, Nick, came to visit me at the group home when I was 13. He interviewed me and asked if I wanted to go live with him and his wife, Aggie. I liked him and said yes, so social services moved me from Stony Plain to Nick and Aggie's farm just outside of St. Paul. They bought me a snowboard, skateboard, and guitar, and encouraged me to develop my skills. They taught me life skills and learning strategies with patience and kindness and enrolled me in public school so I could make friends. No more homeschooled cult bullshit, social services saved my adolescence from de-socialization and brainwashing. Nick and Aggie were pivotal in that save. They were and are the wisest and kindest people I've ever met.

I dropped out of Grade 10 and ran away, four months before my 16th birthday. My high school principal caught me smoking weed, and said I had to attend "alternate education distance learning" (i.e. homeschooling). I stepped outside for a cigarette after and caught Nick's eye. He could see

I was about to run. I said, "Dad, this isn't your fault. You did everything right." He said, "If you change your mind, our door's always open." I took off and used the money I saved from working at McDonald's to rent a room at a drinking buddy's house. He was 27, and a supervisor at the local food processing plant. He got me a job, and I was enjoying being independent... Then I realized that he and his thirty-something year old friends were preying on my drunk teenage friends who came over to drink booze. I moved out to Red Deer and tried to go back to school. But I had a drinking problem. I couldn't concentrate on schoolwork between working for a living and getting drunk.

I moved back to St. Paul and got a job at Boston Pizza in January 2005. I used my roommate's car to drive deliveries between working as a line cook. One day in April, right before I got fired for drinking on the job, my Buddhist manager told me about a place in B.C. called "Summerland." He said that I could live on the beach there, surrounded by fun people who would pay me good money to pick peaches and play guitar. When I got fired (the other manager thirstily mistook my container of Jack Daniels for his container of Iced Tea and chugged half of it...), I packed my backpack and hitchhiked to the Okanagan Valley. I lived on the beach all summer, playing guitar and working construction for money, eating peaches and cherries from the trees. Near the end of summer, I heard about a magical surf spot near Tofino, B.C. from a fellow hitchhiker and left the Okanagan to find it.

Shortly before my 17th birthday, I "found Jesus." I read the New Testament and did everything the red letters said, right down to giving away everything I owned to the poor. I was firmly convinced that I was meant to go to Tofino and surf, and I crossed by ferry to Nanaimo to do just that. I had fasted and prayed myself down to less than 100 lbs, and naively approached random strangers preaching the gospel and talking about my plans to go surfing in a remote location. A forty-something year old career criminal with a history of sexually assaulting minors told me he would go with me to Tofino; I had no idea who he was, so I went with him. When he and I got far enough from town that no one could hear me scream, he brutally assaulted me and tortured me for hours. He kept telling me he would kill me when he was finished. I escaped by running naked through a mile of thick brambles and jumping off a cliff to the embankment beside a highway. I walked in front of an SUV to make the driver stop and call 911. I was willing to get hit by the SUV rather than let the rapist catch me. When the cops arrived with an ambulance, I don't remember anything until I was at the hospital and talking to the doctor after the rape kit.

Shirley saw the opportunity to look like a super-mom in front of her church, so she flew to B.C. to get me; but the first time I woke up screaming, she checked me into the psych ward of the local hospital. When I was discharged a week later with a diagnosis of PTSD, I left for Edmonton to live with my friends. I was in therapy and barely holding down a job to make rent. It was a struggle to stay sober because I had to drink to calm my nerves enough to be around people.

One of the regular, non-cult Christians from St. Paul named John offered me a construction job, on the condition that I stay sober. I started that at the same time as a 6-month long "healing program" at the Mannawannis Native (American Indian) Friendship Center. After I testified at the rapist's trial, he was acquitted because I couldn't prove I didn't consent.

I finished the "healing program" by hitchhiking to the Saddle Lake Indian Reservation. I smudged sweetgrass with a Cree elder (Medicine Man), who asked me who I was. I started introducing myself like an interview, but he stopped me and said, "No. Who are you really?" I told him about my hitchhiking adventure and how one of my friends was too high on shrooms to say "Caleb"; so he started calling me "Kai." I told him that after that, I started introducing myself as Kai wherever I went and felt free to create myself completely free from my past... until I was assaulted and went back to living as "Caleb." He said "Kai is who you really are. You need to reconcile yourself."

After that talk, I was inspired to go door to door on the whole reservation, introducing myself as a half-breed and asking forgiveness for what my white ancestors did. A lot of people forgave me but many said, "I can't forgive you for something you never did."

After that, I hitchhiked back to St. Paul. I kept working construction for John Reid and saved up about $3000 to send to Gospel for Asia to build wells and buy school supplies and livestock for kids in the Third World. He introduced me to the regular Christian leaders of Moose Lake Baptist Bible Camp. I volunteered as a camp counselor for teens the same age as me and made a bunch of friends. These friends, along with John Reid, the people from the Mannawannis, Nick, and Aggie helped me get my high school diploma. At Nick and Aggie's suggestion, I walked into the same high school I was expelled from for smoking weed and told the same principal who suspended me that I wanted to challenge the diploma exam. He said, "Alright. I'll schedule you for two weeks from now."

John Reid gave me two weeks paid leave from work, and my friends from MLBBC lent me their study guides. I studied 12 hours a day every day for two weeks straight, fueled by free coffee from the Mannawannis. I passed with marks so high that I was accepted into the University of Alberta's Bachelor of Science (Pre-Med) program on full scholarship (provided by Social Services on recommendation from Nick and Aggie).

In 2007, for the month leading up to college, I drove to Tofino in my Dodge Omni and learned how to surf.

I got passing grades, and I made good friends, but I felt that something was missing in University. I craved adventure. I started working construction again as soon as finals were over. Instead of going back to pre-Med, I enrolled in paramedic training. In January 2009, I started training at the Canadian College of Emergency Medical Services. Every day after class, I'd either find an open mic or busk on my guitar in the subway mezzanine. I passed all of the written and practical exams for my pre-paramedic "EMT" certification by April. I was working as a fitness consultant at Club Fit and about to start my on-the-job preceptor training, when I met a bunch of hippies who persuaded me to volunteer at a music festival and travel instead.

I hitchhiked to Vancouver Island Music Festival to work security and was totally enchanted by festival culture. I heard about a festival of +12,000 people called "Shambhala," so I hitchhiked to it. The tickets were sold out, but I snuck in anyways and had the time of my life.

I hitchhiked back to Red Deer in August of 2009, after Shambhala. When I first arrived, I found a gig volunteering at a thrift shop that outfits battered women with furniture and clothes to flee abusive relationships. When someone donated an estate that included a really nice suit, the woman who ran the place said, "Hey Kai, you'd look good in this. Do you want it?" I said "Sure!" and did a job interview in it for a bar-tending position at a local 4.5-star hotel. I aced the interview, got the job, and saved up a few thousand dollars in tips in no time at all. I used it to move into an intentional community of hippies in Edmonton in January of 2010. I lived off of my savings while learning from the eco-conscious, spiritually aware social activists that surrounded me. When my savings ran out, I worked construction in the days and played guitar, and learned about Eastern Religions in the evenings. Every weekend there was a tribal gathering with local musicians, locally sourced food, and homemade brews and weed. It was Hippie Heaven. They inspired me to learn more about the forest, how it works, how to survive in it, and how to protect it. To that end, I enrolled in the forest technology program at NAIT, a local community college, for a 12-week wilderness induction course.

I hitchhiked to Shambhala Music Festival again in the summer of 2010 and arrived back at NAIT the day after the last day of Shambhala.

I spent 8 weeks out in a cabin in the Canadian Wilderness, not unlike Jack Kerouac in Dharma Bums. I learned how to navigate in the wild, what goes into a forest, and how to extract most any resource or person from the forest. When I got back to Edmonton, I divided my days between course work and playing music at events. One day near the end of the first semester, I wrote an essay about how Weyerhauser is destroying irreplaceable old-growth rainforest in coastal B.C. An instructor pulled me aside and told me to rewrite my essay because it would get me blackballed in the industry. I said I had signed up for the program specifically to save the rainforest. He told me I was in the wrong place, so I dropped out.

Right after that conversation, I got a call out of the blue from Gilbert, for the first time in years. He invited me to his place in Ontario for Christmas. I drove all the way to Ontario in my van; but when I got there, I found out that he didn't check with Lenora first. He tried to pretend I showed up out of nowhere, but she confronted him with text messages showing him sending me directions to their house. She started beating the shit out of him in front of their 3 kids (On Christmas Day, class fucking act). While this was happening, I had turned the webcam on and was recording the whole thing while pretending to surf the web. Gil called the cops, and when the two female Ontario Provincial Police officers showed up, Lenora pointed at me and screamed, "HE HIT ME!!! I WANNA PRESS CHARGES!!!"

The OPP officers were about to cuff me when I calmly said, "That's a lie. I caught the whole thing on video on the computer. Check for yourself." Lenora took a swing at me, I dodged it, and the female cops arrested her for domestic violence. She spent the night in jail, and the next day she got out and took the kids to her mother's house. Gil, sniveling, pleaded with her to stay; he said he deleted the video and wouldn't press charges. I told them both they were pathetic and hadn't changed a bit since I was a kid, and that I never wanted to see or hear from them again.

I got in my van and drove to Montreal to celebrate New Year's. While I was there, I recorded some videos of me singing and playing guitar, and uploaded them to my YouTube channel as "private."

I drove back to Alberta after that.

I worked construction and lived in my van, using my student ID to shower and train in the college gym and swimming pool. I was dead set on moving to Tofino to surf full-time. I watched videos on how to surf and snuck into underground parking garages to train on my longboard. I trained at the pool until I could swim 2 miles without a break, using flutter boards to simulate paddling on a surfboard.

When spring hit, I got a job pouring concrete and worked 12-16 hour shifts 6 days a week until October. I saved up thousands of hours so I could collect employment insurance benefits all winter and moved to Tofino at the end of October 2011 with $20,000 and a guaranteed income of $2200/ month from EI. I lived in my van in the old-growth rainforest, surfing every day and playing guitar at parties or the bar every evening.

In the spring of 2012, I left for a weekend to go to a wedding in Shirley's family. They treated me like I was less than them, like an outcast from their cult. I was extremely offended at having driven 12 hours through the mountains and spent hundreds of dollars to come see them, only to be reminded of the Munchausen-by-proxy role they created for, and imposed upon, me. I realized I should never have expected anything else. They would never change, and even if they did, it was too late. I disowned them and left them forever. I have no love for them. I'm dead to them, and they're dead to me.

I got back to Tofino and talked my way into a housekeeping job at a 5-star resort so I could still keep surfing... My EI benefits had run out. I met some hitchhiking metal musicians, who invited me to a metal festival; so, I quit my job and drove them to the festival in Kamloops. We traveled around in my station wagon, skateboarding and going to metal shows all over mainland B.C. for all of June 2012. In July, I went to Kelowna and spent the summer working on orchards; busking, skateboarding, and adventuring around lake Okanagan. By my 24th birthday, my car had broke down; I was out of cash; Canadian winter was right around the corner. I was in Osooyoos drinking with a skateboarder buddy, Shawn Andyson, when I spontaneously said, "I'm going to California to surf all winter. Who's with me?" Shawn said, "I'm down." So we left and crossed the border that night.

When Shawn and I got to Medford, Oregon, his cat ran away at a truck stop. After four hours of searching, a truck driver offered us a ride to Redding, CA. He wanted to stay and keep looking; I told him I'd meet up with him in Cali... (he never found his cat). We met up in Willow Creek, CA where we both got jobs on different weed farms as trimmers. In November, I took my earnings to the Bay Area, and he left for Burnside in Portland. I hung around Santa Cruz and Berkeley until Christmas; then I hitchhiked up to Del Norte to steal hitchhiking gear from a Wal-Mart.

I was hitchhiking back south when a Vietnam veteran "tunnel rat" picked me up. He seemed nice at first, but then he pulled out a 9mm handgun and waved it in my face, and made his dog bite me. He said that if I tried to "abandon" him, his dog would chase me down and he'd shoot me. When he slowed down at a truck stop near Tulare, I bailed out of the moving vehicle and ran for my life. I knocked on a trucker's passenger door and explained to him that I had just ditched my backpack and stuff with a crazy guy who had a gun, and I was worried he was going to find me and shoot me. The trucker told me to get in and gave me a ride to East LA. I took a couple rides to Hermosa Beach; then the bus and Metro to Long Beach; then settled into

Venice Beach for the month of January... Skateboarding and surfing it up. I was hitchhiking back North to Humboldt County to find work on a weed farm when I met Jett McBride outside of Bakersfield.

After the Smash Interview, I hitchhiked up to Stockton on the 199. I checked my messages on a hotel computer, and Jessob told me to stay right there and drove up to do the second interview. Then, I hitchhiked through San Francisco to Santa Rosa, where I checked my messages at a library computer. Jimmy Kimmel offered to pick me up in a limo full of weed and pay for me to do whatever I wanted to if I appeared on his show. I was like, "sure"; so, he sent Kardashians producer Lisa Samsky to pick me up. While I was waiting for her, I smoked a blunt with a fan who had seen my video, who squirted about 16 doses (an eyedropper full) of LSD into my mouth. I was already tripping when I met Lisa, and we spent the night at a fan's house in Frisco. The next day we went to Hermosa and I skateboarded down the entire hill from the top to the plaza, then went surfing beside the pier. Later that day, we went to Kimmel's studio and did the skit. The leftover blunt from the fan in Santa Rosa had acid on or in it; so I started tripping again after I smoked it. I got loaded on Jack Daniels and got kicked out of the fanciest hotel in Hollywood for skateboarding in the lobby. The next day, I made the YouTube videos from 2010 "public." Kimmel's people drove me up to Arcata. I partied and skateboarded with Humboldt State University students for a couple weeks, then went to Fresno to testify at Jett McBride's arraignment.

I met some people in Fresno who had made a Facebook page about me, but they were shamelessly exploiting me to promote their own products. I was invited as a headliner to play at music shows but got maybe two songs in after everyone else played. I finally had enough when the promoter interrupted me at a studio someone else had invited me to and told me to play guitar differently. I was like, "You wanna play this? Because I only spent 14 years learning how." She started acting downright nasty so I said,

"Either stop acting like a fucking jackass or get out of my life. I'm sick of being exploited to promote shit; if I wanted that I would've gone with the Kardashians and at least got paid for it." She left in a huff and flamed me on the Facebook page, but when people called her out on it, she removed the page rather than apologize. Other musicians were commenting and messaging me, saying things like "she doesn't represent us at all. You alright with us, Kai." I was like, "Whatever, her loss. Let her find someone else to use." I ditched her and partied with some friendly fans, including some musicians who put together a ska show with me the night after she pulled that shit.

I hitchhiked to Oakland and partied with some freight-train riders I met near the Cafe Revolution, and made a radio appearance on CR's metal station. I met up with many fans like this on my way back up to Arcata. I was drinking too much for my own good, but it numbed my anxiety I felt after McBride attacked those people. That whole incident triggered my PTSD to the max. When I got back to Arcata, I found out someone had stolen my surfboard and gear. I didn't really care because I was getting hella invites to parties with free booze everywhere I went.

I had an inbox full of messages from people all over the world inviting me to surf, play guitar, or party with them. I'll never know how many there actually were, because when I checked it on February 4, it already said "10,000+." Facebook stops counting after that.

All I had to do was search my messages for the city I wanted to visit, and I had a place to stay and with a friendly tour guide.

I made it back to Venice Beach and was walking around the boardwalk when Adam Bauxbaum walked up to me with a sign that said, "Kai the Hitchhiker." Adam was a Rainbow Family organizer, and he told me he "manifested" me because he and his friends wanted to bring me to every Grateful Dead dance between San Francisco and the Mexican Border.

I shit you not, straight outta Kerouac; a modern Neil Ginsburg appeared out of nowhere on a magical mission.

I went with them to San Diego and San Francisco and back to LA, and every happening spot in between. We smoked more hash than I've ever seen before, and fans popped out of the woodwork EVERYWHERE we went, inviting us to random acts of awesomeness.

When we got back to LA, I responded to a too-good-to-be-true invite by Kailani Laigo, to record at Studio 13 off of Sunset Boulevard. I arrived with a 4-pack of Guinness, and he let me use his equipment to record. We smoke a bunch of his weed and my hash, and afterwards he was practically begging me to stay, but I had other plans for a party in Downtown LA. I left Kailani's studio without any idea what a slimeball he was... his podcast 3 months later, where he bribed a crystal meth addict with a bag of meth to make shit up about me, totally blindsided me. I never knew that Kailani was a meth dealer, or I wouldn't have associated with him. Meth is disgusting.

Anyways.

The next day, I responded to a fan's offer to go on an epic adventure from Malibu to Arizona. A week later, I was on the Greyhound from Phoenix to Jacksonville, FL, where a group of comedians (no joke), headed by Jessica Mears, had invited me to play guitar at one of their shows. I found out that I have a lot of fans in Florida. People were inviting me to gigs and to smoke weed and drink beers by the beach, all the time.

After about a week, I bought another Greyhound ticket to NYC. I had messages from media people in NYC who wanted to interview me, including the Gregory Brothers, who invited me to jam with them at their studio in Williamsburg. People in New York were recognizing me left and right: inviting me to posh West Village penthouses to smoke bongs, and to trendy nightclubs where bouncers were like, "HOLY FUCK, IT'S THE SMASH SMASH SMASH GUY!!!" and jumped me ahead of lines, got me in for free, and gave me free drinks all night. I got invited to a party near Albany, where I made a drunken fool of myself at a Karaoke bar. Then I went to Rhode Island for a week to meet some skateboarders and surfers.

I was on my way back to NJ via NYC on May 10 when my ride fell through. I tried sleeping outside near Columbia, but I got rained out, so I had to take a subway to Port Authority and sleep by the Greyhound terminal clutching my ticket stub. I was in Times Square the next day, trying to find the train to NJ so I could hop a ride when the rapist Joseph Galfy walked up to me and asked me where I was from. All these years later, it occurs to me that he was checking to see if I was an immigrant, so he could get me deported if I tried to report him. I was so naive.

—•—

As for that horrific night, I asked Kai what he can remember.

—•—

I don't remember leaving. One thing you gotta understand about PTSD and rape trauma syndrome (RTS) is that sometimes people dissociate, have amnesia, and lose chunks of time. I very clearly remember waking up on the floor and punching him in the face. Then blank. Then he shoved my head into the bed, I grabbed his wrists, pushed back, and moved backwards. I kicked up and hit him from underneath, and he slammed into me. I'm shaking as I write this. I tried to shove his head away from me, he was making movements on top of me as I was trying to get out from under him, then I don't remember anything until I was in the parking lot of Bistro 1051.

Apparently, I tried to call the NJ fan while I was blacked out. I heard a recording of the voicemail I left. But I don't remember leaving it. Same thing when I was raped as a teenager. I was running through the trees, then I jumped off a 30' embankment and rolled down a ditch, threw myself in front of a car to make him stop, naked and bleeding, but after the paramedics got there I can't remember anything until I was talking to a doctor at the hospital. There was a whole ambulance ride and about an hour that I just lost completely, with no recollection whatsoever, even though I apparently answered the paramedics and described what happened. I know I was drugged by Galfy, but I don't think the memory loss is completely from drugs because the same thing happened when I was 17.

—•—

I also spoke to Tony Cantu and another person who met Kai before the events of May 2013. This is what Tony had to say to me:

> Camping in willow creek ridding our skateboards threw Arcata and willow creek bombing his and hitting on all the babes ! We camped with a group of friends and I have a tattoo from that camp trip. On our way back to Arcata we almost died when thr rv we were in back wheels broke loose and we careened into a ditch next to a 200+ft cliff.

Tony said Kai was an "awesome soul" who was "always down to have a good adventure."

One other person I spoke to who had met Kai after the event in Fresno had this to say:

> I think Kai was a cool and charismatic guy. what I meant by the "badass" and "dope" comments was actually trying to convey the voice of sincere reverence amongst the dudes

in Humboldt who saw him ride into town as a drifter with a high moral character. They thought he was awesome in both the Ninja Turtle use of the word, but also the classical sense of the word in "awe inspiring".

I am from a different small university town in California and I think people in my hometown for instance would have been a little more hesitant to give him the same hero's welcome he received in Humboldt because he was (in)famous for having committed a violent act; even if it was a noble violent act that saved lives. Kai is an interesting character in that way because he is a hero I think, but many Americans who even think he did a good thing saving lives feel uncomfortable with the idea of taking violence into your own hands and prefer to defer violence to the state.

CHAPTER 5

LEGENDS, MYTHS, AND MISPERCEPTIONS

Epic heroes embody the cultural ideals of the time and place they spring from. Arguably, Superman and Spiderman could be considered contemporary American counterparts to the likes of Odysseus or Aladdin (though considering the nature of American society and the consumerist values that have subsumed it, a huckster along the lines of L. Ron Hubbard might be more fitting).

Hubbard might be more fitting, but Kai appealed to people because he represented the kind of hero people craved, one people need. In a disillusioned world, just believing in something can be therapeutic, even life-changing.

Earlier we did a quick run-through of some relevant bits of history related to hitchhiking and surfing. That background should simplify understanding the mechanisms behind stereotyping and scapegoating as they apply in this case. So much of Kai's story has been warped by "the telephone game." Occasionally, it seems, as if the misinformation and disinformation may have been deliberately disseminated. In other instances, it's likely just laziness or an attempt to capitalize on clickbait sensationalism. Then take all those incomplete and erroneous narratives floating around and it's no surprise that the truth is hidden behind a murky wall of incomplete or downright false, sometimes conflicting details.

Shortly after Kai's arrest, a reporter played up how Kai almost crashed with him on that horrific night, when Kai was assaulted in Clark. The reporter had briefly messaged Kai through Facebook. He didn't bother until near the end of the article to point out that he "likely" wouldn't have suffered the same fate, as the inciting incident was Kai being drugged and raped. Or the story in which a reporter goes on a rant comparing Kai to the TV character Dexter Morgan, a serial killer who hunts down other serial killers.

The article was eventually corrected noting that Jett McBride was not, in fact, killed with a hatchet. But wouldn't it have been more responsible to just retract the piece entirely once you realize the premise is built on fiction? Then, of course, there's the case of Todd Grande. Grande is no stranger to misperceptions. He markets himself on YouTube as "Dr. Grande" and does psychological profiles of True Crime figures, famous people, and e-celebs in the news. Whatever is trending at the moment.

Grande, like the YouTuber The Rewired Soul, is somewhat controversial in certain circles. The Rewired Soul is an armchair psychologist who capitalizes on trending topics to put his pop psychology spin on things. He has claimed that his goal is mental health advocacy and awareness. But many critics consider him just another gossip and drama channel.

YouTube has been under fire for lack of oversight and moderation related to extremist content, but other issues abound such as child grooming.* Grande

---

* Institutional pedophilia and child grooming are topics covered in my first book *Pedogate Primer: The Politics of Pedophilia*. One chapter is devoted specifically to online grooming facilitated by YouTube and other platforms.

uses the veneer of psychological expertise as the main selling point for his videos. That said, despite his disclaimers that he is not diagnosing anyone, it's obvious that is what he is trying to do.

Many commenters on his videos or in Reddit threads and elsewhere decry his misuse of his credentials (which are, somewhat dodgy themselves as I'll show shortly). Dr. Grande is not a therapist, psychologist, or psychiatrist. He is licensed as a mental health counselor, but his degree is related to training counselors, not practicing.

In one article about the controversial YouTube counselor, John Torous, a psychiatrist at a teaching hospital connected to Harvard Medical School makes it painfully clear. "Even psychiatrists don't comment on the mental health of anyone they haven't examined."[1]

This is the cornerstone of the Goldwater rule. The American Psychological Association created the Goldwater rule in response to professionals weighing in on the mental state of presidential candidate Barry Goldwater in the 1960s. The rule prevents APA members from commenting on the mental health of anyone they haven't personally examined.[2]

Dr. Grande is not licensed to practice medicine, he is not a licensed psychiatrist or psychologist and his doctorate is a PhD, not MD. Though he was licensed by the state of Delaware as a Mental Health Counselor, that does not give him the same leeway in diagnosis as a practicing psychologist.

His sensationalist videos, clickbait tactics, and snarky insensitive humor are also a turn-off to many. In a 2019 article, "Armchair Psychologists Who Ticked off YouTube" Dr. Grande is mentioned as one of the gossip mongers in question.

Even some of his followers from years back have left with a bad taste in their mouths as Grande's content becomes more sarcastic and obviously geared entirely towards engagement farming* and AdSense. From one former fan: "I'm surprised he gets so much universal love, at least from what I've seen. Like you pointed out in your original post, no decent medical professional would make YT commentary videos which go to the level of speculation that he does. Goes to show that if you're a man, speak with authority, and use complex terminology/jargon people will be convinced that you're an expert on the topic.

"Like a lot of YT commentators, he presents himself as unbiased and objective, but he has a clear political/ideological slant in a lot of his videos - the MJ video being a good example of that. What a disturbing and victim-blamey video."[3]

Many others, often former viewers, also note how he has begun to give them "major bad vibes." That something "seems off." Another recurring consideration is his apparent lack of empathy saying they would never go to him for therapy. Luckily, he didn't practice, so harming patients was never a concern. Most people who see his videos likely assume he is an actual psychologist or psychiatrist who went to an actual institute of higher learning. Nothing could be further from the truth.[4]

Grande did a speedrun of higher education, going from undergrad admission to attainment of PhD in less time than some spend on their doctorate alone. How did he do this? Is he some sort of intellectual savant? Not quite. You see, the trick is making sure to find the right diploma mill.

Grande received his BS degree from the "acclaimed" Excelsior College online, in the space of one year. His Master's degree is from another

---

* Using clickbait tactics to encourage more engagement, even "hate views" and comments which at this point just encourages YouTube to serve the recommended video to more people due to the engagement.

online diploma mill "school." He received his PhD from the University of Wilmington (not to be confused with the legitimate University of North Carolina-Wilmington). Unlike UNC-Wilmington, the online college he attended has an acceptance rate of 100%.[5]

Luckily, Grande didn't use his credentials to practice. Instead, he ended up teaching at, you guessed it, the paper mill "university" itself. In one forum discussing the issues with Grande, a PhD in Clinical Psychology takes issue with how he "claims to know things that are untrue." Going on to implore anyone who will listen: "Advice to any students following him for educational purposes...please find a new teacher/mentor. That is, providing you want to pass licensing exams."

The victim-blaming aspect of his videos also impugns his lack of empathy and professionalism. In one he makes snarky jokes about Claudia Conway, blaming the teenager for her mother sharing inappropriate pictures of her online out of anger. His "Snow Shoveling Murder-Suicide" video is another that has been called out for victim blaming.

Fellow mental health YouTuber "Ana Psychology" is a clinical psychology doctoral candidate (at an actual institute of higher learning that doesn't have a 100% acceptance rate). She made a video to share her concerns "as a fellow mental health professional." She raises several issues especially his "constant mocking and taking jabs at people" as well as his unforgivable penchant for victim blaming.[6]

"His video about the victim Rebecca Schaeffer is disturbing. He lacks empathy, victim blames and objectifies women. I'm relieved to see that other people are bringing attention to his unprofessional behavior." The turning point for Ana was when he "made very light about a situation of this man being stalked by a woman he slept with but didn't want to see anymore." The man was stalked, had his house broken into, and was bombarded with thousands of text messages. Grande used this as an opportunity to offer up his trademark deadpan "zingers."

It's ironic that Grande earlier had critiqued Dr. Phil for much of what he is now popular for. In fact, a Google search for Grande brings up the auto-suggested query "is dr todd grande a real doctor." Well, I mean, technically sure, but that's about it.

Robert Pandina at Rutgers comes up regarding seeding disinformation as well. Or perhaps more aptly, refusing to dispel disinformation attributed to him during the Grand Jury hearing. Dr. Robert Pandina was positioned as a medical expert. Misrepresenting his testimony was meant to weaken Kai's self-defense claim and cast doubt on the assault, despite the evidence.[7]

Prosecutor Scott M. Peterson in his questioning of Sgt. Johnny Ho claimed there were "absolutely zero signs that there was ever any kind of date rape drug." Well, of course, when you run it through a dishwasher such evidence is spoiled. And, for the record, spoliation of exculpatory evidence is grounds for dismissal in an ordinary case. Or at least on paper. How often these kinds of things happen is shocking but not entirely surprising.

"You'd be throwing up" is another false claim attributed to Pandina.[8] GHB, zopiclone, barbiturates, burundanga (scopolamine),[9] and other drugs can incapacitate one briefly for drug-facilitated crimes including sexual assault. And cases of sleep-driving on these or other drugs also call into question the claims of Peterson which he falsely attributed to Pandina.[10]

"So you don't get drugged, allegedly raped and have no effects whatsoever. [...] the State at this time doesn't believe any of that ever happened."[11]

"When Kai spoke to us, he put out there he was raped by Joe," Peterson told the Grand Jury. "It doesn't appear that he shows any signs of being raped" (then whose unidentified blood was on the alleged rapist's penis?). Peterson's claim that "no semen was found," contradicting the forensics lab report, which is followed by the claim that there was no semen found on the bedsheets, but the puddle of urine on the carpet where Kai involuntarily relieved himself amid the horrific and traumatic event, along with the hairs mashed into the vertical side of the mattress show that the assault took place on the floor rather than the bed.[12]

It's also interesting that the state never offered a single motive.[13] We are expected to believe that Kai just decided out of the blue he was going to murder a lawyer he'd just met. Despite being far too well known to go on the lam, despite the many opportunities and offers arising from his viral success after his heroic acts, Kai decided for no reason at all to kill this man.

Speaking of the Grand Jury testimony, it's notable that the prosecutor made sure not to bring up anything from the McNamara brothers' interviews. John McNamara noted that Kai seemed off in some way when he met him while Kai was still under the influence. "Hi, I'm Kai the Hitchhiker" was the first thing out of his mouth. An odd thing to do if he were "on the run" as has been claimed. It's also unlikely that a man who committed premeditated murder and was "on the run" would leave scraps of paper with his phone number and email address on them at the scene.[14]

Johnny Ho, Homicide Task Force of the Union County Prosecutor's Office, was the on-call detective. It was Ho who was called in to investigate the case and then put on the stand during the Grand Jury by Prosecutor Scott Peterson.

Peterson asked if Ho is "familiar with all of the witness statements" and "all the reports that have been prepared by various other detectives." Ho answered in the affirmative. Well, then that means he was aware of the

Suter and Gardner investigative report that showed the crime scene had been tampered with. That a dishwasher had been run, rinsing away precious evidence. Evidence that could have supported Kai's self-defense claim.

Just like the "bait and switch" tactic* regarding the rape kit run on Galfy, this allowed the prosecutor to attempt to confuse the jury by pointing out that a rape kit had been run (on the alleged rapist) and that there was no evidence of bottles and mugs being drugged (after being run through a dishwasher during a time none of the police investigators can account for).[15] I too am familiar with all of these reports, which is why I know that Johnny Ho's statement of assent could not be correct. Either he was not fully familiar with those reports and witness statements, in which case it was negligence on his part, or he was familiar with the reports and knew good and well he was lying on the stand.

One issue with the coverage of the case in the media boils down to reporters refusing to question the state's claims. Very few news stories exist that even mention the conflicts between the claims of the Grand Jury transcript and the facts available. If the prosecution and state's witnesses lie, misrepresent reality, or omit relevant details it can skew the perception of the case.

Culturally specific stories play a huge role in societal cohesion. Truths passed down, along with myths and legends are vital to any group's development. Joseph Campbell, originator of the hero's journey concept, once said that dreams are private myths, mythology being just public dreams.[16] But not all myths and legends have a positive effect on the world.

Generalizations, related to misinformed tropes about certain types of

---

* A "bait and switch" is a type of scam. In the case of advertising and sales, the substitution of one less valuable product or service for another is a common example. The idea of the bait and switch can apply to several other fields in which the assumption is that one decision or behavior is being made but deceptive methods result in a new one being suggested last minute.

people can develop into negative stereotypes. They can easily impact the way those groups are perceived. As we mentioned in the last chapter, Kai belongs to multiple groups that have been historically stigmatized. The stereotype of the "dumb surfer" or the "shifty or dangerous drifter" has colored the discourse, especially since the events of May 2013.

Hitchhikers have also received an often-unearned bad name, especially since the 1980s. As far as urban legends go, the classic story of the crazed serial killer hitching his way across the country has no basis in reality. Hitchhiking and picking up hitchhikers is not nearly as dangerous as they are painted to be. In most cases, it's the hitchhiker who is more likely at risk than the person picking them up.

One well-known example of the evil hitchhiker myth would be the classic track from The Doors, "Riders on the Storm." The ominous tune warns of a "killer on the road." The tune was written by Jim Morrison and almost became a set piece for a short film screenplay.[17]

Long before Jim became world-famous as an acid rock pioneer, however, movies like the 1953 film noir picture *The Hitch-Hiker* warned drivers of the potential dangers of picking up a stranger on the road. The film was loosely based on what was probably the most famous case of a dangerous hitchhiker, Billy Cook.[18] But for every Billy Cook there are several more Ed Kempers or Ted Bundys picking up unsuspecting travelers.

The 1945 film noir picture *Detour* also featured themes of the dangers of hitchhiking. In this case, the death of the man doing the picking up wasn't the responsibility of the hitcher. That said, it still ended in tragedy for all involved. 1977 brought us the grindhouse flick *Hitch-Hike*. It also dramatized, nay sensationalized, the dangers of hitchhiking. This was in keeping with persistent misinformation that led to hitchhiking falling out of favor in subsequent decades.

In 1986 Rutger Hauer played the ominous and deadly hitchhiker in the movie *The Hitcher* which was remade in 2007. Four years before that was the film *Dead End* which featured another murderous hitchhiker. The truth rarely makes for compelling fiction though. Of course, there have been incidents of hitchhikers perpetrating violence but they are rare. The most famous example of a "deadly hitcher" in recent times would have to be Ronald James Ward Jr.[19]

Meanwhile, look at the Santa Rosa Hitchhiker murders. Or Lawrence Bittaker and Roy Norris the uniquely sadistic "Tool Box Killers." Names like Donald Henry Gaskins, William Bonin, Ivan Milat, Patrick Kearney, Robert Ben Rhoades the "Truck Stop Killer,"[20] and Keith Jesperson the "Happy Face Killer." All of these men, in addition to the aforementioned Kemper and Bundy, are the most well-known serial killers known to prey on the unsuspecting ride seeker.

The Jesperson case, as well as the murders related to "The Ghosts of Highway 20" also reveal how recalcitrant police action (or inaction) can result in not only the innocent being imprisoned but the guilty being left free to continue their evil deeds.

Keith Jesperson was one of a handful of serial killers who would pick up victims, but his case proves how law enforcement will sometimes choose the simplest path forward regardless of the implications. Keith Jesperson, known as the happy face killer, actually had to fight to claim the murder of Taunja Bennett. Laverne Pavlinac and her abusive boyfriend, John Sosnovske, at first ended up in prison for the crime. Pavlinac had been trying to get her boyfriend locked away for various reasons before convincing Oregon police that Sosnovske was responsible for the unsolved murder.[21]

Laverne Pavlinac called the Multnomah County Sheriff's Department, anonymously at first. She claimed Sosnovske had bragged about killing

Bennett. Pavlinac eventually came forward with a piece of ripped jeans "as evidence." Jesperson believed the police told her what she needed to bring forward. Otherwise, she couldn't have known that a piece of the fly area in Bennett's jeans would be convincing enough to implicate Sosnovske. Victoria Redstall reported how the jeans in question didn't even match Bennett's after being sent to the crime lab. Despite this, Sosnovske was not only a burden to Pavlinac but a "nuisance to law enforcement."[22]

The denim was shown to be the wrong material. Plus, Pavlinac had a history of coming up with "bogus reasons" to try to get Sosnovske locked up. At this point, Pavlinac did the unthinkable. She finally confessed to having been present at the time of Bennett's rape and murder. After Sosnovske and Pavlinac were locked up, Jesperson left some graffiti in a Montana truck stop restroom: "I killed Taunja Bennett and two people are on trial for the killing."[23]

Jesperson, after being caught would admit to the Bennet murder. Pavlinac recanted her confession after being charged with aggravated murder. She admitted to manufacturing the "note" and that the ripped jeans material had belonged to her granddaughter. Jesperson confessed, even produced letters to his brother where he'd admitted the murder of 8 women including Taunja Bennett. It was clear that the police weren't interested in investigating any leads that exonerated Pavlinac.

To circumvent the friction from police reticent to be proven wrong, Jesperson had to placate Ken "Duke" Mensebroten. Mensebroten was the jailhouse snitch. Giving him a body for police to find could shorten his sentence. This would eliminate the threat of police becoming aware while he was in the process of smuggling out letters to seven media sources.

"They were all worried that I held a secret piece of evidence that could prove me to be the real killer. And I did!" he told journalist Victoria

Redstall. Jesperson had to devise a plan to reveal evidence that would prove he was responsible without the police being able to bury it (along with their embarrassment and complicity in the murders that followed Bennett). Jesperson announced he remembered throwing her purse out of the window near where the body was dumped. Law enforcement accompanied by Eagle Scouts "armed with machetes and clippers" scanned the area, cutting their way through blackberry bushes.[24]

In a letter to Redstall, Jesperson explained why this was so important: "This is why the prison don't want you to interview me because they don't want you to expose the truth. Remember, they are in on the whole cover-up, too. We could bring down the whole of Multnomah County if you are willing to expose the truth. But be very careful—they may stop you getting in because they read all my letters to you and record all our phone conversations."

Jesperson's guilt would eventually be proved. Not only by the recovery of the purse but also due to saliva tested on the 1994 confession letter to Phil Stanford, a journalist at *The Oregonian*. Another case of serial murder in Oregon also hinged on the police being disinterested in a thorough investigation. In both of these cases the police's failure to act allowed for a series of murders to happen on their watch.[25]

The Ghosts of Highway 20 story is a heartbreaking example of what happens when police decide to cut corners. John Ackroyd was sentenced to five life terms in prison in 1992 for the abduction and murder of Kaye Turner.[26] He also was charged with the murder of his step-daughter Rachanda Pickle in 2013.[27] Over 2 decades after her 1990 disappearance.

Among other sources, *The Oregonian* has released evidence that suggests that Ackroyd was responsible for multiple other murders that occurred on the Oregon stretch of Highway 20. In the previous case, police wouldn't act on the confession of a convicted murderer. It's understandable to take the word of a cold-blooded killer like Jesperson with a grain of salt. But ignoring the facts in favor of the narrative already invested in is quite another thing.[28]

With the Ackroyd killings, however, there is a possibility that the deaths he is believed to be responsible for could have been avoided if his first victim had been believed. Marlene Gabrielson was a new mother. It was her first time going out after giving birth to a newborn baby. She had no idea the evening would end in a nightmare. Ackroyd pulled her into the woods and raped her at knife point.[29]

Despite Marlene calling police, nothing was done about Ackroyd and he is now believed to be responsible for seven killings. The report of Marlene Gabrielson's unprosecuted rape found in the case file is a grim reminder of how the police's failure ended in tragedy.[30] *The Oregonian* went to court to unseal records of the case which would also show that Ackroyd was afforded a plea deal. The deal related to the disappearance of his 13-year-old step-daughter Rachanda. If not for the years of work freeing the rest of the story, the authorities' role in letting Ackroyd continue his killing spree may have remained hidden forever.

Speaking of ghosts, not all hitchhiker tall tales are so ominous, but even some more innocent variations on the theme also have a dark tint of sorts. The Phantom Hitchhiker is another example of hitchhiking cropping up in urban legend.* One of my favorite examples of the myth would be the Tom Waits song "Big Joe and Phantom 309"[31] which is a musical exploration of the classic tale. One of the most classic pieces of scholarship on urban legends is by Professor Jan Harold Brunvands. His book *The Vanishing Hitchhiker* is named in honor of the classic ghost story. The ghostly

---

* This myth starts with a hitchhiker standing next to the highway, thumbing a ride. When the driver pulls to the side to offer a lift, the hitcher suddenly disappears into thin air.

"vanishing hitchhiker"[32] is obviously less dangerous than that of other urban legends such as the "killer on the road" or the ubiquitous "hook-handed man" targeting teens trying to make out in some shady lover's lane.[33]

Theodore Romankow, the prosecutor in Union County, New Jersey certainly leaned into the myth of the bloodthirsty drifter when he tried to pin multiple "unsolved murders" on Kai.[34]

Obviously, there was no truth to this. After the initial statement it never really came up again. That's the nature of black PR. Spread the lie on the front page and by the time you retract it weeks or months later on page E-5, most everyone has the faulty idea stuck in their head. Romankow, by the way, looms large when it comes to the many conflicts of interest and irregularities in the case, but I don't want to get ahead of myself here.

Another source of confusion related to this case is unfortunately all too common. People just don't understand sexual assault and regardless any progress we've made as a culture, we certainly have a long way to go. Judge Robert Kirsch said it "defies common sense"[35] that Kai would return to Galfy's if he thought he had been sexually assaulted. The problem with this is, first off, Kai wasn't sure exactly what had happened the first night. He was already sleep-deprived after having slept in a train station the night before meeting Galfy. After eating, having a beer, and passing out he woke up. There was some sort of residue on his face that he initially thought was just dried saliva. It wasn't until he woke up, bleeding from the violent rape that occurred while he was passed out that Kai knew the reality behind Galfy's seeming kindness.

That said, it's not too surprising why so few sexual assault convictions are returned. For those who don't concern themselves with matters of sexual assault and harassment, the reality does seem to "defy common sense." It's counterintuitive (not to mention disturbing) to realize that, out of every

1,000 sexual assaults, 975 perpetrators go free.

It starts with about 310 being reported to the police. One reason for that is that the insensitivity of investigators can amount to revictimization for some survivors of assault. That and the fact that out of those 310 reports, only 50 lead to an arrest. An average of 28 cases lead to a felony conviction and only 25 of those serve time behind bars.

The reasons for not reporting include fear of retaliation, and concern that police will not do anything among others. In Kai's case, his lack of official documentation branded him "illegal." On top of that, the man who assaulted him was well-heeled and well-regarded in his community, possessing multiple connections to the police and local justice system.[36]

Another thing that isn't common knowledge (but no less true) is the fact that GHB, certain sleeping pills like Ambien, zopiclone, and other drugs commonly used in DFSA can result in a blackout state in which the victim will have little or no memory of the events that transpired. They may blink in and out of consciousness and even be able to function at high enough levels to operate a motor vehicle despite being technically asleep.[37]

Even in cases of sexual assault that don't involve drugs being used to incapacitate a victim, trauma-induced blackouts can occur. Kai describes a blackout experience that occurred in his teens after being assaulted. Traumatic memory can be volatile and unpredictable. Adding drugs that can induce blackouts can only exacerbate this. In short, blackout and memory loss is far from unusual in instances of DFSA.[38]

In the end, Galfy effectively sealed his own fate. If he hadn't drugged him to the point of stupor and raped him to the point of bleeding then when Kai came to, he might have been more measured in his response. Unfortunately for both of them, Kai woke in the traumatic state of fight or flight, combined with the drug-induced blackout. As James Galfy mentioned in his impact statement, it's a tragedy that Galfy's nieces won't have anyone to go crabbing with them. It's also a shame they will have to find someone else to help them close house deals. The reality is, a sexual assault is not the type of activity that a 73-year-old lawyer would likely pick up out of the blue on a whim. A decades-long history of associating with "drifters." Those weekend trips to NYC. Galfy's reticence to have neighbors see who he was bringing back to his house. All these facts raise some important questions. How long did this go on? How many times did he get away with it?

The prosecution painted Kai as an unhinged maniac. Unfortunately, the media played into this quite a bit. They continually sneered at his "conspiratorial claims" without exploring any veracity. This effectively amounts to gaslighting.

Imagine yourself in his shoes. You already live with PTSD from years of being neglected, abused, and molested as a child. The trend continues with sexual assault in your youth. It is such a formative part of your past that it drives you to attempt to act as a protector. Whenever you see someone else in a situation where they may be victimized, you rush to their aid. But now you've been drugged and raped by a well-to-do lawyer with major crony connections in the local good ol' boy network. Even your own defense, at times, seems to be fighting your attempts at exoneration. Imagine the difficulty of maintaining composure in such a circumstance.

As Kai pointed out in his statement before sentencing in the time he was rambling he met "tens of thousands of people." Not one of whom has come forward with stories of the purportedly dangerous, violently unhinged hitchhiker attacking *them.*

"The hundreds of people I've stayed with [...] now question 'Why didn't Kai hurt us?' because this trial didn't answer those questions, but my character does. My character for helping people is why people were safe with me."[39]

Kirsch further mischaracterized Kai saying he was likely to re-offend, that he was unstable and anti-social since childhood. Again, I can't stress enough that being institutionalized by the state to protect you from an abusive and neglectful household is *not* a character judgment. And it's honestly a shame I have to even say that, much less reiterate it repeatedly. Unfortunately, the likes of Kirsch and his outdated ideas related to sexual assault and trauma are far more common than they should be in our so-called enlightened age.

Pruden also apparently puts words into the mouth of Jessob Reisbeck, the reporter from Fresno who conducted that first viral interview. Reisbeck is one of Kai's longtime supporters to this day, but you wouldn't pick that up from the Pruden piece:

"As Reisbeck quickly learned, McGillivary was impossible to control or predict, and there was something in him that could turn suddenly dark, like a switch had been flipped."[40]

Pruden's article ignores or misrepresents a great deal. She mentions that "public attention and interest was already starting to turn" (a point picked up by Todd Grande). She fails to provide context regarding the role harassment of supporters by a small, but dedicated troll army played in that. The troll army militantly defended Galfy and disseminated disinformation that supported the portrayal pushed by the state. She also brings up Kai's tattoo. Without a single concrete example, remarks that "others concluded McGillivary was stupid or high or mentally ill or just seeking attention." This is another point that was picked up by Grande in his insensitive and inaccurate video "diagnosing" Kai.[41]

The damage done by Pruden's irresponsible and incomplete reporting can't be stressed enough.* Before the article in the *Toronto Globe & Mail*, the only public claim that Kai was impolite dated back to some indie promoter who had hired Kai as a headliner for a music show. Kai felt they were "shamelessly exploiting" him. When Kai spoke up about his problems with the micro-management and other issues, the promoter ran to Facebook claiming he was guilty of "blatant DISRESPECT towards women." This is the sole origin of the spurious and harmful claim in the Pruden piece.

Pruden also downplays (or fails to mention entirely) the many, very real issues related to corruption and conflicts of interest, destruction of evidence, failure to collect evidence, and more. Or even the deprivation of due process that made it impossible for Kai to prove his self-defense case. A case that all hinged on proving that he had been drugged. Hard to do when any evidence of the rape and drugging was never collected or in some cases literally run through a dishwasher within an active crime scene. Something that should have been impossible to manage at a time when no police investigators were present. This alone should be considered highly irregular and grounds for further inquiry.

Pruden notes that Kai "implied and, at times, flatly alleged, collusion and corruption among the police, lawyers and judge." The only example Pruden provides, however, is how the prosecutor would refer to the alleged rapist "casually as 'Joe,' as though they were friends." I can't mention enough the fact that, despite it taking 9 years, Kai finally had a federal judge rule that he was the victim of a conspiracy to deprive him of his due process rights.[42]

No mention of Romankow's connections to Galfy, his damaging claims, or his stepping down after 11 years the very same day Kai was arrested.*

---

* In addition to civil suits against people directly involved in the investigation or court proceedings, Kai has filed suits against Grande and some others who have attempted to misrepresent him in the media.

'No mention of Peter Liguori fighting Kai's attempts at filing motions. No mention of the fact that Robert Mega, a judge from Union County, was a partner at the law firm of Kochanski, Mega & Galfy. Mega was also a fellow member of the Kiwanis, even passing the mantle of club president on down to Galfy who vowed he would "work closely with the Key Club" (putting him in access with high school students). Mega finally recused himself after it was revealed he was on Galfy's speed dial.[43]

Pruden's article also tried to paint Kai as a potentially dangerous and unpredictable character. When talking to Kai's mother Shirley Stromberg, Pruden didn't press the issue regarding the childhood abuse he faced at the hands of her and Gilbert McGillivary except to say "they got help as a family to be healthy," whatever that means.

The article also may have contributed to the judge's remarks at sentencing. Specifically, his claim that Kai had a history of violence going back to the age of 2. Kai and I spoke about this situation in our correspondence:

"The psychological report referred to by the judge at sentencing. It contains bald, unchallenged assertions by my birth mother that I 'had behavioral problems since I was two years old and killed two hamsters when I was four.' Never have I heard such victim-blaming bullshit directed at a small child. She and Gilbert used to keep me as a toddler locked in a small room deadbolted from the outside. I had night terrors (PTSD from abuse I was too young to remember), and she and Gilbert would throw open the door as I was screaming, beat me, then throw me in a freezing cold shower until my lips were blue and I couldn't scream anymore. My two hamsters died because I gave them cold showers (in the bathroom sink) to stop them from

---

* I reached out to Romankow, who says that he stepped down due to the fact his term was up. That still doesn't explain what it was he thanked Governor Chris Christie for allowing him to stay on longer to get some things "tied up." Whatever he needed to be tied up must have been firmly in shackles about the same time Kai was in custody.

being noisy at night; I was scared for them, and I didn't want them to get beaten for crying at night."

Pruden also mentions that many "fan pages and fundraisers are gone." This is certainly true; it might have been responsible to share the reason for that. It didn't take long before I became all too aware of the small (but obsessively dedicated) troll army. They attack supporters. They make fanciful claims with no evidence backing them. They obstinately refuse to accept stark facts as reality when it hurts the narrative they're pushing. Kai's original Facebook page had over 10,000 supporters following it. In April 2016 it was removed after a period of unceasing, targeted harassment of supporters and admins.[44]

At one point, Pruden notes "a sensational afterward to the story." I'm fairly certain she meant "afterword" but misusing a common word is hardly the biggest problem with the article.

Kai shared with me his thoughts on the Pruden fiasco:

"Back in May of 2019, Jana Pruden interviewed me over the phone. She was a journalist at the Globe and Mail, a Canadian newspaper with a large readership.

She seemed eloquent and book savvy, someone with a fondness for language that was evident in how she talked. She chose words for impact, for the emotional contours they created in conversation. She promised to help me overcome the injustice of a false conviction, and we opened up to each other. I told her of my life up to that point. She told me of her experience in the Peace Corps in Africa, and how she became a journalist. It was night in her Peace Corps camp; she was awake by candlelight and straining to hear the radio. Bits of static interspersed the program, hyenas yipped in the background. A light breeze moved the antenna for a moment, and with seeming crystal clarity she heard the radio host pronounce a shining hope for female journalists. This was back when radio shows would have book readings, and the female host was passionately reading her novel with a glow that lit young Jana's eyes with fervor.

As I listened to Jana describe this moment, I was enchanted by the thought of a college student in the 1970s, perched by her cot in her tent on the savanna, tall grass rustling outside the tent flap. She suddenly intimated to me that, years later, she bought the book that the host was reading. She looked high and low for the section that had so inspired her to become a journalist. Laughing, Jana told me that she found it, but it wasn't what she thought it was. As it turned out, she had heard the radio host wrong, with a serendipitous result that propelled her onto the path of journalism.

She was still chuckling, good naturedly I thought, as I blurted out, "Oh, a mondegreen!" Cold silence. I waited. I tried again, "Isn't that what that's called?" "Yes, I suppose it is." As her terse responses met my attempts to rekindle the conversation, I wondered what happened to the woman who was so enthralled with words. Monosyllabic brusque bursts of tense and measured speech replaced the rich vocabulary and graceful charm she introduced herself with.

I was so confused. I thought she loved descriptive words?

A year later, a fan sent me her article about me. It started out like her interview with me: charming, witty, and full of graceful eloquence. Then I saw the Facebook post. The one that was removed 6 years before. She must have dug deep for that screenshot; the original poster was denounced publicly for her false accusations and took it down within 24 hours. The very musicians referred to in the post took my side over hers and invited me as the headliner to a music event the next day. The women at that event remarked at how respectful I was, at how safe they felt with me around.

I was offended, insulted, upset. I tried to explore my options for filing a lawsuit against Jana for slander, but I had no time nor money to pursue one. I was in the midst of a criminal appeal involving a false murder conviction and trying to survive one of the hardest prisons in America.

Two years went by.

A message from Jana, sent April 7, 2020, sat in my jPay inbox, asking in a courteous way for a comment for her upcoming article. It had a prepaid reply.

On October 3, 2022, I was seized by a flash of inspiration. I tried to articulate the damage she did. I first sought to understand, then to be understood by this person who kicked me when I was down. But the point I was trying to make, the end game, was the respect for women she threw mud on. Stopping a man from attacking a woman. Telling women they deserve respect, that mistakes don't define them, that they are worthwhile. Spending countless hours reading feminist books to be a more supportive man to the women in my life. Guys like that exist.

Here's what I wrote her:

"As a journalist, I thought you would appreciate a bon mot, a word that perfectly describes a situation. So when you described the radio program that inspired you to become a journalist, and I blurted out 'oh, a mondegreen!' I thought you might see that as a bid for connection. As a fellow aficionado of the English language, I thought you might even feel some delight at the bon mot. Instead, your silence was cold, and you ended the call shortly after. A year later, you quoted a long-removed Facebook post. One that the original poster recanted after being called out by women who knew me as respectful. You called me, through someone else's voice, 'disrespectful towards women.'

"Never mind the years I've spent learning from feminist authors how to be a more supportive friend to the women in my life.

"Never mind putting my life in danger multiple times to save women from a physically assaultive man (Something I've never been to women).

"Never mind the thousands of dollars I've donated to Gospel For Asia to educate women in the third world.

"You let your feelings cloud your journalistic objectivity, and you clouded my reputation with those feelings too. You also clouded the hope of a lot of other women, who saw in me a man who would stop another man from disrespecting their bodily autonomy. Who saw clearly from my actions in Fresno that day and hoped for more men who would respect women like that.

"I never meant 'mondegreen' as a trivialization of your career, of your powers of observation, or of your cherished memory. That's not what I wanted to do. I genuinely wanted to connect with another person who reads dictionaries for fun, to learn words that perfectly describe the moment. That's all.

"But I could see in your article that you brooded over it. You dwelt on it. You formed your perspective based on how you heard it.

"And you got back at me for something I didn't do.

"You didn't just get back at me, though. You got back at a lot of women who found solace in what I said to them in that video. A lot of women who've never done you wrong. That wasn't fair of you.

"I just thought you should know that."

And as far as Judge Kirsch goes, for a supposedly impartial official, he plainly had a bias against Kai evident in his statements on the record:

"He may be difficult. He may be obstructive. He may be disingenuous. He may be crafty, shrewd, manipulative, et cetera, but he is quite clearly competent."

In case you weren't fully convinced regarding Kirsch's entrenched preconceptions, he continues:

"You are crafty, cunning, disingenuous and manipulative. You are a powder keg of explosive rage."[45] Wow, but tell us what you *really* think, Judge Kirsch!

Judge Kirsch also painted Kai as some sort of cruel egomaniac. He declined to allow Court TV or *Inside Edition* to broadcast the trial (which incidentally would have revealed at least one bald-faced lie by his honor). This was done "for his own sake," Kirsch claimed:

"It is obvious that he plays to the media. He's obsessed with it. I've never seen anything quite like it, quite honestly, and for his own sake, I am removing that intoxicant to him so that he can focus on the matters at hand."

If Kai was so obsessed with the spotlight, wouldn't he have taken up the offer of his own reality TV show offered by the producers of *Keeping Up With the Kardashians*? To believe the state's version of events, you have to seriously suspend disbelief, ignore relevant facts, and assume that Kai decided out of the blue to kill a man. A claim that is challenged by the obvious signs of sexual assault. It's important to remember that as early as the Grand Jury hearing in 2013, the prosecution underscored the fact that they had no obligation to provide any sort of motive. We're meant to believe that Kai, despite bright prospects and no history of assaulting innocents, decided on a whim to throw it all away and kill a man for absolutely no reason.

And further, Kirsch admitted Kai is no dummy. Yet Kai decided to commit premeditated murder with no motive, not taking a thing from the house and making sure to keep things simple for the investigators by leaving his phone number and email at the crime scene? Something doesn't add up here, and it's painfully obvious that this is a reason why it was stressed that the state had no obligation to provide any motive for the actions of that horrific night in Clark, New Jersey.

Lawyer John Cito (as well as some of the people who took part in the trial) pointed out the fact that Galfy often had several young men over to his home. Cito also noted how relevant information was suppressed at the Grand Jury hearing while other information was misrepresented to fit the narrative the state attempted to advance. For instance, in line with Romankow's attempt to seed the idea that Kai was a potential roving serial killer, Prosecutor Scott Peterson played up the fact that Kai was carrying a printout with information about various sex offenders. This was related to a story idea pitched to a Vice reporter he had met in April of that year who, like him, had been assaulted.

Sophie Duensing a *Vice* reporter and producer on *The Jenny McCarthy Show* had claimed that Kai "found the French guy [who date raped her] and had him being watched." Kai says that what he actually suggested was trying to confront the rapist on camera. Kai had also pitched a story for Vice to her just days before the events of May 12th, 2013:

"The idea was to catch sex offenders on camera who were violating release rules regarding staying away from schools. I reached out to Sophie and her agent with no response."

Kai did indeed have a printout of the addresses of sex offenders as part of the background research he'd done for that story. This information was spun by the prosecution to paint Kai as some underground vigilante. The prosecutor's made sure to point out the "knife" Kai was carrying along with that list. Protip: either for camping or living outdoors, on the road or on the street, always have a blade of some sort. Even if it's just for opening canned food, rather than self-defense, it's just an important tool to keep on hand*.

---

* That said, it is always a good idea to keep abreast of local blade laws. In my home state, for instance, a pocket knife under a certain length is not classified as a weapon until wielded as such, though from personal experience I can tell you that authorities will call a box cutter locked in a car trunk a weapon if it suits them.

Kai had met up with Duensing at the New York Public Library. They had previously gone out for drinks and food. At one point, it seems she is pushing forward the "mooch" narrative that is also advanced by the prosecution and the troll army. Pointing out that she paid for all the food and drinks. Well, yes, and in exchange, you were getting a feature story banking on Kai's viral fame.

She invited Kai back to her place after their third outing. She went to her room to put on a movie, asking Kai how she looked. He says this was when he noticed she was standing naked next to her bed. They began making out but when his clothes started coming off, she repeatedly noted, "I'm not sleeping with you," and then went back to kissing him.

This went on for a while. At one point sitting on the bed nude, legs spread, saying: "I'm not sleeping with you."

"At which point," Kai tells me, "I was like, alright you win. Do you want me to sleep outside or something? And she was like, go ahead if you want. You can still stay here. So I was like, alright, I'm sorry for saying you were only doing it for a story. And she invited me to sleep in her bed with her, so I slept beside her, under her covers with her, all night. We didn't kiss or anything after I accused her of doing it for a story, though. We woke up the next morning, and she gave me $20 and told me there was a diner down the way I could get breakfast at. As it turns out, her 'boyfriend' was her FIANCE, who was standing right next to her while the detectives interviewed her. You know, the guy I said I wouldn't tell? Yeah, him."

All this occurred after having just met Sophie first at the New York Public Library. At one point, he tells me she compared his member to that of Black-Eyed Peas frontman will.I.am an evening that (even before the mixed signals makeout session) had featured a candle-lit dinner and some heavy flirting.

Peterson would continue to claim that there was no evidence of Kai being sexually assaulted despite forensic lab results clearly contradicting this. Cito pointed out in court that the prosecutors presented prejudicial and irrelevant material while ignoring anything that didn't fit their story. He also pointed out police investigators found evidence of password-protected websites with pornographic material and contact information for young men on his phone. Perhaps most importantly though, were the obvious signs of assault. The inexplicably untested and unidentified blood on Galfy's penis alone is consistent with a violent and non-consensual assault on Kai's person and dignity.

"Something must have occurred of a sexual nature," Cito remarked, pointing out that Kai "was fending off a sexual assault." This is information that the state made sure was not brought up in the Grand Jury hearing. Peterson repeatedly suggested that, contrary to hard evidence available, there was no sign of a struggle, and "if there was, it wasn't much of one." This is at odds with the idea of this being a brutal, premeditated attack. An attack that, according to the authorities in Union County, occurred only because Kai felt like throwing his life away at a time when the world was his oyster.

"They made him out to be a vigilante seeking out sexual predators," Cito complained. It's not very difficult to bend the truth when you control the information that's released. Lies of omission can be as harmful as lies of commission and in this case, there is a plethora of both.

The YouTuber wavywebsurf scored a viral hit video when he released "Whatever happened to Kai the Hitchhiker." You see the repeated claims of "behavioral and emotional problems." Vague claims he was "causing problems" leading to him having to stay in a group home. Even his claim that Kai was "detained" at a group home until 18 was inaccurate. This was just one example of information that seemed to be pulled out of the blue showing up in a news report, social media post, or YouTube video. The video quickly hit a million views; luckily, I was able to reach out to the YouTuber. He eventually retracted the video and released a second after admitting he had seen my article urging him to check out my interviews and reporting on Kai for an accurate timeline of events that is based on verifiable facts.

To his credit, he not only corrected the video but admitted his errors. He even agreed to donate funds raised from the replacement video to a charity of Kai's choosing.[46]

"So many of you are aware earlier in the month I made a video about Kai The Hatchet Wielding Hitchhiker. Well, that video got really big...and it had some mistakes I was not comfortable with. This should answer any questions you have."

One thing I've never understood is those who choose to embellish the story. The truth is compelling and sensational enough as it is. Wavywebsurf himself admitted in the follow-up video:

"It's way more fucked than I previously thought it to be."

Quite a different story unfolded with Kailani Lagos. Kai met Lagos while in California and even had Kai record some music in his studio. In an episode of his podcast, Metalslut released shortly after Kai's arrest Kailani and his cohost Mo talk about, among other things, just becoming legal to drink alcohol, weed dispensaries, and some candid discussion of their recreational usage of methamphetamines.

The two noted it didn't surprise them that Kai might be a killer all the while making highly insensitive (not to mention entirely unfunny) jokes. Kailani seems to lead his co-host Mo, saying that despite his being "a pretty conspiratorial guy" he believed that Kai was guilty. They also played into the "romp" narrative that authorities smeared Kai with.

They also denigrate the idea that he was raped. Even claiming that if he was raped "it's still murder." Ah, but that's the whole thing. Fighting off a rapist with lethal force is not even manslaughter in New Jersey. It's simple self-defense. The cohost brings up that there were a "lot of gray areas." Kailani seems to notice he's off the narrative and calls that out as a "stupid, white knight* *thing to say."

They speculated that perhaps he was trading in sex and that he "does need to do what he needs to do for basic necessities." For the record, I've been homeless multiple times. I've slept outdoors. I've slept in abandoned structures. I've slept in sketchy people's homes on the couch or floor, but having been homeless doesn't automatically make a person a sex worker.

They go on to make jokes about how maybe he was "gay for pay." Saying there's nothing wrong with it if he "wants to prostitute himself" before admitting that they're "just guessing."

Then they veer into unsupported claims regarding Kai being potentially dangerous. They claimed he had some incident with a homeless woman and that he had supposedly "broken in" to the studio. If he was such a supposedly dangerous person, it wasn't so much so that they felt the need to report it to the police. Or even milk it for podcast content at the time. If this were the case, why wouldn't they have capitalized on this inside dirt on the famous hitchhiker before then?

It's also posited that he had a "flashback of being molested, something goes wrong, trying to steal from the guy, maybe something goes weird, goes wrong." But there was no sign of anything being stolen. There was no robbery and if there had been, then why would Kai essentially leave a calling

---

* White knighting or to white knight is internet slang for providing excuses for someone, often a woman, online.

card for the police? I do agree with Kirsch up to a point, he certainly is "shrewd" and intelligent which is why this major plot hole just doesn't track. Mo, the co-host even joins in despite admitting, "I wasn't there but from what you guys told me…"

They also take the bait from Romankow regarding the "Kai the serial killer" story that disappeared as quickly as Theodore Romankow did from the Union County Prosecutor's Office the moment that Kai was in custody.

Later on, in the same episode, they talk about consuming "crazy amounts of alcohol and all kinds of things" including LSD and crystal meth. Kailani talks about how meth doesn't have much of an effect on him at which point, Mo tells him to do the "Moses challenge" explaining that "there's a science to it."[47]

Daniel Hagen (TikTok user Xanxotic) is yet another who spreads rumors as if they were facts. On his account, which has racked up over 100,000 followers and over 2 million likes he has laundered the "romp narrative" that got a major boost from the publication *Queerty*. Author Matthew Tharrett is listed as an editor of the publication. Neither he nor anyone from *Queerty* has responded to my requests for clarification or retraction despite how their coverage is responsible for very damaging claims:

"Though homeless, McGillivary considers himself 'homefree' and relies on the kindness of strangers for food, shelter, and according to some, hookups. Investigators say surveillance cameras captured the two meeting in Times Square shortly before heading back to Galfy's place in Clark, NJ. Though no official outlets have confirmed the two were meeting to 'hook up,' the details of their meeting seem pretty suspect.

"After Galfy's body was discovered on Tuesday, McGillvary took to his Facebook page (*yes*, this homeless man has a Facebook page) to claim he was drugged and raped by Galfy. This is where anti-violence advocates start raising their eyebrows."

"According to some." Who are these some? Admittedly none of the "some" were reporters. However, that didn't stop others from sharing this story and even in recent years, this same damaging narrative comes up in news reporting regarding the case. *New York Post* claimed that the situation appeared to be a "sexual encounter turned violent." Well, that's one way of saying that the investigators noted signs of a sexual assault even before Kai was in custody. If only they had properly collected and cataloged this evidence. Then there might be a chance at definitively implicating Galfy.[48]

An article from the local news venue *TapIntoClark* also falsely alleges Kai claimed it was a "date rape." Many times a date rape and a drug-facilitated sexual assault (DFSA) are the same, however, not every time a "date rape drug" is used is related to a date.[49]

Rolling Stone reporter Hunter S. Thompson once wrote a piece where he claimed that candidate Ed Muskie was possibly using the exotic psychedelic ibogaine. When pressed on it after it harmed Muskie in the polls, Thompson explained that he had only reported that there was a rumor that he was using ibogaine. Then admitted that, yes, it was he who started the rumor.[50]

The comments section is even worse, claiming that Kai was using a "gay panic" defense. It was more so the "waking up bleeding from your orifice while being actively raped" that caused the panic, not the fact that Galfy was gay, which he was already well aware of at that point. Another commenter points out that prosecutors (specifically Romankow) mentioned: "backtracking Hatchet-dude's recent travels to see if they fit the profile of a serial killer or something along those lines." See how simple it is to get a story completely warped via the social media version of the telephone game?

A recent example of narrative warping in the wild occurred at *Shore News Network*, a New Jersey outlet. The article in question, "Hitchhiking On The Rise in Northern Ocean County" was published in June 2022.

"Shore News Network fact checks its news through several fact checking methods including official sources, authoritative sources and two-source fact checking. If you believe a story is untrue or inaccurate, please let us know so we can investigate."

Obviously, I was going to call them on this. The fact that it was none other than the editor and owner, Phil Stilton who shared the patently false claims doesn't bode well for their supposed commitment to factual reporting.

There is also a rather odd and unsupported comment: "Hitchhiking seemed to die out during the early 1990s after the run of the popular television series, *The Hitchhiker*, which delved into the darkness of society." Okay, for one, that show is just a horror/fantasy anthology series like fellow '80s fantasy/horror anthology *Tales From the Darkside*. While researching this book, I read several sociological and historical studies of hitchhiking. Many factors contributed to hitchhiking's fall from favor, but in none of the essays, papers, or books I read did I see the TV show introduced by a "mysterious hitchhiker" as one of the roots.

"It's also dangerous for the hitchhiker and the driver. One of the more infamous hitchhikers in modern history was 'Kai the hitchhiker,' a hatchet-wielding psychopath hitchhiker. Kai became famous for assaulting his driver with a hatchet. He later killed his defense attorney."

Though it's true that the alleged rapist, Joseph Galfy was an attorney, he certainly wasn't Kai's attorney. Galfy specialized in divorce and later real estate. Also, the alleged rapist, Joseph Galfy died with, according to the forensic results, unidentified blood and his own semen on his penis. As for how this happened, the most likely explanation is that Kai's claim of being drugged and raped is true. It is also likely the reason why the dishwasher was run in an active crime scene so that any results from drug testing the glasses would be inconclusive.

There is a point at which sloppy reporting becomes malicious. Whether through neglect or willful malice, Phil Stilton has helped prop up certain of the completely false narratives surrounding Kai.

The complete absence of any citations or references in the article is note-worthy (especially in light of his lofty claims about the multiple methods of verification). Mr. Stilton expects us to just take him at his word and I have to wonder, whether the monumental misreporting was purposeful or not; it certainly doesn't bode well for the rest of his outlet's credibility.

I tagged Stilton and *Shore News Network*. I never got any reply, but they eventually updated the article to remove the easily disproved details they invented. Of course, an apology and full correction would have been prefer-able, but it's better than nothing.[51]

Legends and tall tales can be positive, negative, or neutral. In the case of hitchhikers and surfers, many of the prevailing tropes are negative which can lead to stereotyping. Something quite evident in this case. On the one hand, the idea of a homefree hitchhiker willing to jump into the fray and risk his life to save people he doesn't know resulted in a glowing response at first. As soon as the events of May 2013 transpired, however, all those negative stereotypes came into play.

Initially, Kai's viral fame grew out of the larger-than-life character he rep-resented. A traveling musician, something like a bard or troubadour, who called out injustice wherever he went held a natural appeal for many.

CHAPTER 6

SOMETHING ROTTEN IN THE GARDEN STATE

The roots of New Jersey corruption and the current state of affairs are too broad a topic to cover in a single volume. A basic survey of the situation should reveal certain recurring trends along the lines of what I've proposed as the unoriginality of corruption. Coming up, we tackle the way things work in "Galfy Country" i.e. Union County. But first, let's explore some highlights of business as usual in New Jersey.

Quite relevant to this story is the potential of some hijinx surrounding $300,000 in donations to two universities that happen to be the employers of the two "expert medical witnesses" in Kai's case.

First, Dr. Robert Pandina who, in the words of Prosecutor Scott Peterson "was basically briefed" (basically?) on Kai's case. The misrepresentation of his testimony coupled with his refusal to take the stand allowed Peterson and Ho to misrepresent the science claiming Kai could not possibly have been drugged. Witness testimony to the contrary would be suppressed at the hearing. The grand jury transcript refers to "the effects of the date rape drug"[1] as if there's only one with only one effect. As if there isn't a drug with a history of utilization in DFSA that has side effects including seemingly lucid blackout states and a metallic taste upon awakening. Identical to what Kai reported.[2]

I am not a believer in guilt by association and I don't feel that the sins of the father should reflect on the son... or vice versa for that matter, but a situation regarding the absent expert witness comes to mind. Robert J. Pandina's son is Gahan Pandina, a researcher at Johnson and Johnson. The younger Pandina worked with Dr. Joseph Biedermann in a university research center that was a thinly veiled attempt to corner the pediatric psychotropics market. Apparently by any means necessary.

Gahan and Biedermann were responsible for a 40-fold increase in off-label prescriptions for the drug Risperdal in autistic children. This was despite serious side effects known of beforehand. Gahan Pandina was also aware that the "significant improvement" seen in children who were trialed with the drug was similarly evident in the control group. Gahan not only knew this, but documents revealed during the litigation showed he had concerns about how to get around this issue. They settled on just not mentioning that the "significant improvement" was identical to those who received a placebo.

The scandal resulted in both civil and criminal charges and fines of $2.2 Billion. Risperdal was pushed by doctors, some of whom received kickbacks to aggressively push the drug despite "heavy risks for children."[3] While Gahan was on the stand, he claimed no knowledge of the danger the drug posed to children. Plaintiff attorney Tom Kline pointed out the "outrageous farce" and warned that continuing to backpedal in an attempt to distance themselves was certain to leave a "record of falsehoods."[4]

Wall Street Journal decried how the "partnerships and financial ties between drug manufacturers and academia undermine the integrity of medical research and, by extension, the practice of medicine." According to documents revealed during the proceedings, the entire university research center program was meant to be a "springboard for a Johnson & Johnson pediatric psychopharmacology franchise."[5]

Dr. Gahan Pandina was a Senior Director of Clinical Research for Johnson & Johnson. Even faced with internal emails and other evidence to the contrary, Gahan tried to claim that Risperdal wasn't being marketed to children and adolescents. Attorney General Eric Holder commented on the case and how it "jeopardized the health and safety of patients and damaged the public trust." Associate Attorney General Tony West demanded accountability over the debacle; which represented Johnson & Johnson "put[ting] profit over patients' health and misus[ing] taxpayer dollars."[6]

In 2008, the *New York Times* reported on the "40-fold increase from 1994 to 2003" in the diagnosis of pediatric bipolar disorder. *The Times* also reported a concurrent "rapid rise in the use of powerful, risky, and expensive antipsychotic medicines in children."

J&J funded the Mass General Children's Center. According to a 2002 annual report, the "essential feature" of its research was to "move forward the commercial goals of J&J."[7] This might be a good spot to point out that, for the time Kai was being held in Trinitas Regional (the hospital Romankow served on the board of) he was prescribed Risperdal. Like many who have been given the drug, it resulted in the side effect of horrible nightmares which manifest as night terrors in some. Romankow was a prominent figure due to his connection to the Union County Improvement Authority and the Freeholders; as well as having a hand in policy and development. Trinitas hospital is where Kai was kept for "observation."[8] Trinitas was the hospital of choice for many Elizabeth detainees* like Kai. I can only wonder how many of them also received night-terror inducing Risperdal as Kai did during his stint.

Robert Pandina's program at Rutgers was the beneficiary of a surprise $150,000 gift from the Galfy estate. Despite this, Pandina claimed that he and Galfy had never met. Quite a coincidence, a rather convenient one at that.

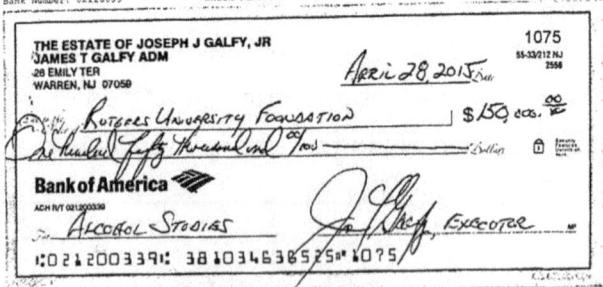

$150k check issued to Pandina's Center for Alcohol Studies paid out by the Galfy estate.

---

* Yet another of the many incarceration deaths in Union County's jail occurred due to the use of restraints by correctional officers on William Pariseau. Pariseau died of cardiac dysrhythmia "due to excited delirium and physical restraint," according to the Union County Medical Examiner's Office.[9]

Another "expert witness" was Dr. Junaid Shaikh. Dr. Shaikh also just happened to have a $150,000 check issued to his program, after testifying on behalf of the prosecution.[10] This wouldn't be the first time that donations to universities had been diverted for bribery, payoffs, or even money laundering. In fact, there are two fairly recent cases in New Jersey alone. One of which, just happens to be the very university where Shaikh worked. In addition to the UMDNJ scandal,[11] contemporary stories of university donation fraud in New Jersey include Rutgers and even Princeton.[12]

A donor's suit charged Princeton with fraud, in 2004. The situation dated at least back to 1992:

"We have considerable evidence that there is fraud involved, and even though this is an august institution, it's clear that something is wrong at Princeton, and we are the primary victims of their wrongdoing," bemoaned William Robertson of the Robertson Foundation (adding fraud and misrepresentation to its list of charges against the university).

The Romankow-linked hospital Trinitas is another institution that has recently been charged with fraud. The hospital had to pay out over $3 million for rampant and pervasive Medicare fraud, which dated back years.[13] A powerful South Jersey political boss (and often foe of Governor Phil Murphy's reformer campaigns) was also swept up in a case of hospital-related fraud.[14*]

"It's clear that something is wrong at Princeton and we are the primary victims of their wrongdoing."

---

* In Mario A. Garcia's *Organized Crime Investigation: A Lecture Series For Criminal Justice and Criminology Students,* Garcia notes several types of common organized crime in North America which include several types that come up in relation to Union County. For instance, monopolies on industries ("industry cartels"), bid-rigging, labor racketeering, and business fraud. One type of business fraud mentioned is health insurance fraud; the book specifically mentions Tricon-associates in New Jersey involved in a conspiracy to defraud insurance companies.

Another recent New Jersey-related university fraud story involves the fake "University of Northern New Jersey" which turned out to be no more than a "pay-to-stay"[15] visa fraud operation. Also this year, Rutgers was busted for "ranking fraud."[16]

Another ongoing scandal has erupted at Rutgers in recent years. Renowned (and, one would guess, like Galfy "well respected in his community") oncology researcher Dr. James Goydos, former director of the Rutgers Cancer Institute, accepted a plea bargain related to a battery of charges. This former director of the Rutgers Cancer Institute was charged with crimes ranging from identity fraud to invasion of privacy. The crimes allegedly entailed taking pictures of students in various states of undress, without their knowledge.

Goydos claimed that he was singled out by the university for, (wait for it, that's right...) his whistleblower status. Now whether these claims have serious merit, remains to be seen. As of now, the civil suit lodged against Rutgers is back on since the criminal proceedings are complete. Goydos accepted a plea bargain admitting guilt for a portion of the 160 charges. Goydos claims he was speaking out on fraud related to grant applications and a new business model. He claims that he was chosen as the sacrificial scapegoat.[17]

Rutgers New Jersey Medical School (NJMS) was at the center of a scandal in 2006 related to financial mismanagement and fraud. Sometimes these scams can even put lives in jeopardy.[18] At this point, you may begin to see a pattern here.

In most media accounts, Kai's claims are categorized as baseless conspiracies. But as you can see, there is plenty of precedent for this kind of behavior. This type of financial fraud and bribery, facilitated through university department donations is not uncommon in New Jersey.

It's interesting that these supposedly "baseless conspiracies" are rarely explicated. Even if they were, they still might seem unbelievable. Unless you take the time to look into the state of academic fraud and realize this isn't so unheard of. Kai's made his case in court that a conspiracy exists already, in spite of years of the Galfy estate and Union County defendant lawyers attempting to characterize Kai's concerns as "baseless" and "circumstantial" up to now. Not only is the conspiracy "sufficiently alleged" according to federal court authority, but it is plain to see these things aren't unheard of in the first place.

And of course, we can't forget Camden, once known as the "most dangerous city in America." Three mayors were busted for corruption during the 1980s and 1990s.[19] The state had to take control of the city.

After three years of municipal self-government, the state stepped in to run the school system. The situation got so bad that local reformer officials had the entire town police force shut down and joined with the neighboring city to set up a new countywide force.[20]

By June 2009, Camden's state hadn't improved as evidenced by another case of university donation fraud. The New Jersey School of Medicine and Dentistry of New Jersey* case ended in a $2 million settlement.[21] The settlement stemmed from a decade of double-dipping Medicare fraud, similar to the situation at Trinitas.

This fraud case led to the conviction of Camden State Senator, William Bryant in 2008. Bryant had a 26-year career in the state Legislature and served one term as majority leader of the Assembly. His role as chairman of the influential budget committee; as well as his "low-paying position" at the University of Medicine and Dentistry of New Jersey; put him in just the

---

* The University Shaikh hails from that was beneficiary of a $150,000 surprise gift from Galfy.[22]

right spot to capitalize on his situation. Literally, millions of dollars of state money were diverted to UMDNJ.

New Jersey's RWJBarnabas ran afoul of the Federal Trade Commission due to an "anti-competitive" hospital deal. The monopolistic arrangement was a recipe for "higher prices, less innovation and lower quality care for patients," according to FTC Bureau of Competition Director Holly Vedova.[23]

Another example of hospital-related fraud involves what should by now be an increasingly familiar name, that of George Norcross. Norcross is one of the preeminent "bosses" of New Jersey politics.

Although Murphy and Norcross locked horns multiple times throughout Governor Murphy's first term, he was forced to make peace with Norcross (and other New Jersey political machine figureheads); just to stay in the Governor's mansion.

Murphy ran as a "reformer." "Reformer" campaigns are a long and storied tradition in New Jersey. Despite his apparent distaste for "bossism" in politics, he may not have eked out the narrow victory in 2021 without millions of dollars backing him and a think-tank (as well as the party bosses) supporting him. It's clear, the support of these unelected "make or break your campaign" power brokers comes with some cost.

Brigid Harrison of Montclair State University expressed her concern:

"We saw it with Corzine, and we're seeing it now. On a gut level, that tells me something is seriously wrong."[24]

New Jersey suffers from what could be characterized as a reformer-relapse cycle. Since the eras of James A. Bradley and Frank "I am the law!" Hague,* the nascent phase of New Jersey corruption set the standard for how public officials (elected or otherwise) rise to power. They rise or fall under the auspices of the political machines and their unelected poobahs.

Cut forward to the time of writing: one of the most recent "reformer candidates" former New Jersey governor, Republican Chris Christie has allied with Democrat George Norcross' machine. All this is due to the *latest* reformer candidate, current governor Phil Murphy.

So, as you see, even the state executive currently raging against the (political) machine had to "work within the system" just to get into office in the first place. To make things worse, an "opaque non-profit" (described as a dark money funding network) has been criticized widely throughout the state. So has his wife's non-profit refusing to disclose donors.[25]

Murphy has also crossed those who initially backed him. At some point, he realized that as popular as his first term was, he likely wouldn't be serving as Governor without the backing of the party bosses. Sue Altman** explained the dichotomy represented by Murphy's reliance on the machines. To be elected in the first place, and for future electoral support:

"If anything, this is a case study in why these machines should be weaker, because you have a governor who's extraordinarily powerful who still feels a need to dance a certain way for their pleasure."[26]

Chris Christie was fairly popular during his first term. It wasn't really until the revelations of Bridgegate ensnared some of his associates, that the

---

* During Prohibition, Mayor Frank "Boss" Hague was faced with the claim: that his will couldn't be done, as it would conflict with New Jersey State law. He famously replied, "I am the law!"

** Murphy supporter and executive director of New Jersey Working Families Alliance.

tides began to turn. To be fair, Christie claims ignorance of the events that led to the George Washington Bridge's Ft. Lee exit being shut off. An email was released with the header "Time for some traffic problems in Ft. Lee."[27]

Before this, in the contemporary era at least, most of New Jersey's corruption scandals were at the municipal level. This is why, for instance, the city of Camden, while under the leadership of corrupt mayor Angelo Erichetti, was diverted to state authority. This situation reverses former Union County prosecutor Theodore Romankow's argument against state involvement (and by extension, oversight in the Union County Prosecutor's Office).[28] This is a situation that we will delve into more deeply later.

The reasons for the systemic corruption in New Jersey are multitudinous and some of the roots have been briefly explored. Baruch College professor Brian Murphy researches political corruption throughout history. He shares another explanation for some of the contemporary corruption in the state.

"It's a small state, it has a lot of valuable real estate, and local governments have very broad authority to declare parcels of land redevelopment areas. A lot of people go into Jersey politics to get rich."[29] That's a recurring theme regarding construction companies and real estate. This could possibly have given Galfy unique opportunities to earn favors from unscrupulous string pullers.

The reformer-relapse cycle continues. After major scandals in 2004, New Jersey attempted a major overhaul to improve transparency. This was meant to stem the flow of graft and influence peddling. For a time it seemed to work. In 2012, the Center for Public Integrity scored New Jersey as top in the nation. A Bloomberg columnist based in Hoboken had the following to say[30] about the surprising turn of events:

"How did that happen? Easy. We bribed them."

AL.com released a video featuring journalists from several historically corrupt regions vying over the title of "most corrupt state." In Alabama, Pulitzer Prize-winning journalist John Archibald cites a mayor in prison for selling out his own constituents and six county commissioners convicted in the largest municipal bankruptcy to date until Detroit took the crown later. On top of this, some other recent scandals include: a "lecherous governor" covering up an affair being convicted, ethics charges against the speaker of the house, and a Supreme Court Justice running against an attorney general who was appointed by the governor he was supposed to be investigating.

New Orleans weighs in describing Louisiana as "1/3 underwater and 2/3 under indictment, or the other way around." Of course, the name Huey Long, the inspiration for *All the King's Men*, is invoked as well as Earl Long's open affair with a Bourbon Street stripper.

In New Jersey, *Star-Ledger* and *NJ Advance Media* reporter Sean Sullivan refers to a "Russian nesting doll of political corruption" and "long, storied history of reformers and crusaders falling from grace." Of course, Christie's Bridgegate scandal is mentioned. Christie perfectly represents a shorter cycle of the reformer-relapse rubric. Though Christie himself was not directly connected to the Bridgegate scandal when several of his close political allies pled guilty or were convicted on corruption charges it definitively besmirched his legacy. Bridgegate is also considered one of the reasons for the failure of Christie's 2016 presidential primary run.

US Senator Bob Menendez's indictment was brought up. Sullivan painted the picture, a dramatic image indeed, of Menendez showing up on the witness stand wearing a bulletproof vest. A former Hudson county mayor worked with the mob to funnel education funds and construction dollars into mob coffers. And of course, the near-legendary state of New Jersey corruption had to be mentioned.

New Jersey corruption is well-established in American pop culture. From shows like *Boardwalk Empire** and *The Sopranos*** to movies like *American Hustle.**** Sullivan argues just going by the numbers game, New Jersey should take the cake. One reason for this is, that despite the small size of the state it has 565 municipalities meaning lots of mayors to put on the take.

Sullivan challenged his debate partners to name a city in his state that doesn't have a mayor who has been convicted or under indictment. He also pointed to the city of Paterson, the third largest city in the state in which the mayor had been recently indicted. That same mayor conducted a campaign fundraiser on a yacht stuffed with wealthy donors and sitting politicians shortly after. "We've got it in every corner of the state," said Sullivan.

But Archibald argued that the numbers don't tell the whole story. He cited the existence of some level of transparency in, for instance, Chicago, that doesn't exist in Alabama. The information necessary to uncover the inner workings of the Alabama good ol' boys is kept under "lock and seal." And good luck finding so much as a basic police report. It's just "swept under the carpet this way."

Speaking of difficulty obtaining files, there are supposed to be strong transparency laws in New Jersey. Transparency mechanisms notwithstanding, I've personally found great difficulty requesting files from the New Jersey Policemen's Benevolent Association related to Clark Local #125. In an attempt to confirm a tip related to Joseph Galfy, I had hoped to secure

---

* *Boardwalk Empire* was a semi-fictional account of prohibition-era corruption in New Jersey. It featured real-life mobsters and politicians as characters.

** *The Sopranos* may be based in part on the DeCavalcante family which has Union County's Elizabeth listed as one of their founding locations.

*** *American Hustle* fictionalized the dramatic story of the sting that netted various New Jersey politicians and even members of Congress accepting bribes. The bribes were from a phony "sheikh" though the mobsters involved were real.

meeting minutes and donation records.

Problem is, the number I found for PBA Clark Local #125 is inactive. The number for the New Jersey state Policeman's Benevolent Association I called with no answer. I was unable to leave a message due to the inbox being full. Another NJPBA contact point referred me to the Clark PD who switched me over to the records department.

To quote the first album by Electric Light Orchestra there was "No Answer." The local Clark PD did finally encourage me to file an OPRA request. I also found some old 990 forms. It appears they tend to file up to five years at a time. One year, they spent over $10,000 on a golf tournament event that after expenses netted -$109 total on paper.[32] Also, a secretary of the Clark PBA for several years was later named in a racism scandal in Clark, New Jersey that is mentioned later.

2007		**Federal Statements**			**Page 1**
		NEW JERSEY STATE PBA ASSOC INC			
		CLARK PBA LOCAL 125			22-0818450

Statement 1
Form 990-EZ, Part I, Line 6
Net Income (Loss) from Special Events

Special Events	Gross Receipts	Less Contri- butions	Gross Revenue	Less Direct Expenses	Net Income (Loss)
Golf Outing	23,943.	0.	23,943.	23,834.	109.
Total	$ 23,943.	$ 0.	$ 23,943.	$ 23,834.	$ 109.

The Clark PBA golf tournament, a purported fundraiser,
yielded about a 2% loss on investment.

This actually brings up an interesting point related to measuring corruption by counting convictions. An article published at ethics.harvard.edu explored this concept pointing out that using conviction data from 1980 to 2010 it would *appear* that the most corrupt state is... South Dakota?

The irony here is that the Dakotas historically have led the nation in the fight against government corruption, a trend that has been going strong since the late 19th century. The prairie states in general tend to be harder on corrupt officials. So it should become evident that the number of convictions alone is not an accurate measure of corruption in a state.

The Harvard essay goes on to note that "perception indexes" might be a way to work around this. Illegal corruption in government is considered "very common" in states like California, Florida, Illinois, Texas, and, not surprisingly, New Jersey.[33]

The Center for the Advancement of Public Integrity did a study on Garden State corruption. They noted the state had some of the toughest anti-corruption laws in the country. These include "unique 'pay-to-play'" laws and multiple watchdog organizations like the State Ethics Commission, State Comptroller, and others. Despite all this, the trend of corrupt politics continues. One factor cited was the closure of the Independent Office of the Inspector General in 2010: a "worrying setback for public integrity enforcement."

A poll in 2015, conducted by Monmouth University, found New Jersey the fourth-most likely state to be named "most corrupt." It was only beat by New York, California, and Illinois. This followed a lull in corruption, resulting from stringent standards enacted in response to a scandal surrounding former governor James McGreevey (who resigned after admitting an extra-marital affair, with a man he rewarded with a spot as homeland security advisor).

The Center for the Advancement of Public Integrity lamented that "municipal corruption is a perennial issue" in the state. They mentioned the Mayor of Hamilton Township, indicted for accepting bribes from a health insurance contractor in 2011. Then there's the 2012 case of Trenton's Mayor. Indicted on federal corruption charges for skirting the law to the benefit of a parking garage developer. The Mayor of Paterson assigned municipal workers to private jobs, working for himself as well as his family. That same year, the mayor of Passaic was sentenced for bribes solicited from developers.[34]

Even the sheriff of Middlesex County, an important hub of New Jersey corruption, sold jobs to the highest bidder. Seton Hall law professor Paula A. Franzese (who helped reform New Jersey's ethics laws in 2005 following the McGreevey debacle); felt the governor's control of the Ethics Commission makes it ineffective. Perhaps a factor in how the Bridgegate scandal managed to put state-level corruption back on the menu during Christie's administration.[35]

2017 saw a probe into corruption in the New Jersey State Police related to a sexual assault case that was covered up. Prosecutors in Sussex County were at odds as to whether or not to pursue the rape case and the suspect was released without charges after interrogation. The woman who was assaulted was told to drop the case as she was "not fully raped."

At least a few state troopers reported the situation to the Official Corruption Bureau believing that the case "had some political involvement."[36] Rather than being punished, one of the officers involved in the cover-up was actually promoted to State Police superintendent. Is it any wonder why so many people don't report cases of sexual assault? Take a look at the depressingly low number of convictions that arise from such cases. Then consider the treatment rape survivors often receive from authorities. In many cases, dealing with the police and other legal proceedings can be as traumatic as the initial incident.

The Center's overall analysis is that the state "appears to be headed in the wrong direction on ethics issues and reform." They still held out hope that governor Phil Murphy "will help it reverse course." As previously mentioned though, Murphy has his work cut out for him as he attempts to take on the boss politics system of New Jersey. He had to play ball with the machine to even get the nod from the influential Democratic leaders who control large swathes of the voter block in the state. The Center's report predates his reelection, the "dark money" allegations, and controversy surrounding his seeming acquiescence to the Norcross machine and county bosses.

The report concludes by noting how New Jersey "has been plagued with both criminal and ethical violations by elected officials and their employees at all levels of government."

A candid confession from George Norcross explicitly reveals the nature of New Jersey's good ol' boy political system. "In the end, the McGreeveys, the Corzines, they're all going to be with me. Not because they like me, but because they have no choice,"[37] Norcross boasted in a secretly recorded conversation in the early 2000s, referring to now former governors James McGreevey and Jon Corzine.

Favors for the favored are a price of doing business in the state and one discounts the power of the unelected "bosses" to their own detriment.

Irwin Stoolmacher at *The Trentonian* had this to say: "It is reminiscent of what occurred back in 2014 when Rep. Rob Andrews announced his retirement. Almost instantaneously Donald Norcross, brother of political boss George Norcross, received the unanimous endorsement of all of the major political players in the 1st Congressional District."

"For me, what's troubling here is not the nepotism. If voters have a choice and decide to go with a candidate whose dad or mother is famous, that's up to them. In Mercer County, we have several examples of sons and daughters of well-regarded Mercer County political families working their way up the political ladder right now (Anthony Carabelli Jr., John Cimino, and Paula Sollami). All of them appear to be very talented and well-regarded elected officials. What is wrong is when the bosses and the party elites are picking the people's representative."[38]

One of the most striking cases of New Jersey corruption since the ABSCAM scandal occurred in 2009 when the FBI arrested 44 people in New Jersey and New York. At the time, it was the largest coordinated operation in FBI history. Like ABSCAM it started with a cooperating witness, Solomon Dwek,[39] a corrupt realtor who was the son of a Syrian rabbi with powerful friends. Dwek agreed to wear a wire and the recordings uncovered massive bribery. The damning recordings exposed politicians, a handful of rabbis, and religious charities engaged in international money laundering and organ trafficking.

Frank Gilliam was one of many mayors ousted for corruption. Gilliam beat incumbent reformer Don Guardian with help from a coalition of "top Democrats, unions, online gaming companies" and other powerful groups in Jersey. The idea was that "there's still money to be made" despite the city's insolvent state at the moment, according to the *Philadelphia Inquirer*.[40]

Dishonest mayors stepping down is "A Jersey Tradition," proclaims a headline in *The Star-Ledger*. It's a regular affair. Municipal corruption and political machines churn out candidates firmly in the back pocket of the people who put them in that position of power. Generally, this goes on at the expense of the people of these poor towns themselves.

"The status quo goes unreformed because Garden State cities are run by one party – a machine party, consisting of politically connected Democrats, government unions, businesses, and nonprofits that feed off government money."[41]

Another fairly recent case, involved thousands of dollars in bribes delivered via coffee cup (hearkening back to the bad, old days of Frank Hague: who had a specially designed lap drawer, for discreet bribe delivery). There is a steady stream of cases like this just in the past decade or two.

It's not unusual for crooked politicians to use their connections to try to worm their way out of trouble either. There's no way of telling exactly how often this works, but consider the case of Essex County Executive James Treffinger. He was a former candidate for the United States Senate.

Treffinger even tried for the position of US attorney for New Jersey in the hopes that he could throw a monkey wrench into the ongoing investigation. Ironically, Treffinger was elected as a supposed reformer candidate promising to clean up the government.[42] Before Treffinger, Essex County Executive Thomas D'Alessio was convicted of extortion. He accepted nearly $60,000 in bribes from a solid waste company, in exchange for a state permit.[43]

Just as mindblowing as the scope of corruption in the state is the reception of corrupt officials. Sharpe James was a state senator and former mayor of Newark, the largest city in New Jersey. After he was convicted in 2008 for helping a girlfriend secure properties that she resold for a profit of over $600,000 James did his next term not in office but in federal prison for 19 months. At his release, hundreds of citizens crowded to greet him.[44]

Bergen County corruption has some Union County ties that will be briefly covered later. State Senator from Bergen County, Joseph Coniglio was convicted in 2009. He used his position on the Senate budget committee to steal millions in state grants via Hackensack University Medical Center.

Yes, that's right, yet another case of "university donations" being used for illicit purposes.[45]

Another story from this year with what seems like an amusing headline until you realize it's not a joke: "Bribery could soon be charged as bribery in N.J." Matt Friedman reported at *Politico* how bribery charges in the Garden State often didn't stick. All owing to a curious loophole where a candidate could promise things "if they got elected" and since they weren't yet a public official this was considered perfectly fine? The bribery statutes only applied to "public servants" not people attempting to use said bribery to become public servants.

Assemblymember Greg McGuckin (R-Ocean) introduced a bill as far back as 2012 that would attempt to expand the law to cover candidates regardless of if they are already in some public office or not. Earlier this year, Joe Cryan (D-Union County) had sponsored a Senate version that will be heard in the Senate Judiciary Committee.[46]

Kai first showed me a lot of the cases of "wire fraud" that I was seeing involving these judges and lawyers and politicians in Union County and elsewhere in the state serve as a euphemism for bribery, graft, kickbacks, and cover-up cash. A former FBI agent turned consultant, podcaster, and True Crime author Jerri Williams and an agent from the FBI public affairs office I spoke to both agreed that when cases like these involve wire fraud it can be an indicator of some other elements of corruption at play. "No-show" jobs and other indications of organized crime and corruption rear their head time and again in New Jersey in general and Union County specifically.

Another recent corruption story that involves Union County (specifically Clark township, former home of Galfy); has pretty much everything you could ask for in a political scandal. Bigotry and racism? Check. Mayor caught on recording? Check. Hush money payout to keep the story quiet?

Check. This is Clark, New Jersey. And judging by the many quote tweets from locals, it doesn't surprise anyone in the slightest that Union County's Clark township suffers from a "culture of racist corruption" as *Star-Ledger* puts it.

Many of the issues that New Jersey faces are found throughout the country, to be sure. With that said, New Jersey's storied corruption is in a league of its own compared to some states. It seems as soon as some new law or regulation is put in place for greater transparency, unelected bosses and business owners will find a way around it.

CHAPTER 7

GALFY COUNTRY

New Jersey has a reputation for organized crime, graft, and corruption. Union County, the home of lawyer Joseph Galfy, is no exception. The county features heavily in multiple incidents of mafia history. From Lucky Luciano and Meyer Lansky to the only native mafia family in the state. The DeCavalcante crime family is, according to some (including members of the DeCavalcantes) the inspiration for the crime family portrayed in the HBO series *The Sopranos*. They also have the dubious distinction of being the only wholly New Jersey-based mafia family. In 2001, in *The New Yorker*, they were referred to as the "and a half" family[1] accompanying the Five Families of New York. Union County is listed as one of the founding locations of the DeCavalcante's criminal organization. In 2017, two Union County members of the crime family[2] were brought in on charges of cocaine trafficking.

From the 80s on, the cocaine route in the US was highly dependent on the Port of Elizabeth. Decades of local news stories, increasing frequency from the 70s on, involve cocaine being smuggled from Colombia via Florida to

Elizabeth.* From there, it would be distributed across the country.[3]

One stash house, run by Colombians, fronted as a car repair shop. This may explain some of the recurring stories of trucks and cars fitted with secret compartments to make the cocaine trafficking more discreet.[4] Elizabeth police gang, The Family, also had a role in protecting cocaine traffickers. A source from the area spoke with me on the condition they could remain unnamed. They told me that in Union County (as well as Newark and Trenton) there are streets where the police are, in essence, enforcers of the traffickers.[5]

The situation has not been ameliorated since the 70s and 80s, however. The Newark-Elizabeth Marine Terminal is still the entry point for tons of cocaine and massive quantities of fentanyl, heroin, and other hard drugs. The overall route has changed a bit. 1.6 tons seized in 2019 came via Chile rather than Colombia,[5] but the fact the port has the largest APM terminal** on the East Coast, (one of the largest in the USA[6]) has not.

In 2011, six Union County residents were netted in the "largest mob takedown in history." The case dealt with the International Longshoremen's Association. Racketeering, extortion, and illegal gambling were among the charges. Among those arrested were mafiosos with connections to the Genovese, Colombo, and Gambini crime families. New Jersey US Attorney Paul J. Fishman remarked on the bust, "Workers should be free to pursue an honest living without being worried that their own union representatives will shake them down. ... Paying tribute to the mob is not an acceptable

---

* During Iran Contra, Elizabeth was said to have the largest Colombian population outside of Jackson Heights in Queens, and Bogota in Columbia. Obviously, most were not involved in trafficking of any sort, but it's undeniable that some had a major hand in the cocaine trade. Especially throughout the 70s and 80s.

** APM Terminals are headquartered in the Netherlands and operated by Maersk which has repeatedly had issues with cocaine, heroin, and human trafficking in the past.

cost of doing business in New Jersey."

One Genovese family associate was protected by a former Union County prosecutor multiple times on behalf of his Union County prosecutor buddy.[7]

The continued existence of waterfront-based organized crime is likely the reason why the state of New York recently had to take the unusual step of seeking support from the Supreme Court to block New Jersey's attempt to dissolve the Waterfront Commission (which we will go into much further in the next chapter).

New Jersey state Senator Joe Cryan (also former Union County Sheriff, who is named as a defendant in motions by Kai) spoke out[8] against the move to block dissolving the Commission founded in 1953 to prevent kickbacks and cargo theft among other instances of waterfront-based crime.

In 1969, the *New York Times* reported on Union County District Judge Ralph DeVita's ties to the Mafia. It was noted that Gov. Richard J. Hughes had already been apprised of said connections to organized crime. DeVita was appointed in 1966 and three years later indicted on charges of bribery involving, wonder of wonders, an organized crime case.[9]

Bruce Paterson, in a letter to the editor, referred to the "corruption in real time"[10] that occurs in the county of Union. Just one recent case is exemplary of how business is done in Galfy Country.

"They are running a con game with the politically connected at the taxpayer's expense," Paterson noted in a letter to the editor about a $100 million+ government facility project. The practice of graft, by no means, originated with the Tammany Hall political machine. But since that process was introduced and spread throughout New Jersey, it has been near impossible to shake its influence.

As a result, we have the Waterfront Commission and statutes such as the Local Public Contracts Laws (LPCL). These are designed to make sure that contract bidding is done in the open to protect against bid rigging, (a major problem in the state of New Jersey that has resulted in multiple major FBI stings such as operation Bid Rig I, II, and III).

Just this year, Ted Sherman of *NJ Advance Media* did an investigative series about a multi-million-dollar government complex at the center of bid-rigging ignored by the Union County Improvement Authority.[11] Galfy acquaintance, Theodore Romankow, also had a role in the Union County Improvement Authority in addition to being a Freeholder. Like party bosses, Freeholders and Improvement Authority representatives have unique opportunities to trade on influence. Romankow, by the way, is also named in a media suppression story from The Reporter's Committee on Freedom of Speech (RCFP). RCFP reported on the case of Tina Renna's fight to keep her sources secret as is her right under the state's journalist shield law.[12]

Kai was initially denied his day due to "suicide risk." Or so the state claimed. Kai's story differs. He says he was not suicidal at the time, but after witnessing and experiencing physical and psychological abuse, he did eventually harbor suicidal thoughts due to the ceaseless torment/abuse. Kai was seen by Dr. Rodemar Perez at Trinitas hospital in Elizabeth, New Jersey. Theodore Romankow was on the board of Trinitas Regional and also connected to local mental health and children's and sexual assault victim's initiatives. Trinitas, as has been mentioned, was made to pay out $3 million in 2008 due to pervasive Medicare fraud at the institution.[13]

Considering how Kai was treated, including the actual felonious refusal of victim's services after he reported being raped, I can't put too much faith in Romankow's proficiency in dealing with abuse victims or the mentally ill. Romankow was also connected to The Children's Advocacy Center. It was funded by the Union County Improvement Authority and county

Freeholders, both of which Romankow was a prominent member of at the time.

Tina Renna had to fight for the privilege of asserting her right to the shield law after county prosecutors attempted to subpoena Renna to get at her sources. For what purposes, one can only guess, though retaliation and intimidation are quite likely. Romankow not only tried to get at Renna's sources. He also impugned her character claiming she may have made up the accusations.

"Personally, I believe she was caught in a lie and chose to waste time and money by hiding," Romankow told New Jersey's *Star-Ledger*.[14] Well, two can play that game. I think the evidence is sufficient to at least note, that the many irregularities in Union County arising about or around Romankow: are signs that this former prosecutor, at the very least, doesn't have the best interests of the people of Union County at heart.

I have dealt with attempts at intimidation regarding stories I've covered. The last few years I have been investigating a con ring in Houston with a body count numbering at least four, perhaps five. A law firm alleged in some news stories to be engaged in media suppression, attempted to have me pull that story. I spent years contacting reporters; with some showing interest, before ghosting me altogether. Alissa Fleck was the only journalist willing to help me get the story shared.

I told Alissa about the law firm's threats and asked her if she would be worried in my shoes. She informed me it wasn't her first rodeo, and she wouldn't be worried about it. So I rode it out. Seeing as they never bothered to offer anything contrary to what my sources and the evidence showed, I refused to fall prey to their petty attempts to harass me or influence my reporting. However, most of the sources I had for that story were admittedly off the record. Go figure. When you have a character who brags about getting away with murder due to consulate connections, it tends to make people want to clam up.

Renna understands the situation just as well. "Who would talk to me if they had to worry about me having to reveal them? I believe that was their goal: to shut down our blog."

Romankow was also quite intent on keeping the matters of Union County's Improvement Authority under county control. Perhaps to escape the oversight of the state? In Camden for instance, extraordinary corruption led to New Jersey intervening in regard to local government matters. Romankow's role also involved public planning projects, another potential area in which access allows for potential corruption.

I have no specific smoking gun to point to in this case; but, as Pulitzer Prize-winning journalist John Archibald said, sometimes it doesn't come down to the number of public officials caught. In the most extremely corrupt venues it would stand to reason that more cover-up, less transparency, and accountability would lead to fewer cases of crooked officials being caught.

Just this year contracting company Dobco exposed bid-rigging in Union County facilitated by the Union County Improvement Authority. They were one of the contractors who put in a bid for the over a hundred-million-dollar government complex. Dobco's bid was the lowest. Ordinarily, this would win them the contract. But this was no ordinary circumstance. That's just not how business is done in Galfy Country.

Dobco Inc. sued, citing the irregularity that skirted the LPCL process. As a result, construction work in Bergen and Union County was stopped. In a 21-page ruling, judges were quite clear in their claims that Dobco had "clearly and convincingly demonstrated irreparable harm... of all taxpayers in Union County."[15]

In many counties in many states that would be the end of it. But not here. After the adverse ruling against Bergen and Union Counties for wriggling their way out of the LPCL procedures, it took only three weeks for the rules to be rewritten "in real time" (as Paterson put it).

Senator Paul Sarlo of Bergen County sponsored senate bill S-1714. It would make county Improvement Authorities exempt from the LPCL. It was none other than Union County's own Nick Scutari, the state senate president who would be responsible for advancing the legislation in the Senate. Now, how convenient for the two counties outed for avoiding laws meant to protect citizens against officials engaging in bid rigging. The timing of the new law springing up, and its being pushed by officials from the two counties in question, is no coincidence.

By the way, Scutari has a rather interesting history that may provide insight into what type of politician he is. When he was the Linden City Court Prosecutor in Union County, he was charged with an alleged theft of $150,000 of services. He also was accused of getting paid for a "no-show" job.* That's right, in at least one case the prosecutor didn't even bother to show up in court. This resulted in the taxpayers being on the hook for a large payout.[16]

Scutari wasn't the subject of just the one inquiry, but "several" investigations into his activities while prosecutor of Linden. The state's Joint Legislative Committee of Ethical Standards also attempted to put the heat on him. Sadly, his corruption was not quelled. Instead, he managed to move his way up from crooked prosecutor to crooked state senate president.[17]

Activist Sue Altman is the director of the New Jersey Working Families

---

* No-show" and "low-show" jobs are mentioned in Garcia's criminology textbook as indicators of organized crime, along with bid-rigging and "industry cartels" freezing out competitors in public works projects.

Alliance. Sue called for Scutari to be removed as chair of the Judiciary Committee, due to the obvious issues posed by such a character having his hands on the lever of the legislature.

"Being removed from the Judiciary Committee is significant because right now, he's the arbiter of who moves up in the judicial system, and that person should have a high ethical standard," Altman told the press. Altman was one of ten who filed an ethics complaint delivered to former New Jersey Supreme Court Justice John Wallace.

The letter read, in part, "This accusation raises serious questions as to Senator Scutari's ability to perform his taxpayer-funded employment and threatens to undermine the public's trust in the Legislature." Scutari's "serial absenteeism" is just another instance of how the now high-ranking official seemed to flout the gravity of the offices he has held. Out of 141 days absent in a two-year period from 2017 to 2018, he only reported five to his superiors.

Law firm Calcagni & Kanefsky wrote up a report on the "no-show" prosecutor. Sue Altman gained access to the scathing, 59-page report through an Open Public Records Act (OPRA) request.

"Unfortunately, we have such a culture of corruption and complicity in New Jersey that is fairly unsavory, and these things go on and on until a group of people says, 'Hey, we need to stop this,'" said Altman.

Scutari also was accused of "widespread malfeasance" by Linden Mayor Derek Armstead on multiple occasions. Through the near-constant shadow of scandal about him, Scutari served as Linden's prosecutor for 15 years. He was first elected to the state senate in 2003, in addition to being the chairman of the Union County Democratic Committee.

In 2019, Scutari was investigated for using a consulting firm that stuffed his pockets with over $147,000. His disinterest in actually showing up to work also led to serious problems in the county courts. On the days he actually did show up he would often excuse himself before the docket was up. When two cousins were brought up on disorderly charges and no prosecutor was to be found, the county had to settle for $575,000. As you can see, even when the money doesn't end up in Scutari's pocket it still stings the residents of Union County.

"This is a criminal justice issue—folks' first entry way to the criminal justice system is often through municipal court," said Altman. "To think we had a prosecutor whose full attention wasn't on the job at hand is extremely troubling."

Hector Osegura, a Hudson County activist, said of Scutari's actions, "politicians... don't think the ethics rules apply to them." He went on to say that he hoped that officials like Scutari would be held to the same scrutiny as others who abuse the system but fears that in the end it will all just be covered up as is the case so often in the county of Union.[18]

Union County Commissioner Bruce Bergen wants to appeal the decision claiming, irony of ironies, that the rules were being changed to their detriment despite the LPCL dating back to 1971 and the senate bill arising three weeks after the exposure of the potential bid rigging scam in Union County.[19]

It's so corrupt it's almost comical. Like a caricature of evil. And the fact that the people involved are under investigation a dozen times and end up floating to the top of the senate should be shocking, but I've seen this sort of thing outside of Union County, outside of New Jersey.

This is not a singular situation. And yes, the role that Union County plays as a hub in overall NJ corruption I think goes back to its geographical location. It's that whole North Jersey Shore thing from Tammany Hall to Atlantic City and Prohibition on. It set up a system that is now so ensconced it doesn't even have to stay too hidden. All this going on out in the open meaning there's much more behind the scenes.

As we've seen, contracting, real estate, and connections to legislative bodies and the judicial system show up time and again. It's just speculation on my part, but I find it interesting that Joseph Galfy retreated from divorce law to work in real estate-related proceedings as well as buying and selling properties himself.

According to his younger brother James Galfy, Joseph also assisted him with "civil suits." The former deputy police chief of Irvington PD turned high school teacher claims he was targeted due to his "deep pockets." As for how and why a police officer generally becomes the subject of civil suits and how and why a police officer turned high school teacher would have such "deep pockets,"[20] these are just a couple of the many mysteries in the case.

I have considered the possibility that, in naming several parties, many of them lawyers and politicians, I might become the subject of a lawsuit myself. In such a case, considering the narrowness of my own pockets I would be forced to defend myself pro se. On the bright side, the discovery process inherent in such a defense might be just the thing to help me gain access to some of the material that might fill in some of the gaps in my research.

Besides, I had to learn a bit about pro se filing already when I was forced to subpoena *ABC7NY* to hopefully find out perhaps who it was removing… something from the active crime scene in Clark. Was this the same person who ran the dishwasher? Why did *ABC7NY* take the video off the internet? Why did the judge refuse to enter a still from the video into evidence? These are questions I ponder that, who knows, might be best answered during discovery process if I were forced to defend my work.

Speaking of having to defend one's work. Tina Renna characterized Romankow's attempt at silencing her as a "political vendetta."[22] The precedent set by her becoming the first blogger to have proved herself covered by the state's shield laws is important in a state with 21 counties, 566 municipalities, and over 600 school districts. A jumble of local political groupings that is difficult to hold accountable without additional help from watchdog organizations.

Generatorgate was another major Union County scandal. Several county employees took home generators during Hurricane Sandy which rocked the northeast coast in 2012.[23] Then there were the stolen chainsaws and the missing funds from Musicfest.[24] It wasn't just these issues, though. Romankow was also "protecting favored employees." Instead of acting on the tips that Renna publicized, Romankow used his position to protect his friends and harass a journalist. She calls into question "Romankow's integrity and independence from political bosses" as well.

New Jersey does have strong journalist shield law protections. But the issue did not hinge on whether or not she was gathering and disseminating information clearly in the public interest. Their weak argument centered on her lack of affiliation with a traditional news media source.[25]

Renna had already proven herself a gadfly in the eyes of some of the Union County "old guard" by 2009. That was the year she called out new employee vehicles for certain government employees, decked out with expensive voice-activated navigation systems. Then there was Musicfest 2010, a week-long festival in Union County which would inspire a five-month investigation. Unfortunately, the Union County Prosecutor's Office dropped it. They claimed there was "insufficient evidence" of criminality.

The whole snafu was just a case of "poorly executed" management, Romankow's office had decided. The investigation began with a letter by

Tina Renna to the Office of the Attorney General. After pointing out that somewhere in the neighborhood of the high six figures was missing, the Attorney General referred the case to the Union County Prosecutor's Office.

The whole thing cost taxpayers over $1.12 million. Romankow argued that the issue stemmed from, among other things, the method used to count cars. Romankow also admitted that having county employees handle and store money raised by charities at the event (especially money that hadn't even been fully accounted for) wasn't the best idea.

Patch reached out to the national event director and press contact for the charity Love Hope Strength (whose board contains multiple local officials) with no answer. The county manager also declined to speak to *Patch*, but Tina Renna spoke up.

"It's outrageous. He holds absolutely no one accountable. It's an obvious smokescreen." Pointing out the issues inherent in such incestuous conflicts of interest, she added, "It's nothing I didn't expect. From the beginning, I said the Union County prosecutor should not be investigating the county."[26]

With the Union County Board of Chosen Freeholders serving meals, Renna argued these should be classified as meetings as per the state's Open Public Meetings Act. In my hometown, similar issues with transparency in local politics abound. A county commissioner revealed ways in which the state's Sunshine Laws designed for transparency of local politics were being circumvented.[27]

Renna attended meetings of the Freeholders. She brought up issues such as a former County Manager recusing himself from projects involving Birdsall Services Group. Later Birdsall would reveal a mass of illegal payouts to local politicians' campaigns. A former employee admitted this practice "regularly won contracts." To get around the issue of campaign donation limits,

Birdsall would have its employees write personal checks to candidates and reimburse them with salary bonuses. Then they lied to the state of New Jersey regarding necessary disclosures.

Christopher Baxter in the *Star-Ledger* described it as "the perfect political machine." And despite having been brought up in 2009 at a Freeholders meeting by Tina Renna, tape recordings of Birdsall employees discussing the practice didn't go public until 2013. This would result in a full investigation into "one of the most expansive and sophisticated criminal pay-to-play conspiracies in recent history."

Hundreds of politicians, mayors, council candidates, and county freeholders (as well as "some of the most well-known New Jersey power brokers") had a hand in the Birdsall criminal conspiracy. From 2008 to 2012, over a million dollars was funneled in secret to candidates and political groups to curry favor and secure contracts. Contracts amounting to over $84 million in taxpayer funds, bought and paid for by dirty political dealing. Birdsall also had ties to the George Norcross political machine.[28]

New Jersey is mostly a one-party state. But corruption is a bipartisan affair, and Birdsall didn't play favorites. They donated to both Democrats and Republicans. Many public officials defended using the contractor, but in the end, Birdsall and its executives would be indicted and plead guilty to campaign finance law violations. Records from March 2011 show Birdsall also spent $2500 on the legal defense fund for Angie Devanney, wife of the former Union County manager George Devanney.

Angie denied ever receiving said funds. That very year, Union County spent several thousand dollars on legal expenses related to a US Department of Justice investigation into George Devanney (incidentally the nephew of Union County state Senator Raymond Lesniak).[29]

In an interview with a reporter, former Union County official, Frank Lehr, explained the extent of Lesniak's pull. "If he (Lesniak) has somebody he wants to get a job, he gets it....I don't think there's any question that he is the boss of Union County." Dina Matos McGreevey also spoke of Lesniak's importance. She first met him when she was twenty-two and a fresh face on the Elizabeth planning board. "If you wanted to secure a state or government contract or run for office, he was the one whose blessing you'd have to get," she revealed in her autobiography.[30]

Lesniak, by the way, was often featured in the *Union County Directions* publication. The state comptroller called out the hefty $1.5 million price tag this free publicity ran the public. It also tended to promote local Democrat politicians (many also Freeholders) connected to Union County's good ol' boys. Comptroller Marc Larkins warned of the self-serving newsletter:

"When a group funded almost entirely by government money, managed by government officials, carrying out a government function is allowed to operate outside of government rules and regulations, accountability disappears."[31]

George and Angie Devanney are currently running Keywood Strategies which promises to help businesses "through the maze of New Jersey politics." They tout the assistance of "several of New Jersey's most influential elected officials." Among those named is State Senate President Nick Scutari. Scutari, the former Union County Freeholder Director, despite numerous investigations, still enjoys an upward trajectory in his political career. Devanney left his career of public service the same year that the Birdsall documents were made public.

Angie Devanney presided as Berkeley Heights' Business Administrator during a "development boom." This resulted from "intensive zoning changes and economic development planning." She worked for Berkeley Heights in a public capacity from 2005 to late 2007. During this period she claims to have assisted several area companies in "navigating to succeed."[32]

In an article about Union County's issues with the organization, *Star-Ledger* highlights how the local political process, especially as far as bidding on public projects goes, is susceptible due to many entangling alliances, family and political and business connections:

"Indeed, politics has long been part of the DNA of the Union County Improvement Authority."

"For more than a decade, the agency was headed by the late Charlotte DeFilippo, who also chaired the county Democratic Committee and ran the UCIA (Union County Improvement Authority) from her home and was paid $160,000 per year."

"Until his recent retirement, the county's spokesman served as the authority's chairman. A former freeholder replaced DeFilippo as executive director for a time. The Union County Improvement Authority is currently being run by Taylor, the wife of former East Orange Mayor Lester Taylor whose law firm also has contracts with the county. Also serving as the county's finance director, she is paid an additional $5,000 a month to serve as the Union County Improvement Authority's 'project manager,' in addition to her current $160,000-a-year county salary."[33]

Star-Ledger reported on Freeholder Daniel Sullivan in 2009. Sullivan attempted to not only make his home county safe for nepotism but also make it verboten to bring up such potential favoritism at public meetings.

When Renna brought up the fact that Sullivan had kin on the public payroll, Sullivan was adamant, "I'm going to tell you right now, do not mention my family."

"We cannot talk about your family who are county employees?" Renna responded. "That's right," was Sullivan's answer. "That's right. You cannot mention my family."

This rightly upset Renna. She was removed from the meeting by a security guard at the request of Sullivan, who "mockingly mimic[ked]" her according to the *Star-Ledger*. Union County spokesman, Sebastian D'Elia, claimed that Renna was thrown out for speaking over the amount of time allotted to her, but, a videotape of the meeting has Sullivan plainly threatening her: "If you mention my family I swear to you, you'll be thrown out of here." Bruce Paterson later utilized his time in part to ask how "all of these freeholder family members get hired." At which time Sullivan advised him it would be best to "move on to your next point."

How's that for transparency?

When the *Star-Ledger* spoke to spokesman D'Elia about exactly how many Sullivan family members are being paid out by the county, D'Elia replied that they "don't know." It took the involvement of the ACLU of New Jersey to amend the next meeting's opening with a disclaimer:

"Comments regarding public employees, whether or not they are related to freeholders or others, will be allowed at this and all future meetings, as protected by the First Amendment."[34]

Freeholders have been implicated throughout the state in various instances of corruption. Just before Christmas in 2019, 8 were arrested in New Jersey over a case of corruption that involved bags, envelopes, and a coffee cup stuffed with cash. Ten grand in the coffee cup alone.[35]

In 2020, former freeholder John Cesaro was one of three indicted in a corruption case. Last year, the coffee cup case resulted in four indictments described by state Attorney General Gurbir Grewal as "old-school political corruption at its worst."[36]

Despite the best efforts of the Union County Watchdog's Association and reporting by Renna, time and again, instead of the guilty parties being brought to justice, they seemed protected by the system. In the 2010 MusicFest debacle, Romankow declined a criminal investigation into potential malfeasance by George Devanney. Instead, he charitably gave him time to retire. Romankow's assistant was in attendance at Devanney's retirement party.[37] A very specifically timed step-down, akin to that of Romankow on the day of Kai's arrest.

These are just a handful of the many stories related to how business is handled in Galfy Country. As of 2022, *Politico* has been closely following the case of political consultant, Sean Caddle,[38] Caddle was already being investigated for charges related to misappropriation of funds from certain super PACs and non-profits. The plot thickened when he pled guilty to hiring a hit man.[39] Caddle hired two men to viciously murder Jersey City native Michael Galdieri, a former friend and associate, in 2014. Caddle had a notable role in developing a "web of dark money groups" that helped Union County political boss Raymond Lesniak, among others.[39] Caddle was allowed "home confinement" in the interim, while reportedly cooperating with federal authorities on another investigation.[40] This has sparked rumors, that he may be on the verge of setting off the actions that could potentially cause the Union County corruption house of cards to collapse under its own weight.

Equally interesting to the local political scene are the geopolitical reasons for Union County corruption. A lot of these issues go back decades to corruption on the docks and also resulted in some shocking news related to the one degree of separation between the Union County Prosecutor's Office and the Genovese crime family.

Even in recent months, Union County has had multiple shameful stories crop up. Clark Mayor Sal Bonaccorso was called to resign after it was revealed the township had agreed to pay hundreds of thousands of dollars to a whistleblower to hush the fact that Clark mayor Bonaccorso, the police chief, and an internal affairs sergeant were using blisteringly racist language. This wasn't the first time Bonaccorso had been accused of racism, but with audio recordings, it was a little far past the point for denials.[41]

That said, it's quite obvious that Clark (and Union County in general) is no stranger to conspiracy and cover-up when it suits them.

"In July 2020, six months after the settlement was signed, the Union County Prosecutor's Office seized control of Clark's police department, citing 'credible allegations of misconduct.' [....]

"Two years ago, the township concealed the allegations by quietly agreeing to pay the whistleblower and his attorney $400,000 under a legal settlement. The whistleblower, Lt. Antonio Manata, was also allowed to remain on the payroll for more than two years without working at an additional cost of $289,700 in salary alone. In exchange, he turned over the recordings to ensure they would not be disseminated and agreed not to file a lawsuit."[42]

Clark's PBA called out for Bonaccorso to be removed from office in a strongly worded letter... that neglected to mention anything about the two high-ranking Union County police officers, including a former Clark PBA officer, also caught using the n-word and other racist and sexist language on the very same recording. Clark PBA was "disheartened and outraged" regarding the mayor, but silent about their brothers in blue, including a former secretary of the Clark PBA also caught on the recordings.

As happens so often in these cases, the whistleblower Lt. Antonio Manata who recorded the remarks in 2020 reports he is being punished for embarrassing Clark, or rather for allowing the Chief of Police, internal affairs sergeant and mayor to embarrass themselves.

Manata's lawsuit argues that the prosecutor's office is now punishing him for blowing the whistle on conduct that he "believed in good faith to be illegal, unsafe, against township policy, against public policy and/or a matter of public importance," meanwhile the discrimination he collected evidence of goes unprosecuted. At the time, a spokesperson for the Union County Prosecutor's Office declined to respond to these claims, saying the office does not comment on pending civil litigation.[43]

CHAPTER 8

ON THE WATERFRONT

In 2019 the *Washington Post* covered a Gambino crime family boss, Francesco "Franky Boy" Cali being assassinated outside of his home. "New York Mafia still active, but flashy 'mob hits' decline as witnesses flip and law hits harder" the headline read.[1] J. Edgar Hoover spent decades trying to deny the existence of the mafia. In the intervening decades since, the FBI was forced to acknowledge their existence, but the myth that "the mafia doesn't exist/doesn't exist anymore" has persisted. It was in 1957 after the Apalachin Meeting in New York that Hoover and the FBI would finally acknowledge the network of families referred to in the agency as "La Cosa Nostra" (LCN).[2]

The *Washington Post* story notes that the hit represented the first major crime boss to be assassinated since 1985. J. Bruce Mouw, a retired FBI agent who had worked on the investigation that took down mob boss John Gotti told the Post that the absence of such incidents was a sign of the decline of the mafia's influence since a peak in the mid-1980s. Mouw cites the FBI taking out top leaders in various organized crime operations as well as working to keep unions clear of mafia ties. "The Gambino family had 10 to 15 unions that they controlled, construction, garbage collection. They may have a few now, but they are few and far between."

A few confirmed examples of union and Waterfront Commission members with mafia ties have a shocking Union County connection whose tendrils extend to multiple people tangential to Kai's case. One reason for Union County's importance in understanding New Jersey corruption is geographical. The fact that much of the industrial waterfront lies in New Jersey's 20th District of Union County makes it an important bit of political real estate. As *Gothamist* reported, anyone who wants to be governor of the state eventually has to gain the favor of the political bosses.[3] And Union County's geopolitical importance, tied to its industrial waterfront, makes those county bosses particularly important. That kind of leverage leaves a lot of room for skimming off the top and political favors. As Union County Democratic Chairman Jerry Green put it, "Governor has to go through Union County."[4]

Nearly a full decade before the Apalachin meeting, journalist Malcolm Johnson would pen a series of articles entitled "Crime on the Waterfront." The series delved into violence, murder, and corruption on the docks in Hoboken, New Jersey. It would, in turn, inspire the classic Elia Kazan film, starring Marlon Brando and featuring one of the most memorable lines in all of cinema history: "I coulda been a contender, instead of a bum. Which is what I am."

The Waterfront Commission owes its existence in part to the Elia Kazan film inspired by the Pulitzer Prize-winning series by Malcolm Johnson. The 24-article series began with an investigation into a murder on the docks which led to the discovery of massive criminal activity surrounding corrupt union officials, organized crime, terrorism, racketeering, and violence related to longshoremen in Hoboken, New Jersey. But the film almost never came to be.

When the story was pitched to Darryl F. Zanuck, he reportedly re-sponded, "Who's going to care about a bunch of sweaty longshoremen?" Johnson's reporting and the subsequent film spurred on the "United States Special Committee to Investigate Crime in Interstate Commerce" in 1953. This chapter in history would be adapted in yet another classic film about American organized crime, *The Godfather Part II.*

What began as a simple report on the murder of a dock worker's hiring boss in 1948 would result in a series of revelations that would shape the history of New York and New Jersey waterfront politics for decades to come. To this very day, in fact. Johnson's journey into the depths of waterfront crime may have begun with a single story, but like with Kai's case, once you begin turning stones over, you're bound to find a can of worms after a while.

Johnson describes the development of the series beginning with the initial murder in 1948:

"The story, in all truth, snowballed. One lead led to another; various sources and contacts were developed, but only after months of hard digging."[5] As with the case of yet another scapegoated figure, Dr. Fletcher Woodward (colloquially referred to as Fletch Woodward) what started as an investiga-tion into a murder and the drive to be exonerated led to Woodward unin-tentionally unveiling a series of dirty secrets.[6]

The Commission was founded in 1953 to prevent organized crime, cargo theft, racketeering, kickbacks, and violence in the New York Harbor. "The original intention was to prevent organized crime influence literally on the docks," said New Jersey state Sen. Joseph Cryan, a former Union County sheriff whose 20th legislative district spot in Union County means he rep-resents some very valuable political real estate. A good portion of the indus-trial waterfront of New Jersey.

"We're in a completely different world. Does it mean that crime has gone to zero? Absolutely not, but we're not meeting the moment with the Waterfront Commission. We think there's a better way to deal with this," Governor Phil Murphy who, like Cryan, supported freeing New Jersey from dependence on the Commission, remarked to a reporter in early 2022.

"The compact made sense in 1953," Murphy, who filed a brief at the Supreme Court over the bill signed by Chris Christie on his last day as governor. "It makes no sense now."[7]

They may have not been correct about the lack of corruption on the docks currently, but at least partly right about the Commission itself. "This was a total agency breakdown," Inspector General Fisch said of the troubling issues revealed by the 2009 Office of the Inspector General report. "Instead of ridding the waterfront of corruption, this agency itself was corrupt."[8]

The waterfront scene is an important backdrop to Kai's story. One of the central figures in multiple waterfront-related fiascoes happens to not only hail from Union County but is also a close friend of Albert Cernadas, Jr. Cernadas is integral to several scandals that erupted as a result of Waterfront Commission General Counsel Jon Deutsch's misconduct, revealed by the New York Office of the Inspector General (OIG). According to the report, Mr. Deutsch "fashioned a scheme" to allow a felon, Frank Cardaci, who had been convicted of federal charges of illegal domestic sales of goods intended for foreign shipment, to hide his ownership of a waterfront warehouse by placing it in his wife's name[9] among several other major issues that proved those tasked with keeping corruption at bay were already thoroughly corrupted themselves.

It also found that none of the 53 stevedoring companies supervised by the commission had been granted permanent five-year licenses, as required.[10] On top of that, numerous fiscal issues arose from payroll audits which were as much as 14 years behind. What is perhaps most relevant to this particular story is the peculiar relationship Deutsch had with both Union County prosecutor Albert Cernadas, Jr. and his family, some of whom were "related" to a very different sort of family.[11]

Deutsch would assist the Genovese-affiliated father of his Union County prosecutor friend for years. Deutsch acted as head of the Commission's Licensing Division at the time that the Eastern District of New York and Waterfront Commission began a joint investigation into certain members of the International Longshoremen's Association (ILA). The Waterfront Commission would interview Cernadas, Sr. in March 2000 and October 2003.

"For simplistic purposes of the record," Deutsch announced, "I will ask the questions." The then-acting police chief of the Waterfront Commission of New York Harbor, Kevin McGowan, who assisted Deutsch in the 2003 interview has said he was aware that Deutsch had worked with Cernadas, Jr. but wasn't aware of the full extent of their relationship. Deutsch wouldn't divulge just how close they were until after Cernadas, Sr. was eventually arrested and revealed to be connected to the Genovese crime family. Deutsch claimed that the conflict of interest only arose after Cernadas, Sr. was indicted in connection with organized crime.

McGowan, by the way, isn't above scrutiny either. He was discovered to have been diverting detective personnel for the all-important task of... guarding the prime parking spots in lower Manhattan for the benefit of executive staff. Meanwhile, Commissioner Michael Axelrod was also taking advantage of his position. Axelrod would give official "police" placards to his wife and a wealthy friend who wasn't even connected to the Commission apart from friendship with Axelrod.[12]

The OIG report establishes not only that Deutsch helped out Cernadas on multiple occasions in multiple ways but also that the definition of conflict of interest is rather loose in some people's minds. Check out this doozy of a question from the OIG report.

```
Q: But a civil RICO investigation wasn't enough?


Deutsch: No, I think it was the - I think it was -
no, no. With the civil RICO, God, that went on for
months. They were just trying to build a case. They
didn't say, oh, we got a sure-shot thing here, this
guy is a member of organized crime. They were trying
to build their case.
```

Now we could certainly assume that Deutsch was just acting on his own accord in some of these cases. After all, this is a man he'd invited to his daughter's bat mitzvah, so they were quite close. He might feel protective of his friend and coworker. There is, however, no excuse for why Cernadas lied about soliciting help from Deutsch as is also made clear in the report:

"Although Cernadas, Jr. initially stated that he had only discussed general reporting requirements with Deutsch; once confronted with telephone records, Cernadas, Jr. admitted to Commission investigators that he told Deutsch at dinner that members of the Waterfront Commission were looking for his uncle."

Why lie if you have nothing to hide? Unless that is, you know that what you're doing is both illegal and unethical. Cernadas wasn't planning on volunteering information that would have incriminated himself and his friend Deutsch. Only when faced with proof of his lies did he relent.[13]

As Union County corruption watchdog and investigative journalist Tina Renna pointed out, at no point was Cernadas, Jr. publicly censured either by his immediate boss Theodore Romankow or by Romankow's boss the Attorney General. It's honestly no wonder that the many conflicts of interest related to Kai's case didn't seem like a big deal. In Union County, they "know people."[14]

Cernadas was a long-time luminary of the International Longshoremen's Association (ILA) at both the Port of New York and New Jersey. Cernadas was previously Executive Vice President of the ILA and President of the ILA Local 1235 chapter. He wormed his way out of a 2006 conviction involving mail and wire fraud picking the pockets of union members. Stealing directly from their health care fund that he was a trustee of.

In addition to the two years of probation, Cernadas was also booted from the ILA altogether. It wouldn't be until 2009 that an indictment would reveal Cernadas was, in fact, an associate of the Genovese crime family, one of the notorious "Five Families" in New York City.

Of the 127, 18 were from New Jersey with one-third of those indicted from New Jersey hailing from Union County. Albert Cernadas, Sr, Anthony Alfano, Stephen Depiro, Tonino Colantonio, John Hartmann, and Guiseppe Pugliese represented the County of Union in the case. Cernadas had already slunk away with only two years of probation after pleading guilty to diverting thousands of dollars of union money to a pharmaceutical company with mob ties.[15]

Cernadas, Sr. was indicted along with fellow ILA leaders Harold Daggett and Arthur Coffee, and Lawrence Ricci (a reputed Genovese family capo) connected to the health care fund fraud. Despite pleading guilty to wire fraud, mail fraud, and criminal conspiracy he received a paltry two years of probation. As Deutsch pointed out, sometimes it's all about who you know. Jack Arseneault, a friend of Harvey and McGreevey, presented US District Judge I. Leo Glasser with 292 letters of support urging leniency in sentencing.[16]

Arseneault had nearly been appointed Attorney General under McGreevey. He was also the lawyer for one of the influential political bosses and Norcross gang ally, John Lynch.[17] Lynch and Norcross often found themselves at odds with Union County's Ray Lesniak. Lesniak, not to be underestimated, convinced McGreevey to wait out the clock past the point of the special elections favored by Lynch and Norcross. Lynch's official political duties ended when a "covert operation" employed against the current Whitman administration to McGreevey's advantage was made public. Lesniak admits that the occurrence was a sign that "we [party bosses] have too much power. [...] When you talk about the bosses, I'm one of them. I can't deny it."[18]

Former General Counsel Jon Deutsch used his spot on the Commission to issue a license to Brendan McDermott, son of a family friend, despite his drug conviction. Deutsch also made sure that Cernadas Jr. got advance notice regarding the investigation. Another major conflict of interest uncovered by the Inspector General's investigation stemmed from his failure to disclose his connection to consultant, Dennis M. Kelly Associates, LLC when recommending the company in his official capacity as an employee of the government agency.

Where it gets really interesting as far as our story is concerned, is when Deutsch "engaged in a series of improprieties involving his relationship with Al Cernadas, Jr," who is listed in the report as Cernadas Jr.'s "former co-worker and friend." Deutsch not only leaked information regarding a probe into the Union County prosecutor's father, Albert Cernadas, Sr. but even intervened on behalf of his friend. Deutsch failed to recuse himself from questioning Cernadas, Sr. who was then targeted by the United States Attorney's Office, Eastern District of New York. Deutsch stepped in again and "inappropriately intervened" on behalf of Cernadas' family friend, Jimmy Zamuz. Deutsch, when asked why he took it upon himself to pull police records regarding the case rather than the Commission's police division as per protocol remarked, under oath: "I was a prosecutor in Union County. I mean, New Jersey's a little different than New York. I mean, we know people."[19]

Cernadas Jr. has claimed he was "unaware" that Deutsch would be questioning his father. This could be so, however, there is no question that Deutsch would step in a third time on behalf of Cernadas' family and friends by leaking private information regarding Cernadas family members who were then being investigated concerning a bar fight. Deutsch also sought the suspension of one of the parties involved in the fight who was "estranged" from the Cernadas family at the time.

Deutsch also assisted convicted felon Frank Cardaci in evading the Waterfront Commission Act by helping him set up a warehouse in his wife's name. This cover-up implicated "several former senior officials" including the aforementioned Nastasi. Ironically, the Cardaci warehouse operation which involved goods meant for international sale being sold domestically at lower prices was, according to the report, "the same type of criminal activity the Commission was created to combat."

The Deutsch and Cernadas connection goes back to the early 1990s when Deutsch was working as a prosecutor in Union County. The Inspector General's investigation noted that Deutsch and Cernadas, Jr. met frequently for lunch or dinner and that Cernadas, Jr. had been invited to Deutsch's daughter's bat mitzvah. Cernadas, Jr., and Deutsch were also on the board of Crime Stoppers of Union County. Quis custodiet, et cetera...[*]

Another Genovese family associate with connections to Cernadas, Sr. is

---

[*]   "Quis custodiet ipsos custodes" is a Latin phrase meaning who watches the watchers or who guards the guards, from Roman poet Juvenal's Satires.

Jose "Pepe" Rodriguez. Pepe is mentioned in the case of Manuel Rodriguez (aka Manny Rod, AKA Manny Guitarbarr). Guitarbarr was accused of extortion, racketeering, illegal gambling, and involvement in gangland violence as well as misrepresentation while being interviewed under oath by the Waterfront Commission in matters involving Albert "The Bull" Cernadas, Sr.

"The Bull" Cernadas, Sr. was tight with Manny Rodriguez. Similar to the relationship between Cernadas Jr. and Deutsch, "The Bull" attended Rodriguez's wedding, was good friends with the in-laws and the two were also friends on Facebook. Rodriguez lied on the stand for his friend, Cernadas, Sr. At the time he was "aware of the organized crime ties, allegations, and criminal history of Cernadas and Guitarbarr." The Administrative Law Judge (ALJ) found that he "lied during his sworn interview despite being warned that revocation of registration could be a consequence." Rodriguez "then failed to retract a single false statement despite being offered the opportunity to do so at the conclusion of his sworn interview."

The ALJ found that "during the Hearing, he persisted in claiming ignorance about the organized crime ties of both Cernadas ... and Guitarbarr." The ALJ also noted that, during the hearing, he retracted prior admissions, contradicted prior testimony, and "offered incredible excuses for his Facebook friendships with Cernadas and Guitarbarr."

Less easy to explain was why Rodriguez posted "snitches get stitches" as a comment on Manny Guitarbarr's Facebook page. Apart from the obvious explanation that the ALJ came to. The Judge noted that Rodriguez's "message threatening informants on the Facebook page of a Genovese crime family associate under indictment, gives a clear perception of corruption."[20] So it was clear that the waterfronts, and even the Waterfront Commission for that matter, were not free of organized crime influence. But there was a new item on the agenda in the early 2000s.

Thomas Leonardis was president of ILA Local 1235 after Cernadas. Leonardis was also one of those indicted in the massive 2011 sting. He also supported Lesniak's bill to shrug off the influence of the agency as it had "outlived its usefulness."[21] The timing of this grand declaration was premature, to say the least as just over a week later on January 20, 2011, FBI and Secret Service agents accomplished the largest one-day Mafia arrest in history. 127 individuals suspected to be associates or members of all five Mafia families in New York as well as New Jersey's DeCavalcante crime family were brought in on federal indictment.

Thomas Leonardis, the president of ILA Local 1235 one of those indicted in the massive January 2011 sting also testified in support of Lesniak's bill the Autumn prior.[22] It was not long after Deutsch was fired that Lesniak sponsored the bill. Right about the same time as the nearly 800 FBI and Secret Service agents and law enforcement officers arrested 127 suspected members and associates of the Mafia from all five of New York's Mafia families as well as New Jersey's DeCavalcante family.[23]

So much for Leonardis's theatrics presenting an old cargo hook to demonstrate how outdated the Commission was.[24]

New Jersey US Attorney Paul J. Fishman remarked on the bust, "Workers should be free to pursue an honest living without being worried that their own union representatives will shake them down. … Paying tribute to the mob is not an acceptable cost of doing business in New Jersey."[25]

The recent and recurrent nature of such waterfront-based organized crime led the state of New York to take an unusual step this year. They sought support from the Supreme Court to block New Jersey's attempt to dissolve the Waterfront Commission. This despite Democrat Governor of New York Kathy Hochul and Democrat Governor of New Jersey Phil Murphy generally being allied.[26] The Commission was formed via a bi-state compact in the 1950s. A New York and New Jersey lawsuit from 1931 was also related to waterfront property.[27]

"In light of current geopolitical uncertainty, the termination of the Waterfront Commission would cause immediate and irreparable harm to New York State, from increased crime to higher prices to employment inequalities," Hochul said in a statement announcing the lawsuit. "It is our responsibility to New Yorkers to stop New Jersey's unlawful actions and preserve the ongoing work of this law enforcement agency."

Like Lesniak, Cryan, Christie, and others, Murphy (also a friend of the ILA) was determined to put an end to what they saw as an overbearing Commission that involved New York where New York had no business.

Lesniak also looms large as far as characters in close orbit to those implicated via a conflict of interest concerning Kai's ordeal. Lesniak, an admitted "county boss" knows how the game is played and doesn't deny the long history of racism and mafia connections in Union County. In chapter 3 of Raymond Lesniak's recent book about his life and political career, he makes it clear that mobbed-up local government is nothing new to the county.

"My mayoral campaign picked up momentum after the fire because Elizabeth residents were fed up with their city being treated as a dumping ground. People believed that surely the city government knew what was going on at Chemical Control all those years, but no one had the courage to stand up to the mob. And Dunn had his associations with mobsters. In the 1980s, he put Mafia soldier JoJo Ferarra on the city payroll as a municipal code inspector. JoJo was the personal protector of Giovanni 'John the Eagle' Riggi, a member of the DeCavalcante crime family. Riggi was the leader of the 'Elizabeth crew' in the family where he was a caporegime. Only in New Jersey."

Lesniak also decries the rampant racism that existed under the Tom Dunn administration that preceded his election to Mayor of Elizabeth. Considering the scandal about the lies, cover-up, and racism from the mayor of Clark (and high-ranking members of the Clark PD.) just earlier in 2022 it's clear that neither the organized crime issues nor the racism has been fully excised from the county since Lesniak's coming into his own as a local power broker in one of the most important counties of New Jersey.[28]

It is nonetheless interesting to hear Lesniak reveal the inner workings of Union County machine politics. At one point in the excerpt published by *New Jersey Globe,* Lesniak shares how "one of my presumed allies, the chair of Rahway's organization, had sided with the Dunn faction after being promised a $10,000-a-year part-time job as a legislative aide."

One thing that becomes clear after spending enough time watching how politics works in New Jersey, corruption is a bipartisan affair. Republicans will support Democrats (or vice versa) if it means a favor gets paid off or a connection is made happy. Chris Christie's support of Norcross waging a war against fellow Democrat, Governor Phil Murphy is just one of many examples of this phenomenon.[29]

Lesniak reminisces about turning his petitions over to James Devine, who "was an ardent enemy of Dunn because of a tussle Dunn had with his dad." Lesniak and Cryan fell out in 2011 in part due to the Elizabeth Board of Education is another similar case. Devine was frank with Lesniak when returning from putting in his petitions:

"If Dunn was willing to promise the Rahway Democratic chair ten thousand dollars to knock you off the line, how much do you think I could have gotten to toss your petitions in a trash can and knock you off the ballot." Lesniak notes that Devine "would later become a controversial political consultant with a particularly devious side to him."

New Jersey state election records show that Albert Cernadas Sr. donated to corrupt senator Bob Menendez's campaign* as well as to Union County politician Joe Cryan.[30] Cryan was sheriff of Union County in 2013 when Kai was arrested.

What's more, he is also the son of John Cryan who was sheriff in Essex County when it was indicted as a RICO racketeering operation. Cryan was indicted but not convicted due to a technicality. The elder Cryan ran a tavern and was a local party boss in addition to his role as Sheriff which involved shakedowns, kickbacks, and extortion. Cryan led the department in a "long-standing 'system' of annual cash political contributions." His associate Lerner even had a "secret safety deposit box" (far more sophisticated than the ten thousand dollars delivered via coffee cup in another recent New Jersey story, Lerner's solution rivals that of the special drawer Frank Hague had designed).

In the RICO case involving Union County politician and Sheriff Joe Cryan's father, the "Enterprise" was composed of the Essex County Sheriff's Office which was accused of a "pattern of racketeering activity" including bribery and extortion. Cryan's involvement ended in a mistrial declared January 15, 1980.** Harry Lerner was charged with three counts of perjury

---

* Menendez was implicated in multiple scandals and incidents of corruption but was instead "severely admonished" when all charges were dropped due to a mistrial hinging on McDonnell v. the United States which strongly limited the definition of public corruption and bribery. Absolutely no consequences for the, around one million dollars he received in exchange for being the "personal senator" to Salomon Melgen including obtaining visas for those close to Melgen. Melgen, unlike Menendez, would have charges stick, though he was eventually pardoned by Donald Trump.[31]

** Over $100,000 was seized from William Leonardis in the Essex County Sheriff's Office. The warrant was executed by agents of the FBI trial in January 1980, mistrial declared "Court found that this Lerner transaction was not sufficiently linked to the overall conspiracy, involving Lerner's co-defendants, to annually extort money and issue bribes... but rather constituted evidence of a separate conspiracy."
Counts one and two were dismissed. It was claimed that the "two conspiracies were charged in the same count." The "impermissible amendment of the Indictment" led to the Third Circuit Court of Appeals. Lerner's perjury counts were "stayed, pending the outcome of the appeal."

arising out of his testimony before the grand jury."[32]

Cryan's indictment alleged he "conspired to conduct the affairs of the Sheriff's Office through a pattern of racketeering activity, by extorting money and receiving bribes, in excess of $100,000, from employees of the Sheriff's Office, in return for awarding salary increases, promotions, preferred job assignments, and other job-related benefits." He was charged for (among other things) creating a secret cash fund used for illegal campaign expenses.

John Cryan, Sheriff of Essex County since 1970, Harry Lerner Chairman of Essex County Democratic Party from 1968-1978, William Leonardis, Chief Inspector of the Essex County Sheriff's Office since 1972, Rocco Neri, Undersheriff of the Essex County Sheriff's Office since 1975, were charged in a five-count indictment with conspiracy to commit racketeering (RICO) and racketeering through the commission of bribery and extortion in violation of State law. Additionally, Harry Lerner was charged with three counts of perjury arising out of his testimony before the grand jury."[33]

Though I haven't been able to conclusively confirm a relation, there is a William Leonardis in New Jersey with a son named Thomas Leonardis whose ages line up but apart from that I was unable to definitively prove the crooked cop William Leonardis and mobbed up Thomas Leonardis who succeeded Cernadas as head of ILA Local 1235 are father and son. Thomas Leonardis was initially indicted around the same time as Cernadas. Leonardis had previously testified in support of Lesniak's bill meant to end the Waterfront Commission and would be sentenced to two years in prison for Mafia extortion in 2014.[34]

It's also unclear why the indictment against Cernadas over the violent shakedowns to obtain "Christmas tribute" money funneled to the Genovese family was unsealed sans fanfare (or even the usual press release). Generally, such indictments would be announced. Keeping it quiet wouldn't work for long anyway; soon Cernadas, Sr. was found to be embroiled in a "far larger conspiracy dating back more than two decades." During his stead as a major figure in the ILA, Cernadas forced cash payments from members every year around Christmas aided by "actual and threatened, force, violence and fear."

The US Attorney's office in Newark initially offered no comment regarding what got it interested in Cernadas or why he was quietly indicted with no fanfare, no press release even. A week prior, Robert Ruiz, 51, international representative and delegate of ILA arrested and charged in New York for extortion conspiracy "similar payments."[35]

Around that same time, the FBI happened to dig up nearly $52,000 from the backyard of an unidentified union member from New Jersey who went to authorities after being threatened with loss of their jobs, or even lives, if they didn't hand over the cash demanded by the Genovese-affiliated ILA chapter.[36]

Stephen Depiro, another reputed mobster from Union County was also indicted in New York in the massive waterfront sting. Depiro helped move money from the union member shakedowns into the Genovese mob's coffers. Court records show that Edward Aulisi, president of Local 1235 after Cernadas was given the boot, made a phone call where he assures Michael Coppola, reputed mob boss, that the money will still be filtering in despite Cernadas being indisposed. On the contrary, the payments actually doubled under Aulisi.

Aulisi was a witness at a special hearing of the Waterfront Commission related to his "no-show" job at Port Elizabeth. Apart from invoking his Fifth Amendment rights, Aulisi was tight-lipped. The Cernadas shakedown operation spanned all the way back to 1982 according to an article in the *Star-Ledger* where the fact that Cernadas, Jr. was 1st assistant of Union

County is mentioned almost as an afterthought.[37]

Indicted along with the elder Cryan was Thomas Leonardis. Especially interesting considering his younger namesake's role in working with Union County party boss Raymond "Ray Ray" Lesniak, considered the "architect" of the bill meant to dissolve the Waterfront Commission.

The Lesniak-sponsored bill's supporters included "groups that have directed hundreds of thousands of dollars in campaign contributions to state lawmakers." Lesniak was noted as not only the "architect" of the original bill but the "single-biggest champion of eliminating the agency" according to a 2017 article at *Politico*. That said, he was not a sponsor of the 2017 version that Christie supported. Perhaps because Lesniak was "among the governor's fiercest critics." Christie had vetoed Lesniak's original bill in 2015 for fear it was "legally dubious." Christie was concerned it may violate federal law, though he would later support the position that the Commission was outdated and a hindrance to New Jersey's waterfront-based industry.

In another article, Cryan claimed that dissolving the commission would fix the waterfront-related issues. Now, though it is perhaps true that the waterfront is no more corrupt than any other institution in New Jersey, that is a far cry from claiming there isn't a great deal to be concerned about. Both on the waterfront and the Commission meant to oversee it.

When asked to explain himself regarding that action, by the way, Jon Deutsch (who actually mentions his work at the Waterfront Commission on his website under job experience, though with no mention of how he was terminated for being one of the most crooked of the crooks during his tenure there) glibly responded that things were "a little different" in New Jersey.

Well yeah, that whole "multiple Union County Prosecutor's Office staff being no more than one to two degrees removed from actual mobsters" bit sure seems to suggest that. And maybe I'm just old-fashioned but, say, having a crooked government official step in to try and shield your 5 Families-affiliated dad isn't exactly behavior befitting an officer of the court, much less a 1st assistant prosecutor, but hey, maybe I'm just behind the times.

I mean, technically, I'm not. On paper anyway. Investigative reporter and Union County corruption watchdog, Tina Renna, noted on her County Watchers website that Cernadas Jr. appeared to be flaunting the Union County Prosecutor's Office Law Enforcement Code of Ethics:

".... I will keep my private life unsullied as an example to all and will behave in a manner that does not bring discredit to me or to my agency...... Honest and thoughtful in deed both in my personal and official life, I will constantly strive to achieve these objectives and ideals, dedicating myself before God to my chosen profession...Law Enforcement."[38]

Deutsch looked into why the Commission's detectives were interested in Ray Costa, another relation of the Cernadas family. Deutsch knew that he should have observed the chain of command but circumvented Acting Chief of Police McGowan by calling Lieutenant Politano instead. He admitted doing this after having dinner with Cernadas, Jr. He also admitted knowing it was a "personal request" regarding Cernadas's uncle. After obtaining the information regarding the investigation from Politano, Deutsch immediately reported back to Cernadas. Politano noted that Deutsch asking him for information was odd enough, odder still to call in the evening.

When McGowan learned of the special favor, he initiated the investigation that led to Deutsch being suspended, but again, it looks like Deutsch was primarily chosen to take the fall along with two police detectives who were also suspended after lying to the Commission throughout the investigation. Cernadas seemed to benefit from Deutsch's multiple actions on his behalf and certainly knew of some of it, even requesting certain actions but for whatever reason, this was deemed perfectly fine.

In a stroke of irony, Deutsch got entangled in a violation of the Waterfront Commission Code of Ethics… that he had written himself. In other words, no one should know better than Deutsch that it was wrong to release confidential Commission information or use one's official position to "secure unwarranted privileges or advantages for himself, herself or others."

Deutsch also tried to worm his way out by claiming ignorance of basic chain of command. First, arguing that the incident was related to lack of any official chart listing the chain of command. He later admitted he was well aware of the protocol.

A Detective David Bistacco gave Deutsch warning of what was coming down the pike after being questioned by McGowan. Bistacco, one of the two detectives who lied to the investigators regarding this case, called Deutsch warning him to "watch out" claiming "this is De Maria's doing." Bistacco was suspended for lying under oath, but covering up evidence of corruption wasn't grounds for termination according to Commissioner Madonna. Madonna also tried to blame Commission problems on former Executive Director De Maria who would be replaced by William Arsenault.

Madonna was also a former state police union president with the New Jersey Policemen's Benevolent Association which represented Commission detectives. Doing so was clearly a conflict of interest, as pointed out in the report. Madonna also got DeCotiis to write a recommendation letter for a friend's promotion making sure that there was no mention of how Michael DeCotiis (then-Chief Counsel to Governor McGreevey) was related to said candidate. That friend was none other than Jon Deutsch, the Cernadas Sr.-protecting General Counsel of the Commission. Dubious pick Deutsch owed his appointment to nepotism facilitated by Madonna and DeCotiis.

Mayor Jon Corzine, who replaced the disgraced McGreevey, would remove Commissioner Madonna from his position in response to the spate of issues uncovered by the Inspector General. Deutsch was terminated for his actions and many other officials implicated resigned in the wake of the scandal.

Former Governor McGreevey, by the way, like many of the Union County "politicians of interest" and current Governor Phil Murphy have in common a kinship with the ILA. McGreevey, before resigning in disgrace after a sexual harassment allegation and news that he'd given the object of his affection a spot working with Homeland Security, had an all-expense paid trip to Puerto Rico for himself and his family paid for by the Longshoremen's union.[39] It was none other than Albert Cernadas, Sr. then-president of Local 1235 in Newark who made the invitation.[40]

This trip occurred at the same time as the Angelo Prisco parole investigation (a case that involves Steven Seagal seeking the help of an imprisoned mobster to try and take care of some issues he was having with a Gambino family-funded movie he was shooting) did nothing to help McGreevey's case once all the rest came out.[41]

There are many legitimate issues with the Waterfront Commission compounded by the $11-million per year bill footed by taxpayers. As seen with the New Jersey County Improvement Authorities, Freeholders, and LPCLs they are not above being bought off by organized crime and white-collar criminals, but that isn't even the only concern at the docks.

After 9/11 the Waterfront Commission's concern extended beyond that of organized crime. With the new Patriot Act and the Department of Homeland Security it had created, terrorism was now a top priority. Enter Bob Buccino. Buccino raised a few eyebrows when the veteran of New Jersey State Police and the Union County Prosecutor's Office seemed to give the mob a pass.

"The mob isn't what it used to be," Buccino remarked, "I don't see it as any threat to our security, and the crimes associated with Cosa Nostra never really impacts on terrorism."

He went on to underscore how the mobsters' love of country would prevent any threat from organized crime on the waterfront.

"They do raise the American flag in front of their house, and they participate in American society," Buccino went on. "I hate to say it, but they are patriotic, and they believe in the American way."

In the *ABC7 News* story referencing the quote, retired customs official Joseph King, who teaches courses on terrorism and organized crime at John Jay College in New York gives his take on Buccino's optimistic assessment:

"I don't believe the old idea that they're loyal Americans. They're in business, they don't care what it is, they're looking for money."

King conceded that the evolution of dockworker duties resulted in less direct access to cargo but warned that didn't mean there weren't officials with the power to decide what containers end up where.

"Everybody says: they (the mob) would never do that," King said of allowing terrorists access to the ports; "But if you agree to get a container through for a guy and he says: `It's hashish,' what about the second time, when it could be nuclear material? They don't exercise customs, they don't open it and say: `Yes, it's all hashish, thank you very much,'—they let the cargo through."[42]

Buccino, a 51-year law enforcement veteran who is currently listed as president of Corporate Integrity Consultant Service, LLC,[43] even wrote a book: *New Jersey Mob: Memoirs of a Top Cop*.[44] Despite his decades of law enforcement experience and many run-ins with associates of organized crime, what he claims flies in the face of what I've heard directly from retired FBI agents as well as two other sources who are veterans of the "Global War on Terror." As frightening as the prospect is, white-collar crime and organized crime often fund or are funded by enterprises with ties to terrorism.

"Sophisticated criminals like white-collar crimes," I was informed by one former intelligence officer. "Transnational terrorists tend to be involved in white-collar crime even if it's just counterfeit goods."[45]

The United Nations Office on Drugs and Crime (UNODC) has also noted the similarities and cross-over between organized crime organizations and terrorism funding.[46]

As for Buccino's improbable claim that white-collar criminals or mobsters would never risk funding terrorism out of a sense of "patriotism," one concrete example of how union funds have been diverted to international terrorists implicates none other than General David Petraeus. The disgraced general was made head of KKR & Co. by its founder Henry Kravis.[47] KKR ran a large investment fund. One of the largest unions in America, the Service Employees International Union (SEIU), with around 2 million members in total, had its pension funds tied up in KKR. The private equity fund and intel firm was a major player in several other pension funds as well.[48]

This would be unremarkable if not for the fact that KKR & Co. was involved in funding "moderate Muslims" in Syria that, it would later be revealed, had morphed into ISIS[49] under the auspices of the CIA, Saudi KSA, and bookoodles of black budget money and funds from private organizations such as KKR. General Petraeus and KKR's Project Timber Sycamore was vital to the initial build-up of ISIS. And union pension funds were absolutely a part of the KKR cash that quickly converted to dividends of death and destruction.[50]

It's important to point out here that there is a great degree of disconnect between "rank and file" union members and some corrupt officials who enrich themselves on the back of dues-paying union members. Even in crooked union organizations, it's the average worker paying their dues getting the shakedown or having pension and healthcare funds raided for nefarious purposes. In some cases as with Cernadas, funneled directly to the mob or even international terrorists.

Even taking the concerns surrounding national security, trafficking, and other very real issues, just the cost to the states of New Jersey and New York (as well as the federal government) make both the issues on the docks and those tasked with overseeing them important to all United States citizens regardless of where they reside.

As obvious as it is that the issues that created the need for the Commission are still present, it is also painfully clear that the agency is as susceptible to corruption as any other institution in the state. $170,000 in federal grant money meant for the Commission was used to purchase a boat meant to prevent possible "waterborne attack." It ended up being "rarely used" apart from floating V.I.P.'s around during Fleet Week.

They also received over $600,000 from DHS for "Project Safe Port." The Commission had informed DHS that they had used the money to update their wireless capabilities to be more capable against a potential terror attack. Commission employees would eventually admit to the Inspector General that this was not the case.[51]

Former Union County Sheriff Joseph Cryan, who is named as a defendant in motions by Kai, now serves as a New Jersey state Senator. Cryan spoke out against the move to block dissolving the commission founded in 1953 to prevent kickbacks and cargo theft among other instances of waterfront-based crime.

"The original intention was to prevent organized crime influence literally on the docks."

In short, things have not changed much since the era of Prohibition or the golden age of Godfather-era mobsters in the region. In many cases, there doesn't even need to be any connection to gangland shenanigans. Municipal corruption in New Jersey in general and Union County specifically is brazen and out in the open.

CHAPTER 9

CODE OF SILENCE IN THE HOUSE OF HORRORS

Early in 2022, Kai referred me to the Edna Mahan sexual abuse scandal in Union Township, New Jersey. Union Township is in Hunterdon County, not to be confused with Union County where Galfy lived and worked.* A formal inquiry and a small number of arrests took place a few years back. Up to that point, the "code of silence," lack of any oversight, and any complaints from correctional officers or inmates potentially leading to even more abuse loomed large in the how and why of this situation festering for so long.

Guards, both male and female, took part in the brutality and one especially

---

* A county that multiple lawyer predators worked in going back over 30 years. Lawyer predators who received no more than a slap on the wrist consisting of probation, therapy, and 6-month bar suspension for sex crimes including sex crimes against children. Lawyer predators who, all but the few whose charges were federal, managed to keep their name out of the papers. The only paper trail is New Jersey's Disciplinary Review Board reports. And even these use euphemisms like "child endangerment" along with the legal code unless you look this up and see "oh, that's molestation, oh that's child pornography" you might think they were busted for driving with a kid in the back of a pickup. Dangerous perhaps, but nowhere near the level of "endangerment" that robs a child of their innocence forever.

heartbreaking case involved guards tormenting a woman in the throes of a psychotic break. Even basic commodities like feminine hygiene products were used to coerce sex from inmates, some of whom would gain or lose weight or even disfigure themselves to be less attractive to the guards.[1] Last year, Governor Phil Murphy announced he would do his part to end the years of abuse at the Edna Mahan institution. But as of 2022, there is still no timeline or plan of action. This promise only materialized after a federal inquiry regarding dozens of cases of assault and abuse[2] of inmates and correctional officers alike. Abuse at the hands of both correctional officers and civilian staff was an "open secret" at Edna Mahan for years.

Inmate rape and abuse have been reported in Union County multiple times and in the case of Jesse Collins (again no local coverage), a man was raped by a guard and then told he was not able to sue for his permanent PTSD because the scars were psychological rather than physical.[3] The only mention of this in papers is an article in the *New York Times* regarding the criminal and deplorable way that the state got out of the suit that Collins brought forward.

Kai also opened up on the "well-documented"* code of silence among law enforcement and correctional officers[4] that multiple inmates, correctional officers, and law enforcement in Union County have described:

> You know about Jesse Collins. That Union County Jail inmate was forcibly raped by a guard from Joseph Galfy's sex predator ring. I've released videos and reports showing that that sex predator ring includes judges, prosecutors, and politicians in Union County, NJ.

---

*   Crossing the Thin Blue Line: Protecting Law Enforcement Officers Who Blow the Whistle by Ann C. Hodges published by the University of Richmond references the Lords of Discipline cop gang mentioned by New Jersey police whistleblowers Samuel Clark and Justin Hopson.[4]

But I've done more research, and found something horrifying…

They don't just destroy evidence of rape they kill their victims to get rid of the evidence.

They've been doing this for generations…

Raping and torturing vagrants; then either psychologically and physically torturing them until they kill themselves, or inciting other inmates to kill them, or just plain killing them: to get rid of the evidence.

Let's start with 'the code of silence.'

On December 23, 2016, Guilio Mesadieu was asleep in his cell when officer Wilson opened the door and began brutally beating him. Wilson grabbed his legs and yanked him out of his bunk, pulled his pants down, and brutally assaulted him.

I watched from across the hall as over a dozen UCJ officers pepper sprayed and beat and 'burk'-ed* William Pariseau to death in his cell, in a situation creepily similar to Mesadieu, in 2014.

In 2017, UCJ officers held me face down in a puddle of pepper spray and tried 'burk'-ing me to death, too.

In June 2014, Officer Johnson wrapped his handcuffs over his fist and beat Jamil Hearns so bad he fractured his skull.

---

* Prison slang for strangled.[5]

(See "Hearns v. Johnson" 2016 US Dist Lexis 120716)

UCJ guards beat Laquan Kearney so bad they ruptured his eardrum. (See "Kearney v. Union County Jail" 2014 US Dist Lexis 69229).

In every single one of these incidents, the UCJ officers falsified reports and denied medical treatment. To quote the court in "Mesadieu v. Union County" 2019 US Dist Lexis 76287*,

"Defendants purported cover-up of the assault was done while operating with a 'Code of Silence' policy between all defendants. Pursuant to this 'Code of Silence' policy, UCJ officers would not report the misconduct of other UCJ officers. The Code of Silence has a long history of being practiced within the Union County Administration and the UCJ. This policy allows the officers of UCJ to falsify, spoliate records, and to cover up their misconduct; and to act without fear of reprimand, discipline, or termination.

That's how UCJ Officer Gayeland Robinson was able to forcibly rape the dozens of inmates BEFORE Jesse Collins. That's how UCJ officers Pablo E. Chavez, Sonny Heyder, Nick Calas, Christopher Calas, and Joey Garcia, under UCJ Sgt Chris Schmidt, were able to turn the Medical Isolation

---

* Mesadieu's suit named then-Union County Prosecutor Theodore Romankow as well. Romankow was alleged to have "suppressed evidence of racial profiling."[6] A situation that multiple news stories from 2022 alone reveal is still a major issue in Union County law enforcement. Romankow and Attorney General Christopher Porrino were specifically called out for the fact that despite their supervisory roles they "permitted, encouraged, tolerated and knowingly acquiesced to an official pattern, practice or custom of police officers." James Cosgrove, also named as one of the offenders in the suit would eventually be outed for his racist and misogynist language.

Unit into their own personal dungeon of brutal and sadistic abuse of inmates. Waking male and female inmates up to strip searches and brutal assaults; pepper spraying them then strapping them into restraint chairs for hours; beating them and leaving them in cold, empty cells with severe injuries and no medical attention... and they threaten nurses with brutal violence if they attempt to help the injured inmates crying out in agony from pools of their own blood.

It's only once every decade that a whistleblower brings this to light; but up until now, it's always quickly swept back under the rug.

Jesse Collins blew the whistle back in 1996, but it came out a decade later that literally THE DAY AFTER Gayeland Robinson was fired over a dozen of his fellow UCJ officers participated in the abuse, assault, and torture of scores of INS detainees at the Union County Jail. The one UCJ officer who spoke out against the sadistic abuse got fired... and he was so scared that he waited almost a decade to blow the whistle. (For details, check out "Espinosa v. County of Union" 2005 US Dist Lexis 36563).

But it's not just physical torture, rape, and brutality.

They psychologically torture inmates into killing themselves.

Just like they tried with me in 2013.

They usually do this as either retaliation for filing a lawsuit or because the inmate is homeless and therefore they think they can get away with it (they enjoy and laugh about causing inmates to suffer and commit suicide).

In 2018, UCJ officer Melendez psychologically tortured a homeless man until he hung himself.

In 2014, the UCJ officers from the Medical Isolation Unit psychologically tortured a homeless inmate until he drank a half gallon of cleaning solution. That inmate was released (all he did was not pay fines, because he was poor), and he killed himself shortly after.*

In 2013, the UCJ officers psychologically tortured me until I attempted suicide.

In 2010, they psychologically tortured a homeless inmate until he killed himself. (For details, check out "Dawkins v. County of Union" 2010 US Dist Lexis 58368).

In 2008, they watched a homeless inmate die from a treatable medical condition while threatening nurses who wanted to help. (For details, check out "Pittman v. County of Union" 2006 US Dist Lexis 49721).

In 2006, they psychologically tortured a homeless guy until he hung himself. (For details, check out "Lazarsk v. County of Union" 2006 US Dist Lexis 55018).

As you can see, hardly 2 years go by without the UCJ officers torturing someone who's struggled with homelessness... to

---

* I found multiple cases of people in Union County detention facilities dying by suicide, or at least being reported as suicide deaths despite fairly insignificant crimes.

death. Not a decade goes by without Union County being exposed for dozens of systemic rapes (Google "Edna Mahan Sex Abuse"; located in Union Township).

Union County Jail is literally "House of 1,000 Corpses" meets "Deliverance"...

In Real Life.

You may be wondering what is meant by "psychological torture."

First, they take away all your clothes and mock your appearance. They have words like "fat" and "ugly" and "worthless" written in masking tape that's visible from the cell.

There are no mirrors, so after a month you forget what you look like... and start to believe what's being said.

Then, they sleep deprive you for weeks, knocking on your door whenever you begin to doze off.

Then, they begin their brainwashing. They use hypnotic language and repetitively command the inmate to agree with statements about themselves and their families that are demeaning and degrading. If they catch an inmate masturbating, they stand outside the door and repeatedly say "babyfucker." They watch inmates of either sex use the toilet and ridicule the inmates' genitalia while threatening sexual assault. They threaten to let male inmates into female inmates' cells if the female inmates don't perform sexual acts for the guards.

I watched them hypnotize a homeless guy who was sleep deprived for two weeks, and they made him eat his own shit.

They got one guy to castrate himself with his fingernails under hypnosis.

And what sickens me is that some of these people were there for fucking TRAFFIC violations. But after the guards chanting "babyfucker" at them, I'm extremely concerned about what they did after they got out. And the guards want that kind of thing, they ENCOURAGE that kind of thing because they have a protection racket going with the public. "If you don't have us, look what'll be unleashed on your community."

They do that to the nurses, too:

"Tell on us, and we'll leave you alone with a bunch of rapists."

They're brutal and totally self-serving.

But that's not all.

I told you how they incited another inmate to attack me after I filed a lawsuit, right?

As it turns out, the tactics they used on me are the same as they've used before.

Allen Farmer was brutally beaten by UCJ officers in retaliation for filing a medical request to document an assault on him by a UCJ officer. In 2011, he filed a civil rights lawsuit about it, "Farmer v. Riordan" 2011 US Dist Lexis 18130. The UCJ officers, as part of their 'Code of Silence,' psychologically tortured him in retaliation: causing him to attempt suicide. Think of it like a rabbit chewing his own leg off to get out of a painful trap.

Farmer was taken to the hospital, where a doctor ordered that he be transferred to a psychiatric hospital, where he could be treated for the effects of psychological torture.

Sensing the evidence that would produce, the UCJ Administrators defied the Doctor's orders; brought Farmer to a Max Unit in GP; then got him raped and tried to kill him using another inmate:

1.) They broke a padlock so another inmate could both get out of his cell; and use the padlock as a weapon;

2.) They removed all officers and witnesses from the unit; then

3.) They incited the inmate to brutally assault Farmer; while no one was around to hear him scream.

Check it out for yourself: "Farmer v. Lanigan" 2017 US Dist Lexis 66317

Brutal and sadistic rape and torture rings like the one that's been running UCJ for decades(if not since it was built) only exist because of a failure to screen State Government Officials properly. Federal Law Enforcement Officials undergo GKT's and GS-5 level (or higher) screenings, which weed out virtually ALL sexual predators from Federal Law Enforcement positions. The only reason we don't have this in State Governments is because the technology to do these screenings didn't exist back when the State Administrative Codes were written.

Those brutal rape and torture rings have been "grandfathered in," and your tax dollar is paying for their terrorizing of homeless people and vulnerable populations, with brutal assaults and torture.

Whistleblower, Juan Espinosa worked at Union County jail from 1982 to 1984 and from 1988 to 2001. On June 18, 1995, Espinosa saw 25 to 30 UCJ correction officers "beat, harass and abuse INS detainees." When he reported the incident to his superior Lieutenant Salay, he replied that he "didn't care."[7]

According to a grand jury report from 1998, nearly one-fifth of the 370 on the police force were members of "The Family." Testimony from officers involved tales of "bizarre initiation and excommunication rituals." Physical abuse and false arrests, often inspired by racism were hallmarks of "The Family." The 2000 article from *The New York Times* pointed out that at the time the entire department had only four Hispanic officers and no Black officers among the 60 or so "superior officers."

Patrick Maloney, the Director of the Elizabeth police from 1995 to 1997 told *NYT,* "The Family was originally formed as a study group." What started purportedly as a way for officers to study together for promotion exams "soon became a specialized unit within the department that had its own insignia." Once again, shades of the Lords of Discipline police gang that New Jersey police whistleblower Samuel Clark has spent years working to expose.

Christian Bollwage and James M. Cosgrove, Mayor, and director of police at the time acknowledged the group's existence but claimed their influence and danger were a matter of debate. "Hopefully, this group is not with us anymore," Cosgrove (the Chief of Police who would be forced to step down due to racist and sexist language) told *NYT.* The article, however, referenced "a dozen current or recently retired officers" and church and neighborhood leaders who disagreed.[8]

Reverend Michael Granzen, minister at Second Presbyterian Church in Elizabeth and the author of *Breaking the Plate Glass Window*, published in May 2022, explained how he knew that racism and misconduct were not a relic of a bygone era in Elizabeth, noting beatings and false arrests. Retired lieutenant Daniel Wood said that Elizabeth PD "had no interest in investigating the Family or its activities."

In Reverend Granzen's book, he relates how the day "Blue Shadows" was released you "couldn't find a single *New York Times* anywhere. They had all disappeared." In addition to this, all the cars parked in front of the church had been ticketed, a warning from the corrupt police regarding speaking out it seemed. Far worse, retaliation against churchgoers included beatings, harassment, and worse. It was after the article's publication however that Granzen reports that some members of the Family were forced into retirement, others demoted or reassigned, and the federal prosecutor and FBI "began to return our calls."[9]

"The police in Elizabeth like in many other urban cities were bent on shake downs, intimidation, corruption, and abuse. The 'Family' clique inside Elizabeth Police Department didn't like me and my name was on a 'hit list.' My work on exposing police brutality around New Jersey got me many death threats and attempts at intimidation..." Salaam Ismael is quoted in Rev. Granzen's book.[10]

Elizabeth police officer Lt. Bill Dugan called the church to see if the police could play basketball two afternoons a week in their new gym. "At first, I was suspicious, but then I realized he was one of the good police officers. We wanted to work with them." Sister Jacinta at the church, one of the first to expose The Family "saw the best and worst of the Elizabeth Police Department."[11]

Lt. Edward Szpond was sent to the property room after an investigation that led to him being singled out as one of the leaders of the white supremacist gang operating within the Elizabeth Police Department. Not unlike the RICO-worthy Essex Police Department run by Union County official Joe Cryan's father John, law enforcement itself was lawless in the area. Operating in the open as a criminal enterprise.

"Blue Shadows" may have been the first major reporting on the cultish law enforcement gang, but years earlier in 1994, a dozen officers protested the shadowy group claiming it was abusing its influence and intimidating officers who weren't part of the clique. This mirrors the case of Samuel Clark* and the Lords of Discipline gang within the Newark Police Department.[12]

Sgt. John Guslavage and Thomas were both police officers on the Elizabeth force who attempted to take on the Family. October 1998, a Black Elizabeth police officer Leon Thomas, allegedly shot himself in the head under "suspicious circumstances."

Thomas had been arrested the day before by Elizabeth PD at a drug

---

* Samuel Clark is the author of *Total Misconduct: a factual account of police and political corruption*. The book is in part an exposé of the Lords of Discipline police gang. In the book, Clark gives his frank opinion on Internal Affairs: "The overt purpose of Internal Affairs is the prevention of police misconduct. The covert purpose of Internal Affairs is the prevention of police whistleblowers."

store. He had been working as a security guard. While leaving shift, he was arrested for supposedly stealing items that they said he placed under his car. Now first off, it stands to reason that hiding stolen items under your car is not the best way to hide them. Not to mention anyone else could just "steal it back." Plus, it's pretty easy to set someone up by placing items under their vehicle and then claiming that they put them there.[13]

But being framed is not even the worse that can happen. One scenario mentioned by whistleblower Samuel Clark: the department might get a particularly dangerous call and backup just might be late. This, along with constant harassment for minor or non-existent infractions are ways of having "troublemakers" on the force neutralized in a plausibly deniable manner. This may be why Galfy's home of Clark, New Jersey has such a history of whistleblower cops recording material to back up their claims.[14] Historically, racism and hush money go hand in hand in Union County.

Thomas left behind a nine-page letter illustrating numerous instances of police planting drugs on suspects. His mother and sister say he kept a journal of racist practices by Elizabeth PD that he wanted to eventually give to prosecutors. Sadly, Union County prosecutor Thomas Manahan claimed that the office checked into the claims but that the investigation was closed due to insufficient evidence to warrant prosecution. An occurrence reminiscent of the Generatorgate and Musicfest scandals under Romankow that Tina Renna reported.

Thomas shared his fears with his family and some other Black police officers, Tracy Finch, and Michael Brown Sr., who at the time were "unconvinced." Lateef Banks said before his death he told them of notebooks full of detailed information regarding false arrests, violence, and planted drugs involving Black and Hispanic people in Elizabeth. Thomas's sister Tawana said the Elizabeth PD took the notebooks after his death and only one page was left: a 1996 arrest, brutal beating, and drugs planted to justify the arrest after the fact.

Tawana Thomas, Leon's sister had this to say: "The notebooks had logs detailing police wrongdoing and discriminatory treatment by the Family since the day of Leon's hiring." Certain police officers' names happened to come up again and again when racist and corrupt misconduct was mentioned. "There are a number of Elizabeth police officers who usually work in teams who account for an excessive amount of very suspect drug busts," James Kervick, public defender's office in Elizabeth during the 90s explained.[15] A pattern of inconsistencies in police reports backs up the claims of his clients disputing certain officers' accounts of drug arrests in Elizabeth. Certain elements in Thomas's case are reminiscent of the apparent murder presented as suicide in Sean Suiter's case.[16]

Guslavage, corroborated the Family's protected status, racist behavior, and involvement in distributing drugs in the community. Eventually, evidence surfaced revealing certain narcotics officers, all members of "the Family" being present during the deal. Federal prosecutors turned over the information to local prosecutors who referred it to the Elizabeth police. Fox and the henhouse.

"What amazes me is that they have gotten away with this for so many years," retired police officer, Lt. Daniel Wood lamented. Hassen Abdellah, a Black lawyer in Union County also shared his experience. "I hear frequent reports that the police use excessive force [...] use the derogatory N-word while on duty and plant drugs on suspects. This has produced widespread feelings of fear and apprehension."

Police planted drugs on Richard Mixson, in Rahway, New Jersey in Union County while he was working nights as a janitor for Merck. Mixson was acquitted at the trial and later sued the police.[17]

It was a sick-out in 1994 that resulted in Lt. Szpond being banished "to the basement" in the property room coupled with an assault case involving officer William F. Burdge attacking a 67-year-old woman and her brother that brought local attention to The Family again. Sadly, there was little in the way of reporting on the situation outside of the *New York Times* article. Szpond was known to regularly use racist slurs, spoke glowingly of how Hitler would have awarded him the Iron Cross, and even referred to police cruisers as his "panzer columns."

Guslavage received a $600,000 payout in 2006 when he went on the record about what happened when he "violated their code of silence." Guslavage reported a suspected drug abusing cop to Union County Prosecutor's Office in 1999 and suffered "years of retaliation" as a result. Edward Kologi, the City of Elizabeth attorney called the ruling "totally erroneous." This is a pattern in these cases, even when Union County is forced to pay whistleblowers, sexually harassed corrections officers, or others, they refuse to take responsibility or admit guilt even when enough evidence exists for hundreds of thousands or even millions of dollars to be paid out in settlements.[18]

Guslavage, a 36-year veteran of the Elizabeth police department reported to the court how he was "belittled and driven into depression, suffering a nervous breakdown that led to 18 months of medical leave." The jurors in the civil suit agreed with Guslavage that he had been targeted, harassed, and punished by his superiors. The second incident occurred in 1999, once again related to dirty cops operating under the cover of the police department. Guslavage informed the US Attorney's Office of two dirty narcotic cops associated with the Family.

While technically, Guslavage was protected by the Conscientious Employee Protection Act (CEPA), as fellow New Jersey police whistleblower Samuel Clark has pointed out, there are limits to that protection. Running out the clock and other tricks are employed by the department to wear down potential whistleblowers.

Guslavage sued Elizabeth police Chief Gene Mirabella, Deputy Chief Mary Rabadeau, Chief John Simon, acting Police Director Michael J. Orak, and Lieutenant Patrick Shannon. In 2001, Guslavage would file a second CEPA complaint against the City of Elizabeth, the EPD, Police Director Cosgrove, Chief Simon, and Captain Mark Kurdyla involving other incidents of retaliation related to his whistle-blowing that occurred in 1999.

It was in his third CEPA complaint from 2002 related to his demotion and attempted disciplinary actions for breaking the "code of silence." Guslavage claimed in his suit that he spoke to Chief Mirabella about a call from Michael Zidonek, an assistant prosecutor in the Union County Prosecutor's Office regarding Ruotolo assigning him to the US Attorney's Office to assist in the Cervantes investigation. Zidonek confirmed making the call, Mirabella claims not to remember this and says that transferring him from Narcotics Division after he reported dirty cops was "because plaintiff was detail-oriented and a good administrator" and he was "not getting along very well with the other officers in the Narcotics Division."

Well yeah, I'd say that if you're the clean narco cop pointing out that other cops are getting drunk at the bar of a coke dealer and then happen to show up during his arrest, that could cause some friction. It's worth mentioning that the same department that attempted to discipline Lt. Szpond by sending him to the property room claimed that Guslavage's move to the basement was just because he was such a great, "detail-oriented" police officer. For fans of *The Wire*, Lt. Daniels being exiled to the property room as punishment for attempting to do good police work may come to mind.

Another interesting situation in the Guslavage case perhaps owed to the "unoriginality of corruption" is that of false testimony provided by an "expert medical witness." That's right, shades of Dr. Junaid Shaikh and

Robert Pandina rear their head here. Dr. Meyer, the expert witness called by the state, had claimed on the stand he was "not being paid at all." It was later revealed that he was paid $2,410.65 in total.

The Family and their "code of silence" brings to mind recent stories related to LASD gangs[19] which are themselves, nothing new. The Department of Justice determined at one point[20] that the LAPD was eligible for RICO treatment,[21] due to widespread misconduct and corruption in the force.

As for whether things have changed in Union County? It appears unlikely. As of August 2022, a lawsuit alleges a "boys club"[21] that protected cops accused of having sex on duty, drunk driving, and more. So long as they were white and in with the good ol' boy network.[22] Similar to what I learned from New Jersey police whistleblower Samuel Clark, the suit alleges that not being a part of the club or at least being silent about what they do can have very negative repercussions. The in-crowd "will not hesitate to come after one's livelihood with full force."

In addition to a "history of discrimination" which in Union County alone would result in material for a full-length book, the complicity of the Chief of Police is noted: "Debbie condones having sex on duty in police vehicles, engaging in prostitution, drunk driving, crashing/ damaging County vehicles, deleting information on County run databases, harboring missing juveniles, losing firearms and assault rifles while failing to report the loss of same, and perjury."[23] As I've heard in other cases from New Jersey, especially from correctional officers and law enforcement personnel who happen to be women and/or people of color, if you're not "personally liked by" or have "pledged your loyalty" to the Chief and the inner circle who are running wild and dare speak up you will be hounded and harassed.

Like Elizabeth's The Family or The Lords of Discipline in Newark, these lawless law enforcement gangs tend to have an intense racist element. This is pointed out by Homero Almanzar in his lawsuit[24] and evidenced in the treatment of whistleblower, Blake Clay, in 2013. Clay, a Black police officer, reported Union County Police Chief Debbie and other officers for racially profiling drivers. Shortly after, he received a picture of a drowning slave in his workplace mailbox. This in addition to constant administrative offenses being filed, is consistent with Mr. Clark's personal experience.

Also in 2022, a report of "major discipline" of New Jersey cops resulted in a handful of names from Union County, one of which was fired after being caught interfering with a witness. As for whether the bigger issue to the authorities over him was the illegal activity unbecoming an officer of the law or the audacity of managing to get caught, it's hard to say. One Elizabeth cop, Officer Lamar Boone, received a few days' suspension for "improper handling" of a domestic violence case. Other suspensions came for drunk driving and then refusing to submit to a breathalyzer test, violating body-worn camera policy.[25]

The Elizabeth Public Information Officer declined to comment to *Tap Into Westfield* reporters who covered the story. Clark Police and the Union County Prosecutor's and Sheriff's Office were among the 17 Union County law enforcement agencies that did not report any "major discipline." Considering what is reported in lawsuits and coverage such as the *NYT* exposé and Dr. Granzen's book, this is just as likely a sign that the perpetrators are protected, as that there are no issues in said departments.

It's not even just inmates, correctional officers, and police officers who have complained about the dangerous and deplorable conditions in the Union County carceral system.

Angela Hoag, a licensed clinical social worker (LCSW) brought a civil suit after corrections officer Richard Sheppard "threatened her and physically and verbally abused her." The suit failed, but only "because the State was not vicariously liable for Sheppard's conduct; and second because plaintiff failed to meet the TCA pain and suffering verbal threshold. NJSA 59:9-2d." That and the fact that they determined she was not a state employee.[26]

The response from Sheppard after she spoke with prison administration about him is shocking, but sadly not surprising once you've read enough of these Union County cases: Sheppard asked if she had "been talking to anybody," and threatened her, warning: "You better not be talking or else." Continual sexual harassment and threats of physical and sexual violence weren't deemed enough of an issue to do something in Union County.

Throughout all this time, Sheppard continued to receive positive performance evaluations. Despite his repeated use of the n-word, antisemitic and sexually demeaning language according to his assistant supervisor who said he and others had been "getting away with it" for years. A doctor on staff also backed up Hoag regarding the threatening and inappropriate behavior of Sheppard. Thanks to the precedent set in the Jesse Collins inmate rape case, permanent PTSD was not considered sufficient "pain and suffering" since there were no physical marks visible.* Convenient.

It wasn't even the first time he'd threatened violence. As far back as 1990 he had threatened to "fuck up" a coworker. Not uncommon in these cases, a racist component was heaped on to add insult to injury. The threats, abuse, and sexual and racial harassment continued for months.[27]

And again, remember her suit failed, not because there wasn't this huge issue that should be taken care of, but because of technicalities. For instance: "because she was an employee of CMS, an independent contractor, and not an employee of the State." A search of Google news and newspapers.com

---

* In the modern history of torture since the Cold War leading up to the era of "enhanced interrogation" many ingeniously evil ways of inflicting pain and suffering without ever leaving a mark have been developed.

returns 0 results related to this story.

Another way that cover-ups are facilitated in the carceral system in Union County is by skirting the Open Public Records Act (OPRA) and attempting to claim exemption by misfiling reports (or not filing them at all). The Union County OPRA compliance manager was taken to court by Conrad Benedetto after Union County attempted to stymie a probe into "suspicious deaths" including apparent suicides or drug overdoses by claiming that they could not release information due to privacy concerns. The County tried to use health privacy laws to prevent being compelled to turn over records. They further tried to advance the notion that the only records of suicides and drug overdoses would be health records as if there are no logs of such incidents kept by the correctional facility itself.[27]

In October 2018, Sgt. Augustin Alvarez received a 28 day suspension when he and others on duty were found to be negligent in their duties allowing an inmate to die by suicide. Sgt. Augustin Alvarez, Lt. William Gargiles, C.O.'s Jakari Lee, Wesley Peters, Antonio Melendez, and John G. Esmerado, Esq. Special Duty Attorney General/Acting Assistant Prosecutor, and Union County Prosecutor's Office were all named in the Final Administration Action of the Civil Service Commission ruling on the situation. Eight out of ten scheduled checks that day were not done, despite the logbook being filled out to the contrary.

The Commission noted "the irony of the fact that errors in the logbook continued even on the afternoon of the event, with the 4:00 p.m. security check not being initialed by the officer performing it." Lee, Peters, and Melendez were all found to be guilty of violations that resulted in an inmate being found hanging in his cell. According to Lt. Gonzalez, the shift commander, there were cameras available for supervision throughout the day so that supervisors could "check in" on their officers. Though Gonzalez admitted these are "real time" only and can't be rewound or reviewed after the fact. Gonzalez saw Alvarez tour the unit, speak to Melendez for "a minute or two" and sign the logbook.

The fact that the logbook was signed off on despite minutes later an inmate's body being found hanged is just one of multiple infractions for which the buck kept being passed. Melendez had written "all secure" in the logbook after Officer Peters claimed that there were no issues. Lt. Gonzalez charged Alvarez with "neglect of duty" due to his "failure to observe" and "failure to advise the shift commander."

Det. Dennis Donovan, Sergeant, Special Prosecutor's Unit, Union County Prosecutor's Office was asked to step in as they were "swamped" in the internal affairs department for the prosecutor's office already. In coordinating with the prosecutor's office the goal was "to do whatever they could to get him back to duty." Alvarez showed up around 12:41 p.m. and signed the logbook at 12:53 after being told all was clear. At 1:03 p.m. during the next scheduled check (both noon and 12:30 security checks were marked as complete despite never having been performed) Alvarez found the inmate hanging. Emergency personnel arrived at 1:05 and he was removed by 1:27 by the EMS.

The Civil Service Commission's findings regarding Alvarez included incompetence, conduct unbecoming a public employee, neglect of duty, and "other sufficient cause"[28]

The body of CONRAD J. BENEDETTO v. MARLENA RUSSO decided in June of 2018 reveals that even the judge "expressed disbelief that the County Correctional Facility did not maintain records related to inmates who died in jail." As with the years of numerous mysterious and suspicious

---

[*] NJAC 4a:2-2.3(a)(12) does not define 'other sufficient cause', but this phrase is generally interpreted to mean violations of rules, regulations, policies, and procedures such as Post Orders.

deaths out of Ft. Bragg that have begun to finally make news, failing to report suspicious deaths is one way of keeping the "code of silence" intact.

The so-called "code of silence" is even mentioned in a 2004 report from the State of New Jersey Commission of Investigation: The Changing Face of Organized Crime"[29] In the section on law enforcement training:

"They should receive constant reminders that their oath is more important than adherence to any unwritten code of silence. The system should ensure that after alerting authorities about corruption and other problems, the whistleblowers come out of the process appreciated, possessed of good career opportunities, and financially and psychologically whole. We should make heroes out of our patriots and not promote the myth that New Jersey folk heroes can be found in the ranks of television's 'Sopranos' or from rogue cops as portrayed in the media. "

Benedetto is mentioned in an article from January 2021 related to Federal authorities' "reasonable cause to believe" that New Jersey's Cumberland County Jail "failed to take measures to prevent inmate suicides and provide adequate mental health care." Their actions "likely contributed to the death of several inmates" according to an official report. The facility had been the focus of a series from *NJ Advance Media* that covered multiple suicides between 2015 and 2018. The DOJ investigative report also found the facility did "not provide adequate treatment because of inadequate staffing, inadequate staff coordination, and inadequate programs that place prisoners at risk of serious harm – including deteriorating mental health and, at worst, suicide."

Inmates told investigators what happened to anyone who would report suicidal ideations: "They'll torture you. It's a punishment – it's not helpful. They treat you like an animal. It's not help. It's torture." Suicidal inmates were "essentially stripped naked" the report reveals, then kept in a tiny cell with a rubber sleeping mat and nothing else. Even toilet paper must be specifically requested from a correctional officer who "tears the paper off the roll and hands it to the inmate." This is the kind of treatment that could eventually break anyone, much less someone dealing with severe mental anguish or suicidal thoughts. Prisoners are kept in these conditions "until they simply stop saying they are suicidal."

Sadly, there is little accountability for those responsible. In the Cumberland County case, Benedetto was involved in, two of three officers who were accused of complicity and cover-up related to the rush of inmate suicides got an offer to have their charges dismissed, record cleared, and no jail time in exchange for agreeing to a pretrial intervention program.[30]

As mentioned in the Benedetto lawsuit against Union County's OPRA compliance manager, officers have been charged criminally with falsifying and tampering with public records to cover up suicides (or "suspicious" deaths in general) in 2017. Benedetto also represented Eddie Waters in a federal civil rights lawsuit filed in Camden in 2019. Benedetto made a statement in the Waters case:

"The allegations that a number of correctional officers ganged up and beat a defenseless inmate are bad enough. But it is unconscionable that after they allegedly beat Mr. Waters, they then allegedly refused to provide him with any medical treatment for the serious injuries he claims he received at the hands of those same officers."[31]

It's almost no wonder why these situations persist. The idea of secret societies, codes of silence, and rampant abuse from authorities have deep and unsettling implications. It would certainly be easier to consider it no more than wild conspiracy theories and call it a day. The sheer number of claims and the amount of supporting evidence available, however, make it clear that Union County and several other county correctional facilities and police departments in New Jersey do indeed operate essentially above the law protected by a code of silence that, if challenged, can result in harassment and disciplinary action against police and correctional officers or far, far worse for inmates like Kai who are unwilling to keep silent about what they've seen and experienced.

CHAPTER 10

DEFENSE FOR THE PROSECUTION

PROSECUTOR:

Everything I'm talking to you right now, Kai, is about the night when you killed Joe; okay? Is that less ambiguous?

THE WITNESS:

No, that's actually argumentative. And you need to stick to the specific time frame. Are you asking me about the time I can't remember from the sexual assault to when I came to in the parking lot or are you asking another question?

PROSECUTOR:

I am asking for a clarification. Kai, let me ask you this—

THE WITNESS:

Now you're raising your voice. You need to clarify
the question.

MR. CITO:

Objection.

THE COURT:

I am going to sustain the objection. Mr. McGillvary
and Mr. Peterson, I am, again, instructing you to
please answer the questions. And, Mr. McGillvary,
you're adding information and you're arguing with
the prosecutor. Your role is a simple one. You must
answer the questions which are posed. If it's an
objectionable question, you've got a very capable
lawyer —

THE WITNESS:

I was answering the question.

THE COURT:

— excuse me for a second — who has no hesitancy, nor
should he, in leveling an

objection. It is not appropriate for you to engage
the questioner with your own editorial feelings about
the prosecutor's conduct, etc.

THE WITNESS:

But that goes directly to the question.

THE COURT:

Answer the questions.

THE WITNESS:

That's what I am doing.[1]

Caleb McGillivary, better known to the world as Kai the hitchhiker, spent nearly five long years in solitary confinement at the Union County Jail while awaiting trial. Twenty-three hours a day, seven days a week, in segregation—circumstances considered "cruel and unusual punishment" in the United States.[2] This is of course a gross violation of constitutional rights, not unlike the inherent violation of the sixth amendment right to a speedy and fair trial that Kai was subjected to.

It all began with two fateful rides, only weeks apart. The first would catapult him to fame and epic hero status, and the second would plummet him into the depths of a nightmare that continues to this day. Kai gained viral fame with a ride he thumbed that resulted in him saving the lives of a utility worker and a woman in Fresno, California in 2013. His emotional and heartfelt message catapulted him to viral fame. His 'catchphrase' of "Smash, smash, suh-MASH!" resulted in him being invited on the Jimmy Kimmel show and featured on an episode of Stephen Colbert's show, among others.

It all changed in an instant, shortly after Kai shared the following status on his Facebook account:

"What would you do if you woke up with a groggy head, metallic taste in your mouth, in a stranger's house . . . and started wretching [sic], realizing that someone had drugged, raped . . . you?" This was one of the last posts beloved viral star Kai the Hitchhiker made to social media before his arrest. From viral fame after being interviewed shortly after saving the lives of a man and woman, Kai's rising star seemed to be crashing quickly. Not long after that though, the nightmare would begin, a nightmare that continues to this day.[3]

Kai alleges he was drugged and raped. Evidence available suggests he was then subjected to a sloppy frame-up job. After the "investigation," he was detained without trial and held in solitary for years. When the trial finally came, in keeping with the investigation and detention, it could be characterized as nothing less than a massive miscarriage of justice with the defense, at times, seeming to work on behalf of the prosecution.

Major conflicts of interest abound in the case, including officials of the court who should have recused themselves. Eventually, one judge assigned to the case would step down rather than recuse himself. This was after Kai pointed out that he was connected personally to the alleged rapist lawyer, Joseph Galfy. The prosecutor, Theodore Romankow also resigned after 11 years before any connections with the deceased were disclosed. Incidentally, he "call[ed] it quits" on the same date Kai's arrest was announced.[4]

New Jersey's *Star-Ledger* reported the following:

> "In court, McGillvary told Superior Court Judge Joseph Donohue last month that Robert Mega, Union County's presiding Criminal Court judge, had the phone number for the victim's son, Joseph Galfy III Jr., saved as contact no. 18. He later learned that Mega was listed in Galfy's cell phone from the evidence that the prosecutor's office provided to Liguori. Donohue said Mega has recused himself from the case, but he understood the defendant's concern about the other judges."[5]

Oh dear, not another conflict of interest! This is starting to look like a pattern. Not unlike the pattern of abuse inherent in the New Jersey penal system and specifically the Union County jail and Juvenile Detention Center which have been responsible for multiple deaths and an environment of sadism that is beyond the pale. Systemic cruelty resulting in suicides and unexplained deaths.

There are numerous issues with the investigation, detention, and trial of Kai. Kai accused the proceedings of being a kangaroo court and sham trial. Many media sources portray his claims as unhinged and conspiratorial but what then of the fact that evidence supports many of those claims?

The Gardner and Suter investigative reports reveal that the dishwasher had been run between May 13 and 15th,[6] while the home of Joseph Galfy, the wealthy lawyer and accused predator, was an active crime scene. Also, Galfy was found with his own semen mingled with "unidentified blood"[7] on his penis. Kai was denied a rape kit, but they ran one on the deceased. The cups with which Kai is said to be drugged were washed by investigators so no results from the alleged drugging incident could be recovered. A rape kit was run on Galfy but not Kai. Obviously, it came up negative. It was performed on the wrong person. So at this point, the prosecution can claim that a rape kit was run[8] and that there was no evidence of Kai being drugged. That certainly would seem to make Kai out to be a liar had this not been the result of a brazen bait-and-switch.

Why would a dishwasher be run in a house subject to an ongoing investigation concerning an alleged murder and/or rape? And to explain the "and/or" in New Jersey, lethal force is authorized in the case of sexual assault so accidentally killing someone who is raping you in the state is not even manslaughter.[9] Now if the evidence of Kai being drugged and raped hadn't been destroyed ('spoliation of exculpatory evidence,' in legalese[10]) then this would be an open-and-shut case. If the public defender was more interested in defending Kai rather than playing ball with the Union County system then perhaps there would have already been a more favorable dispensation.

Oh, and who was allowed in the house around the time that this mysterious dishwasher incident occurred? None other than the former deputy chief of police brother of the deceased, James Galfy. James Galfy, according to investigative documents released in discovery, notes his concern that some drifter was involved when he was told his brother was dead. Apparently, not the first such case of a "vagrant" of some sort being involved in Galfy's life.[11]

Why would James Galfy immediately assume his wealthy lawyer brother might have a "drifter" in his home the night he died before Kai was even a suspect?[12] In another interview with a witness who saw Kai, he was described as looking "under the influence"[13] of something when he saw him after the incident. The audio of Kai's interrogation has him emitting an audible sigh when he discovers that the man he accuses of drugging and assaulting him is dead.

Considering that James Galfy was informed of certain things by Peterson or someone from the UCPO* before his counsel further suggests a coordinated cover-up. As of late Summer 2022, federal judge Madame Cox-Arleo conceded that Kai had sufficiently proved a "conspiracy" to deprive him of his due process rights, so this shouldn't be especially surprising.[14]

"At this early, stage, Plaintiff sufficiently alleges a conspiracy among the individual Moving Defendants to deprive him of his due process rights," Madame Cox-Arleo ruled on July 28, 2022.

Meaning Kai had successfully proved "that the favorable evidence [suppressed and destroyed in this case] would have produced a different verdict."

---

* Galfy estate lawyers seemed to be kept abreast of certain matters even before Kai's own defense, suggesting a cozy relationship with someone in the prosecutor's office. An office we've seen multiple problems in thus far.

The due process and conspiracy claims, though viable according to the Federal Judge's ruling, are "barred by the favorable-termination rule of Heck v. Humphrey."

This effectively results in a Catch-22 scenario where Kai can't move his case further until he has vacated his conviction or served his time. The court won't even look into the potentially criminal actions related to the conspiracy to deprive him of due process "in the absence of a viable federal claim" which, again, can't be brought forward until he has been legally exonerated or finished his sentence. Quite convenient for those responsible for the cover-up. Also, due to SCOTUS precedent, a plaintiff "cannot bring a fabricated-evidence claim under §1983 before favorable termination of his prosecution."[15] In short, it's not that Kai cannot prove the conspiracy to deprive him of due process, but that the federal court can do nothing about it until he can exonerate himself or finishes his sentence.

On top of this is the expert doctor Robert Pandina who the prosecution claimed asserted Kai could not have been drugged and raped despite obvious signs of sexual assault. Pandina claims he did not know Galfy. This strikes me as odd considering, as per a document from the Prosecutor's Office, Pandina "unexpectedly received charitable funds from the Estate of Joseph Galfy."[16] Well, what an unexpected turn of events, but who among us hasn't received a windfall from deceased persons after being asked to act as an expert witness (then declining after your findings are misrepresented) in trials involving them?

Refusing proper services and processing for a victim of sexual assault is a crime in New Jersey. One of several laws broken here: for one, undermining the New Jersey Attorney General Standards for providing services to victims of sexual assault. By ignoring what Pandina found, Sgt. Ho and Prosecutor Peterson assert Kai could not have been drugged.

Unfortunately, Kai's motion to dismiss could not be heard. At least not with his own public defender fighting him all the way. The stakes are incredibly high, not only for Kai but for Union County and the state of New Jersey. The Federal civil suit itself will be a slam dunk, that is if Kai is exonerated. Until then the case is in limbo as it can't be heard while he is incarcerated.

If Kai wasn't raped, then why are there signs of rape in this case? New Jersey law states "sexual assault is a form of serious bodily injury, the threat of which would justify the use of deadly force in self-defense," NJSA 2c:3-4.[17] Mismanagement of evidence, evidence of sexual assault, conflicts of interest (the alleged rapist's prominence in the legal community of Union County).

In my original article about this case for *Inquisitr*, I note that the case was "eerily reminiscent of the Cleveland Street Scandal from London in the 1890s." In that case, a high-profile pedophile ring that reached as far as the court of Queen Victoria. The whole affair was covered up for decades. During the Oscar Wilde trial, Wilde was surrounded by predators who were tied to the Cleveland Street case. I had no idea how prescient that statement would prove.[18]

In this case, no nobles or royals are implicated, but Kai discovered through the use of the law library in prison that a 30+ year tradition in New Jersey of sex criminals, including child sex criminals being given a slap on the wrist consisting of six months' probation, therapy and a 6-month suspension from practicing law in many or most cases.[19] In all but very few of the nearly two dozen cases, I've seen a complete media blackout despite those involved being not just lawyers, but politicians, legislators, District Attorneys, and Assistant Attorney Generals.

In one case, a sexual predator judge, James F. Boylan, who assaulted women by coercing sex from them in exchange for lessened sentences comes up. This same Judge Boylan's son was previously charged with molesting a 5-year-old girl. Neither shows up in state or federal sex offender registries and disciplinary bar reports and a lawsuit are the only extant paper trail.[20]

I've been in contact with Kai for a few years now and have written multiple articles, conducted several interviews, and kept in touch via correspondence. The massive number of issues in the case precludes the possibility of covering each issue in anything less than several hours, but it's possible, in a few pages, to at least scratch the surface.

The reversal of the phrase "innocent before proven guilty" to "guilty before proven innocent" didn't begin on April 23, 2019, at the murder trial of Kai the Hatchet-Wielding Hitchhiker. Rather, this inverted maxim has always been understood by those at the top and the bottom of the American legal system. But on April 23rd, 2019, in Elizabeth New Jersey, "guilty before innocent" became the official maxim of law and order in America.

Of course, the issues had been evident for years before Kai would get his day in court, finally, in 2019. These nagging little inconsistencies and "coincidences" pop up throughout the investigation, the detention, and the eventual trial. The Voir Dire (jury selection) itself was quite enlightening as to how things would proceed in that courtroom in Union County. It becomes clear that jurors who might be sympathetic to Kai are quickly booted by Kirsch while connections to Union County powerbrokers like Scutari or Cryan don't pose a problem. Being associated with or friends with Galfy's former law partner also not an issue. Two jurors with connections to investigators on the scene are also permitted. In short, anyone who seemed like they would bring back a favorable verdict for prosecution was a shoo-in. Meanwhile, even having a loved one who experienced sexual assault gets you booted.[21]

An eyewitness at this trial states that defense counsel, John G. Cito, Esq. stood askance from the jury, looking slyly sideways at them; under other circumstances, he might have been telling them a secret. The moment was cinematic; all it lacked were cameras. Judge Robert Kirsch had banned all video reportage of Kai's trial on March 21st, two weeks before it began.[22]

This was perhaps because video documentation would have shown the public that something was amiss. On April 16th, 2019, Union County Prosecutor's Office Sgt. Johnny Ho was on the witness stand. A video was about to be played on a large screen for the Jury. Judge Kirsch stepped down from his bench and walked to the gallery to sit near the jurors, saying "Dim the lights, folks. I'm going to move so I can see the screen closer." Keep in mind that the record shows what you have just read above when present-ed with Judge Kirsch's statements about witnessing what happened next 'from his perch on the bench.' To put this in context, Kai claimed that the Sheriff's officers behind him began to laugh derisively in front of the Jury as soon as the video reached the part where Kai described waking up to find Galfy, the man he is accused of murdering, sexually assaulting him. Judge Kirsh, however, denies this, stating:

"I categorically reject that two Sheriff's officers 'laughed' during his tes-timony regarding his claimed sexual assault by Mr. Galfy, and that this alleged conduct somehow may have influenced the jury [...] I was in the courtroom the whole time, watching Mr. McGillvary and the Sheriff's officers from my perch on the bench."[22]

It seems obvious from the judge's own statement that Kirsch was not on his "perch on the bench." How could he have been, after he had "moved to see the screen closer?" Kai subsequently requested a review of the court-room security video footage; such a review, of course, would show Judge Kirsch's blatant falsehood for the lie that it was. This request was refused by none other than Judge Kirsch, of course. To quote Hizzoner from an earlier ruling during Kai's case, "I know they have security cameras in here and they're being viewed as we speak [...] but there's no basis for me to do so and I'm not doing it." Kirsch stated this in response to Kai's earlier request to review courtroom surveillance after Prosecutor Scott Peterson altered the position of a laser pointer indicating the injuries on Mr. Galfy's chest x-ray.

In my 2022 article from City University of New York's graduate news-paper *The Advocate*, I cited sections of the trial transcript that hadn't been reported elsewhere. One section has the judge refusing to allow courtroom surveillance tapes. Had they been allowed we could prove the impossibility of one of the judge's claims. In the court transcript, the judge mentions watching a video from "his perch on the bench." This is wholly inaccurate. It may seem like a small thing, but it was significant. That wasn't the only possible reason for Judge Robert Kirsch to suppress Kai's request to have the courtroom tapes reviewed.

"I know they have security cameras in here and they're being viewed as we speak [...] but there's no basis for me to do so and I'm not doing it." Kirsch had a second possible reason to make sure the tapes weren't entered into the record. At one point Prosecutor Scott Peterson changed the position of a laser pointer when showing the injuries to Joseph Galfy. Why is this relevant? Galfy was discovered with his body face down on the floor. Kai claims to have woken up beneath him, with a strange taste in his mouth potentially indicating being drugged.

Sadly, the investigators found that the bottles had been run through the dishwasher around the same time former Deputy Chief of Police and brother of the deceased James Galfy was allowed unprecedented access to the crime scene. This occurred before the investigation had even been completed.[23] Perhaps some of this missing (and/or destroyed) evidence was removed from the home by the mystery man caught by *ABC7NY*'s cameras. The video was pulled by *ABC7NY*[24] however, and a still from the video was not allowed to be entered into evidence. In layman's terms, spoliation of exculpatory evidence means destroying anything that could prove a defendant innocent.

And how about the laser pointer and the location of injuries? The injuries that led to Galfy's death could have only been effected by someone underneath their potential assaulter. Kai's hairs found on the side of the mattress also corroborate his account.[25] Remember that in New Jersey lethal force is authorized in the case of rape and sexual assault. Sadly, the police refused to run a rape kit on Kai (despite running one on the deceased Galfy so they could say they did run a rape kit). For the record, it's also a crime to refuse to run a rape kit on a victim of sexual assault when they request it. Just one of many cases where the investigation goes far beyond merely shoddy. Union County authorities ran afoul of proper protocol and even state and federal law, time and again.

Without suppressing and destroying evidence, the state's case is paper thin.

Kai claims that Galfy slipped drugs into Kai's beer, and he woke underneath him. If the potential evidence of drugging hadn't been destroyed (around the time Galfy's brother, the former Deputy Chief of Police was going to be "securing the scene" as he puts it) proving self-defense would have been a cinch for Kai.

Crime scene photos also include pill bottles. No toxicology screen was performed on those or the items in the dishwasher, and certain drug-facilitated sexual abuse (DFSA) agents such as GHB are very hard to test for. This is especially so if several hours or days have passed.[26]

---

* When I explained my purpose for requesting the video, I was told I'd need to subpoena them. As of this writing, I am in the process of doing so.

Another case of the defense team acting in concert with the prosecution would be Kai's defense attorney, John Cito, playing bait and switch briefly referencing the glassware in the sink and the dishware then going on to say that "I am not sure how you can test fibers for drugs."[27] Mr. Cito's expertise, as it turns out is as a lawyer and not a scientist. It's unknown why Cito would assume that he would have the same knowledge a scientist would. He didn't bother even doing a simple internet search for "test fibers for drugs" because if he had taken 30 seconds to do that, he would have seen multiple scientific papers on various methods used to test fibers for drugs.[28]

You might wonder why it would matter to a jury where the victim's injuries were precisely located. After all, a man was dead, wasn't he? Wasn't that the point? Consider that Mr. Galfy was found face down on the floor and that Kai said he woke up underneath him. The fatal injuries were on the center of Mr. Galfy's chest, unreachable from anywhere but underneath him. This corroborates Kai's testimony. Mr. Peterson, however, moved the laser to the side during his testimony, deceiving the Jury into thinking that Kai had been standing up and kicking Mr. Galfy in the side.

What happened is this: Kai kicked upwards at Galfy while lying on his back. This is important to the veracity of Kai's defense, which follows thusly:

1.) Galfy slipped drugs into Kai's beer, causing him to lose consciousness.

2.) Kai woke on the floor underneath him.

3.) Galfy died due to Kai's legal forcible self-defense. The law in New Jersey states that you can use deadly force to defend against a sexual assault.

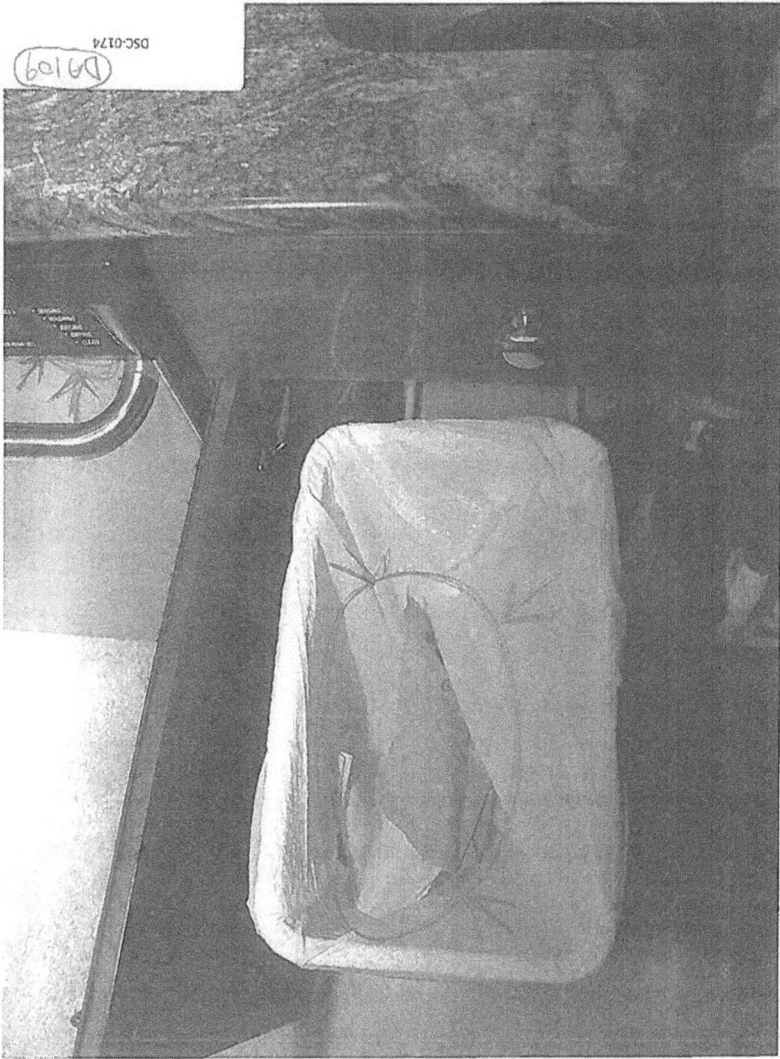

Crime scene photo DSC-0174 [DA109]. The folded paper in the trash can that may have been used to funnel powder into the beer mug was never tested.

Common sense would suggest that a pill bottle full of GHB, zopiclone, or whatever else was found in Galfy's fridge would be fairly convincing evidence in Kai's favor. As would GHB residue in a glass and GHB metabolites found in the urine involuntarily excreted by Kai upon his coming to. Not to mention the fact that, contrary to Pandina's claims, multiple drugs that have been utilized in DFSA cases result in blackout states similar to what Kai described.

Dr. Pandina stated acute effects of date rape drugs typically last two to four hours despite Johnny Ho's grand jury testimony misrepresenting Pandina's claim and ignoring lingering effects. This was admitted in Peterson's March 23, 2016 letter to Liguori (Kai's then-public defender) regarding Pandina's statements. The science being misrepresented was especially damaging when taken in conjunction with the testimony of witnesses who corroborate testimony related to Kai's lingering effects.[29]

Image of the check cut to Pandina's CAS program at Rutgers and still from Galfy's last will and testament that stipulates another $150,000 payment to Shaikh.[30]

It remains to be seen if the $150,000 endowment left to the program Pandina runs at Rutgers had anything to do with this. All this evidence together would clearly support Kai's statement that Galfy drugged him and would convince almost any jury that Kai used legal force in self-defense. Yet Judge Kirsch ridicules such common sense, as evidenced by the following excerpt from the courtroom transcript:

```
MR. CITO:
I think we talked about the glassware in the sink
itself, not the dishwasher. I believe the glassware
should have been collected. The last thing is the
carpet or the carpet fibers. That whole area should
```

have either been cut out or, at least, preserved or the fibers preserved to determine the combination of whose DNA was in the fluid; was it blood, was it urine, was it semen and that would have, at least, confirmed what type of assault or what actually occurred, especially if there was semen in the carpeting. Also, if there was urine in the carpeting, that would determine that it was my client's, and it would have confirmed his position that he did urinate at the time and that Galfy had ejaculated in that area. My client is also noting that it could also be tested for drugs, but I am not sure how you can test fibers for drugs.

THE COURT:
Thank you very much, Mr. Cito.

THE DEFENDANT:
The pill bottles.

MR. CITO:
I know we went over the pill bottles in the fridge, Your Honor.

THE COURT:
Sure.

MR. CITO:
The pill bottles in the fridge, they were never opened, and it was never determined what actually was in the pill bottles; that determination should have been made. It could have been one of the illicit

drugs.

THE COURT:

I mean, by that argument, honestly, shouldn't the State then be required to bring in canines to scour the entire premises? Maybe there is a pill box - - I am being semi-facetious, but not really. Maybe there is a hidden compartment in the home which would warehouse supposed drugs, rape drugs. At what point does common sense indicate—

Sometimes common sense is exactly what jurors are required to suspend to follow the instructions of the judge. For example, we all know that a person is presumed innocent until proven guilty beyond a reasonable doubt. The Burden of Proof is supposed to be on the prosecutor to prove the guilt or innocence of the defendant. However, a special loophole exists in New Jersey; if the defense asserts an Involuntary Intoxication Jury Charge (known as 2C:2-8(D)), the Burden of Proof shifts from the accuser to the accused.

MR. CITO:

I wanted to put in something my client requests which I am differing from. He wants me to not present to the Jury the defense of involuntary intoxication.

THE COURT:

On what grounds?[31]

For Kai, the "maxim of innocent before proven guilty" became "guilty before proven innocent." Kai had asked Mr. Cito to not include that jury instruction because Judge Kirsch ruled that the jurors weren't allowed to infer evidence of date rape drugs from the pill bottles, glasses, or carpet stains. The Jury, then, was therefore instructed to suspend common sense. Bear in mind, that a person can still assert that someone drugged them without asserting the defense of Involuntary Intoxication [2C:2-8(D)].[32] All it means is that the fact of a defendant's assailant drugging them will not alone result in an acquittal; it only factors into their state of mind. Nevertheless, the presumption created for Judge Kirsch's defendant on April 23rd, 2019, effectively stated that if As per Madame Cox-Arleo's July 28th ruling, without Pandina's testimony, Kai couldn't prove intoxication by clear and convincing evidence, the jury had to assume that he was stone cold sober. The jury must therefore infer his state of mind from that presumption onto all other charges.

Conversely, an instruction indicating the Constitutional Burden of Proof[33] would say that unless the prosecutor can prove that Kai was stone-cold sober beyond a reasonable doubt, the Jury must assume that Kai was intoxicated even if not to the point of establishing a defense under 2C:2-8(D). The self-defense instruction should have come into play simply because the evidence of drugs was destroyed. With just the self-defense charge, the burden to prove[33] whether Galfy drugged Kai would have remained on the Prosecutor, not Kai. This is key. Kai's defense of self-defense hinges upon the fact of his intoxication; so much so that a reasonable jury could find their decision formulaically simple. If Kai was intoxicated by date rape drugs, then Kai acted in self-defense against a sexual assault. If Kai was not intoxicated by date rape drugs, then Kai did not act in self-defense against a sexual assault. But the instruction Mr. Cito and Judge Kirsch included— over Kai's objection— reads, word for word: "The Defendant must prove by clear and convincing evidence that he was intoxicated."[34]

As Kai put it himself in his sentencing speech to the Court:

"It's important to point out how manifestly unjust it was to admit that any evidence of drugs was lost and destroyed, but in the next breath to belabor me with the burden of proving the existence of drugs, by clear and convincing evidence. That's the equivalent of saying [...] we cut off your legs, but if you don't run a mile, we will end your life."[35]

To this day, Kai deals with friction involving multiple public defenders who refuse to allow him to move forward with motions for dismissal, change of venue, or citing other glaring issues throughout. One public defender who refused to allow Kai to move forward with his motions was Peter Liguori. Liguori was one of many who allowed the idea that Kai's claims of a cover-up were nothing but wild conspiracy or the last gasp of a guilty man. Liguori did deem a suspected terrorist worthy of a change of venue due to excessive negative media coverage.[36] Abdul Khan Rahimi[37] would be found guilty of a series of bombings in New York and New Jersey.[38] How does this case differ from Kai's? Apart from the video evidence of culpability[39] of one of the defendants in Rahimi's case, and the evidence of a cover-up in Kai's,[40] obviously the lack of "appropriate zeal" applied in Kai's case as opposed to Rahimi's.

Why would the defense counsel, who is supposedly on Kai's side, and the supposedly unbiased Judge, show such a clear bias in working together against Kai? One explanation might be the fact that Galfy was a wealthy and prominent attorney in Union County. A further explanation might be the fact that the investigation, detention, and trial were conducted by those tied to Galfy in personal and professional circles. A final explanation might also be the fact that on April 17, 2019, in front of every Union County judge gathered in the courtroom, Kai stated, "This is a kangaroo court. Why don't you put on your pointy hats and burn a cross out front; you're trying to lynch me."[41]

Kai has since spent years filing motions against the various figures who played a role. James Galfy, Cito, and Liguori's separate complaints were joined on December 21, 2021, with a second motion to dismiss filed on February 16, 2022. Peterson, Romankow, and the UCPO filed their motion on January 21, 2021, and Pandina on February 14, 2021. UCPO, Peterson, and Romankow, rather than attacking Kai's allegations moved to dismiss "for lack of subject matter jurisdiction" and their entitlement to "sovereign immunity."*[42]

Whatever the reasons, we are all affected by the officiation of the formerly unofficial guilty until proven innocent doctrine. We've all heard this phrase before, whispered in civil rights groups, in groups dedicated to gun control measures or to open carry rights, in left and right-wing groups, and in any kind of organization concerned with the rights of people residing in the United States of America: guilty until proven innocent. But to see it in a cold transcript, to hear it shouted from the Judge's bench, to feel the Judge's gavel hammering this nail into the coffin of our Constitution is wrong. The American legal system is, theoretically, about providing security to our persons and our property in a fair manner acceptable to our community. Locking people up for six years without trial, and destroying the evidence of their innocence (while telling them the only way to prove their innocence is with the destroyed evidence) is unfair.

It is unacceptable. It puts all persons and all properties in danger of being subject to the same treatment if left unchecked. I love America because we (purportedly) have checks and balances in place to safeguard against the kind of corruption evidenced in April of 2019 in Judge Kirsch's courtroom from destroying our free society. Even as you read this, Kai has appealed his unjust murder conviction to a higher court. The higher court will challenge the injustices they see, and if that fails us, there is another higher court. Kai is so confident in this that he used his allocution** to defiantly address every

---

* Sovereign immunity refers to the principle that the government cannot be sued without its consent. UCPO also relied on prosecutorial immunity which protects prosecutors even in such cases where they lie, misrepresent cases, or even suppress exculpatory evidence as we've seen throughout this case.

** A short speech at sentencing, usually used to beg for mercy from the judge.

judge in Union County, New Jersey.

THE DEFENDANT:

Despite the bias of the cronies on the bench, I will overturn your false conviction, and your worthless sentence. This has been nothing but a sham trial, and you have railroaded an innocent man. Shame on you.

During the last nine years since Kai was arrested, many people have rallied around him in support of our Constitution. Kai's YouTube channel[43] has hundreds of videos he's made in prison, and his Facebook blog[44] has thousands of followers. Supporters have even started a fundraiser for Kai. However, questions remain. Will the Appellate Court overturn Kai's conviction? Will they move his new trial to a different county? Will they defend our Constitution, our property, our persons? Only time will tell, but to paraphrase Winston Churchill, one thing is for certain: This isn't the end for Kai the Hatchet Wielding Hitchhiker. And somewhere something similar is just beginning for someone. As horrifying as this single story is, what's just as frightening is that perhaps the most singular thing about it is that there's any publicity at all. And it's not just a Union County thing, or New Jersey thing, what happened to Kai is emblematic of a condition, that of systemic rot.

CHAPTER 11

A SLAP ON THE WRIST

Outside of discovering Genovese family ties to Romankow's second in command at the Union County Prosecutor's Office when Kai was arrested, one of the most shocking revelations while researching this book would have to be uncovering the 30+ year tradition of tolerating, even harboring sexual predators. If, that is, they have passed the New Jersey bar examination. We're not just talking lawyers, but judges, District Attorneys, a New Jersey state Deputy Attorney General, assemblymen, and other politicians. No news stories for 90% of the incidents and almost none of the men are listed on state or federal sex offender registry databases. The only paper trail that exists is a series of Disciplinary Review Board (DRB) reports and a civil lawsuit that shows that one of the sexual predator judge's sons also skated despite molesting a small child.

I can't take credit for this blockbuster discovery. Kai actually clued me in regarding the decades of judiciary corruption and media blackout related to several cases involving prosecutors, judges, state legislators, and other prominent persons receiving slaps on the wrist for sex crimes related to children...

for over 30 years. Not all of these cases are specific to Union County. This is a statewide issue.

I'm sure New Jersey is not the only state to have protected predators in positions of power and public trust, but thankfully a search of my home state of Tennessee's bar disciplinary actions proved that not every state will regularly let a sexual predator retain the *privilege* of practicing law.

I mentioned the Cleveland Street Scandal in my first article about Kai's situation in the *Inquisitr* back in 2017. The Cleveland Street Scandal embroiled Oscar Wilde, in which at Wilde's indecency trial the prosecutor, judge, and others were shown decades later to have been involved in a child trafficking ring that catered to the well-to-do elites and may have extended as far as Prince Albert himself.

The Cleveland Street Scandal is mentioned in chapter one of my book *Pedogate Primer: the politics of pedophilia*.[1] There is also a chapter on the 7th-floor group ambassadorial sex crimes cover-up and Operation Flicker which exposed multiple people distributing and downloading child pornography on the Department of Defense networks. This included people with top security clearance at the NSA and elsewhere.

This issue came up occasionally in the news off and on since Hillary Clinton's stint as Secretary of State under Barack Obama.[2] Even a bill was written, the END Network Abuse act of 2019, a bipartisan bill. The End National Defense (END)Network Abuse Act was a bipartisan bill. Introduced to the Senate in 2019, it was then referred to the Committee on Armed Services. There was scant mention of it in the press between July and December 2019, and no actions to report since then.[3]

As it turned out, my initial comparison of the odd chumminess and conflicts of interest in the courtroom may have been somewhat prescient. Early in 2022, Kai shared a list of names he'd uncovered during his research in the prison law library. A sickening trend of sexual predators receiving no more than a slap on the wrist despite their execrable behavior meriting disbarment.

KAI:

> I found some extremely disturbing news. Joseph Galfy and his brother James weren't the only ones in the Union County Legal Community preying on the innocent. When head prosecutor Theodore Romankow said he was "in the same circles" as the Galfy's, he was apparently talking about a sex predator ring that goes back DECADES.
>
> You may be wondering why I haven't brought this up before now.
>
> The fact is, I wasn't able to find out until recently.
>
> For years, in Union County Jail, I was never allowed to access a law library computer.* I had to put in a request form, and an employee of the jail would decide what, if anything, I would receive.
>
> After arriving at New Jersey State Prison, I spent over 2 years perfecting my appeals, so that I'm now ready to bring my case before a federal judge.
>
> I recently got 4 free hours at the law library, after all my work

---

* This is not the first example of a complaint regarding difficulties related to not being allowed direct access to the law library while in Elizabeth Detention Center.

was done. I decided to use the opportunity to answer the burning question:

"How many more Galfys ARE there in New Jersey?"

I tried looking up criminal cases, but those sneaky creeps hide the proceedings. Then I had a "Eureka!" moment.

I checked the Bar Disciplinary Proceedings.

I was like, "Holy Shit."

First of all, I found "In Re Legato 229 NJ 173 (2017)"; a case involving 3 lawyers from those "circles," who were each caught masturbating in front of kids from 9-12 years old... and attempting to lure them into secluded areas. In that case, the New Jersey Supreme Court held, verbatim:

"The Court refrains from establishing a bright-line rule requiring disbarment in all cases involving sexual offenses against children." Legato 229 NJ at 182

The Court then admitted that, up until recently, they didn't really care about lawyers sexually abusing children:

"In the fifteen years since Ferriaolo, we have recognized changing societal attitudes towards child sexual offenders." Legato 229 NJ at 186

There were DOZENS more cases like that.

There were AT LEAST dozens more Galfys.

And these are just the ones with so much evidence and so many witnesses that they COULDNT cover it up.

(remember how hard they worked to cover up the Galfy in my case: destroyed evidence, perjured cops and judges, witness tampering, shifted burden of proof, etc, etc)

These are just the tip of the iceberg; we'll never know how many they covered up. The Newspapers wouldn't even report any but ONE of THESE ones!

Don't just take my word for it; use Google Scholar or Leagle to look up these cases for your own self.

And I did just that. Trawling through the New Jersey Supreme Court rulings and Disciplinary Review Board reports from the Office of Attorney Ethics (OAE) made my jaw drop. And despite the lack of press coverage, there were several DRB complaints for some of these folks. Some of whom are no small potatoes. For instance, a judge whose predatory action escaped public scrutiny before helping his child rapist son also managed to keep his name clear. (No news reports, no sex offender registry records either).

It's a decades-long stream of sex offenders and pedophiles in New Jersey with their crimes kept from the public, a slap on the wrist in the courtroom, and a few months suspension. Almost all cases resulted in no incarceration, and only three on the sex offender registry.

It's not a smoking gun regarding outright media blackout, but like with the Jeffrey Epstein case or that of politically-connected millionaire and murderer Ed Buck,[4] powerful people with connections get stories quelled all the time. As of this writing, Peter Nygard is to be in a courtroom soon, but for years he had stories about his trafficking ring suppressed.[5] Joseph Galfy, the man Kai alleges drugged and raped him, was a lawyer and brother of a former New Jersey deputy chief of police (who was inexplicably allowed in the active crime scene as likely crime scene tampering occurred). We know this much for sure.

I've wondered for a while why no reporters apart from myself seem interested enough to look into the discovery documents, crime scene photos, and other evidence that bears out Kai's claims. Whether it's a media blackout to keep Kai in prison so he can't move forward with his civil suit for the 4+ years he spent in solitary in Union County (New Jersey's 20th district, which, incidentally, shows up several times in the following cases).

Again though, as Kai told me: don't take my word for it. Let direct quotes from the disciplinary board and New Jersey case law speak for themselves.

In the first case here, the only reason there is any mention at all is a civil lawsuit, Prudential Property & Cas. Ins. Co. v Boylan 307 NJ Super 162 (App Div 1997). In this case, the son of James F. Boylan, a New Jersey judge who would be quietly outed as a sexual predator himself, escapes infamy as a child rapist. Despite having raped a 5-year-old girl, he managed to avoid jail time and kept his name out of the papers. The sole record I could find in the aforementioned civil suit.[6]

Sure enough, I found no news coverage related to the molestation of a child by the judge's son. The same judge was involved in defrauding the state and having sex with women in exchange for diminished sentences.

In this case: "The motion judge ruled that Prudential's homeowner's policy provided coverage to James and Linda Boylan and that the policy's business pursuits exception did not apply because this was a 'one time only casual accommodation to babysit in an emergency.' The judge also ruled that the insurance policy covered fifteen-year-old Ryan Boylan as a matter of law because he was deemed to lack the requisite intent or mental capacity to understand the nature of his acts."

That's right, this high school-aged rapist of a child barely old enough for Kindergarten was deemed too young to understand that molesting a small child is wrong. Prudential Insurance applied for but was denied access to Ryan Boylan's juvenile court records. As a result, whether there are other examples of this type of behavior we will never know. I did search for Ryan Boylan in New Jersey state and federal sex offender registries. No record of Boylan exists on the Registered Sex Offender list.

The case ended with a judgment in favor of the plaintiffs for nearly $400,000 plus prejudgement interest. Ryan Boylan "babysat" the 5-year-old girl and her little brother, taking them upstairs where they "played some games" and then went to bed. The daughter was taken to a bedroom where Ryan Boylan forced the little girl to perform oral sex on him. Boylan admitted to this act.

The defendants in the case argued, "that we should declare the law of New Jersey to be that in cases where a minor sexually abuses a much younger child it is the minor's subjective intent that should apply, rather than the objective intent standard that would apply to adults."* Now yes, the judge's son was a minor, but there is a *major* difference between a 5 and 15-year-old.

Perhaps a case of the apple not falling far from the tree, the judge father of the child rapist makes the list as well. James F. Boylan, a few years later, would face charges of coaching female defendants to lie in court to reduce their fines and penalties in exchange for sexual favors. Former Municipal Judge Boylan admitted these actions to the court. In addition to coercing women into having sex in exchange for reduced sentences, Boylan defrauded

---

* In the suit it's argued that "N.J.S.A. 2C:4-11a(1) creates a presumption of maturity for an individual over the age of fourteen; it is manifest that this fifteen-year-old boy knew what he was doing to this five-year-old girl."

the City of Jersey City to the tune of somewhere between $10,0000 and $20,0000. This was also admitted openly to the court.[7] Judge Roman Montez of Union County also was accused of impropriety for inappropriate sexual relationships with someone whose case he was overseeing.[8]

For some strange reason, the court ruled that "the offense level is not determined under [section] 2C1.7(c) (1), (2), or (3)." U.S.S.G. §2C1.7, comment. (n.4). Since the offense level is not determined under any of these subsections, the abuse of position of trust or use of special skill adjustment is not applicable." As for how a judge using his position to coerce sex from women is not an abuse of power and trust, I have no clue. It's also interesting that Boylan was ruled financially unable to pay a fine and "not likely to become able to pay any fine in the future."

Boylan at the very least was disbarred and a very short article at the *New York Times* was written up on the case.[9] This is one of the scant examples out of the nearly couple dozen names on this list to have had any media coverage of the major crimes by these various men in positions of power. Judges, politicians, prosecutors, public defenders, as well as Union County jail staff have committed awful crimes without so much as a drop of newspaper ink on coverage.

With Harry Parkin, similar to Boylan, we have, in addition to sex crimes, an indictment in regards to "a scheme to defraud the public of his honest services in his role as Chief of Staff to the Mercer County Executive." Parkin was indicted on twelve counts of mail fraud as well and was also accused of extortion.[10]

Parkin tried to argue his sentence received was "unreasonable" by nature of his standing in the community and prior military service record. This is reminiscent of how Theodore Romankow, long-time associate of Joseph Galfy and former Union County prosecutor referred to the alleged rapist.

In Parkin's case, even the District Court itself noted that Parkin was "very highly respected" and that "[p]eople say a lot of good things about him . . . ." (Id. at 240.) The District Court read from a letter Parkin wrote to the Court in which Parkin cited his long years in public service as well as his military service. (Id. at 243.) The District Court considered this letter as well as "the letters of all the people that knew Parkin and spoke well of him."

Parkin appealed the sentence of 90 months followed by three years of supervised release and a $26,000 fine. $26,000 isn't much when you consider that the amount Parkin defrauded the taxpayers ran well into six figures.[11]

Next up is another case similar to that of Boylan and Parkin. Quatrella 237 NJ 402 (2019) is also cited in the Matter of Angelo M. Perrucci by the Disciplinary Review Board of New Jersey, decided as recently as late August 2021.

David L. Quatrella was temporarily suspended after one count of wire fraud. Quatrella failed to appear on the Order directing him to show cause why he should not be disbarred. It appears that it was Quatrella's failure to attempt to defend himself and not the fraud, corruption, and sex crimes that resulted in him being disbarred.[12]

The Quatrella Matter is cited in a New Jersey DRB decision in February of last year. Another recurring theme I've noticed is insurance policies and fraud involved in multiple of these examples.[13]

In conversation with current and retired FBI agents* who have worked in the field of white-collar crime and public corruption, I've been told that living above one's means and charges like wire fraud can be indicators that something untoward is bubbling beneath the surface.[14]

---

* Specifically, Agent Raymond Hall and former Agents Jerri Williams and Myron Fuller.

Meanwhile, the 2020 New Jersey Courts Disciplinary Summaries shows that the situation has far from abated. Eval Katzman "solicited high school-aged girls for sex in exchange for money. He showed no remorse for his conduct and attempted to shift blame to his victims."[15] Brian P. Meehan entered a no-contest plea regarding "statutory sexual assault, victim 11 years or older."[16] Jeffrey Toman "engaged in sexually explicit text messages with a fourteen-year-old girl whose mother he was representing in a child custody proceeding." Guess what? No news coverage of any of the above cases.[17]

Yes, you heard that right. Not even the case of a lawyer molesting a middle school-aged girl, his client's daughter, amidst a custody hearing was considered worth reporting. This sort of disgusting conflict of interest shouldn't be possible, but as we see over and over again though things operate just a little differently in Galfy country. We also have the crooked public defender Andrew Michael Carroll "engaging in a sexual relationship with a client while appointed her public defender."[18]

New Jersey lawyer, Tobin G. Nilsen, was finally disbarred after a federal court conviction of enticing a minor to engage in sexual activity and a state court conviction of second-degree child luring.* Nilsen had bought a ticket to fly from New Jersey to Atlanta to meet up with what he believed to be a 32-year-old mother of a nine-year-old daughter who he expected to have sex with. He had been arrested previously by New Jersey law enforcement for soliciting yet another "mother-daughter pair for sexual activity." Why was he not disbarred immediately? It seems this is just the way business is taken care of in New Jersey. As per usual, the Nilsen cases weren't deemed "newsworthy" either.[19]

Despite a "2010 conviction of lewdness and years-long pattern of

---

* A trend emerges if you'll take note. In general, it's only federal charges that result in disbarment, regardless of the seriousness of the charges.

inappropriate sexual conduct" including repeat instances of public masturbation, Todd C. Sicklinger only received a three-month suspension.[20] John
Rex Powell was disbarred in 2016 after "one count of engaging in child pornography enterprise and two counts of sexual exploitation of a minor." He
was discovered to be involved in an international pedophile ring.[21] David J.
Witherspoon in 2010 received a one-year suspension "for offering discount-
ed legal services or fee reductions to three female clients and the daughter of
another client in exchange for sexual favors, practicing law while ineligible
to do so for failure to pay the annual assessment to the New Jersey Lawyers'
Fund for Client Protection, and failing to maintain the books and records
required of attorneys."[22]

William S. Wolfson got a paltry six months suspension after pleading
guilty to an accusation of fourth-degree criminal sexual contact. What's
more, he assaulted a "female employee at his doctor's office." He admitted
that he had a habit of this having "touched six female employees at his
doctor's office between 10 and 15 times." As we've learned here, New Jersey
doesn't seem to be too concerned with judges, prosecutors, public defenders, and local or state politicians being accused of sex crimes, even against
children, even multiple instances of such. Wolfson lucked out with a "Pre-
Trial Intervention Program."[23]

James W. Kennedy is another case of the six-month suspension slap on the
wrist despite fourth-degree endangering the welfare of a child involved in
his admission of downloading between 20,000-30,000 images of children
under 16 engaged in sexual acts.[24] Salvatore J. Maiorino was "reprimanded"
before the review board for fourth-degree sexual assault of a minor. The
Supreme Court of New Jersey "held that a reprimand was the appropriate
discipline for an attorney who pleaded no contest to an information filed in
the state of Connecticut" related to the sex crime against a minor.[25]

Terry G. Tucker also received no more than a "reprimand" from the NJSC related to "unwanted, sexual advances to a bankruptcy client."[26] If behavior like that or these numerous crimes against children isn't behavior unbecoming of a member of the court's bar, I honestly don't know what would be considered such.

James I. Peck, IV received a whopping 21-month "time-served suspension" as discipline for his charge of child pornography possession. Like several other cases noted here, this wasn't Peck's first rodeo. He had been temporarily suspended two years earlier in October of 2001 (In re Peck, 170 NJ 4).[27]

A one-year suspension from law practice was deemed sufficient and appropriate discipline for Donald M. Ferraiolo for "attempted endangering [of] the welfare of a child" and sexually explicit chats with "Jay" who he believed to be a 14-year-old boy. Ferraiolo repeatedly asked Jay to come to his home "to engage in numerous sexual acts, some of which were explicitly stated."[28]

Then there's Gerard Gilligan, the New Jersey Supreme Court finally found a second-degree aggravated sexual assault charge enough to disbar (after a temporary previous suspension the year prior).[29] Unlike with Ty Hyderally,[30] where a "reprimand was the appropriate discipline for an attorney whose certification to practice of law before Navy courts or boards was suspended by the Judge Advocate General of the United States Navy for two years as a result of sexual advances that the respondent made to two women who were his legal aid clients while he was in the Navy."[31] In between Joseph Galfy and this lawyer both being revealed to be JAG predators it kind of ruins the end of *A Few Good Men*, doesn't it?

It was revealed in Collins v Union County Jail 291 NJ Super 318 (Law Div 1995), that Union County correctional officer Gayland Robinson anally raped inmate Jesse Collins. Not only did Robinson never see any time for this, but there was also no local news coverage. The only major coverage of the case came from the *New York Times* years later and that was just related to the ruling that Collins couldn't sue for PTSD and other issues arising from being violently assaulted and violated. The state argued that the inmate had no civil recourse because the PTSD and psychological scars weren't physical and visible. Thus, no compensation was deemed worthy.[32]

Another astounding case of a repeat offender who was actually caught distributing child pornography from his office at the New Jersey State Legislature is also worth mentioning. Now, as hard as it is to believe, Neil M. Cohen spent only a very short amount of time behind bars despite distributing sexually explicit images of children.[33] As outlandish as it sounds, Cohen accessed, printed out, and shared the material directly from his government office. Cohen was turned in by his receptionist who found printouts on his office desk and alerted the press. This and the Collins case are atypical in that there were eventually brief mentions in the news about it. That said, the fact that multiple people who worked with Cohen knew about his perverse predilection and did nothing about it doesn't bode well.

As for Cohen, the court reported that the "facts of this case are undisputed." It was July 2008 when several printouts of the pornographic image, some of "young female victims" were found in a receptionist's drawer at the district office of New Jersey's Twentieth Legislative District. (That's Union County for those of you taking notes).[34]

Cohen was at the time an assemblyman representing Union County. New Jersey State Police got involved which led to the discovery that this was far from the first time that Cohen had left the child abuse images laying out where people might see them. Staff reported there were multiple times they found such images, often during morning work hours or after returning from the weekend. The Office of Legislative Services was quick to act... they decided to put passwords on the computer. Yeah, that'll stop him!

Cohen admitted that he had viewed and printed the pictures and explained that at least some of the material was legal pornography featuring adult models. He had to get the password of another staff member to use his receptionist's computer for his sick hobby. Multiple members of staff interviewed cited multiple occasions they saw Cohen "viewing pornography on the receptionist's computer."

Police found thirty-four CSAM* images. Nineteen girls under the age of 16.

This was one of the few cases where some semblance of punishment was applied. The court noted that disbarment was "the most severe punishment, reserved for circumstances in which 'the misconduct of [the] attorney is so immoral, venal, corrupt or criminal as to destroy totally any vestige of confidence that the individual could ever again practice in conformity with the standards of the profession." In my opinion, there is little you can do that is more immoral than seriously harming a child. For Cohen, however, a plea agreement saw the state drop the official misconduct charge and three of the four child pornography counts.

As for the "official misconduct," in addition to being a lawyer, Neil Cohen was a legislator. And Cohen's political career is nothing to scoff at. He was Deputy Majority Leader of the New Jersey Assembly from 2002 until his resignation, Deputy Minority Leader from 1996-2001, and Minority Whip from 1994-1995. It shouldn't be too surprising to find out that Cohen lived in and represented Union County.[35]

Cohen didn't even have to pay bail once busted. Superior Court Judge Gerald Council in Trenton decided the politician and child predator didn't pose a flight risk and he was released on his own recognizance despite solid

---

* Child sexual abuse material

evidence including the images themselves and multiple witnesses as well as his confession. Cohen would have faced up to 10 years in prison for each of the three dropped charges,[36] had they not been dropped. In 2014 it was reported that Cohen would not be disbarred but would receive a 5-year suspension of his law degree. Despite Justice Faustino Fernandez-Vina's opinion that in the future, perhaps being a child predator should disqualify you to practice law "in light of society's increasing recognition of the harm done to the victims of those offenses."[37]

The article at the *Star-Ledger* noted that two sources said that a legislative staffer first found the images and then informed Raymond Lesniak and John Cryan.[38] Cohen did not comment on the story as he was "under psychiatric care" at the time. That's a theme you'll notice. Time and again these predators with law degrees when they finally do get caught, slip through unscathed apart from, at worst being disbarred. More often the result is just a simple suspension and sentence of therapy. Either way, no more than a slap on the wrist considering the seriousness of the charges.

Star-Ledger notes that Cohen was in his 17th year in the Assembly, having continuously served from 1994 on. Cohen was chair of the Financial Institutions and Insurance Committee and one of seven deputy speakers. Ironically, he was also a long-time member of the Legislature's Joint Committee on Ethical Standards. The article goes on to speak of Cohen's law practice in Montclair where he worked alongside Senator Nia Gill (D-Essex).[39]

Past that point, however, the piece devolves into an odd sort of hagiography, whitewashing the actions of this serial pedophile:

"Among the more than 100 laws Cohen has sponsored is one that created a 24-hour hotline for members of the public to report computer crimes, including child pornography. He also co-sponsored a law that retroactively removed immunity from churches, schools, and other charities that negligently hire employees who sexually abuse children.

"He also supported measures to support stem cell research, provide health insurance for mammograms, restrict strip searches and expand eligibility for the Pharmaceutical Assistance for the Aged and Disabled program. [...] one of the leaders last year of the effort to save the life of Congo, a German Shepherd condemned as a vicious dog after mauling a landscaper." Also, take note of the "community service" associated with some of these legal and political predators at large,* none of which are listed on state or federal sex offender registries for whatever reason.

His staff seems to have liked him anyway apart from the receptionist who reported the child abuse images on her desk. Unless she just finally got tired of it having happened multiple times even there at the office.

"Let me just give you one statement. This is how I feel. I have nothing but respect for Neil. I have no comment on any of the accusations," said Gleshia Givens, his chief of staff.

He did one year, two months of a five-year sentence. 14 months for multiple counts of possession and distribution of CSAM of very young children. He faced up to 30 years. He was only sentenced to five. Of that five years, he served just one year and two months. Contrast that with Kai's pretrial detention which lasted over five years with more than four of those served in 23/7 lockdown in an isolation cell.

---

* Using community service as a cover for grooming and molestation isn't even confined to predators who have passed the bar in Union County, as witnessed by the case of Gregory J. Akers. The major difference in the Akers case is that it was picked up by the federal government and ended in years of prison time charged. Another more recent federal case from 2022 involves a teacher distributing CSAM.[40] That wasn't the only case from 2022 involving a teacher.[41] At a certain point, the excuses of being "respected in the community" that many of the predator lawyers used and that were applied to Galfy ring a bit hollow here.

The New Jersey Supreme Court was quite forgiving of the former politician. After "weighing the circumstances" and taking into account Cohen's "alleged mental illness, his own experience being sexually abused as a child and his cooperation in seeking treatment" the Court decided that they would impose an "indeterminate suspension" with a five-year wait before he could seek reinstatement.

I have to wonder if this case resulting in, albeit minimal incarceration, is due to the fact it is the rare exception to the media blackout that went on for over 30 years in New Jersey. All the while the problem was festering. Often right in the open, in Union County, New Jersey.

In the matter of Cohen, another New Jersey case is cited where an attorney was disbarred after ten years of viewing child pornography. He was eventually caught with 753 images he had distributed and traded. Donald S. Burak, another New Jersey lawyer, possessed "particularly unsettling" material related to child bondage and "sadistic or masochistic conduct and other depictions of violence" was interspersed with the already deplorable and unforgivable acts decimating the innocence of the child victims.

Burak was sentenced to ten years, but only after the court "took into account that the attorney had been indicted for criminal sexual contact with a minor female relative during the time that the FBI was investigating his child pornography activities."[42]

Steven C. Cunningham was eventually disbarred, not so much due to his guilty plea of attempting to entice a twelve-year-old boy for the purposes of sex, but rather "following his failure to appear on the return date of the Court's Order to Show Cause." The kicker, the Disciplinary Review Board had concluded Cunningham's attempt only merited a two-year suspension. Cunningham made plans to meet the boy but since they weren't "finalized" the DRB was inclined to just suspend him.[43]

Another attorney was disbarred after pleading guilty in the United States District Court for the District of New Hampshire to felony possession of child pornography, a violation of 18 USCA § 2252A(a)(5)(B). In re Sosnowski, 197 NJ 23, 961 A.2d 697 (2008). The attorney admitted to possessing sixty-seven images of child pornography and eight sexually explicit video files of children engaging in sexual acts and exposing their genitals. In addition, the attorney had placed hidden cameras in a child's bathroom and bedroom. He was sentenced to 37 months in prison, with five years of supervised release, and was ordered to pay a $100 assessment.[44] Again, 37 months is just about half the time Kai spent in the hole waiting for his trial.

Another case that comes up in New Jersey case law or the Office of Attorney Ethics (OAE) or Disciplinary Review Board (DRB) reports is that of Charles P. Wright. In 1997, Wright was disbarred after being convicted of aggravated criminal sexual assault of his own daughter.[45] This is just one case of incest on the books, though apart from this book, New Jersey case law and DRB and OAE reports, most of these stories weren't deemed "newsworthy." And without ever being initially reported, it is harder to see the pattern that emerges as you dig deeper.

"In re 'X'" from 1990 also has a lawyer, thankfully at least disbarred after sexually assaulting his three daughters over eight years.[46] Three years before that Steven Allen Herman received only a suspension of three years despite the sexual assault of a ten-year-old boy.[47]

It should be mentioned, in Sosnowski, Thompson, and "X" the disbarments are related to convictions under federal law related to sexual exploitation of minors.

Another attorney, Paul Frye pleaded guilty to improperly touching a nine-year-old child in 1999 with the intent to "impair or debauch the morals of the child." Frye would be sentenced to five years of "non-custodial probation" and community supervision in addition to being forbidden to have any contact with the child victim. Frye wouldn't be disbarred for years after he was found guilty of probation violation. Frye had missed six probation meetings and was not attending mandated sex therapy. For this evasion, he was sentenced... you guessed it, to continue probation.[48]

For whatever reason, five of the stories related to Cohen's crimes that are linked in his Wikipedia article seem to have been pulled from the internet entirely.[49]

It's not even just lawyers and legislators. Joseph J. Haldusiewicz[*] was a Deputy NJ Attorney General busted with 996 images of small children being sexually exploited. As with Cohen, this was done right on the computer that New Jersey taxpayers bought. Unlike Cohen, no one was fed up enough to leak the news to the media, or if they did it must not have been a slow enough news day to find time to point out that the Deputy AG was a pedophile.[50]

Considering the process of "trading up" that Nicole Weisensee Egan revealed related to the Bill Cosby case,[51] it's quite possible that the predators named here (and those unnamed as of yet) kept clear of the media by offering something else to papers. In Cosby's case, a side effect of "access journalism" resulted in the trail of victims being silenced.[52] Checking the state of New Jersey against my home state of Tennessee made it painfully clear that this kind of predator shielding is definitely "a Jersey thing."

Haldusiewicz also got off easy. After entering his guilty plea on charges of fourth-degree endangering the welfare of a child (quite a mouthful of a euphemism for downloading child pornography) as well as a violation of the

---

[*] In Re Haldusiewicz 185 NJ 278 (2005)

Rules for Professional Conduct.* Haldusiewicz was sentenced to three years probation, made to pay fines, and prohibited from unsupervised contact with any children under the age of sixteen.

Former AG Haldusiewicz died in 2016. In his obituary, he's listed as a "career attorney" who "served as New Jersey Deputy Attorney General under Governor Christine Todd Whitman."

Haldusiewicz was fired from the NJ Department of Law and Public Safety, Division of Law "for misuse of his internet privilege." A fitting understatement considering the state's continual desire to walk on eggshells so as not to call a spade a spade. Judging from the fact that he continued to be a "career attorney" for years beyond being outed as a predator, his actions didn't impact his life nearly as much as the children harmed by the creation of the materials he was downloading. As for the numbers, 996 sounds like a lot, and when it comes to images of children being assaulted it certainly is. However, during the investigation, S.I. Syzmanski reports having "terminated the examination because of the volume of suspected child pornography found but stated that if the examination was continued more would be found."

No news sites covered these, but the judicial watchdog blog No Ethics[53] brought up at least a few of those listed. Including that of Haldusiewicz:

"A forensic examination of Joe's desktop computer found a total of 996 images of child pornography. The examination also observed numerous homosexual and adult pornographic images. The examiner concluded that because of the volume of suspected child pornography found, much more would be discovered if the examination continued.

---

* R.P.C. 8.4(b) criminal act that reflects adversely on honesty, trustworthiness or fitness as a lawyer.

6 mo. suspension of law degree, Judge Harold W. Fullilove of the Superior Court criminally punished Joey by presenting him with three years of probation and a $1500 fine. The real punishment in Joey's opinion was Fullilove's order that he was prohibited from having any unsupervised contact with children under the age of sixteen."

Yet another case where the horrendous acts were committed in his office, on state of New Jersey computers:

"Mr. Haldusiewicz was using the shared computer when a BPU employee walked into the office. The defendant appeared 'pale and surprised' and immediately shut down the computer with the power button instead of doing a proper shutdown.

On July 18, 2003, Judge Fullilove sentenced respondent to a three-year term of probation.$1,500 and total costs of the court also imposed a fine of $157 and further ordered that respondent have no unsupervised contact with children under the age of sixteen. Respondent was also directed to continue psychological treatment."[54]

Even examining dissenting opinions is worrying. In some cases, the only dissent is a suggestion that maybe the court should suspend their license a few more months than the standard "six months to two years"* that several New Jersey attorneys who have pleaded to or been found guilty of sex crimes received:

"We respectfully dissent from the majority's determination that respondent should receive a six-month suspension for his misconduct. Our disagreement with the majority is two-fold. First, we do not agree with the

---

* From Haldusiewicz's DRB: "In New Jersey, attorneys who have pleaded to or been found guilty of child pornography offenses have been suspended for periods ranging from six months to two years."

majority's premise that respondent's illegal conduct was not related to his duties as a public servant. Second, although disciplinary cases are fact sensitive and must be decided on a case-by-case basis, possession, of child pornography is a very serious offense that, absent special circumstances, should be met with a long-term suspension. In our view, the six-month suspension imposed by the majority is insufficient. In two child-pornography cases decided by the Court in 2003, In re Rosanelli, 176 NJ 275 (2003) and In re Peck, 177 NJ 249 (2003), we expressed our opinion that at least a two-year suspension is warranted for this serious crime, which demeans and exploits children."[55]

Oh wow, you mean two *whole* years in addition to being sentenced to therapy. Pretty rough stuff!

The dissent stemmed from the review board being "unable to agree" with the Office of Attorney Ethics that the discipline should be "enhanced" because Haldusiewicz had served as a deputy attorney general. "We do not believe we should create two levels of discipline, one for the private bar, another for state employees, for the same offense." So as you can see, the general "dissent" found in the Supreme Court of New Jersey isn't so much related to "shouldn't we be disbarring predators" so much as "why are we suspending these predators for so long."

The case of In Re: Fink, 181 NJ 350 (2004) involves a three-year suspension levied on an attorney who had already been disbarred in the State of Delaware for felony possession of child pornography and fifteen counts of unlawful dealing in child pornography.[56]

Donald Rosanelli is another case that shows up in the citations of some of the others. In 2009, Rosanelli was required to file an affidavit of compliance after he had been temporarily suspended in 2009 and again in 2010. Rosanelli was suspended for six months and offered a Pretrial Intervention

Program and examined by a psychiatrist after it was revealed he had twenty-three CSAM images downloaded on his computer that involved small children "engaged in various sexual acts."

Rosanelli would be reinstated in 2004 with future suspensions related to a district fee arbitration committee and a $500 sanction to the Disciplinary Review Board. Rosanelli claimed to the DRB that, despite signing up for a site with his credit card and downloading "about a thousand pictures" he was merely "turned on by the illicit process, the pictures didn't excite me that much."

They certainly excited him enough to print out the nearly two dozen that slid out of a phone book when a friend who had been staying with him found them. Rosanelli imparts how he was called by his friend who told him about finding the pictures and that he should seek help and go to the police. Rosanelli says he initially balked telling his friend "that would destroy my career and life." His friend responded that he'd already spoken with the police and that they weren't interested in prosecuting. Much like so many other of these cases.[57]

Rosanelli's comments to the DRB even reference the, all too familiar by now, media blackout:

"They booked me and released me on my own recognizance. I signed a release, got a computer, was transported to the police station. There was no newspaper coverage. The police were concerned that I would become suicidal."

Donald S. Rosanelli died a year before Haldusiewicz, but like him, there was no mention of pedophilia, crimes against children, or his long delinquency from the bar for multiple violations:

"Don was involved in various non-profit organizations and causes dedicated to the environment and national policy."[58]

Community activism is another thread I see multiple times in these cases. Especially concerning when in one of the crimes against children, victims were groomed and targeted when the wrist-slapped child molester was a "volunteer" coach for a charity league.

Like Haldusiewicz, Rosanelli was handed a 6-month suspension. No newspapers, no jail or prison time. He was ordered "restored to law practice" after being ordered to pay administrative and other costs to the DRB.[59] Rosanelli did receive one mention in the *New York Times*. In a February 2004 letter that he wrote to the editor, that is.

Frank L. Armour is yet another New Jersey attorney who evaded serious consequences for his predatory actions. Yet another case of a lawyer caught with images depicting the assault and exploitation of children. Yet another six-month suspension and then right back to practicing law. Not a single line of print covers this case, like most of the rest. Armour was general counsel for the Newark Housing authority at the time.[60] Like so many previous cases here, Armour was downloading child pornography on a government computer during working hours. Just the fact that the public was paying for these predators to indulge themselves should be enough to make these stories in the public interest.

If you'll recall from just earlier in this chapter, a precedent was set that there was no "bright-line rule" preventing a sexual predator, even one who preys on children, from continuing to practice law. This came quite in handy for Jeffrey P. Ruddy. Despite sexually molesting *several* preteen boys, Ruddy faced no more than a two-year suspension from the bar. The court notes how they took into account Ruddy's "unblemished legal career" and "letters from friends and family attesting to his otherwise good character." I have to wonder how you even begin a letter like that. "Oh sure, Jeff is an exemplar of fine and upstanding moral character. I mean, apart from that whole raping several preteens thing, he's a great guy!"

Ruddy's 1992 case stems from June 1987 when the Essex County Grand Jury returned a fifteen-count indictment against him. Seven counts of second-degree sexual assault and eight counts of third-degree endangering the welfare of a child. What's even more disgusting is that Ruddy was using his position as a volunteer athletic coach to get close to the boys. The children were between the age of 10 and 12 and the abuse occurred over a two-and-a-half-year period.[61]

On June 28th of 1991, Ruddy would finally be sentenced to four concurrent terms... of five years' probation. That's right, sentenced to probation and psychotherapy and ordered to have no involvement with youth groups (many of these predators were involved in "charitable groups" and "activism," as I mentioned earlier, likely for reputation laundering in part, as well as access to victims in some cases). That bare minimum was only ordered "while on probation."

It was in Ruddy, I ran across "In re X" which perked my ears up. Why don't we have a name for this lawyer who raped his daughters for years? I can only hope his name not being listed was to protect the child victims, his own children. "X" admitted to raping his daughters, one of whom was currently under the age of thirteen and the other two between ages sixteen and eighteen at the time of the abuse. "X" was sentenced in 1989 to "three concurrent terms of five years at the Adult Diagnostic and Treatment Center at Avenel."[62]

In re Witherspoon from 2010 is yet another of the examples uncovered. David Witherspoon was charged with sexual harassment, sexual discrimination, and conflict of interest. This in addition to other charges related to practicing law while ineligible and "recordkeeping violations comprised of failing to maintain fully descriptive client ledgers, failing to conduct monthly trust account reconciliations and failing to maintain a running balance in the trust account checkbook ledger" which he argued was not a sign of any funny business but merely "oversight" on his part. The record plainly relates the casual attitude of the New Jersey Supreme Court when it comes to predators in public office and practicing law:

"We have, in the past, imposed shorter periods of suspension as the sanction for other types of sexual criminal convictions."[63]

The matter of In re Legato also makes it clear that this is a long-standing issue in the state. Legato was sexually chatting with, what he believed to be, a twelve-year-old girl. In addition to graphic sexual chat, Legato also "unzipped his pants and exposed his erect penis." Luckily, Legato was speaking with an undercover law enforcement officer rather than an actual preteen.

In a surprising move, even the DRB unanimously agreed on disbarment. That said, after a "psychosexual evaluation and risk assessment" Legato was deemed "not a risk for any offending." Legato would be sentenced to "a special sentence of parole supervision for life" in addition to being required to comply with Megan's Law. One of the rare instances where, even without any media coverage of the case, the offender was at least put on a sex offender registry. Again he was also court-ordered to continue therapy and his Internet and computer access were purportedly restricted "solely to work-related needs."

Justice Timpone, speaking for the court in the matter of the three predator lawyers, Legato, Kenyon, and Walter:

"These consolidated matters involve attorneys, with no previous disciplinary history, who pled guilty to sex offenses in which their intended victims were children ranging in ages from nine to twelve. Respondents Mark G. Legato and Regan C. Kenyon, Jr., each pled guilty to third-degree attempted endangering the welfare of a child. Respondent Alexander D. Walter pled guilty to third-degree endangering the welfare of a child. Each respondent was sentenced to parole supervision for life (PSL), NJSA.2C:43–6.4, and subject to the registration requirements of Megan's Law, NJSA 2C:7–1 to –11. Under Megan's Law, the respondents must, among other requirements, register their addresses, provide community notification, and submit to Internet registration. PSL subjects the respondents to supervision by the Division of Parole for at least fifteen years and to conditions such as counseling and limited Internet access and use."[64]

Later on: "Although discipline for sexual offenses has occasionally been as mild as reprimand, *see, e.g., In re Pierce*, 139 N.J.433, 655A.2d 438 (1995) (attorney convicted of lewdness for exposing his genitals to a twelve-year-old girl)..." Ah, you don't say. So it isn't as if the court isn't aware that a reprimand, suspension, and court-ordered therapy represent getting off a bit light for one of the most heinous crimes a person can commit.

The case of Mark G. Legato, Regan C. Kenyon, and Alexander D. Walter, by the way, dates back only to five years ago and cites the precedent related to there being no "bright-line rule" preventing predators who are accused of sex crimes against children from practicing law. It's unclear exactly where the line exists for the DRB and the Supreme Court of New Jersey. At least in a few cases, full disbarment occurred as in the case of Walter after being convicted on child endangerment charges after he "masturbated in the presence of a nine-year-old girl who had been living in his house."[65]

Yet another case of a simple suspension is that of Donald M. Ferraiolo. The attorney was suspended for one year after being convicted of third-degree endangerment of the welfare of a child. It is lucky that the "fourteen-year-old boy" that Ferraiolo was arranging to meet was a law enforcement officer. It does beg the question, how many of these cases are unknown? As we see with Cohen, some of these predators weren't exactly working hard to keep their sickness hidden, it's hard to believe that there haven't been several other cases that were more thoroughly covered up. Incidents with no paper trail in civil suits, DRB reports, or New Jersey Supreme Court rulings.

But even in cases where a child is harmed, so long as the feds aren't involved it seems to be the same pattern. The trend continues with Richard C. Gernert's one-year suspension for "petty disorderly offense of harassment by offensive touching."[66] Gernert was inappropriately touching a teenage client.

As of mid-August the time of this writing, several cases in the past few weeks involving northern New Jersey, and in some cases, specifically Union County dealt with child molestation and distribution of child pornography. In one case a former teacher convicted of molestation and possession of CSAM got absolutely no prison time, perhaps in part due to his well-to-do family.[67] A second case involves a teacher from Elizabeth, New Jersey. In the third case, a teacher collecting and distributing CSAM and taking pictures and videos of minor children without their knowledge also cropped up in the August 2022 news cycle in New Jersey.[68] These are just a few of the highlights from a very short period,[69] and with predators, like cockroaches, when you see one you can be certain that hundreds or thousands are hidden away.

A case from 2020 had a New Jersey correctional officer convicted of distribution of CSAM.[70]

Elizabeth in Union County, by the way, holds the dubious distinction of claiming the number 9 out of the top 10 list of most residents on the sex offender registry in the state.[71]

Was Kai the single instance of Joseph Galfy taking home an apparently indigent young man with the intent to drug and rape him? We may never know for certain; what can be confirmed, however, is that if you want to be a sex predator in a position of public power and keep your legal credentials, New Jersey seems to be the state to do it in.

CHAPTER 12

NIGHTMARE ON SKYLITE DRIVE

"You look lost." These were the first words uttered by Joseph Galfy when he found what appeared to be just another hitchhiker or homeless young man in his early 20s. It's likely that Joseph Galfy had no idea the young man he was picking up was world-renowned. It's also quite possible this is far from the first time that Galfy had picked up a young man who appeared lost, hungry, or in need of a roof for the night. I somehow doubt that this would have been done purely out of the goodness of his heart either.

Joseph Galfy offered Kai a ride to New Jersey. He already had plans to run into some people in the state and so he gladly accepted. They would arrive at Galfy's home in Clark, New Jersey on Starlite Drive.[1] Kai was under the impression he was in Newark, New Jersey as per text messages sent during this time.

Galfy prepared burgers and offered Kai beer. Kai recalls an especially bitter taste but assumed it was just an especially hoppy beer. Certain stouts, such as Old Rasputin Imperial Stout, for instance, are as or more bitter and strong tasting than certain adulterants that could be added to them making it more difficult to ascertain whether they have been contaminated.

When I reached out to Romankow, the former Union County prosecutor, he claimed that he and Galfy were not friends. That said, considering the small world of the Union County legal world and the fact that they surely ran into each other at events like the American Legion. Galfy managed to be "connected" to several people without being close to pretty much anyone.[2]

According to his younger brother, James Galfy in an interview with police, Joseph Galfy had owned the home in Clark on Starlite Drive for around 20 years. When asked if he was close with his brother, it becomes clear that Joseph Galfy was a guarded man, fiercely protective of his privacy who very few knew well.

They saw each other on holidays and birthdays, they shared Giant's season tickets. Sometimes Joseph would invite James to the Seton/Rutgers football matches. They were "football friends" as James puts it. Apart from these brief instances where their paths crossed, James admitted they "were kind of on opposite ends of the spectrum. [...] Just, just very different." He also admits that "he never told me much of anything, you know." James "knew as much about his business as his clients did, and that was about it." They just had "very, very different lifestyles that didn't necessarily match."

The interviewer with the police department asks if James ever met any of his brother's boyfriends. James mentions one "long term friend" he knew who had passed away a few years earlier.

"The only thing I know about is that he spent weekends... Saturdays I think in particular in New York City." But "what he did there, I never asked, he never said." They just had "different agendas." It appears that a daughter of James Galfy attempted a relationship with Galfy. Despite her repeated attempt to invite her uncle over it seems that any try at a get-together "fell through."[3]

Something I think is worth noting, is that James claims his brother wasn't "Mr. Handy" which would explain away young men coming and going. As for housework, cleaning and whatnot though, James was "sure he had people do it. I just didn't know who they were." Galfy rarely if ever used his front door. Perhaps this was just a side effect of being somewhat closeted due to his coming of age in "another era."

Galfy's former Deputy Police Chief brother admits that his older brother was known for cruising down to New York City on Saturdays. As for what these trips entailed, he doesn't know. Galfy engaged in what his brother refers to as an "alternate lifestyle." One of the few living persons his brother names that knew Joseph well is Norman Springer, a fellow lawyer who had moved to Las Vegas.[*]

Springer and Galfy served in the army together in the 70s according to his brother. Then "when the partnership split up maybe 5 years, 6 years later, uhm Norman moved to Las Vegas and he's been there ever since." Apart from Springer, Andy Baron is named as someone who might know Joseph Galfy's "business friends." The police interviewer also points out that in a city like Clark many of the attorneys and officials of the court tend to run in the same circles. This appears to be the case here. Especially judging from the many connections between people on both the defense and prosecution and even a judge having to recuse himself due to multiple conflicts.[5] Keep in mind how Union County judge Robert Mega only recused himself after Kai pointed out the many conflicts of interest there, including Galfy taking over as president of the Kiwanis Club from Mega and being partners at the

---

* According to the obituary at Neptune Society cremation services, Norman Harold Springer passed away Monday, March 21, 2022, around the time I began working on outlining this book, so I was unfortunately unable to reach out for a comment.[4]

same law firm for years.[6]

Andy Baron was one of about 30 people who showed up at Joseph Galfy's 70th birthday party at Luciano's in Rahway.[7] (Executive Chef Joseph Mastrella's restaurant has no known connection to Lucky Luciano, apart from the house salad being referred to as Lucky Luciano's,[8] just to be clear).

Oddly enough, James Galfy also brings up an incident with a vagrant or drifter who Joseph Galfy had had a run-in with "years ago." He claims "there was an issue" with a homeless man who Joseph Galfy maintained tried to rob him. Bear in mind, at this time, Kai was not a suspect so it's especially interesting to me that James Galfy seems to have been open to the idea that his brother had another "run in" with "some kind of a vagrant guy." Though he admits this incident was decades earlier and that in the end: "It could have been anybody."

He seems to start down a road that the interviewer abruptly shuts down:

8	JG:	And I mean years ago, we're talking early 70's probably uhm my parents had a
9		shore house.
10	TH:	Okay.
11	JG:	And initially he was living there uhm and there was an issue with some kind of a
12		vagrant guy who robbed him when he was down there.
13	TH:	Okay.
14	JG:	That was like 45 years ago if not more so what type of people he ran into and who
15		they were...
16	TH:	Uh-huh.
17	JG:	It could have been anybody.

(handwritten in left margin: I EVEN A SUSPECT AT THIS POINT)

From Detective Harrison's interview with Joseph Galfy's brother, James.

"And I don't know what, what the..." is immediately interrupted by the police interviewer's interjection.

"Cops tend to be very suspect... most other people tend to be more naive and if your brother was a... an alternate lifestyle attorney. God knows what kind of..."

"Right," James Galfy replies.

One of Joseph Galfy's trips to New York City, he had a heart attack and instead of immediately seeking a doctor's treatment decided to drive himself home. The grand jury transcript notes that the medication and pills in Galfy's home were consistent with those used by someone with a heart condition. I was unaware that the erectile dysfunction prescription, Cialis, is a "heart drug."[9]

Cialis, by the way, has often been combined with amphetamines or cocaine during "PNP" (Party and play) which is popular in some sectors of the gay cruising scene.[10] NBC and other major media have covered the "epidemic" of "chemsex" in a subculture of the gay community which can involve mixtures of GHB and crystal meth.[11] Another rich predator who used his connections to prey on the homeless and marginalized was political super-donor Ed Buck who was found responsible for at least two deaths over a period of several years.[12]

James Galfy seems to go on a fishing investigation at one point. Asking for any available information that might help with "funeral arrangements." He also makes a strange statement regarding "securing" the scene.[13] Now, yes, this is a man who was a police officer for 31 years, but he is not investigating this case. His being allowed into an active crime scene is a potential explanation for the mysterious circumstance of the dishwasher being run. Destroying any evidence of the glasses or mugs being drugged. Prosecutor

Scott Peterson echoes this same turn of phrase, "secure the house" to describe officers at the scene after Galfy is found dead due to a welfare check when he didn't show up to work that Monday.[14]

Crime scene photo DSC-0156 [DA114].
Photo of the dishwasher before it was mysteriously run during the active investigation.

What led Kai to that house, that horrible night, in Clark, New Jersey started with him planning to visit the state to see a fan, Kimberly Conley. He had contacted her while he was in New York City May 2013. After the Kimmel show, he headed east.[15] He ended up in Newport, Rhode Island. From there he took a bus to Providence. From Lovecraft country, Kai headed into the Big Apple, New York City. He had already messaged Kim from the Providence Public Library. There was a five-hour layover on the Peter Pan bus before he pulled in.

Kai already knew Times Square somewhat. He walked from the Port Authority up to Columbia University and ended up spending the night in the city that never sleeps sheltered by a cardboard tent that got rained out. The next day was May 11th. Little did Kai know this was one of the last days before his life would change forever again. This time for the worse.

To raise a few bucks he went busking. He had a bit at a restaurant by Tompkins Square Park and came back to the area of Times Square he landed in. Later that day around five o'clock, Galfy approaches outside of the Red Lobster in Times Square.

When explaining to the court, Kai was constricted in what he could actually say.

"Mr. Galfy approached me. A Do I have — am I kind of tied on what I can answer? Like, what can I say?"

Kai explained that he had asked officers of the NYPD how to get to the train to New Jersey because the plan was still to head that way to meet Kim Conley. The police informed him he'd need to go back up to 7th Street and over to Penn station. Once he made it to 7th he was checking street signs to see if he was on the right track. It was then Galfy approached him asking if he was "lost" and needed help.

Kai explained he was on the east coast in from Dogtown, originally from Canada, headed to New Jersey.

"Oh, I'm headed to New Jersey," Galfy responded. At the time it may have seemed like a stroke of good luck. It was certainly a sort of luck, far from good. As he pointed out, hundreds of people who had seen his videos often approached him. Regularly offering him rides, inviting him back to hang out, taking him out for food or beers. He was something of a sensation due to the incident in Fresno and the mentions on multiple late-night shows and news around the world.

Kai stepped into the PT Cruiser and they began driving away. Galfy asked what he does and Kai responded explaining he's a traveling musician who works in construction. He responded, "I am a lawyer in construction and I have friends who are contractors." Kai asked him if he knew anyone looking for a skilled carpenter.

Kai goes on, "And he looked at me and was like, I am sure somebody could find a use for you. And then he was like telling me about he didn't have — usually have friends from Canada over and asked which part of Canada I was from."

They exchanged pleasantries, a situation not out of the ordinary for anyone who has ever hitched a ride or picked up a hitcher.

At one point, Kai begins to speak, "Yes, there was one incident that stood out in my mind. He stopped —" but Peterson objects before he can finish his thought.

Kai goes on in the court transcript to describe getting off the freeway ("or the parkway or something you call it here.")

"Yeah, but anyways, he got off at the main freeway and he stopped at this residential street and this was right at a corner lot and he pointed out the corner lot house and he said, 'As long as you leave two walls standing at any point in time, you can completely rebuild a house on a renovation permit, instead of a construction permit and save yourself tens of thousands of dollars on municipal taxes,' and he went on about this for a while, but I remember that because he actually parked there to show me and it had to do with construction so…"

They pull into the garage behind the house. "I don't usually park out here because I have nosy neighbors who don't mind their own business," Galfy explained to him.[16] It's a two-port car garage with a shiny BMW, rarely ever driven, in the right-hand port. A fridge is in the garage and beyond that a landing heading up inside the house.

While inside the house, Kai gave Kimberly a call as Galfy called a restaurant. "Let's watch some TV and wait for the food," Galfy decided. He turned the news on and in about ten minutes said, "All right, let's go get the food." The two drove around the corner to Mijo's Pizza.

It was around a quarter to 7 p.m. when they headed out considering the 6:30 call to Kim.

They got to Mijo's. Galfy warned Kai to stay put. "Stay out here, I don't want anyone to see I have a guest." Kai assumed it was because of the extra time it takes doing introductions. Meanwhile, he asked if Kai had any cigarettes. "Because I probably smelled like it at the time," Kai reasoned. They stopped at a convenience store around the corner from the house, Galfy went in got a pack of Newports and they drove back to his house. After about a 5-to-10-minute ride they were back at Galfy's home on Starlite Drive.

Galfy carried the food in, placed it all on the island counter. There was an l-shaped counter set into the walls with a serving counter on top with two different sides. He plated up some food and told Kai to have a seat on one of the barstools. At this point, he asked if Kai would like a beer. Kai accepted.

While sitting at the island on a barstool, Galfy pours himself some wine and turns to Kai. "Do you know what, beer always tastes better in a glass. Here, give me your bottle." Kai obliges.

"At that point, I didn't have any reason to distrust him, so..."

Galfy gave him his first beer and food, put the plate on a serving counter. Then Kai went outside for a cigarette. He asked where a bathroom could be found. Last door on the left, Galfy explained. It was the second door on the left, just past his bedroom.

When recounting this, the judge admonished Kai for speaking too quickly. He explained that he was nervous about saying the wrong thing considering some factual elements that add context to the case were not allowed to be heard by the jury. In addition, even on phone interviews, Kai has difficulty going into detail relating what he recalls from that nightmarish night. As most assault victims naturally do.

Kai went to use the restroom, washed his hands, and walked down the hallway. He saw Galfy standing inside the kitchen pouring another beer into a glass.

"'Hold on a second there,' and he handed me my beer. And the way he handed it to me, I thought maybe he was Greek or something. I was like 'Oh thanks, man.' 'All right, let's watch some TV.'"

Kai sat on the right-hand side, Galfy on the left and they watched TV as he sipped his second beer. They watched TV for a couple of hours as Kai texted Kim on his phone.

Trouble arose during the trial when he tried to explain showing Galfy the interview:

"Well, first of all, I said, Hey, I got this video that is trending with millions of views, do you want to see it?"

Peterson, the prosecutor whipped into action: "Objection, Your Honor."

The judge was quick to relent to the state, sustaining the objection. Kai went on to explain that they watched several YouTube videos while engaged in conversation. The prosecutor asked if the conversation veered into the inappropriate.

"Not that I thought of at the time. Hindsight some of what he said about his vacations out of the country could be like kind of creepy." Kai explained further, "I have to provide a full context for the conversation. I don't know if I'm allowed to do that."

The judge asked them to move on to the next question, Cito, the court-appointed public defender was quick to assent and the judge explained his reasoning.

"I view this as irrelevant. Where Mr. Galfy may have vacationed is irrelevant." Even if it's a hotspot for child trafficking? A location in Thailand not only considered a hub of worldwide child sex tourism[17] but also a spot that a former mayor of Clark mentions[18] as having been a favorite vacation spot of Galfy, irrelevant?

Galfy poured another beer. "He told me about this young friend he had living with him before, who whenever guests came over, he got really drunk.

and the way he said it was weird, so I asked him what do you mean by he got really drunk."

From the sounds of it, a young man who frequented Galfy's may have been inebriated past the point of consent with something untoward being possibly hinted at.

Galfy pours another beer and hands it to Kai with a flourish ("placed ceremoniously" are the words he uses during the trial.)

Galfy said that he would give Kai a ride to Newark. Up till now, Kai assumed he was in Newark. Conley had warned him that Newark after dark was unsafe when on a call with her. At the end of the night, Galfy still seemed just like a friendly, good Samaritan. "Just leave the lights off. I don't want any of my neighbors to see that I have young guests over."

This "didn't seem weird at first" Kai explains. After all, it could just be busybody neighbors.

Plans fell through with Kim the next day. It was Mother's Day weekend so she was spending time with her family.

"I have such a bad feeling about where you are right now, you shouldn't stay there tonight" she had told him on the phone. "Kai tried to assure her by explaining he'd slept in downtown LA at night, in areas where there were 'Vatos Locos, MS-13, Hell's angels... And I'm not racist or looking for trouble, so I didn't get any trouble with that. It's like 'Leave it to Beaver' out here."

Right in the middle of saying this, he looked down and she wasn't on the phone, "I'm like, Oh, my God, I didn't take her advice, I must have pissed her off. So I called her, I left a message. I texted her. I was like, did your phone die. And I finished my cigarette. She called again, she thought it was sketchy that a lawyer from New Jersey would offer—" at this point again, he was cut off by the court before he could go into further details. Potentially salient details regarding intentions of a lawyer who randomly picks up homeless people in Times Square to spend the night at their house. Any mention of that was stricken from the record.

Kai went ahead and made plans to meet after her Mother's Day lunch at noon. He headed back into the house and asked Galfy if he could charge his phone. He went to the bathroom, used the toilet and washed his hands. He walked up the hall towards the kitchen. This was a little after 10 p.m.

Kai came out of the bathroom a second time and was offered another beer, again "really ceremoniously." Again, it had already been poured out of Kai's line of sight. "Thanks man," Kai replied. They sat down, watched more videos on YouTube for about an hour. Then Kai made his way outside for a cigarette. He returned to the house around 11 p.m. and headed to the bathroom. As he walked back down the hallway from the bathroom, he saw Galfy standing in the kitchen. Galfy had a dark beer in his hand

"Hey, Guiness," Kai said. He took a drink.

"[I]t was disgusting, he said, I know how much you appreciate beer, so I know you'll appreciate this beer because it's a special German beer."

Another 15 minutes or so of watching videos. Kai says he "drank that beer very quickly because it was disgusting." It left a metallic taste in his mouth. At the time he pondered whether a filling might have come loose in his mouth. All of a sudden, he was feeling really drunk. Perhaps similarly over-intoxicated to the "young friend" Galfy had hinted at earlier. "Hey, I'm feeling kind of drunk. I think I should probably go to bed; where is the guest room?"

"Well, don't you want to have a shower first." Kai is about to say yeah when Galfy finishes his sentence. "With me," he replies. "No, no thank you, sorry, I'm, I'm hetero."

Before now he had not realized Galfy was gay. It hadn't registered, considering Kai never had difficulties with people based on race or gender or sexual orientation, why would it be a situation. It did come out of the blue, such bluntness without any obvious hints leading up to it. "[He] wasn't dropping any innuendo" or "running any game on me at all," Kai explained. "[It] didn't set off alarm bells because I stayed with gay people before."

Once more Kai headed to use the bathroom and was shown the guest room. A long hallway leads to the other end of the house. If you turn right, a shorter hallway leads to the guest bedroom.

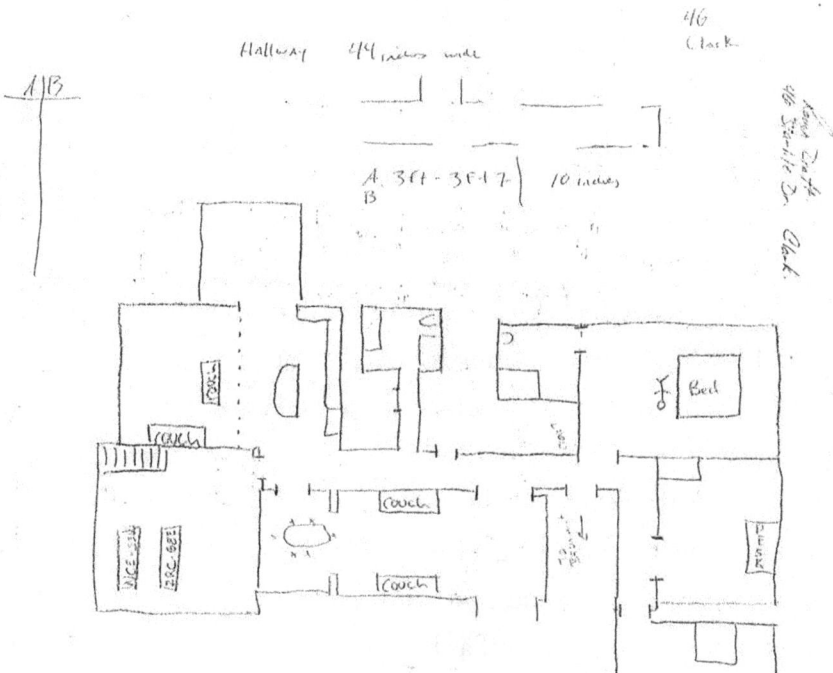

Rough draft of Galfy residence drawn during investigation.

"This is where you're going to be sleeping tonight," Galfy told him. "All right, thanks," Kai replied.

Speaking of things that didn't register at the time but seem ominous in hindsight. Galfy directed Kai to, "just make sure you leave the door unlocked, so I can wake you up in the morning." Kai says he passed out as soon as he hit the bed.

When asked in court if he disrobed, he explained he "didn't want to send any signals." From personal experience, I've learned that gay guys are, in the end, still just guys. Meaning, a significant percentage of them either don't know how to read obvious signals or just don't care.

Kai passed out heavily layered. Wearing sweater, shirt, jeans. He'd taken his shoes off at least but was even still wearing his socks. This is some time around 11 p.m. to 11:20.

He woke up with Galfy in the room, no warning, no knock. Just Galfy, in a reddish polo shirt and jeans, standing over him. "It's time to get up." Kai didn't hear him come in, open the door, not a sign that he was on his way in.

Kai got up, stretched. Quick trip to the bathroom and a glance in the mirror. It's while he was washing his hands that he saw it. The glint catching his eye, there it is. Some sort of a residue on the side of his face. It tasted salty. In addition to the salty residue, his whole mouth was full of a bitter metallic taste that lingered throughout the day. Kai says he was used to smoking about a pack of cigarettes a day at that point. Regular smoking weakens senses of smell and taste, so it must have been fairly rank for him to register it. He washed it off as best he could and walked back to the end of the hall by the kitchen where Galfy was standing.

"Thought you might be hungry, so I made you a muffin."

Galfy asked how to get a hold of him. They exchanged email and phone numbers as well as Facebook profile information. It's this info casually left in the house that led to his arrest.** Galfy told him the info and he wrote it down while Kai was eating.

He asks how long it takes to get to Asbury. He's still hoping to see Kim that day. "I'll take you to the train station, you should be there about eleven o'clock." He texts Kim to say he is on the way. The PT Cruiser leaves the cul-de-sac, turns left, and goes straight.

Finally, he ended up at Rahway. On video Kai was seen vigorously yet absent-mindedly brushing his teeth. He's told me that the metallic taste** **lingered all day long. Zopiclone, a powerful sleeping pill used in Canada and the UK. It is known to create blackout states and has a side effect of a metallic taste.[19] Though it's not prescribed in the US, the early 2010s was the heyday of easy access to pharmaceuticals and research chemicals ordered online from Canada and elsewhere.[20]

They were parked outside the Rahway train station. There's a large quonset outside, a roof with no walls on three sides set into the place. They were parked a ways back and walking past were a group of 20-something Black folks having a casual conversation. Galfy warns Kai, "Stay away from those, n*****s like that will only get you in trouble." It seems that being excessively closeted isn't the only baggage Galfy picked up from his past. Then again, considering what I've learned about the justice system in that region it's not

---

* If he's so "calculating", then why would he leave a direct trail back to himself if he believed that he had killed Galfy? This along with the fact the prosecution could never come up with any motivation for a young man who had the world on a string to throw it all away to have his rights deprived by a group of corrupt cronies in Union County.

** Zopiclone has a similarly bitter and metallic taste to that of the oddly bitter beer the night before. The night Kai woke up with what he had hoped was just dried saliva on his face and a strange taste in his mouth that persisted throughout the day, again consistent with what people who have taken Zopiclone have described.

surprising when the mayor and the chief of police and sergeant of public affairs are all openly using the n-word and even berating their own minority employees.

Galfy and Kai got off the elevator and headed up to the ticket machine, "Could you help me out with this? I've never used one of these before." This claim, by the way, is disproved by Galfy's financial records, specifically a purchase from two weeks earlier from the same machine.[21]

Still unaware of what all had happened while he was passed out, he simply thanked Galfy and gave him a hug. Galfy tells him any time he's in the area to let him know and he could stay in his guest room. For now, nothing quite clicking yet. Kai still gave him full benefit of the doubt and despite some odd moments, Galfy seemed friendly enough if a little overeager in the attempted eroticism department. Galfy waited there with him for the train to arrive.

Kai headed to Asbury Park, changing trains at Long Branch. He got to Asbury Park shortly after 11, called, and left a message with Kimberly. Just waiting around in the transportation center for about an hour until noon. At one point a guy on a bike offers some food. "Hell yeah," Kai replied enthusiastically. He asked him to meet him on the other side of the tunnel at a church where he was able to grab some sustenance.

He asked to take some dinner rolls with him. One of the ladies at the church obliged, bagging them up for him. Walked back to the transportation center and received a text from Kimberly. She informed Kai she was still at brunch and had missed the call and wouldn't be free for a bit longer.

He sat there on the benches outside the transportation center for hours eating dinner rolls and scrolling through Facebook. At one point he exchanged messages with Erin Wagner who he was planning to stay with the night after he had planned to see Kim.

Kai was not used to the relatively hot New Jersey summer, he was more accustomed to Canadian summers where the heat generally doesn't break the upper 70s. He took off his sweater and when that didn't do the trick, decided to cut his hair, especially since a future stop planned was (even hotter and more humid) Atlanta to meet a producer and record some music. Coming from the subtropical south, I can confirm that having long hair during the hottest and most humid months in that area can be genuinely oppressive.

Kai takes his indigenous ancestry very seriously though and hair is an important part of that for him. "Whenever I cut my hair, I make a braid out of it and I take it out into the wilds, to the prairie or the mountains and I make a — I make an offering to Kise Manitou with it and I leave a gift of tobacco there." Oddly enough, the frames showing this are among the ones "missing" according to the police who requisitioned the closed-circuit footage. This was helpful for them considering they ignored the short hairs in Galfy's car or mashed into the vertical side of Galfy's mattress to try and make the claim he cut his hair after the fact.

For them, it's reasonable that a person who couldn't go into public without being recognized would cut his hair to make his distinctive facial tattoo more visible because he's "on the run."[22] It's also reasonable that said viral celeb would introduce himself in a semi-groggy state and sign autographs while "on the run." These, we are led to believe by the state, are the actions of a "calculating" man to cover the tracks of his "premeditated" act.

Time passed slowly. He called another friend in California while waiting around. Now he's feeling a little awkward and insecure. That feeling when you're waiting somewhere unfamiliar seeming out of place. Feeling a bit overwrought, in addition to the heat, he cut his jeans into shorts and worked out for about an hour to burn off extra energy and keep his mind and body busy until around 3 pm.

After this, he headed to wash up in the bathroom. Afraid to stay in this area that Kimberly had warned him about but torn about whether to contact Galfy, Kai considered his options. Though he was in Asbury Park, he was under the impression he was in Greater Newark, perhaps because Galfy had mentioned living in Newark on their trip from Times Square. He resigned himself to heading back to escape potential danger after dark in what he thought was Newark. Took the train back up closer to where Galfy stayed, stopped at Long Branch. He had been hiding in the bathroom due to not being able to afford a ticket. He walked over to Dunkin Donuts to charge his phone which had run down while talking to friends on Facebook, then called Galfy. He answered and Kai asks if he could stay another night in the guest room as opposed to staying in what he believed to be a dangerous area after dark.

He left a message with Kimberly, "Hey, I think this guy is Greek. If I don't eat food with him, that's the biggest insult you could do to somebody from the Mediterranean, if they prepare food and stuff." Told her he still wanted to hang out the next day, to go for supper or something perhaps at her friend Erin's place.

Kai walked up a ramp to find a map similar to the one that Metro transit in L.A. has. He had a conversation with Kimberly on the phone. He got a call back from Galfy, put on his bag, and headed to the ticket booth where Galfy told him to wait for him. A bit later he received a text saying he would be arriving in about 10 minutes. He heard a honk and saw the red PT Cruiser.

Kai thanked him for picking him up on short notice since he'd been "ghosted." Galfy's response was to ask if the friend was a girl. "Oh that figures," Galfy replied. "You shouldn't trust girls, they aren't as trustworthy as boys are." Considering what would happen later that night, this is a tragically ironic statement.

Kai asked him about what New York City was like, but Galfy quickly changed the subject. He instead asked Kai about his experience on the boardwalk. Kai responded that he hadn't visited the boardwalk. Galfy told him he had work the next day and would need Kai to get to bed early so he assumed this meant no staying up to 11 watching TV. "In hindsight," Kai related on the stand, "that has a completely different meaning."

It was Sunday, May 12th, Mother's Day. The holiday was the reason plans fell through with Kimberly since she had an engagement with her family. They made small talk. Galfy talked about work he was doing regarding licensing a commercial project for natural gas, how superior natural gas was to nuclear power.

It was about 20 minutes to 7 p.m. when they pulled in again, to the left-hand side of the two-car garage. Kai put his bag around the corner where he had stored it the first night, turned on the TV and Galfy offered to cook some food.

Kai recalled seeing some news about a Mother's Day parade in New Orleans that was shot up. Again, Galfy offered Kai a beer. He first handed the beer to Kai in the bottle. Kai absentmindedly peels the label until Galfy again offered to "pour it into a glass like last night." From his seat watching the TV Kai couldn't see the beer being poured from the island behind him.

From the first sip, he again recognized the bitter taste. "It was that nasty beer from the night before," he explained. He only took a couple of sips at first, waiting for the burger Galfy prepared to help mask the caustic taste.

They had their burgers, Galfy offered yet another beer. The second was poured in front of him, a lighter beer than the one from earlier and the previous night. This was the only beer Kai actually saw being poured in front of him.

From here on, Kai recalled feeling "warm and fuzzy and like relaxed and stuff." Galfy rinsed the plates and dropped them in the dishwasher (the same dishwasher that any evidence of Kai being drugged would be destroyed in).

"The last thing I remember is hearing the Jeopardy theme and then I was on the floor of his room on my back."

When he woke, everything was spinning, light was oppressively bright and painful, he felt Galfy on top of him, tugging at his jeans. Kai was lying on his back, sat up, and punched him in the face as hard as he could from his position. All the while, his head shrieked in pain, his cognition cloudy.

Kai's face was shoved into the mattress, resulting in the freshly cut short hairs being embedded into the vertical face of the mattress rather than the top of the bed. This is another reason why carpet materials and the stains, along with the "unidentified blood" on Galfy's penis should have been tested, rather than blatantly ignored.

Galfy was "humping and grinding" against him, his penis out. Kai remembered trying to fight his way out from under the much heavier Galfy. He remembered potentially kicking him away from him at some point. He felt suffocated, the amount of fear that occurs when you are being choked out and unable to breathe is impossible to describe if you've never had it happen. Suffice it to say, it is one of the most painful and frightening experiences a person can be subjected to. Same with sexual assault. Combining the two, on top of a drugged semi-conscious state is a recipe for disaster. Whatever happened in the blackout state, even the prosecution agrees it didn't take long.[24] The fact that the rest of the crime scene was mostly clear also shows that Galfy didn't move far. The activity was confined to a small area.

Another clue regarding the area in question is the urine stain. The way it's positioned on the floor is consistent with Kai lying on the carpet, emptying his bladder in response to the assault in a drugged state where he had limited use of his faculties and control of his body. With his groin on the spot where the stain was, Kai's head would have been mashed into the mattress.

The police and prosecution made a show of mentioning how there are no signs of semen or other evidence of assault while conspicuously making no mention of the evidence that the assault happened on the floor with Kai's head directly against the side of the mattress, not the top of the bed. The crime scene photos of the area also disprove the theory that he cut his hair after the fact "on the run." As you should be realizing by now, the more you take a look at the facts of the case and the context of the county and state it occurred in the more sense it makes that a federal judge would rule aspects of the farce of a proceeding a clear conspiracy to violate his due process. No theories here, a federal judge ruled that Kai had made his case for conspiracy to violate his rights.

Crime scene photo DSC-0270 [DA104]. A urine stain is visible on the carpet that could have been screened for presence of drugs.

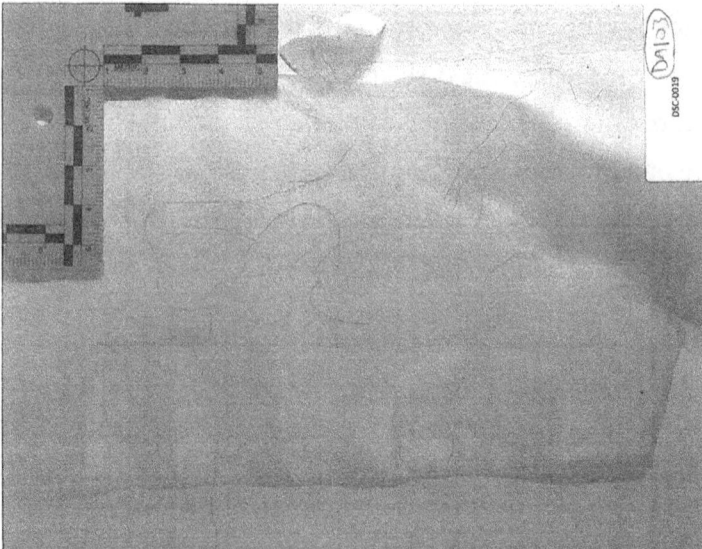

Crime scene photo DSC0019 [DA013]. You can clearly see short, dark hairs firmly attached to the side of the mattress, consistent with Kai's claims regarding his location on the floor in Galfy's bedroom and his hair being cut before the incident.

The room was neat and orderly, bed made. If there had been a tussle from a standing position, the 220-pound lawyer would have knocked things over. Shelves and other items in the room would have been knocked out of place. Hitting upwards from underneath is the only reasonable position that Kai could have been in to prevent the large lawyer from being knocked backward into things.

The prosecution wanted the jury to believe that despite a bright future Kai would throw it all away on a murder with no motive. Galfy, a wealthy lawyer, had cash, gold ingots and valuable coins in his house.[25] Prosecution even tried to allege that the act was premeditated since he went back the second night. If so, then why would he have left all the evidence including his email and bag. It boggles the mind that the judge could rightly note that he is a bright young man but ignore these glaring inconsistencies in their claim.

As pointed out by the exhibits and not disputed by the prosecution, there were tracks of blood heading down the hall from the bedroom.[26] This lines up with Kai's recollection of waking up, finding his pants down, and Galfy above him. He had a rug burn from his supine position, laying on his back below Galfy. This conflicts with the picture painted by prosecution, despite agreement on the rest of the details. The abrasions that resulted in Galfy's ear being ripped were likely from the jean fabric dragging against his heel making contact with him as he struggled to get away from the much heavier, over 200-pound lawyer.

Perhaps a medical examiner who hadn't received a generous payout to his department might have had a different "professional opinion" but contrary to Dr. Shaikh's claims evidence supports Kai laying on the ground. If he had stood over Galfy grabbing his head and yanking it as the state's case repeatedly claimed there would be grab marks and bruises. The only grab marks evident on Galfy are at his wrists which is consistent with Kai's claims of trying to fight him off as he awoke, face mashed violently against the vertical side of the mattress.[27]

Checking the forensic reports, the autopsy, nowhere is any mention found of grab marks or bruises on his head or neck. His face was found face down, neck broken in three places.[28] This is consistent with frontal blows as Kai was kicking upward as the shorter, but much stockier lawyer hovered above him. Kicks upward could cause the damage evident, but the grabbing and yanking claims are not supported by forensic evidence.

The type of force the yanking would have required would have left bruises or marks of some sort that simply did not appear. Galfy's injured ear showed signs of abrasion, think of a rope burn, it's tissue damage from friction. Again this is consistent with the jean fabric scraping across his ear as Kai tried to kick his way loose.

A rag was also found at the scene. Kai believes it was used to wipe off semen. It was entered into evidence, but conspicuously never analyzed.[29]

While fighting him off, his jeans down to his ankles, no underwear, he fought off Galfy as quickly as possible and left the residence. Kai doesn't even remember leaving the place, his next clear memory is being in a parking lot with fingers burned on some matches.

Kai regained most of his consciousness over the next few hours. He found himself in a parking lot. Every muscle in his body on fire, a pounding headache and that same nasty metallic taste on top of the vague memories of the nightmare he'd just escaped.

Kai asked for a glass of water at a restaurant and was told to "kick rocks." Then he wandered off to a diner and then a 7-Eleven. At the diner, he met with brothers John and Rob McNamara whose testimony of how Kai seemed drugged was suppressed not only in the grand jury but also the trial itself.[30]

In the diner, looking in the mirror there's a flashback scenario. The same residue, the same sickening taste of dried semen. At this point, Kai vomited in the toilet. Or tried to at least, all he was able to muster was dry heaving.

Up until now, it was possible to believe that spot on his face was just dried saliva the night before. Now it was just one more piece of evidence that he had been assaulted by Galfy.

Kai splashed water on his face, trying to clear the fog. He downs some water, trying to relieve the disgusting metallic taste that zopiclone users have said tends to persist throughout the day. Kai took pictures with the McNamaras, they talk for a bit, have dinner and go outside to have a smoke as they talk about the video related to Kai's heroic act in Fresno.

When Kai pointed out on the stand that the interviews with the McNamaras corroborate his claim of being drugged, Prosecutor Peterson objected. "He is asking for facts that weren't put into evidence at all." Ah, so he's expected to prove self-defense by proving intoxication but all evidence of being drugged and raped is either not collected, destroyed, or not allowed into evidence?[23] Sure, seems fair.

John McNamara offered Kai money for the train station and pointed out the way. His phone was now ruined, smelling "like urine and burnt plastic." Likely damaged during the assault and while fighting off the rapist. With no phone, Kai made his way walking for what seemed like forever, feeling dead tired due to the traumatic events and lingering effects of the rape drugs he was slipped hours earlier.

Walking past the 7-Eleven, he tried asking a guy for directions relative to the train station at which point the man "gave [him] the run around."

"I already had a headache, and I was like, do you know what, thanks anyways, and I turned to walk out the door and he called out after me, Oh, maybe you could try going back to the center of Clark."

Suddenly, there's an unbidden flashback: Kai envisioned Galfy getting up and coming after him with a gun. There was no way he was going to head back in the direction of where Galfy was. Kai headed to the Rahway train station not far from the 7-Eleven. Sitting on the bench was uncomfortable with his posterior still sore from the recent events. His head was still cloudy and was concerned with making sure he had his ticket.

While trying to find a way to charge his phone he couldn't fight the evocation of memories of Galfy every time the pungent scent of urine entered his nostrils. He threw the malfunctioning phone out, though unable to shake the painful memories they brought up.

Kai was at the Rahway station for about 45 minutes and got on the train and headed back to Long Branch where he spent the night under a box car with a makeshift cardboard mattress. He borrowed a phone from a train conductor later, tried to call Kim. He didn't want to leave a message about the rape in front of the conductor. It was around 1:30 or 2 a.m. when he finally pulled into Long Branch.

When he finally got a hold of Kim he explained the damage to his phone but going into details was difficult as it caused flashbacks of the fright and degradation experienced under Galfy's weighty frame. The conductor told Kai that the train would stop at Long Branch. There would be no connecting train to Asbury until the morning. Kai got off the train at Long Branch and slept under a railcar, which had been converted into a diner. The next morning, he got on the train to Asbury. At the Asbury Park Transportation

Center, he asked someone for the location of a Salvation Army to get some food and if there was somewhere he could use a public computer. He was pointed towards a Salvation Army near a library. He availed himself of both, and tried to contact Kim on Facebook via the internet.

She asked Kai where they should meet. When they got together, they headed to a friends of hers in Philadelphia. Once face to face with Kim, he told her about what happened. Bringing up the fact he was raped by Galfy to Kim was stricken from the record by the judge despite it being central to his self-defense argument.

Kai explained his reticence to call the police was due to his illegal immigrant status. Not to mention the fact that the rapist was a rich lawyer with connections, which, as can be seen with the likes of Ed Buck who also had a penchant for bringing indigents into his home to drug them, have sex with them, and occasionally kill them via overdose, the wealthy and well-connected all too often just get away with horrific crimes. Whether it's Harvey Weinstein, Jeffrey Epstein, Peter Nygard or the DuPont heir put on house arrest for viciously raping his 3-year-old daughter,[31] laws just don't seem to apply to the rich and politically powerful as they do to average persons.

In order to prevent even more trauma on top of what he'd already dealt with, Kai just told Kim that he had called the police about the incident already. He had hoped to confront Galfy later with a reporter friend, perhaps Shane Dixon Kavanaugh. At this time, Kai had no idea that Galfy was no longer alive.

Kai spent another night with friends of friends. Specifically, Erin the friend of Kimberly's in Philadelphia and her boyfriend. That morning, it was just Erin and her friend Bob.[32] He woke up, did some yoga as per his traditional routine. He was thinking of how he did need to confront Galfy somehow. Perhaps contacting some people from the media who had reached out to him in the past, could help with that, he thought. "Hey, creep, how many other homeless people were there, you know."*

Kai asked to use her computer, logged into his Facebook account and suddenly in the midst of another flashback of the previous night just had an outpouring of emotion that expressed itself as that last Facebook status update.

Caleb Kai Lawrence Yodhehwawheh
May 15, 2013 ·

what would you do if you woke up with a groggy head, metallic taste in your mouth, in a strangers house... walked to the mirror and seen come dripping from the side of your face from your mouth, and started wretching, realizing that someone had drugged, raped, and blown their fuckin load in you? what would you do?

931   38 Comments 275 Shares

Kai's last Facebook post

After spending more time with Erin and her friends, they head to a mall, have pizza, and drop him off at a train station in Philly. There he meets a woman, Sam Blaker, who asks him to walk with her to work and offers for them to hang out later.

Blaker worked at a gentleman's club; she had one of the other dancers there drive them to the train station. They took the train to a place near her grandparents' house where he slept in the garage.

Kai was sent a Western Union transfer that couldn't be claimed in Philadelphia as it was sent to New Jersey. After that, he and Sam went to

---

* This, not surprisingly, was stricken from the record.

Rittenhouse Square where they hung out, had some beer, doing some street performing.

It was when Kai headed into a Starbucks that he was recognized and came to the attention of law enforcement in Philadelphia.[33] He had offered to sing a woman's favorite Beatles song in exchange for a coffee ("All My Loving"). Then headed to the Greyhound station.

Lounging on a bench, a uniformed man tells Kai to get up. "Are you Kai?" He "looked like a security guard" and Kai at first assumed it was yet another person wanting a selfie. Kai was put under arrest. He was told that some people in New Jersey were seeking him.

Kai's first assumption was that Galfy may have tried to get him arrested on some "made up shit story" such as robbery to explain whatever black eye or other injuries sustained while Kai was fighting him off. During that first interview Kai used words like "blacked out," "dazed," "confused," and "black hole" to describe the fuzzy, unreachable spot in his memory from the traumatic assault and drugging.

During Prosecutor Scott Peterson's cross-examination, he referred to Galfy affectionately as "Joe" impugned Kai's claims and spoke sarcastically of the panic attack Kai described occurring when he was first being interviewed by Detective Johnny Ho.

Peterson even brings up how when asked to take a picture with fans at the White Diamond Diner he is seen smiling. "That's not a real smile. That's, that's not being a jerk."[34] The classic sex offender's excuse of "but look at this picture with us, the supposed victim is smiling" somehow has managed to persist even into the post-#MeToo era.

On cross-examination, Kai brings up yet another striking bit of evidence ignored. Namely, the rug burn on his back that came from the tussle while he was on the ground.[35] Head mashed into the side of a mattress, urinating in pure terror.

When all was said and done the most vital pieces of evidence that could have exonerated Kai and proved exactly what happened that night were ignored, not collected or destroyed. Four hours of surveillance footage[36] and even testimony from witnesses were not allowed to be entered. This material supported Kai's claim of being drugged by Galfy. And all the while, Kai was expected to prove himself despite the best efforts of Union County authorities in ensuring Galfy's dirty secrets died with him.

CHAPTER 13

TWO SETS OF LAWS

In the United States, we are taught that justice is blind and that all have equal access to and protection under the law. In reality, that access to the law is highly dependent on multiple factors. It's like the old joke of how we operate under a capital punishment system: if you don't have the capital, you get punished. In recent years, this disparity has become more and more obvious.

If you look at the great lengths that rich and powerful people have gone to cover their dirty deeds, trends such as media suppression and abuse of the legal profession show up time and again. The disparity between "legal persons"[1] (i.e. corporate entities) and "natural persons"[2] is another worrying trend related to this phenomenon. Unscrupulous members of the media and the legal profession are responsible for sheltering the perpetrators of massive corruption and criminality.

Previously in this book, we've dealt with police and prosecutorial misconduct, bribery, and corruption throughout Union County and New Jersey as a whole. I do not mean to propose that New Jersey is unique in its culture of corruption. I asked police whistleblower Samuel Clark about regional corruption and he feels, as do I, that there are "flavors" of corruption[3] that change from time to time and place to place, but the root situation: greed for power and money, stays the same.

The issue of prosecutorial misconduct is hard to fight. What's worse is when you see figures with a history of corruption ending up being promoted to their level of corruption. Journalist Brian "BZ" Douglas has spent over a year and a half reporting on multiple cases of corruption and misconduct related to Dan Kasaris. The issues date back to the 2000s when he was a county prosecutor. Since then he's become the Ohio assistant Attorney General for the state.

It started with Douglas finding a story posted by Kelly Patrick to the People's Archive of Police Violence in Cleveland. Kelly relayed how a prosecutor dropped a case of domestic assault against her. The catch? The violent offender was the brother of said prosecutor.[4] This was just the tip of the iceberg, it turned out. Douglas had already noted Kasaris's name coming up in another case that the prosecutor declined to pursue. A case involving a young man being shot dead by an off-duty Cleveland police officer. Again, it was Kasaris's fingerprints on the case. Kasaris was also involved in the Tony Viola case that would eventually result in Viola being freed after years of wrongful imprisonment.[5] Can you guess who the culprit is? I'll give you a hint: first name Dan, last name Kasaris.

Like Nicholas Scutari going from "no-show" prosecutor to ranking state senator attempting to streamline corruption in Union County or deputy state Attorney General Haldusiewicz named in the chapter on shielded predators in New Jersey, it's always concerning to see corrupt individuals move up, as Jason Goodrick, head of the Cleveland Community Police Commission, put it in an interview[6] with BZ and I on Walking the Wire* podcast: at some point, you have to decide whether you want to make a difference or move up.

One of the major issues driving corruption is inequality. Inequality is the elephant in the room that we have to come to terms with to understand what drives greed and corruption and both white-collar crime and crime committed out of desperation by those who might not otherwise be able to subsist. As for the elephant in the room, maybe it's more about the "elephant's head."[7]

In Katherine Pistoria's *Code of Capital*, a graph of different income groups is described. "The elephant's head" represents the growth rate and amount of wealth globally by different income groups. 50% of the population is in the "forehead" and is responsible for 12% of the growth in global wealth. The 1% sits at the crest of the tip of the trunk. This is where 27% of the new wealth grows. If you look at "[t]he valley between the forehead and the trunk" you'll see where lower-income families have their meager holdings squeezed out and harvested.

As of May 2022, billionaires in the US saw a net gain of $1.74 trillion in wealth. That's a gain of over 58% since the beginning of the covid pandemic. Even the number of billionaires in the US grew from 614 to 745 by October.[8] The top five billionaires, (Elon Musk, Jeff Bezos, Bill Gates, Larry Ellison, and Larry Page) had their fortunes grow most dramatically over the difficult period in which 89 million Americans lost their jobs. The global economic crisis rivals anything the world has faced since World War II and the middle class has been the driver of the growth in billionaires' holdings. The trillions of dollars siphoned from the middle class in the last 2 years may be greater

---

* BZ and I were introduced by a mutual on Twitter. At the time, he faced similar baseless and toothless legal requests as I was over a case involving a Houston Ponzi ring that I cowrote with journalist Alissa Fleck.

than normal, but *Time* reported in September of 2020 how around $50 trillion has moved from the middle class to the wealthiest individuals in the past few decades.[9] Other analysis of the pandemic period has the total loss at around $9 trillion which would make it the worst global economic collapse since the Great Depression.[10] It doesn't take an MBA or Ph.D. in Economics to surmise: if trillions were lost during the covid era, but the richest are getting richer then continuing at this rate could have us hurtling straight into neo-feudalism in a matter of generations at best, years at worst.

It's all been shaping up to this for decades. The 1980s saw a "surge in economic and legal reforms" in the markets putting markets over the government or "the people" the government is supposed to be by, of, and for. Katherine Pistoria posits how a major factor in this increasingly growing disparity is "capital's legal code." By manipulating financial instruments, such as the relationship between assets and the legal code, lawyers and legislators are able to "fix" the game.[11] It's like a casino, the house always wins in the end because it's set up to do so. Even when the financial wizards do misstep (take a look at the housing bust or the Panama Papers) they are more likely to be rewarded than censured and receive prison time, even for actions that are negligent or criminal.

The weaponization of the legal codes against the have-nots becomes increasingly baroque with the evolution of more convoluted financial instruments. All of these financial instruments evolve from such basic, legal concepts as contract law, property rights, and collateral law. Trusts, corporate law, and bankruptcy law are shaped into "modules" to code the conditions that ensure we continue along this trajectory.

Legal historian, Bernard Rudden introduced the idea of "feudal calculus" that accounts for some of this:

"The traditional concepts of the common law of property were created for and by the ruling classes at a time when the bulk of their capital was land. Nowadays the great wealth lies in stocks, shares, bonds and the like, and is not just movable but mobile, crossing oceans at the touch of a key-pad in the search for a fiscal utopia. (. . .) In terms of legal theory and technique, however, there has been a profound if little discussed evolution by which the concepts originally devised for real property have been detached from their original object, only to survive and flourish as a means of handling abstract value. The feudal calculus lives and breeds, but its habitat is wealth not land."[12]

Rudden's feudal calculus is "alive and kicking" according to Pistoria even in democratic societies that, at the surface, claim to prize equality before the law despite such glaring differences in the treatment of someone with money and standing. It can be as simple as the choice of legal venue. I learned a bit about pro hac vice and "venue shopping" after looking into Lambert Worldwide law firm. Lambert is mentioned in some reporting on Daphne Caruana Galizia due to attempted media suppression.[13] An individual involved in the offshore industry named in Galizia's reporting employed Lambert after Galizia was murdered by a car bomb following her reporting on corruption in the Maltese offshore banking industry.[14]

Lambert Worldwide worked to protect the offshore industry-loving Azeri, Turab Musayev,[15] who was named in her reporting by harassing newsrooms and reporters).* Pistoria explains how the ability of domestic parties to resort to foreign law while still retaining the protection of local courts is yet another way that the legal field works more efficiently for the rich. Now contrast that with the difficulty, near impossibility even, of Kai getting a fair hearing in Galfy Country.

---

* I first learned about Lambert when I received a "courtesy request" to pull down factual reporting related to a Houston-based Ponzi ring responsible for millions in fraud and connected to multiple murders.

London and New York City are "leading global financial centers"[16] resulting in English common law and the New York State code being the two dominant legal codes in global finance. As we will see shortly, offshore industries housed in Panama or elsewhere are also quite important to the shadow economy.

Max Weber wrote of the state monopoly over the means of violent coercion. This can be economic coercion or physical force. State coercion is enacted through the so-called "justice system" and the courts, bailiffs, police forces, and municipal, state, and federal laws.[17]

Pistoria notes that lawyers are "the true masters of the code of capital." Not surprising when it is lobbyists with legal experience, the K Street types who schmooze and fund your elected officials.[18] Pistoria puts it plainly and succinctly: "In principle, anybody has access to lawyers and their coding skills, but the market for legal services ensures that only the best-paying clients can hire the most skillful among them."

As far back as the 19th century, Lord Campbell warned the House of Lords of the growing power of the legal class: "There is an estate in the realm more powerful than either your Lordship or the other House of Parliament, and that [is] the country solicitors."[19] This unheeded warning came shortly before a major depression in 1870s England. In the 2008 housing bubble bust that nearly blew up the global banking industry, we saw how operating "technically legally" isn't enough. It showed us what happens even if everyone is playing "by the rules" in a manner that isn't sustainable, (however legal).

Pistoria writes, "Indeed, one of the great ironies of the litigation frenzy that followed the 2008 crisis is that some of the big players in the market sued each other, each claiming that they had been misled—even though many of them had engaged in similar conduct themselves, were sophisticated players in financial markets, and had been advised by equally sophisticated lawyers."

What's more is that increasingly, some lawyers worldwide act as "corruption brokers." And who can blame them? Situations where lawyers who are caught breaking the law and indicted for them are rare.[20] Partially because lawyers can "use law in two crucial ways: to seize an opportunity for quick gain, and having done so, to cover their tracks."

And perhaps you think you're inoculated against this. After all, you may be thinking, "but I'm a law-abiding citizen." Well, as it turns out the legal code has been going through another disturbing transformation, again related to the mercenary use of the legal profession, the coding of corporate entities as "legal persons" and the impending global depression resulting from, among other things, the covid pandemic.

"Anti-camping laws" are sprouting up here and there. In some cases, as in L.A., the anti-camping laws are incidentally occurring at the same time as shelter closures ensuring a fresh stock of people illegalized sheerly for the sake of lack.[21] We are in the midst of a period where the middle class has been bled for trillions as major corporations are having record earnings.[22] Contrast the $3 trillion or so that moved from the lower and middle class to the richest between 2020 and 2022[23] with the $2 trillion the "global war on terror" cost taxpayers from 2001-2019.[24] But maybe you're not one of the many people who lost their job or small business during the lockdown. Maybe you're one of the people who didn't have to mortgage or sell their home* as Wall Street fat cats Hoover up real estate.

As the law continues to bend towards the protection of "legal persons" it

---

* Taking advantage of the economic downturn, venture capital funds, and other Wall Street heavy hitters have bought hundreds of thousands of homes in the past year, a number that had reached $60 billion by October 2021, according to the *New York Times*.[25]

looks to even more ways of criminalizing common people. The anti-camping regulations and laws are a vigorously revamped version of indigency and vagrancy laws that were initially put in place to replace the no longer constitutional slave codes.[26] Once you're caught in the revolving door of justice it's easy to get swept up. Finding work can be hard. Finding work homeless is much harder. Finding work homeless with a felony record is far more difficult.

Jeffrey Reiman's 1998 book *The Rich Get Richer, The Poor Get Prison*, exposes ways that the law and legal system enforce a stratified society that benefits the haves at the expense of the have-nots. Despite the myth of "all equal before the law" it shouldn't surprise anyone that poorer people are more likely to be arrested, and when arrested more likely to be sentenced to prison. This shouldn't be surprising to anyone considering, that with more money you can afford more capable legal representation, and the way the laws are set up favors those with the best defense team. But the cost of freedom is prohibitive. It's not that poor people necessarily commit more crimes.

Our legal system is set up to "weed out the wealthy" from the point of arrest on. Several studies suggest that richer people are less likely to even be taken in than poorer individuals, even for the exact same charges.[27] As our society becomes more stratified with the middle-class disappearing, this economic bias should be concerning.

Public defenders are often overworked and underpaid. As a result, it's not surprising that their main concern is often encouraging plea bargains for the innocent or guilty alike. I was the target of a raid while on campus in the dorms of the University of Tennessee-Chattanooga campus over the sale of "red rock opium" (a common name for dragon's blood incense, derived from the Daemonorops draco plant). It contains no opium or opiates of any sort and was completely legal. I came prepared with a manila folder full of information on what it was and wasn't. The public defender just seemed cha-grined and still tried to pressure me into pleading guilty to a crime I didn't commit. A charge that would keep me from ever receiving federal funds for college, safety net support, and other benefits.

Class and other issues may result in vastly different outcomes despite "equal protection under the law." Everyone is afforded as much justice as they can afford.

Simply look at the way white-collar crime is treated. White-collar crime and corruption are not victimless crimes. The housing bust of 2008 resulted in no arrests in the United States. On the contrary, many of those respon-sible received "golden parachutes" and substantial bailouts. They were prac-tically rewarded for plummeting millions of people into deep debt and dire financial straits, resulting in poverty, food insecurity, and homelessness.

Sara Lee recalled tainted meat in December 1998. This was only after killing at least 15 people in addition to making dozens more seriously ill and resulting in six miscarriages.[28] Did anyone responsible for the deaths go to prison? Of course not, the corporation was fined, however. Johnson & Johnson faced a massive class-action lawsuit in 2020 over carcinogenic baby formula containing asbestos.[29] The next year, a study published in Chemical Research in Toxicology showed that 2400 sunscreen products on the market contained carcinogens.[30] The popular smoking cessation prescrip-tion Chantix and several other drugs got hit with cancer lawsuits in recent years.[31] This is actually fairly common in the pharma industry. Knowingly keeping information about a dangerous product from the public resulting in prison time may be rarer than a unicorn.

Recall the J&J connection to Harvard university and how Gahan Pandina was insulated from any repercussions despite knowingly putting children in harm's way. All this over a pharma product whose risks easily outweighed (lack of) benefit.

In fact, since the 90s Holder Memorandum "too big to jail" keeping corporations accountable is harder than ever. The 1999 memo, "Bringing Criminal Charges Against Corporations" set the stage for the bust of 2008. Then-deputy US attorney Eric Holder argued that prosecutors should keep "collateral consequences" in mind when considering charges against major corporations.[32]

"There's all kinds of problems with the applications of this policy which began with the Holder memo and got more formalized," John Coffee, Columbia University law professor and white-collar crime expert said in 2013. "You are going to send a message that we don't really care significantly about misconduct within those institutions."[33]

The standard was set for the "deferred prosecution arrangement." In the wake of the economic carnage of the 2008 housing crisis, Holder doubled down admitting that some megabanks are so large and tied into the global economy that it's "difficult to prosecute them."[34]

So as you can see, the division between the middle class or poor and the wealthy and the "legal persons" and "natural persons." A "legal person" refers to corporate entities that, thanks to Citizens United get all the benefits of "free speech." This means they can donate unlimited money to campaigns. But if a person willingly acts in a manner that is likely to result in the death of multiple humans (natural persons in legal parlance) that person, pending they can't afford sufficient legal representation to get them off the hook, may find themselves in handcuffs.

Even the FBI's Unified Crime Reporting (UCR) is lacking in many ways. According to a paper by Cynthia Barnett published by the Department of Justice's Office of Justice Programs (OJP) "it is impossible to measure white-collar crime with Uniform Crime Reporting (UCR) data if the working definition revolves around the type of offender."[35] Not only does law enforcement have difficulty classifying and quantifying WCC there are major difficulties involved when it comes to arresting and prosecuting these offenders.

As per statistics from 2021, only 5,000 out of 100,000 people get arrested for white-collar crime annually. Of that small amount, only 3% were prosecuted. And that number is shrinking, it's already down 53% from the last decade.[36]

People who worry about the influence of "gangs" rarely are aware of law enforcement gangs like the Lords of Discipline or The Family in New Jersey or LASD gangs. They also likely don't consider how collusion between white-collar criminals results in corporate sponsorship of organized crime. Consider how many murders were aided and abetted by Hong Kong Shanghai Banking Corporation (HSBC).

HSBC, Europe's biggest bank, was made to pay a $1.9 billion fine in addition to a five-year "deferred prosecution agreement (DPA)." Deferred prosecution and non-prosecution agreements are fairly standard since the Holder Memorandum's "too big to jail" philosophy infected the DOJ. As far back as 2008, a drug lord in Mexico recommended HSBC as the "place to launder money." The bank blamed "lapses in anti-money laundering controls" for the at least $881 million cleaned by HSBC for the Sinaloa and other cartels in Mexico and Colombia.[37]

"While we still have improvements to make and work to do, this shows the DPA has worked in the way intended which was to lead to a transformation in the way HSBC manages financial crime risk," Stuart Levy, Chief Legal Officer at HSBC. But did it though?

In 2012, the DPA was signed promising to "upgrade compliance systems." The International Consortium of Investigative Journalists (ICIJ) reported that the bank had "moved vast sums of dirty money" while under the terms of the DPA. In fact, between 2013 and 2017, HSBC processed over $900 million through shell companies with links to criminal networks. No indictments ensued. Ponzi schemers and drug traffickers continued to find that HSBC was the place to clean dirty money while supposedly on probation.[38]

Coffee, the law professor at Columbia pointed out the double standard with HSBC and the banking crisis: "There were reasons in 2008 to say maybe we shouldn't indict any bank we can because it will just add to the systemic risk. But we were in 2012 to 2013 with HSBC — that risk wasn't there and we weren't dealing with something that was relating to the activities that produced the 2008 crisis."

HSBC moved around $31 million between 2014 and 2015 for companies found to be moving stolen government funds from Brazil. Over $292 million was transferred via HSBC to a Panamanian entity known to US authorities as a major launderer for cartels. According to FinCen Files documents, HSBC was aware that regulators were investing their involvement with a multi-million dollar Ponzi schemer. They were confident enough to continue doing so, however. And why not? Funding cartels is a minor thing for "legal persons" like HSBC, but try being broke and caught with a nickel bag of weed in the wrong state and see what happens.

Think I'm kidding? Ask the dozens of non-violent offenders who were handed down a life sentence for marijuana-related offenses.[39]

The book *Cárteles No Existen, Los Narcotráfico Y Cultura En México* by Oswaldo Zavala was translated into English this year. The title, *Cartels Do Not Exist* sounds sensationalist, but the point Zavala makes is that these major trafficking entities directly responsible for murder, bloodshed, torture, and indirectly responsible for misery via flooding the streets of Mexico and the USA with drugs could not exist without complicity of corrupt government officials and corporations like HSBC.

In an interview for *The Nation*, Zavala was asked if the title was just "provocation."

"I really do believe that. That's not to say that drug traffickers aren't real or that the violence isn't real—of course they are—but that our understanding of all that has been filtered through what UNAM [National Autonomous University of Mexico] sociologist Luis Astorga calls the 'narco matrix.' This is the idea that drug traffickers are a separate entity from the government and that they've amassed so much power that they pose a threat to the state. That's completely wrong."

Zavala points out how both US and Mexican law enforcement "created a national drug network out of the city of Guadalajara" during the Operation Condor years. Operation Condor propped up dictators like Auguste Pinochet. The Central-American version of Condor was Operation Charly. Charly saw Nicaraguan personnel trained covertly, in the secret war effort funded by the Iran-Contra affair. Iran-Contra saw CIA agents help usher tons of cocaine into California just before the genesis of the crack-cocaine epidemic.[*40]

"Officials didn't just cut deals back then," City University of New York professor Zavala explains, "they dominated traffickers."

In the book *Blue Mafia: Police Brutality and Consent Decrees in Ohio* Tim

---

[*] After learning of a "60 Minutes" investigation set to broadcast on the topic of the CIA's role in importing tons of cocaine, they released a statement characterizing it as a "most regrettable incident" that should be chalked up to "instances of poor judgment and management on the part of several CIA officers." Most people when caught trafficking tons of cocaine would likely regret it, the difference here is, that those responsible here were insulated from repercussions.

Tolka shares bloodcurdling stories of those charged with the responsibility "to serve and protect" engaging in jaw-dropping criminality such as the case of two cops hiring a hitman to kill a state's witness. This occurred while the department was already under intense DOJ scrutiny. Not intense enough, however, for the officers involved to even be forced to resign, much less face time.[41]

Criminology doesn't pay, I once quipped to a New Orleans-based criminology professor. He groaned a bit at that, but it's at least truer than the inaccurate, but better-known adage "crime doesn't pay." As it turns out, there are multiple ways to invest in crime and have it pay off without the least concern of imprisonment. Ironically, one of the safest ways to do this is just to invest in the for-profit prison industry.[42]

The 1980s satire *Robocop* was an over-the-top dystopian sci-fi story about Omni-Consumer Products (OCP) and the privatization of law enforcement. Joel Dyer's Perpetual Prison Machine notes how Corrections Corporation of America (CCA, as opposed to OCP) legally profits from rising crime by investing in the prison industry. The HBO series Oz may have been fictional, but the episode dealing with the way that districts with prisons siphon funds from poorer areas is right on the money.[43]

Disenfranchising felons while counting them as part of the population for prison districts is, in essence, a legalized revamping of the 3/5th vote rule that benefited plantation owners.[44] Considering how people like billionaire and former mayor and presidential candidate Mike Bloomberg* took advantage of nearly free labor in his campaign, it almost seems as if the 13th amendment, rather than abolishing slavery enshrined it, making it constitutional in certain cases.

---

* Ironically, Bloomberg's news outlets reported last year on Russian prisons returning to forced labor. They were referred to as "gulags." The prisons he outsourced his low-cost or no-cost campaign labor from are different for unspecified reasons.[45]

Privatization of the prison industry began as a means of offsetting the cost of running correctional institutions. As it turns out, it was not really that efficient at that either. Meanwhile, the rise in profits of for-profit prisons correlates with rising crime. Military, law enforcement, and prison spending are where the bulk of your tax dollars go. And US spending in these arenas dwarfs every other nation on earth. Factor in the for-profit probation and parole industry and the result is nightmare scenarios that, in some cases, amount to legalized extortion.

2021 federal spending on law enforcement and prisons at the federal and state level was over ¼ of a trillion dollars. That breaks down to about $259 million per *day*. Nearly 8 billion taxpayer dollars went to the Bureau of Prisons alone last year.[46] That said, for-profit prisons result in longer sentences and more inmates according to a 2020 study. This shouldn't be surprising; any industry seeks to keep its market share by retaining customers and drumming up new business. When that business is locking away people for crime things begin to become a bit problematic. In addition to higher incarceration rates, for the communities near the prison district, crime actually increases correlated with the increase in for-profit prisons. Other studies show that private prisons can even influence sentencing decisions by judges.[47]

Eric Schlosser put it bluntly, "The prison-industrial complex is not a conspiracy, guiding the nation's criminal-justice policy behind closed doors. It is a confluence of special interests that has given prison construction in the United States a seemingly unstoppable momentum. It is composed of politicians, both liberal and conservative, who have used the fear of crime to gain votes; impoverished rural areas where prisons have become a cornerstone of economic development; private companies that regard the roughly $35 billion spent each year on corrections not as a burden on American taxpayers but as a lucrative market; and government officials whose fiefdoms have expanded along with the inmate population."[48]

Abuse by police runs the gamut from abusing authority and discretion verbal slurs, profiling, brutality, and, as witnessed in Tolka's book, even murder.

In addition to being vigilant for earmarks and indicators of corruption, as per Agent Raymond Hall, recently of the White-Collar Crime division of the FBI, demanding that our public officials hold themselves accountable and to a higher standard is of extreme importance. After all, it's these executives and legislators at all levels who are helping mold and shape the system we live in. Predators should have no part in politics and hold no positions of power. Not just because abusive sociopaths are likely not going to have the best interests of the people at heart but because of the very real, "clear and present danger" that a compromised official represents.

And we can't just depend on the media to do the work for us. Look at how long Jeffrey Epstein, Harvey Weinstein, and Peter Nygard were allowed to go on. Or even what happened to those who did try to cover the story. A *Forbes* reporter was paid $600 to put his byline aside a press release from Epstein's team.[49] Meanwhile, around the time the magazine started pursuing a story on Epstein, Graydon Carter, editor at *Vanity Fair*, woke up one day with a dead cat's head outside his home reminiscent of the horse head scene in *The Godfather*.[50] In addition to employing companies like K2 Intelligence and Black Cube, powerful predators engage in "trading up" as Nicole Egan author of *Chasing Cosby* puts it.[51]

You don't have to be a multimillionaire to use your status to shield the most awful deeds though. In September 2022 another major human trafficking bust netted teachers, Disney staff, and even a chief of police. This was the second of its type this year netting Disney staff and employees. In 2017, a Disney exec was busted on child pornography charges.[52]

In addition to the obvious human cost or even the economic cost of child abuse, when it comes to people with positions of power the "clear and present danger" not only to the children but to the fragile fabric of democracy itself, routing out corrupt and compromised individuals is of paramount importance.

I want to make sure to leave readers with the understanding that this kind of blatant corruption is not something that only happens in Union County or New Jersey as a whole. This perversion of justice is not a once in a lifetime affair. It happens more often than you could imagine and often goes unreported in major media. Sometimes there aren't even the types of paper trails like the DRB reports and lawsuits I scoured.

There are things you can do. Letter writing campaigns are effective. Write your representatives, whether you voted for them or not doesn't matter. I've written multiple letters to representatives, never once after signing off "your constituent" was I asked, "but did you vote for me." And no, not every letter had a positive result, but continually writing letters on a subject eventually led to a positive disposition on some concerning issues in my experience.

In addition to that, keep an eye on your local and state politics. Look for the signs of corruption as mentioned by the FBI agents I spoke with. And we must demand that our elected (and appointed) officials are held to a higher standard and keep them accountable. We can't let the Romankows, Scutaris, and Kasarises and all their ilk who keep advancing despite scandal after scandal. Diligence and vigilance are your friends. Keep up the pressure and don't stop believing.

Now that you've heard the true story of Kai the Hitchhiker, let's contrast that with the tale the prosecutor managed to get the jury to swallow:

Now that you've heard the true story of Kai the Hitchhiker, let's contrast that with the tale the prosecutor managed to get the jury to swallow:

Once upon a time Kai the hitchhiker decided instead of taking Kardashian producer up on the tv offer he would commit premeditated murder after getting a face tattoo and cutting his hair so it was more visible. while on the run he posed with people smiling (if slightly drugged looking according to interview material never heard at the grand jury or trial for obvious reasons): "Hi, I'm Kai the Hitchhiker."

He was both calculating and premeditated and sloppy enough to stay in town for a while talking to locals, posing for photos, leaving his phone number and address and he did this all with zero motive. Yup, just was like "wonder what throwing my life away would be like."

Oh, and that blood on the deceased alleged rapist's penis commingled with the alleged rapists' semen? We don't need to test that, they said. And those cups that he says were drugged? Uh oh, they're washed in the dishwasher now, another said. And still another said: just fume them.

The End

This is the literal fairy tale the prosecutor and the state somehow got to pass a jury of 12 citizens. But now you've heard the true story, a lot of the story that was suppressed for whatever reasons at court and in the media. You can't make this stuff, well you can but you'd likely make it more believable if you do fiction for a living.

I rest my case...

APPENDIX

Sketch by NZ

A CALL TO ACTION

I'll leave you with the body of Kai's petition at Change.org, a shortened bitly URL at the bottom of the page will take you to it and Kai's other petitions if you want to have your say heard.

We, the undersigned, petition the State House of Representatives and State Senate to introduce a bill that requires all state government officials to undergo SSBI/SCI and GKT screenings. We are aware that the GKT (guilty knowledge test), when used by trained security personnel, has an over 95% accuracy rate. We recognize that compromised government officials pose a grave national security threat; both personally, and in the hands of foreign governments.

Our system of law, which protects our safety and security, needs to be free of security threats. Over many decades, a steady stream of sexual predators has flowed into government positions. Although some have been caught and disciplined (however effectively or ineffectively), they were in positions where they could affect social policy, before they were caught: in many cases, for decades.

Sexual offenders against children should never be allowed to hold such positions in the first place.

Technology such as the GKT and SSBI/SCI screenings are available and already mandated by the federal government, with scientifically proven effectiveness. We, as people who visit, live in, and/or care for the United States of America, deserve to benefit from the security that these technologies provide. Our children, families; and selves deserve to be protected from rapists and sexual offenders against children; who infiltrate positions of policymaking, law enforcement, judiciary, prosecution, and administration of justice.

For all these reasons, we ask the representatives in the State House and Senate to submit bills mandating GKT and SSBI/SCI screenings to be administered by qualified and appropriate security personnel: to every State government official, member of the State Bar, law enforcement officer, and recipient of any pension or benefit intended for such State Officers.

You can sign the petition online by following the link bit.ly/kaipetition if you'd like to donate to Kai you can do so at bit.ly/fundraiserkai or you can reach out to Kai through the mail: Caleb McGillvary #1222665, New Jersey State Prison, PO Box 861, Trenton, NJ 08625 or on Jpay.com #000102317G

AFTERWORD
BY BRIAN "BZ" DOUGLAS

When I met Philip Fairbanks in early 2022, I was only two years into a mid-life career shift into journalism. At the time I was dealing with the first legal threat I'd received that actually gave me sleepless nights (the Dan Kasaris story mentioned in Chapter 13). Fairbanks was getting similar threats at the time, which is why a mutual friend on Twitter introduced us. We talked on Zoom for nearly six hours about our work, lives, and perspectives. That first meeting was, without hyperbole, one of the best conversations I've ever had. It laid the foundation for a friendship and professional respect that would land me here, writing my first afterword to a book.

This is just any book, but an essential book, one that I fully believe needs to be widely read, discussed, and acted upon. Fairbanks, like myself, is as independent as journalists come. There's no team of PR folks arranging podcast appearances and morning talk show spots, no slick marketing website, no social media managers riding trends and scheduling targeted ads. If there is one thing I want to impart to you, it's to humbly ask that you do everything you can to help spread the word about this book.

I have always loved this quote from Tom Robbins' *Still Life With Woodpecker*:

> "There are two kinds of people in this world: those who actually believe there are two kinds of people in this world and those who are smart enough to know better."

While I still appreciate the truth of this as it applies to the totality of an individual, I do believe that firm delineations do exist in the roles individuals play in society. There are journalists who only care about breaking the news, and those who take the time to fix it. There are journalists who serve themselves: prioritizing careers, prestige, and access to powerbrokers, and those who serve the public interest by exposing the abuses of the powerful.

In both cases, Philip Fairbanks has shown himself to be firmly in the latter category. The pages of this book are littered with lowlights of the other types of journalists. Careerists who can't be bothered to see Kai's humanity, and won't allow their minds to be disturbed by seriously considering his allegations of corruption and conspiracy.

Fairbanks is also the kind of journalist who allows Kai all the space he needs to share his story directly with the reader. What's more, Kai contributed vital research and insights that Fairbanks didn't hesitate to consider, scrutinize, and build upon. It would be to the detriment of any journalist to do the opposite, but sadly this attitude is not universally shared in our field.

Shortly before writing this, Fairbanks and I discussed bias, objectivity, and personal attachment. Both of us believe that far too many journalists have a bias towards the status quo, and a lack of personal attachment with the subjects they work with. Fairbanks and I are not constitutionally capable of being indifferent to the pain and suffering of an individual whose life has been mangled by a corrupt individual or system. We look at the sheer volume of injustice that is never reckoned with by the majority of the press and understand that something is objectively broken.

Neither I nor Fairbanks know how to fix a system so broken that it continuously churns out farcical tragedies like Kai's. What we do know is that the solutions must arrive from an honest accounting of the facts, no matter where they lead.

THANKS AND ACKNOWLEDGEMENTS

First and foremost, I have to thank my friend Rachel Cochran. She actually encouraged me to interview Kai in 2017 and has offered emotional support, advice and helped with some of the costs of creating the book. Next up, Virginia Randall (aka Skye). I actually met Skye through the Facebook Legal Support Page. All that I have uncovered on my own was rooted in the painstaking research already done by her and Kai.

Also, of course, huge thanks to Kai for offering me access for these past years. He also offered invaluable help on the end notes section, especially related to the many motions, exhibits, evidence, and court transcripts. Tony Cantu, a member of the Kai the Hitchhiker Facebook group provided some background for The Early Years chapter that really added something to the book. Great appreciation is owed to Wendy S. Painting, PhD., Alissa Fleck, BZ Douglas for contributing material to the book as well as designing the book and website, Darren Herridge of Uncooked Media for additional support on the design front and an amazing cover concept, and to NZ for the awesome sketch of Kai. Can't forget to mention Isaac, the co-producer on the Walking the Wire podcast who clued me into the connection between KKR and SEIU.

I'd also like to thank two fearless, Texas journalists whose dedication to fighting carceral injustice inspires me: Barrett Brown and Keri Blakinger. And to Nicole Weisensee Egan, another major inspiration, who also showed interest in seeing the book. Other indispensable resources in the research and writing of the book were the Marshall Project and Prison Legal News. Also, thanks to Matt Friedman, Chris Baxter, Tina Renna, Sean P. Sullivan, and other journalists who made this work possible by covering corruption in Union County and New Jersey in general. Thanks to Rev. Michael Granzen, PhD for having the bravery to expose and document corruption in Elizabeth, New Jersey. Big thanks as well to the CUNY Advocate who published a story I wrote about Kai's case this Summer. Kai and I both also wanted to express our thanks for organizations like RAINN which provide support for sexual assault survivors.

There was a lot of work that I couldn't do on my own. Hours of audio transcription, data entry, help on the end notes, and with editing were provided from Fiverr by Jellyn Joy Gaspar, ahsan62, misstranscript, taffelet, omer_hassan2194. Thanks to Rachel Ayotte for helping me with the market analysis and comparable titles section of my book proposal. And thanks to Langton's International for taking the time to read the proposal and the drafts from this Summer and December.

Great appreciation is owed to Ben Razon and all the staff and regulars of the Oarhouse Pub for always making me feel at home and no one ever minding I'm usually nose-deep in a notebook in between sips and bites until someone gets me on a rant. A few nights were spent switching back and forth between notebooks and scrawling ideas while sitting there at the bar. Thanks to Heather Harman, Hutch, and Chris Francese, who provided emotional (and financial) support at times when I really needed the help.

Hanz, who decided to send me a laptop he was retiring after having seen me posting about device issues I was having. And I definitely can't forget the brain trust at ma[0].

Thanks to P**y D**e, and everyone else who was there for me (both in the Philippines and back in the US) that frightening year when I was in intense pain, bedridden with a spinal injury. That definitely includes my friends Vie and Kathleen Taguinod who helped me keep my house clean while I was laid up in bed and several times this year when I couldn't find time to get to it myself as well as my friend Celina who was there for me when I checked out of the hospital and saw me home and my friend, writer and disability advocate, Miranieva Buen.

And also thanks to a lot of folks who are in part responsible for the trajectory of my life at present. Shane Watson is an artist and motivational speaker. I discovered his site Silverladder.com over 20 years ago and took part in a strange, Dada-inspired Alternate Reality Game/art project. The whole community that grew around that event were instrumental in convincing me to get back to creative endeavours.

Bob Freville, who I've shared multiple mastheads with going all the way back to Ink magazine in the late 90s, and GetUnderground, wav, and Kotori in the 2000s. And I can't mention those outlets without mentioning Wasim Muklashy. Wasim got me my first press passes to Bonnaroo a couple decades ago and set me off on a path of journalism that I am still on. Another of the GetUnderground and Kotori alumni who I'm glad to have kept up with is Kurt Broz of Nerdbot and WLFK productions.

Thanks to Josh McBride, the Ashleys, and Matt Harbin, all my McMinnville and Smithville friends, and everyone else who offered me couch or floor space (not to mention, friendship and support) during that rough patch that was my 20s. Definitely want to mention my very good friends Chelsea Nunley and Ashley Crowe who are always there for me when I need a friend. And thanks to my mom and dad who raised me right despite a rebellious, prodigal phase from about 17 till my late 20s.

Mrs. Chambers, my high school librarian. My Humanities professor from University of Tennessee-Chattanooga whose name escapes me but whose advice ("As the older poet said to the younger poet: 'Nice piece, but save some of the universe for your next work,'" stays with me still. Mrs. Glenn, Mrs. Hitchcock, Ms. Clark, Mr. Mullican, Mrs. Mullican (no relation as far as I know), Ms. Dial, Mrs. Willmore, Mr. Northcutt, Coach Fisher, and all the teachers who inspired and encouraged me.

I definitely can't forget author William Ramsey of William Ramsey Investigates, one of the first people to interview me when I released my first book back in 2020.

Also, thanks to all the GoFundMe donors without whom this book would have been delayed, perhaps by months: Dylan Tumey, Collin Boyer, Jared Fischedick, Zack Collier, GraphFollow (who also has helped me out a few times powering the data science and making amazing Mark Lombardi-inspired interlocks). Jonathon Shippling, Hannah Shaw, V**** R****, James Bennett, Nikolai Schulman, N*** R******, and my mother Barbara, my sister Sarah and my cousin Angela Schonter, M**** R*****, R*** H***, K***, C******, Ashley Akers, and Martin Wright.

SOUNDTRACK NOTES

The soundtrack of this book (i.e. the jams I played while writing, research-ing and editing) also helped keep me going so big thanks to Deerhoof, Sun City Girls, Smoke City, France Gall, The Pet Shop Boys, John Zorn, Tori Amos, Freddie Hubbard and Mimaroglu, Serge Gainsbourg, Gary Jules, Weather Report, Pat Metheny, Frédéric Chopin, Saga, Steely Dan, Supertramp, Genesis, R.E.M., Pink Floyd, Outkast, Parliament (and Funkadelic), Chicago, George Brigman, Amon Tobin, YĪN YĪN, Joy Division, Miles Davis, Echo & the Bunnymen, John Coltrane, Macroblank, Enigma, Leonard Cohen, Tommy Wright III, Lil Jack Manson, Psycho, Claude Debussy, Erik Satie, Alcatraz, Shaolin Afronauts, Frank Zappa, the Sound Defects, Blind Melon, Soul Asylum, Longmont Potion Castle, New Jazz Underground, Allah-Las, Bill Lasswell, Reilly Stroup Sheppard, Macintosh Plus, Tom Waits, Pharaoh Sanders, Jimi Hendrix, Flight of the Conchordes, Electric Light Orchestra, Townes Van Zandt, Thelonious Monk, Curtis Mayfield, Yoko Kanno, Akino Arai, postXam-erica, Roxy Music, the Walker Brothers, Glass Candy, Aretha Franklin, Pizzicato 5, Fantastic Plastic Machine, Momus, Todd Rundgren, Haircuts for Men, Jonathan Coulton, Peter Gabriel, Elis Regina, Ministry, Khun Narin's Electric Phin Band, Cibo Matto, Ennio Morricone, OSCOB, MF Doom, Charlie Parker, The Cramps, Difang, Elliot Smith, Jazz Emu, Badlydrawnboy, ABBA, Brian Eno, Ren,Stone Temple Pilots, Alice in Chains, Olias, Yes, Marty Robbins, Haslinger, Ace of Cups, and that's just the highlights from my browser history between mid-August and late December.

In all honesty though, music has fueled this project especially during those difficult final months of trying to coax something decent from the long stretch of words.

LEGAL AND ETHICAL DISCLAIMER:

In the past decade or so, the idea of the place of subjectivity and emotion (or emotional distance) in journalism has changed quite a bit since the hard and fast rules of the 20th century. I will be the first to admit that I have a strong emotional connection to this story. Not only the situation with Kai, but the fact that this goes on every day to so many people affects me strongly. The trick here is to make sure that doesn't affect my objectivity. This can be aided by making sure your work is solidly founded on evidence and that you take a more critical eye toward the sources you tend to trust than the ones you have doubts about.

In this book, I have done my best to stick to the facts. In some cases, however, the lack of evidence is evidence of a sort itself. As mentioned before, even a federal court has ruled that a clear conspiracy and cover-up has occurred here that deprived Kai of his due process rights. Years of claims from the state, defendants in Kai's civil motions, and the press that Kai was merely espousing "conspiracy theories" must be reevaluated as a result.

In any case, where I do make inferences based on the evidence, I make it clear that it is speculative. The truth is, with some of the most important evidence destroyed or never collected we have to read between the lines in some cases. Considering the depth of my research into this case, I am confident enough to welcome the discovery process should any of the persons named in this book have any issues. The main persons related to the case were reached out to and offered the right of reply. James Galfy, Romankow, Cito, and many others either had nothing to say or next to nothing to say in their defense but I reiterate, I welcome the discovery process seeing as there are some things I have not been able to access that this could aid me, that along with the fact that I have no assets and therefore nothing to lose I simply say to anyone who is unhappy about their appearance in this book:

bring it on.

It's always the sources you trust that you have to work especially hard to evaluate and verify because of your implicit biases. If I didn't work to compensate for my biases then I'm no better than the reporters who "reported on" the story by simply repeating what Peterson, Romankow, and the cops said rather than looking at the court filings, the crime scene photos, reading the interviews and investigative reports which is where you see evidence of the cover-up and conflicts of interest.

I will disclose the fact that Kai was instrumental in the production of this book. Several of the leads I pursued came from him. I managed to track down some things he hadn't uncovered yet but likely never would have made it that far this soon without the amazing headway from his legal research. I must also disclose that, over the years, I have definitely developed a closeness with "my subject." In fact, as unconventional as it may be, like most of my "subjects" I think of him first as a human being rather than as story fodder.

I honestly believe that some of the commonalities in our experiences have led me to a greater understanding of Kai than could be gleaned by people who maybe haven't ever been mugged, attacked, slept on rainy cardboard, squatted in abandoned structures, spent time with the Rainbow Family, lived on a commune in the mountains, etc. I've also dealt with mental illness and had to learn to cope with multiple traumas that affect my health to this day. It's exactly these "had to be there" experiences that not only resulted in a fondness and friendship being fostered but also helps me to share these sorts of experiences that are so alien and foreign to a large percentage of the population who, unlike me, may have never been hungry enough to eat a piece of pizza out of a box thrown in a trash can.

One day I'll tell my own story perhaps, give my perspective on what it's like carrying a heavy duffel and wondering where I'd be sleeping once the sun went down but for now, I am applying that valuable (if not always fun) lived experience to this case and believe this relationship and my personal experience and access to Kai to be what sets this book apart from any other piece of media dealing with Kai's case.

The facts were all there, sure. But no one bothered to trudge through a thousand pages, and spend a few thousand hours to expose the inconsistencies throughout. I'm very proud of the effort that went into this book. Years of effort and months of planning and outlining led to this and I can only hope that readers will find themselves just as outraged by the failings of the system as I am. Outraged enough to make their voices heard.

I did allow Kai access to early drafts of the work. He made some suggestions, in the cases where clarity, grammar, or accuracy and also offered some advice regarding approaching certain subjects more sensitively. I also gave Kai a chance to speak out about some issues in his own words here, but any claims I make up are backed by evidence cited in the end notes.

Of course, it's the sources you trust that you have to work doubly hard to evaluate and verify. This is true because if you don't compensate for your implicit (or explicit) biases, then I would be no better than some of the sources listed in chapter 5. Reporters, podcasters, and others who merely made the truth murkier, more obscured.

You don't have to accept any opinions or speculations from myself or Kai to see that there are major issues in this case. Issues that even federal courts have agreed amount to a deprivation of civil rights.

FURTHER READING ON HITCHHIKING SUBCULTURE

In addition to Roadside Americans, I read several ethnographic and sociological studies related to hitchhiking among them the following: "Hitchhiking and Missing and Murdered Indigenous Women: A Critical Discourse Analysis of Billboards on the Highway of Tears" by Katherine Morton, "America's wandering youth: a sociological study of young hitchhikers in the United States," by Walter F Weiss; Mike Carmichael, "Becoming intimately mobile" by Paula Bialski,"Aspects of civil attention: an ethnography of hitchhiking" by Peter J McGivern, "Who picks up whom: the fleeting encounter between motorist and hitchhiker" by David S Alcorn; Spencer J Condie, "The neglected art of hitch-hiking: risk, trust and sustainability" by Graeme Chesters Graeme; David B. Smith.   As far as academic texts related to hitchhiking, Bear Scott's Field Methods and Ethnography research paper, Two More and a Dog: Folklore of the American Hitchhiker is well worth checking out.

Scott's paper directly references Kai and the assault. Laura Chavez's "Marketing a Panic: Media Coverage of Novel Psychoactive Drugs, NPDS and its Relationship with Legal Changes" also briefly mentions Kai in an article that dispels some disinfo related to the idea that Jett Simmons McBride was under the influence of "bath salts" a colloquial term for stimulant research chemicals that were often connected in the media with grisly crimes, sometimes with cannibalistic undertones. In 2016, Forbes published "The Legend of the Miami Cannibal Provides Lessons in Shoddy Drug Journalism" (later republished at Reason) which dispels the myth of some quasi-legal, face eating cannibal drug being responsible for the horrific events.

A NOTE ON FLETCHER WOODWARD

"I think I have gone far enough through the storm to know something as to who and by whom this officer was murdered, and why I was drawn into the vile current, and how and why convicted."

Fletch Wood'ard

Dr. Fletcher Woodward was colloquially known as Fletch Wood'ard. It's the name on the cover of his book, Fletch Woodard. His Fights with those Bad, Bad Town Boys. A drive for the life of a human being! The Accusation, Arrest, Imprisonment and Trials of Himself and the Flynns, charged with the Murder of Enoch Cooksey.

Cooksey, by the way, was the first peace officer to be shot in the line of duty... as he was leaving the brothel downtown. Woodard was the perfect scapegoat. An inventor, a poet, a man with strange perhaps heretical spiritual philosophies, and on top of that an early dabbler in the wizardry of photographs and magic lantern shows. Dr. Woodward was also one of the foremost pioneers of stereoscopic images (best described as the original View-Master).

Cooksey, was a bit of a busybody I've been told. As was Fletch, so killing the one and pinning it on the other definitely made it easier for the good ol' boy network. Some of whom still have deep ties to the region in which I grew up.

The book is distinguished by passionate and fiery prose. Woodward broke out of the Nashville prison and proceeded to use his journals and memory to prove his case, his alibi, and the inconsistencies of the false witness borne against him and point out multiple instances where the state's witnesses, at the behest of "those bad, bad town boys" had perjured themselves in the name of pinning the eccentric Dr. Wood'ard to the wall.

Dozens of witnesses slated to testify in his defense were not heard. The Odd Fellows' fraternal order seemed to be connected. Woodward also wrote a letter to the newspaper charging the jail guards in Nashville with cruel treatment to himself and others.

Fletch did not set out to uncover the dirty secrets of the town. He expressed regret saying it "pains me to have to uncover and re-expose to the world the faults of my native home, but self-preservation impels me in self-defence." Similar to Kai's case, the media was also content to share the accepted version of events set forth by the state. "The above article is false in every particular nearly. It is a fair sample of the spirit of the prosecution, and we cannot believe it ignorance; no, but to the contrary, a well-studied and premeditated plan, more infamous than the crime they accused me of."

The judge and a handful of (mostly related by blood, business, or other ties) folks pretty much ran things in the smoke-filled backroom style of the era, a style that apart from fashion and fads and lip service played to diversity, hasn't changed all that much since the Gilded Age of the Robber Barons.

Like Fletch, Kai painstakingly went point by point, through the many irregularities evident. He did so in order to free himself. In doing so he ended up revealing the dirty secrets of those who had conspired against him. Proving the Jonathan Swift quote from which John Kennedy Toole borrowed his title, "A confederacy of dunces." Because wherever, Swift tells us, a genius is to be found you will know them by the fact that a confederacy of dunces is out to get them. Thus, was the case for Dr. Fletch Wood'ard, a man whose real-life history sounds like the stuff of tall tales. Also, based on the years I've spent poring over the evidence (and lack thereof) thusly with Caleb "Kai the Hitchhiker" McGillivary.

SELECTED CLOUD DRIVE HIGHLIGHTS

There is so much more to the story than I had room for in one volume. That said, this is certainly not the last installment in Kai's story, much less the last written by me. I encourage anyone who has made it this far to read through the end notes as well as explore the court documents, exhibits, civil motions, interview and trial transcripts, and more. All those materials will be stored in a cloud drive at bit.ly/kaidocs as well as at my personal site philfairbanks. com at the following shortened link: https://bit.ly/smashsupplement

Some interesting highlights from documents that didn't make it directly into the book or the end notes follow.

Case 2:22-cv-04185-MCA Document 1-7 Filed 06/22/22 Page 3 of 25 PageID: 63

Brief in support of Defendant's Motion to dismiss indictment based upon spoliation of evidence; or in the alternative, motion for issue preclusion and reduction of charges; and motion for designated facts to be taken as established or, in the alternative motion for adverse interference. Da2

Case 2:22-cv-04185-MCA Document 1-7 Filed 06/22/22 Page 8 of 25 PageID: 68

Exhibit N (statement to Ho) Defendant's position as to the events that occurred are as follows, as noted in his statement to Detective Ho (Exhibit N)

Case 2:22-cv-04185-MCA Document 1-7 Filed 06/22/22 Page 10 of 25 PageID: 70

An oddly rolled paper napkin in the trash can was photographed at the crime scene [DA 107, 110] (quite possibly an improvised paper funnel that has come unrolled. It could have been used to put crushed pills or powders in the glass of beer he gave Kai). No analysis was done on any of the items. No testing was done on carpet fibers [DA 4-13] which could have been tested to see if it contained any drug residue. The CCTV footage for the New Jersey transit system conveniently has frames unaccounted for allowing them to advance the narrative Kai changed his appearance despite the fact that short hairs found on the vertical side of the mattress and hairs in Galfy's car corroborate his claim that he cut his hair at the train station [DA 15-19].

The mysteriously missing footage from between 12:44 and 4 p.m. [DA 111, 112] was never recovered. The state claims the video was accidentally deleted.

Case 2:22-cv-04185-MCA Document 1-7 Filed 06/22/22 Page 11 of 25 PageID: 71

More misleading information regarding the pill bottles and other potential exculpatory evidence that was never tested: Johnny Ho swore to the Grand Jury that "The pill bottles are being tested by the lab." [DA 43-44 P25 L24-25]; "There was also some empty beer bottles that were collected." [DA 45 P35 L22-23]; "At this time, [the beer bottles] are still being examined by the [...] lab."

Judge Regina Caulfield opined in an earlier motion to dismiss the indictment

that "[L]ab technicians did not find semen on the master bedroom beddings submitted for testing, thus, the physical evidence to substantiate Defendant's allegations [that Joseph Galfy raped him on the floor] was lacking." [DA 70 P22] This is disproved by Forensic Lab Report Number

2 which shows that not only was semen found in Galfy's underwear but so was blood which was never identified.

As for the hairs? She thought it was "reasonable to conclude that [Defendant's] hair could have simply fallen from his head while he was staying at Galfy's residence. Moreover, the State had evidence proving that Defendant cut his hair shortly after Galfy's death." That "evidence" was the CCTV footage that shows him the day prior with long hair. The same footage with hours of missing footage that was "accidentally deleted" by the State.

Case 2:22-cv-04185-MCA Document 1-8 Filed 06/22/22 Page 4 of 13 PageID: 89

Kirsch assured that "any and all motions" were to come through Cito and Cito alone. The judge notes that Kai's previous motion to dismiss was denied in "a rather voluminous opinion" by Judge Caulfield (issues with which are addressed elsewhere in these end notes).

Case 2:22-cv-04185-MCA Document 1-8 Filed 06/22/22 Page 9 of 13 PageID: 94

Judge Kirsch should be fully aware of the issues, he complained Kai's complaint regarding the Brady violation matter (bad faith/willful spoliation of exculpatory evidence) was "nearly four inches thick" before denying it and ordering all motions to go through Cito from then on (see Case 2:22-cv-04185-MCA Document 1-8 Filed 06/22/22 Page 9 of 13 PageID: 93).

The judge goes on to claim that "getting an expert pharmacologist to render an opinion on the effects of a so-called date drug on Mr. McGillvary, I am not sure if there are sufficient facts to support the rendering of an expert opinion, as I understand this case. There is no corroboration for Mr.

McGillvary's belief that he was drugged, so an expert would be really hamstrung in terms of rendering an opinion as to not knowing the quantity, what was -- he was supposedly drugged with, et cetera."

Case 2:22-cv-04185-MCA Document 1-9 Filed 06/22/22 Page 22-24 of 87 PageID: 120-122

Exhibit C

June 3, 2020

Kirsch put Kai in "the hole" just before Kai was to take the stand. It's well established in medical literature that solitary confinement can have a very deleterious effect on the cognition, cogency, mood, and mental stability of inmates. Even in the transcripts, Kirsch's tone tended to be negative when addressing or responding to Kai. Kai notes multiple instances where Kirsch berates Kai, interrupts him, or addresses his testimony with doubt, dismissal, or skepticism.

Case 2:22-cv-04185-MCA Document 1-9 Filed 06/22/22 Page 27 of 87 PageID: 125

A $55 million lawsuit regarding destruction of exculpatory evidence that Peterson was involved with is mentioned. Kirsch said that for Kai "to impugn [...] bad faith [...] [to prosecutor Scott Peterson] is inappropriate." [13T125-4 to 13]

Case 2:22-cv-04185-MCA Document 1-9 Filed 06/22/22 Page 54 of 87 PageID: 152

Ho admitted that "[t]he purpose of testing for DNA would be to develop a [murder] suspect, so, therefore there wouldn't have been any [purpose] for

DNA." [13T129-8 to 10] This makes it clear that once Kai was developed as a suspect in the death of Joseph Galfy, interest in the sexual assault they were initially also investigating went out the window.

Case 2:22-cv-04185-MCA Document 1-9 Filed 06/22/22 Page 57 of 87 PageID: 155

Kai speaks on the record of a: "brazen attempt by Kirsch to game the system; was shrewd, manipulative, and disingenuous. It was designed to disrupt the criminal justice system: by deliberately deceiving the Reviewing Court, as to the true facts of this case. It was yet another example of the Honorable Robert A. Kirsch, J.S.C. 'talking, frankly, out of both sides of his mouth.'" [19T52-14 to 17]

Case 2:22-cv-04185-MCA Document 1-10 Filed 06/22/22 Page 49 of 101 PageID: 234

As to the question of how mention of "stomping" and "blunt force trauma" affected the understanding of the jury, the state argued that "possibly" Shaikh's testimony misled the jury. But since he was "not rendering an opinion to a medical certainty" it was within the bounds of the law. Though the testimony was not "clearly capable of producing an unjust result" rather it was merely potentially capable of such.

Case 2:22-cv-04185-MCA Document 1-11 Filed 06/22/22 Page 3 of 8 PageID: 289

A black iPhone, watch, wallet, cash, and keys to the Chrysler were all found near Galfy's body. The many valuable items in plain sight and the presence of gold, valuable coins, and more make it clear that Kai did not take anything of value before leaving.

READER NOTES

ENDNOTES

Chapter 1: Two Fateful Rides

1.   63% humidity, 5km/h wind, low 3C (33.7F), high 13C (55.4F)

Time and Date. "Past Weather in Fresno, California, USA - February 2013." 2022. https://www.timeanddate.com/weather/usa/fresno/historic?month=2&year=2013.

2.   On February 1, Nelson Pereira, an equipment operator for Pacific Gas and Electric Company (PG&E), was working with Rayshawn Neely, Kenneth Simon, and Nicholas Starkey on a project at Marks and McKinley in Fresno. Around 2:00 p.m., they were on the northwest corner of the intersection, getting ready to perform a task on a corner pole. Neely and Simon were scheduled to go up in the "bucket," while Pereira and Starkey were going to remain on the ground.

People v. McBride, F068949, 3 (Cal. Ct. App. Jan. 27, 2016)

"A broken right leg, and a scarred left leg, has left him bed-ridden. With his wife by his side, Neely is beginning a lengthy recovery process after being attacked while at work."

ABC7. "Fresno PG&E Worker Describes Bizarre Attack: ABC7 Chicago." ABC7 Chicago, 2013. https://abc7chicago.com/archive/8983259/.

3.   "'This is a guy who is undergoing an incredibly traumatic experience, and then he becomes this ironic folk hero,' O'Connell says." Hesse, Monica. "Kai the Hatchet-Wielding Hitchhiker: Why Did We Love Him?" *Washington Post*, 2013.

"His stoner inflection and dramatic storytelling turned him into a folk hero."

O'Connor, Maureen. 2013. "Meet Kai, the Hatchet-Wielding Hitchhiker: Viral-Video Star, Murder Suspect, Fugitive." *New York media*, 2013. https://nymag.com/intelligencer/2013/05/viral-video-hero-flees-murder-charge.html.

4.   6'4" 290 pound Jett McBride picked up Kai then shortly before the attack confesses to raping an underage girl in the Virgin Islands before claiming he is Jesus and pinning Rayshawn Neely.

Kavanaugh, Shane Dixon. "A California Utility Worker's Leg Is Crushed by Crazed 290-Pound 'Jesus Christ,' Who Is Then Hatcheted by Far-out Drifter after Trying to Hug Woman Bystander to Death." *New York Daily News*, 2019. https://www.nydailynews.com/news/national/jesus-hatcheted-drifter-bizarre-roadside-scene-article-1.1255491.

5.   On February 1, Nelson Pereira, an equipment operator for Pacific Gas and Electric Company (PG&E), was working with Rayshawn Neely, Kenneth Simon, and Nicholas Starkey on a project at Marks and McKinley in Fresno. Around 2:00 p.m., they were on the northwest corner of the intersection, getting ready to perform a task on a corner pole. Neely and Simon were scheduled to go up in the "bucket," while Pereira and Starkey were going to remain on the ground.

People v. McBride, F068949, 3 (Cal. Ct. App. Jan. 27, 2016)

6.   "I am God. I am Jesus. I was sent here to take all the [racial slurs] to heaven."

Geiger, Dorian. 2019. "Kai The Hatchet-Wielding Hitchhiker's Father Vows To Fight Murder Conviction." https://www.oxygen.com/crime-time/kai-the-hatchet-wielding-hitchhikers-father-gil-mcgillivary-interview-after-murder-conviction

7.   McBride attacked a woman at the scene. Kai prevents a "hella lot more bodies" on the ground at the scene.

Vadala, Nick. "Kai the Homeless Hitchhiker with an Ax Is Hero for Millennials: The Philly Post." *Philadelphia Magazine*, 19 Sept. 2013, https://www.phillymag.com/news/2013/02/08/kai-homeless-hitchhiker-axe-hero-millennials/.

8.   Tanya Baker is the woman attacked by McBride.

Beaman, Lucinda. "'Hatchet Wielding Hero' Arrested for Murder." *The Times*, 17 May 2013, https://www.thetimes.co.uk/article/hatchet-wielding-hero-arrested-for-murder-3fnx0kshp80.

9.   Jessob Reisbeck interview.

Reisbeck, Jessob. "Kai, Hatchet Wielding Hitchhiker, Amazing Interview." *YouTube*. Accessed November 6, 2022. https://www.youtube.com/watch?v=ckfBGdZoR_0.

10. Kai's viral fame was swift and fast spreading after the interview made the rounds he quickly achieved "meme status."

The San Joaquin Valley Sun. "Kai The Hitchhiker, of Fresno Viral Interview Fame, Has Murder Conviction Upheld on Appeal." The San Joaquin Valley Sun, August 5, 2021. https://sjvsun.com/news/fresno/kai-the-hitchhiker-of-fresno-viral-interview-fame-has-murder-conviction-upheld-on-appeal/.

Abramovitch, Seth. "Viral Sensation Kai the Hitchhiker Sought in Man's Murder." *The Hollywood Reporter*, May 16, 2013. https://www.hollywoodreporter.com/tv/tv-news/viral-sensation-kai-hitchhiker-sought-524067/.

11. Kai was referred to by Jessob as a "world class hero." February 7, 2013 follow up interview

Reisbeck, Jessob. "UPDATE! KMPH Exclusively Talks Again To Kai, The Hatchet-Wielding Hitchhiker [OFFICIAL VIDEO]." *KMPH FOX26 NEWS*, February 7, 2013. https://www.youtube.com/watch?v=lbONqAjdHSg

12. Philadelphia magazine "Kai the Homeless Hitchhiker Is the Hero Millennials Need"

Vadala, Nick. "Kai the Homeless Hitchhiker Is the Hero Millennials Need." *Philadelphia Magazine*, August 2, 2013. https://www.phillymag.com/news/2013/02/08/kai-homeless-hitchhiker-axe-hero-millennials.

13. Kai gets autotuned, Autotune the news.

Huffpost. "Kai, Hitchhiker Hero, Gets Autotuned (VIDEO)." *HuffPost*, February 7, 2013. https://www.huffpost.com/entry/kai-hitchhiker-hero-gets-_n_2639370.

14. Kai meets with Philadelphia Inquirer and covers "Wagon Wheel"

Bertha, Mike. "Video: Shirtless Kai the Hitchhiker Covering 'Wagon Wheel' (plus, the Auto-Tuned Interview Song)." *The Philadelphia Inquirer*, February 7, 2013. https://www.inquirer.com/philly/blogs/trending/Shirtless-Kai-The-Hitchhiker-covering-Wagon-Wheel-Shirtless-Kai-The-Hitchhiker-auto-tuned-covering-

Wagon-Wheel.html.

15. IndieGogo campaign to get Kai a new surfboard and wetsuit

Indiegogo. "Get Kai the Hatchet Hero a New Surfboard and Wetsuit.," 2022. https://www.indiegogo.com/projects/get-kai-the-hatchet-hero-a-new-surfboard-and-wetsuit--6#/.

16. After his appearance on the Jimmy Kimmel Show, Kai was handed an envelope full of a "significant amount" of cash which he handed back to the security guard. "He's one the most intelligent people I've met, one of the most bizarre humans I've ever come in contact with and will ever come in contact with, but he can do the most crazy thing and then the most good hearted thing after," Reisbeck said of the night.

Nieto-Munoz, Sophie. "Kai The Hitchhiker's Strange Journey from Hatchet-Wielding Hero to Convicted Killer." *Star-Ledger*, April 27, 2019. https://www.nj.com/news/g66l-2019/04/592fc95a5d6709/kai-the-hitchhiker-from-straight-outta-dogtown-hatchetwielding-hero-to-convicted-killer.html.

17. McBride spoke glowingly of Kai to his wife: "Defendant admitted that before he knew what McGillivary said regarding the incident, defendant told Donna that he loved McGillivary to death and thought he was the "coolest son-of-a-bitch" defendant ever met. Defendant also talked to Donna about bringing McGillivary up to live with them and wanting to adopt him."

People v. McBride, F068949, 26 n.25 (Cal. Ct. App. Jan. 27, 2016)

18. "Kai is star witness and scapegoat in attempted murder trial." ABC30 January 7, 2014.

ABC7. "Former Internet Hero Kai Is Star Witness and Scapegoat in Attempted Murder Trial." *ABC7 San Francisco*, December 17, 2013. https://abc7news.com/archive/9361827/.

19. Baly "won't say whether it hurt or helped"

ABC30. "Jett McBride Found Not Guilty of Attempted Murder." *ABC30 Fresno,* January 7, 2014. https://abc30.com/archive/9383501/.

20. Defendant packed his bags and got in the car that night. He planned to go to New Orleans, where the Super Bowl would be held that Sunday, to warn people there would be an explosion. He broke his phone in half in a parking lot and threw the pieces in some bushes. He did not want any contact with his wife, and did not want to be tracked. He thought the government, CIA, FBI, and Department of Defense were tracking him.

People v. McBride, F068949, 18-19 (Cal. Ct. App. Jan. 27, 2016)

"Prior to reaching Bakersfield, defendant had been passed by two or three white utility trucks. He felt they were the Illuminati following him, and that they were going to try to kill him. "

People v. McBride, F068949, 19 (Cal. Ct. App. Jan. 27, 2016)

21. Vagabond Inn describes itself on the website as a "charming, Fresno CA Hotel" that "is located off the 99 Freeway at South East Avenue and Jensen."

Vagabond Inn. "A Charming Fresno, CA Hotel - Vagabond Inn Fresno." Vagabond

Inn Hotels, October 26, 2022. https://www.vagabondinn.com/vagabond-inn-fresno.

22.   The two traveled to Fresno, with defendant driving the whole way. During the trip, they discussed religion. Defendant cited numerology in a way that was "shaded by his own prejudicial kind of mainstream fundamentalist Christian views." He did not refer to himself as Jesus during this time. Defendant said he was a successful custom motorbike mechanic who shipped to people all over the country, and that he had a Japanese wife. He also said he was involved in Christian organizations, although he did not elaborate on their nature, and that he was from Tacoma, Washington, and was headed back there. Defendant did not talk about the color of people's skin; had McGillivary "known about that," he "would have hopped on out."

People v. McBride, F068949, 11-12 (Cal. Ct. App. Jan. 27, 2016)

23.   "In Fresno, the two men stopped in the Tower District, where defendant gave McGillivary money with which to buy them some marijuana. McGillivary purchased a baggie of it, which he placed in the console at defendant's direction, then they drove to a recycling depot and shared a joint while they waited for the car radiator to cool down. McGillivary put some water in the radiator and advised defendant to turn on the heating core, and they were able to get the car back on its way. Defendant smoked about a quarter of the joint; McGillivary, who rated the marijuana's potency as two or three on a scale of one to 10, with 10 being the most potent, was feeling '[g]narly and mellow.'"

People v. McBride, F068949, 12 (Cal. Ct. App. Jan. 27, 2016)

24.   In addition, they had a "deep" conversation. They talked about family and where both were from. In addition, defendant told McGillivary about a girl he slept with in the Virgin Islands about 30 or 35 years earlier. Defendant then held McGillivary's hands and kind of leaned over and gave him a hug. McGillivary hugged him back. Defendant was depressed and distraught. He was crying, because he was upset about his wife.

People v. McBride, F068949, 21 (Cal. Ct. App. Jan. 27, 2016)

25.   He was thinking that he had the Holy Spirit in him, and that he could at least take away some of Neely's pain and heal his leg if he could not move the car. At this point, defendant believed, to some extent, that he was Jesus Christ.

People v. McBride, F068949, 23-24 (Cal. Ct. App. Jan. 27, 2016)

26.   "Defendant admitted telling the detective that he hit the truck on purpose and tried to kill Neely. He denied doing it because Neely was Black, but agreed he did it because Neely was Illuminati."

People v. McBride, F068949, 26 (Cal. Ct. App. Jan. 27, 2016)

Starkey saw defendant walk over, grab Neely under the arms, and start pulling on him. Neely was screaming in pain and asked someone to get defendant off him. Starkey heard defendant say, "I am God. I am Jesus. I was sent here to take all the niggers to heaven."

People v. McBride, F068949, 6 (Cal. Ct. App. Jan. 27, 2016)

27.   Defendant did not recall saying anything to Neely, although he may have said "God bless you" or something similar. At no time did defendant make any racial

statements to Neely or use a racial epithet.

Neely turned around and said, "Get this fucker off of me."

People v. McBride, F068949, 23-24 (Cal. Ct. App. Jan. 27, 2016)

28. "His victims were not in court Thursday, but they tell Action News they're just trying to recover from their injuries and move on from the crash. One of them, though, said he hopes McBride does not get off without real consequences."

ABC7. "Jury Finds Jett McBride Insane in PG&E Worker Attack: ." *ABC7 Chicago*, January 17, 2014. https://abc7chicago.com/archive/9395230/.

29. Kirell, Andrew. "Colbert Hilariously Proves That 'Hatchet-Wielding Homeless Hitchhikers Are People Too'." *Mediaite*, February 6, 2013. htttpps://www.mediaite. com/tv/colbert-hilariously-proves-that-hatchet-wielding-homeless-hitchhikers-are-people-too/.

30. Romankow claimed to me he was not "friends" with Galfy but in addition to professional connections they certainly ran into each other outside of work. For instance, Clark Memorial Day Parade May 26 American Legion Post honored "Post member" Galfy.

Romankow spent years raising money for the Veterans Memorial Park Committee in Union County and attended multiple American Legion events in the area. Galfy was a member of the Clark American Legion post in Union County.

Bobbie Peer. "Berkeley Heights Honors the Fallen with a Memorial Day Parade and Ceremony." *TAPintoBerkeley-Heights*, May 27, 2019. https://www.tapinto.net/towns/berkeley-heights/sections/giving-back/articles/berkeley-heights-honors-the-fallen-with-a-memorial-day-parade-and-ceremony.

Abramovitch, Seth. "Viral Sensation Kai the Hitchhiker Sought in Man's Murder." *The Hollywood Reporter*, May 16, 2013. htttpps://www.hollywoodreporter.com/tv/tv-news/viral-sensation-kai-hitchhiker-sought-524067/.

31. "As they traced Kai's steps -- from Fresno across the country -- police say they've uncovered unsolved homicides along the way.

Kai's not a suspect in those cases yet, but police will take a closer look.

"Any time you get a drifter and then all of the sudden he's being charged with a homicide, it would be a lack of responsibility for us not to look into that possibility," Romankow said.

6abc. "Kai Arrested in Philadelphia for New Jersey Murder." *6abc Philadelphia*, May 17, 2013. https://6abc.com/archive/9105613/.

32. "Romankow had been in a hold-over position since his term expired in January. He was told earlier this month that a new prosecutor was selected.

Romankow announced his resignation May 16th, the day Kai was arrested. He claimed that Governor Chris Christie had selected a replacement already. Oddly, a spokesman for Christie "Michael Drewniak said nobody had been appointed to the post and he would not confirm an appointment before submitting a notice of intent to nominate with the Legislature." Romankow would stay in office until June 16th "and said Christie had 'been extremely indulgent' in giving him a month to tie up matters in his office."

Haydon, Tom. "Former Assistant Federal Prosecutor Tapped for Union County's Top Law Enforcement Job." *Star-Ledger*, May 23, 2013. https://www.nj.com/union/2013/05/former_assistant_federal_prose.html.

33. "Kai's stream of consciousness delivery – a mixture of Bill and Ted and The Big Lebowski – meant footage of his interview was watched more than one million times and it made him a star."

34. "Kai the Homefree Hitchhiker: The Early Years, North Coast Journal. Why does this matter to you, Humboldtian? As the *Lost Coast Outpost* noted earlier today, Kai's personal Facebook page lists 'Eureka, California' as the place Kai "lives in." -- so feel free to claim him as your hometown hero and check out the following picture from Kai's Facebook page taken on the Arcata Plaza.

     Feb 8, 2013"

     Goff, Andrew. "Kai the Homefree Hitchhiker: The Early Years." *North Coast Journal,* February 8, 2013. https://www.northcoastjournal.com/NewsBlog/archives/2013/02/08/kai-the-homefree-hitchhiker-the-early-years.

35. "But Kai was still out there. He even said as much in Facebook post: 'I'm sleeping in a hay field across I99 from the chevron/days inn in Lathrope CA. Do any, uh, new friends feel like sharing couchspace?'"

     Zimmerman, Neetzan. "Where Are They Now: News Reporter Tracks Down Kai, the 'Hatchet-Wielding Hitchhiker'." *Gawker.* July 2, 2013. https://www.gawker.com/5982533/where-are-they-now-news-reporter-tracks-down-kai-the-hatchet-wielding-hitchhiker.

36. "I've totally ran into this guy before. So I went back through my photos and, sure enough, found our hero in a series of shots I'd taken for the *Journal*'s End of the World Issue "Plaza Prophecies" piece back in December. Kai kept quiet on his thoughts on Armageddon that day. Perhaps he knew better.

     Congrats on the fame, Kai. And if you do end up, as rumored, on Jimmy Kimmel Live in the near future, remind him that he owes us a visit."

     North Coast Journal ibid

37. Bates, Daniel, James Nye, and SNEJANA FARBEROV. "Did Hitchhiker Kai's Tattoo Do Him in? Former Web Hero Arrested Thanks to Sharp-Eyed Starbucks Barista." *Daily Mail Online,* May 17, 2013. httpps://www.dailymail.co.uk/news/article-2326311/Did-Hitchhiker-Kais-tattoo-Former-web-hero-arrested-thanks-sharp-eyed-Starbucks-barista.html

38. In the weeks that followed, Reisbeck said he assumed the role of McGillivary's de facto agent, fielding and filtering interview and appearance requests since the reporter was one of the only "people on the planet" who had the vagabond's contact information.

     "Every show you could think of was trying to get him on the show — late night, day time," said Reisbeck, who appeared on Kimmel's talk show with McGillivary.

     Producers for the Kardashian family even approached McGillivary for his own show, the ABC anchor claimed.

"It breaks my heart how this whole story ended. It was a fantastic, cool story, how big it got — how big he could have been. He could have had everything," Reisbeck added.

Geiger, Dorian. "Kai the Hatchet-Wielding Hitchhiker's Father Vows to Fight Murder Conviction." *Oxygen.* April 26, 2019. https://www.oxygen.com/crime-time/kai-the-hatchet-wielding-hitchhikers-father-gil-mcgillivary-interview-after-murder-conviction.

39.   U.S. Embassy & Consulates in Canada, First Nations, and Native Americans: "The Jay Treaty, signed in 1794 between Great Britain and the United States, provides that American Indians may travel freely across the international boundary. Under the treaty and corresponding legislation, Native Indians born in Canada are entitled to freely enter the United States for the purpose of employment, study, retirement, investing, and/or immigration."

U.S. Embassy & Consulates in Canada. "First Nations and Native Americans," August 14, 2017. https://ca.usembassy.gov/visas/first-nations-and-native-americans/.

40.   "He's certainly being a lot more careful than many of the people we tried to trick into handing over their names and dates of birth on the streets of Bristol a few years ago…"

Cluley, Graham. "Kai, the Hatchet-Wielding Hitchhiker, Tells All but His Name [Video]." Naked Security, February 5, 2013. https://nakedsecurity.sophos.com/2013/02/05/kai-hatchet-hitchhiker/.

41.   "I'm just gonna be Kai any way it goes. Obviously I was put in a situation for a reason. I would hope, I do hope, that people don't become obsessed with this because there's still so much more that we can do."

Kosur 10 years ago9 years ago, James. "Kai The Hitchhiker Revealed: Homeless Drifter Gives First Official Interview." *Social News Daily*, March 23, 2014. https://socialnewsdaily.com/8631/kai-the-hitchhiker-revealed-homeless-drifter-gives-first-official-interview/.

41.   "Revealing an enormous back tattoo and suggesting he has some severe scarring, Kai alluded to a childhood of abuse and molestation. Reisbeck said many of Kai's 'darker, gut-wrenching' stories cannot be repeated on television. […] 'All of these scars have healed, but they're still scars,' he solemnly said. 'I don't want to go back to being a certain way. This inner-child that I've guarded his whole life is still right here and intact. And I love this inner-child very much. I respect this inner-child, I value this inner-child. And I am the dad that I always wanted.'"

In the same article, Mediaite attributes some of Kai's viral fame to their reporter Meenal Vamburkar sharing the Reisbeck interview on that site. It also references Reisbeck mentioning Kai being trilingual.

Kirell, Andrew. "Behind the Hero: Kai the Hatchet-Wielding Hitchhiker Gives Intimate Interview about 'Dark' Past." *Mediaite*, 10 Feb. 2013, https://www.mediaite.com/tv/behind-the-hero-kai-the-hatchet-wielding-hitchhiker-gives-intimate-interview-about-dark-past/.

42.   The. Schmoyoho auto-tune version of "Smash, smash, smash" uploaded February 7,

2013, currently has over 11 million views and over 110,000 likes at Youtube.

Smash, Smash, SMASH! - Songify This. YouTube, 2013. https://www.youtube.com/watch?v=wDQTvuP1Dgs.

43. What's Trending, Feb 8, 2013 "What's Trending" YouTube channel lists the Gregory Brothers' auto-tune of Kai as the top trending video.

Bros, Gregory. "Gregory Bros. Auto-Tune Kai the Hatchet Hitchhiker Plus Top YouTube Videos of 2/7/13." What's Trending. Feb 8, 2013. YouTube Video, 4: 13. https://www.youtube.com/watch?v=ocBCC8HOdAs

44. The original song from the Feb 8, 2013 video from KMPH Fox26 YouTube channel.

Reisbeck, Jessob. "Kai The Hatchet Wielding Hitchhiker's Original Song [Official Video]." KMPH FOX26 NEWS, Feb 8, 2013. YouTube Video, 4:13. https://www.youtube.com/watch?v=sDxKp22hmBY

45. "He's kind of like a superhero." Reisbeck, Shrouded in Viral Mystery, Kai the Hitchhiker Gains a Cult Following

Laird, Sam. "Shrouded in Viral Mystery, Kai the Hitchhiker Gains a Cult Following." *Mashable*, March 11, 2022. https://mashable.com/archive/kai-the-hitchhiker.

U.S. Embassy & Consulates in Canada. "First Nations and Native Americans," August 14, 2017. https://ca.usembassy.gov/visas/first-nations-and-native-americans/.

46. Gaskell , Jessie. "Leftover Soup 2/8/13." E! Online, February 9, 2013. httpps://www.eonline.com/news/386627/leftover-soup-2-8-13.

Stucknut. "Stucknut Takebox - Jim Rome Audio Archive.," May 2, 2013. httpps://www.stucknut.com/.

47. Christian Worzalla's quote.

ibid *Mashable*

48. Paul. "How Kai the Hatchet Hitchhiker Proves We Would Embrace a Real Life Dexter." *Unreality Mag*, February 13, 2013. httpps://unrealitymag.com/how-kai-the-hatchet-hitchhiker-proves-we-would-embrace-a-real-life-dexter/.

49. IBEW (International Brotherhood of Electrical Workers) offers Kai all expense paid surfing trip as thanks for saving the life of Rayshawn Neeley.

"We decided we need to do something to honor Kai." "Since he loves surfing so much, we want to give   him a surfing weekend. All expense paid, by the union." IBEW was offering to pay for a 2 night stay ($700), $1000 for travel and meals and $300 spending money.

"His act of heroism, courage, touched all of us." The IBEW spokesperson announced. Unfortunately the surfing trip and the meeting would not occur before the events in New Jersey sent his life in a tailspin.

Reisbeck, Jessob. "Kai is Offered Surf Trip from Injured PG&E Worker's Union, KMPH Exclusive." *KMPH FOX26 NEWS*, 2013. YouTube Video, 2: 24. https://www.youtube.com/watch?v=HlTTTYDL_eg

Whitehurst, Winston. "Workers Union Offers Paid Surfing Trip for Kai, the Hatchet-Wielding Hitchhiker." KMPH. KMPH, September 28, 2015. https://kmph.com/archive/gallery/free-surf-trip-for-hatchet-wielding-hitchhiker.

50. After McGillivary testified at defendant's preliminary hearing, but before defendant's trial, McGillivary was arrested in New Jersey and indicted for murder. The prosecutor was unable to secure his attendance at defendant's trial, and his preliminary hearing testimony was read to the jury. (Evid. Code, §§ 1290, 1291; see § 240, subd. (a)(4).) The prosecutor moved, in limine, to exclude evidence of the arrest and indictment as irrelevant. Defendant sought to impeach McGillivary's credibility with that evidence and with McGillivary's demeanor while testifying at the preliminary hearing.

People v. McBride, F068949, 27 (Cal. Ct. App. Jan. 27, 2016)

51. "God being Sophia, yes" "Plastic, made out of dinosaurs"

"Q And did you bring [the marijuana] back to the car?

"A Yes, I did.

"Q Is that in a baggy of some type or a bag?

"A That is correct.

"Q Okay. What type of bag?

"A Plastic, made out of dinosaurs.

People v. McBride, F068949, 34-35 (Cal. Ct. App. Jan. 27, 2016)

"THE CLERK: Do you solemnly state, under penalty of perjury, that the testimony you are about to give in the matter now pending before this court shall be the truth, the whole truth, and nothing but the truth?

"THE WITNESS: God being Sophia, yes.

People v. McBride, F068949, (Cal. Ct. App. Jan. 27, 2016)

52. "The foregoing are only three of numerous examples. The jury did not need visual aids to ascertain McGillivary's demeanor or attitude toward testifying, and in fact defense counsel commenced his summation by forcefully arguing McGillivary was not a credible witness."

People v. McBride, F068949, 35 (Cal. Ct. App. Jan. 27, 2016)

53. We now hold: (1) The trial court did not abuse its discretion by excluding certain impeachment and demeanor evidence; (2) The trial court did not abuse its discretion by overruling defense objections to expert opinion testimony on the White supremacist nature of defendant's hospital remarks, and if it should have excluded references to defendant's admissions of statutory rape, the error was harmless; (3) Defendant is not entitled to reversal based on cumulative prejudice; but (4) Certain clerical errors should be corrected. Accordingly, we order correction of those errors and affirm the judgment.

People v. McBride, F068949, 2 (Cal. Ct. App. Jan. 27, 2016)

54. When Lomeli asked defendant his name, defendant yelled out "88" two or three times. From his training and experience in the gang unit and from speaking to

White male adults in and out of custody, Lomeli knew 8 stood for the letter H, the eighth letter of the alphabet; hence, 88 stood for HH, which in turn stood for Heil Hitler.

California Highway Patrol Officer Vaccarezza responded to the hospital to stay with defendant, who was transported by ambulance. Defendant was unruly and belligerent. He was thrashing around on the gurney, yelling and screaming. He kept saying "88" and asked a male nurse in the emergency department "if he was a Jew." As a gang investigator with the gang unit, Vaccarezza had had classes that included the topics of White gangs and White supremacist groups. He learned that 8 represented H, the eighth letter of the alphabet, and that 88 stood for Heil Hitler. White supremacist groups said "88" and tattooed it on their bodies.

People v. McBride, F068949, 10-11 (Cal. Ct. App. Jan. 27, 2016)

55. "Pursuant to Penal Code section 1026, the trial court committed him to Atascadero State Hospital for a maximum term of nine years."

People v. McBride, F068949, 2 (Cal. Ct. App. Jan. 27, 2016)

56. Ed Kemper was released from Atascadero at the age of 21 after being held since 1964 at the age of 15. He would go on to become "the Co-Ed killer" after being released.1

Ferrarin, Elena. "Ed Kemper Was Released from a Forensic Hospital after Killing His Grandparents and Went on to Murder 8 More People." A&E, August 1, 2022. https://www.aetv.com/real-crime/ed-kemper-hospital-release.

57. Kai's attempts to assert his Sixth Amendment right to a speedy trial and his constitutional right to represent himself in court were denied by the court.

CALEB L. MCGILLVARY, THE DEFENDANT, AFFIRMED

THE DEFENDANT: I'd like to affirm.

THE DEPUTY: Okay, state your name for the record.

THE DEFENDANT: Caleb McGillvary.

THE DEPUTY: Alright.

THE DEFENDANT: For the record, judge, I assert my Sixth Amendment right to litigate my motion pro se and I have requested pro se to argue my case.

THE COURT: Sit down.

THE DEFENDENT: Thank you. For the record.

Case 2:22-cv-04185-MCA Document 1-6 Filed 06/22/22 Page 17 of 23 PageID: 54

Kirsch also casually exposes his bias along with Cito's complicity in just going along with Kirsch's "kangaroo court" as Kai put it:

THE COURT: His testimony certainly alluded to what he viewed to be the odd manner in which Mr. Galfy poured his beer. He went through a number of descriptions that he would turn his back; and much of your cross-examination, Mr. Cito, to a number of State's witnesses, went to did you test the vitamins in the refrigerator, did you test the empty bottles. I think you even opened on this aspect.

MR. CITO: Yes, Your Honor. And also the other thing is when Dr. Wang -- he even testified about the combination of alcohol and heart medication pills could cause dizziness and the like so --

THE COURT: Much of the defense's case is an attempt to portray the State's investigation as shoddy slip-shod.

MR. CITO: Correct, your Honor.

Kirsch goes on to denigrate Kai's story, reducing it to being all about bitterness of the beer and that one of the beers was poured out of his presence. He was "frankly very surprised that Mr. McGillvary would seek the Court not to include that instruction. It's so clearly in his interests and it's so clearly consistent with your defense throughout, Mr. Cito, and I believe there's ample evidence in the record and so you've indicated as a representative of the court that you seek it."

MR. CITO: I seek it. I was putting the record clear what my client's position was for appellate reasons, but I believe it should be in.

THE COURT: And I couldn't agree with you more, Mr. Cito. It's clearly in Mr. McGillvary's interest's to do so.

Kai was ruled competent though, so denying him the right to represent himself pro se, present his own motions, etc. is unconstitutional. No matter how much the judge, the state, and the defense agree, it's unconstitutional.

Case 2:22-cv-04185-MCA Document 1-10 Filed 06/22/22 Page 95-96 of 101 PageID: 280-281

58. Kavanaugh, Shane Dixon. "Kai the Hatchet-Wielding Hitchhiker Nearly Slept on My Couch, Says Daily News Reporter." *New York Daily News,* January 10, 2019. https://www.nydailynews.com/news/crime/brush-kai-hatchet-man-article-1.1346184.

59. The Sad Tale Of Kai The Hatchet-Wielding Hitchhiker, July 14, 2016, was one of the first positive pieces of coverage for Kai in some years and one of the last before I began covering it in 2017 first at the *Inquisitr* then elsewhere.

Kavanaugh, Shane Dixon. "The Sad Tale of Kai the Hatchet-Wielding Hitchhiker." *Vocativ.* July 14, 2016. https://www.vocativ.com/335097/kai-the-hatchet-wielding-hitchhiker/index.html.

Kavanaugh, Shane Dixon. "Kai the Hatchet-Wielding Hitchhiker Reads a Poem from Prison." *Vocativ.* May 20, 2016. https://www.vocativ.com/culture/celebrity/kai-the-hatchet-wielding-hitchhiker-2/index.html

60. I mentioned the Cleveland Street Scandal in my first article on Kai's case in 2017. I had no idea how prescient it would become until 2022. Oscar Wilde's trial was full of people (from his own defense to those prosecuting and judging him) involved in the infamous sex trafficking scandal that utilized young boys disguised as telegraph operators. For more on how apt that story is head to Chapter 11 "A Slap on the Wrist." For more on the Cleveland Street Scandal itself, you can refer to the first chapter in my book *Pedogate Primer: the politics of pedophilia.*

"The Cleveland Street Scandal started in 1889, when police discovered a homosexual male brothel on Cleveland Street in London's West Side, made up of largely underage, lower-class male sex workers. The government was accused of covering up the names of aristocrats and other prominent figures that frequented the brothel. The rumors went as high up as Prince Albert Victor, the eldest son of the Prince of Wales and second in line to the throne. This was never directly proven, but has remained a conspiracy. Lord Arthur Somerset, a major in the Royal Horse Guards and equerry to the Prince of Wales, was also named. He fled to Hamburg, Germany before charges could be brought against him."

Kingston, Bridget. "Cleveland Street Scandal." COVE, February 16, 2021. httpps:// editions.covecollective.org/chronologies/cleveland-street-scan   dal.

61.   "Preliminary indications of blood were detected on the penis swab (Item 98) […] using a chemical presumptive test. Due to the limited sample size, no confirmatory testing was conducted." Ah, so *that's* why they didn't test the blood on Galfy's penis despite being informed of the rape.

Union County Prosecutor's Office Forensic Laboratory, Lab#: L 13-2765 Report Number 2

May 15, 2013, Kai's last Facebook post:

Caleb Kai Lawrence Yodhehwawheh. "What would you do if you woke up with a groggy head, metallic taste in your mouth, in a strangers house…" Facebook. May 14, 2013. https://bit.ly/3XiM5Ga

62.   April 27, 2019, NJ Advance Media, Kai the Hitchhiker's strange journey from hatchet-wielding hero to convicted killer

Munoz , Sophie Nieto-. "Kai The Hitchhiker's Strange Journey from Hatchet-Wielding Hero to Convicted Killer." *Star-Ledger*, April 27, 2019. https://www. nj.com/news/g66l-2019/04/592fc95a5d6709/kai-the-hitchhiker-from-straight-outta-dogtown-hatchetwielding-hero-to-convicted-killer.html.

63.   Reisbeck, Jessob.   Interview, 2013

64.   Reisbeck: "When we went to Jimmy Kimmel's show, they put him up in The (Hollywood) Roosevelt, a very nice hotel. He had a bag, it had everything he owned, even his sleeping bag," Reisbeck said. "And he takes the backpack off and leaves it outside, and said 'I'm staying in this hotel, someone needs this more than I do.'"

Sheldon, Chris. "How 'Kai the Hitchhiker' Went from Internet Sensation to a Convicted Killer." *Star-Ledger*, June 2, 2019. https://www.nj.com/news/g66l-2019/06/0bedf924466292/kai-the-hitchhiker-went-from-viral-video-sensation-to-a-convicted-killer-how-did-it-happen.html.

65.   May 11, Galfy runs into Kai in Times Square on one of his weekend trips to NYC. Considering he didn't recognize Kai when he picked him up, along with his brother James Galfy's cryptic mentions in his police interview suggest he had a history of picking up young men decades younger who appeared to be indigent and taking them into his home.

AP NEWS. "'Kai the Hitchhiker' Heading to NJ in Murder Case." Associated Press, May 28, 2013. https://apnews.com/article/2347629f06ec4206958eb403ac205f2b.

66.   Page 16, line 11: JG (James Galfy): And initially he was living there uhm and there

was an issue with some kind of a vagrant guy who robbed him when he was down there. TH (Terrance Harrison): Okay. JG: That was 45 years ago if not more so what type of people he ran into and who they were... TH: Uh-huh. JG: It could have been anybody.

Galfy, James. "Police interview transcript." By Terrance Harrison. *Docket/Case: 13001703*. May 13, 2013

Chapter 2: Brief Histories

1. James Cook was the first European to witness the practice now known as surfing. Like bungee jumping, the modern pastime is adapted from centuries-old indigenous practices.

    SurferToday. "Captain James Cook: The Explorer Who 'Discovered' Surfing." *Surfer Today*, July 3, 2020. https://www.surfertoday.com/surfing/captain-james-cook-the-explorer-who-discovered-surfing.

2. In Jessica Zehr's "Surfing Subculture" paper she cites Drew Kampion's 2003 book *Stoked! A History of Surf Culture*. Kampion states that "the Polynesian relationship to the sea was beyond European comprehension." Europeans were shocked by what appeared to them as "nakedness, sexuality, [...] shameless exuberance, informality, ignorant joy, and freedom"

    Zehr, Jessica. "Surfing Subculture." Academia.edu, May 25, 2014. https://www.academia.edu/3508604/Surfing_Subculture.

3. A Sociological Study of the Surfing Subculture in the Santa Cruz Area, was the Masters thesis written by Stephen Wayne Hull at San Jose University in 1976.

    Hull, Stephen Wayne. *A sociological study of the surfing subculture in the Santa Cruz area*. San Jose State University, 1976.

4. Dick Dale's Misirlou set the stage and the term "surf music" was adopted followed by hits from bands like Jan and Dean, The Ventures, Surfaris, Beach Boys, and others set the tone for "surf rock" in the early and mid 1960s.

    CalimaSurf. "Blog." Surf Rock, the Classics of the. Accessed November 14, 2022. https://calimasurf.com/news/surf-rock-surfers.

5. Zehr, Jessica, "Surfing Subculture" page 14, The lifestyle of a serious surfer was one spent constantly in the ocean, traveling around the world in search of new waves to ride, often sleeping in cars and on beaches, saving every possible cent for the necessities — food and surfing equipment (Reed 1999). Because of this way of life, there is little room for an occupation, and "surfers will often work at jobs which maximize their free time" according to Hull's sociological study from 1976 as quoted in Zehr's paper.

    Zehr, Jessica. "Surfing Subculture." Academia.edu, May 25, 2014. https://www.academia.edu/3508604/Surfing_Subculture.

6. "According to Jon Stratton, the American surf subculture as it emerged after World War II was 'rearticulated as the living of a myth of leisure.'"

    Maples, Wendy. Surf culture, July 19, 2010. https://www.open.edu/openlearn/body-mind/health/sport-and-fitness/sport/surf-culture.

7. "The decline of trust and rising concerns for personal safety, in tandem   with the changing character of those on the road, combined to alter understandings of the danger associated with hitchhiking. Even though violent   acts were perpetrated by and against hitchhikers in the 1930s and 1940s,   Americans overall perceived these events as isolated instances. Yet as trust   eroded and hitchhiking became associated with new and often subversive   individuals, Americans more and more began to perceive soliciting rides as   inherently dangerous. My focus in this regard is to assess how reactions to   violence changed over time and to determine how this influenced popular   perceptions of hitchhiking."

    Reid, Jack. *Roadside Americans: the rise and fall of hitchhiking in a changing nation.* UNC Press Books, 2020.

8. *Fast Times at Ridgemont High* introduced the world to an "iconic part of 80s culture" in the form of the character Jeff Spicoli. Sean Penn's portrayal of the "surfer dude slacker" would color the image of surfers in pop culture throughout the decade.

    Ballard, Ryan. "Jeff Spicoli – the Classic Character than Shaped the Surfer Stereotype." Surf Researcher, December 15, 2021. https://centerforsurfresearch.org/jeff-spicoli/.

9. In between Bill & Ted's Excellent Adventure and the "Teenage Mutant Ninja Turtles craze" of the late 80s and early 90s terms like "radical," "bodacious" and more entered into the slang vernacular. The word "tubular" features in both pieces of media, showed up in Frank Zappa's 1982 song "Valley Girl." According to Mental Floss, the 80s saw the Oxford English Dictionary add a new meaning to the word tubular (from the Latin *tubulus*) as a surf term denoting "a cresting wave: hollow and curved, so that it is well-formed for riding on."

    McCarthy, Erin. "15 Totally Tubular '80s Slang Terms." Mental Floss. February 20, 2020. https://www.mentalfloss.com/article/617530/1980s-slang-terms.

10. In 2005 in San Jose Del Cabo, Mexico 400 representatives from surf companies, law firms, investment banks store met together to discuss how to manage the speed of their growth to "preserve the environment, brands and surf culture."

    Apparel News. "Surfwear Makers Want Acceptance-but Not Too Much." May 20, 2005. https://www.apparelnews.net/news/2005/may/20/surfwear-makers-want-acceptance-but-not-too-much/.

11. Surfers, like hippies, were often assumed to be no more than "long haired rebels that were impartial to work or a career." Their lifestyle and appearance led to them being ostracized

    Surf Culture. "Perception," 2022. https://socalsurfing.weebly.com/perception.html.

12. Reed explores the relationship between the commodifiation of a culture and its acceptance.

    Reed, Michael Alan. "Waves of commodification: A critical investigation into surfing subculture." Master's thesis, San Diego State University, 1999.

13. Zephyr Competition Team (also referred to as Z-Boys) was highly influential in surfing and skateboarding culture based in Venice and Santa Monica, California.

    SurferToday. "Z-Boys: The Story of the Legendary Zephyr Skateboarding Team."

Surfer Today, October 20, 2021. https://www.surfertoday.com/skateboarding/z-boys-the-story-of-the-legendary-zephyr-skateboarding-team.

14. In 2002, just over a decade before Kai's viral moment, Micah Peasley achieved meme status with his spirited description of his surfing experience. Peasley admitted he was not anything like the "dumb surfer" people assumed.

   Wavelength Surf Magazine, and Luke Gartside. "Fifteen Years on, What Ever Happened to the 'so Pitted' Viral Surfer?" *Wavelength Surf Magazine - since 1981*, May 6, 2017. https://wavelengthmag.com/so-pitted-viral-surfer/.

15. *Roadside Americans*, p31 "Hitchhiking first became common in the 1920s. Although the nation's motor vehicles were largely in the hands of rural farmers -- 70 percent of automobiles in 1927 were in towns with fewer than fifty thousand people -- the ride solicitation culture of this era was predominantly urban, white, recreational and youthful in nature."

   Reid, Jack. *Roadside Americans: the rise and fall of hitchhiking in a changing nation.* UNC Press Books, 2020.

16. . loc. cit. p36 prospective social and moral dangers "Many declared hitchhiking unsafe and warned about the dangers of offering rides. [...] some fretted over the prospective social and moral dangers."

   Ibid

17. "In 1926, the New York Girl's Service League took it upon themselves to warn young women of the dangers of picking up rides from strangers. Hitchhiking was a 'special problem' and 'true ladies' do not accept rides."

   loc. cit., pg 37

18. New Deal "worked to enlarge the nation's highway infrastructure."

   pg 40 loc cit.,

19. loc. cit., p59, in 1937, Samuel Zeidman, for example, characterized hitchhikers as admirers of "hard work" and "free-enterprise capitalism." Praising ride solicitation as a force of good, he declared: "To the hitchhiker himself there is one final word. Hold your head high—not arrogantly but proudly. The road develops characteristics in you which are requisites for entrance into business and professional life."

   Ibid

20. "For instance, the sheer volume of so-called Okie farmers leaving Oklahoma in search of stable work frightened many within California's agricultural communities who saw them as outsiders competing for jobs and absorbing limited resources. At the same time, Americans judged tramps even more harshly."

   loc. cit. p44

21. "Polling data from 1938 suggests that roughly 43 percent of Americans offered lifts."

   loc cit p4 9

22. Corrosion of Conformity released a 1996 album entitled Wise Blood. Punk rockers Gang of Four released "A Man With a Good Car" in 1986. Both are references to the story of Hazel Motes, a story that on one level plays out as the struggle

for mobility (often in the form of automobility) which itself represents a sort of fundamental freedom. The most basic sort of freedom: the freedom to move from place to place.

loc. cit. pg. 82

23. Jack Kerouac's *On the Road* was "arguably the seminal text for rock rebellion."

Kerouac, Jack. "On the Road (1957)." *New York: Viking Penguin* (1991).

"No man with a good car needs to be justified": Preaching Rock and Roll Salvation from O'Connor's Wise Blood to Ministry's "Jesus Built My Hotrod"

Miller, Monica. "No man with a good car needs to be justified." *Flannery O'Connor Review* 12 (2014): 82-98.

24. Artists Von Dutch and Ed "Big Daddy" Roth's "Kustom Kulture" involved pinstriping cars, van murals, and underground "komix" that despite arising in the 50s were highly influential on the 60s counterculture scene. They were featured in Tom Wolfe's *The Kandy Kolored Tangerine-Flake Streamline Baby Artforum*, November 1993

Kraft, Charles. "Mechanical Dreams: Von Dutch and Kustom Kulture." The online edition of *Artforum International Magazine*, November 1, 1993. https://www.artforum.com/print/199309/mechanical-dreams-von-dutch-and-kustom-kulture-33746.

Boczkowska, Kornelia. "The Outlaw Machine, the Monstrous Outsider and Motorcycle Fetishists: Challenging Rebellion, Mobility and Masculinity in Kenneth Anger's Scorpio Rising and Steven Spielberg's Duel." *Text Matters: A Journal of Literature, Theory and Culture* 9 (2019): 81-99.

25. "Evocative of the era's informal and trusting culture, numerous Americans appearing in Hoerger's travel diary do not think twice about interacting with or helping a stranger. Highroad Number "Z" is unique in offering a detailed portrait of months spent on the road, but similar stories abound in local newspapers throughout the country during this era."

Ibid, p. 55

26. 26. Reagan as hitchhiker was a "true American story" according to radio personality Jim Zabel. Reagan had returned to the station where he'd hitched to find a job doing sports broadcasting on WHO Radio in Davenport, Iowa.

Reid, Jack. *Roadside Americans: the rise and fall of hitchhiking in a changing nation.* p. 10 UNC Press Books, 2020.   Ibid, p. 10

27. By the 1980s hitchhikers were generally assumed to be "unsavory individuals." It was not so much car ownership or crime rates that affected this perception (though that did lessen the number of hitchers and affect their type).

Ibid, p11

28. In the 1930s and 1940s hitchhiking was common and necessary (it was also a relatively safe period for hitchhiking according to crime blotters of the period).

Ibid

29. "During the years 1941 through 1947, American serviceman was the predominant

hitchhiker."

Ibid, p. 25

30. Ibid, p. 10

31. "A smaller segment of young people paired this search for authenticity with more controversial and politicized forms of mobility, such as hitchhiking to civil rights demonstrations. At the same time, the beat movement gained widespread admiration among young people by the early 1960s. As we will see, the success and popularity of Jack Kerouac's On the Road inspired a generation of teenagers and twenty-somethings to see hitchhiking, and the world, in new ways. By 1968, this politicized youth culture expanded tremendously and hitchhiking grew more popular than ever.

Counterculture youth, however, rejected the traditional values of the Protestant ethic and embraced hitchhiking as part of a subversive and communal lifestyle, fueling resentment among Americans."

Ibid, p. 27

32. Hitchers were painted as "untrustworthy and dangerous transients and darkening the discourse surrounding hitchhiking." Fracturing of the New Deal social order was one factor in a more conservative national climate being birthed in the 1980s.

Ibid, p11

33. .Ibid, p. 14

34. The early 1980s brought a new variety of hitchhiker.

"These individuals faced strikingly different circumstances than their Depression-era counterparts. In a society increasingly preoccupied with individual well-being and safety, motorists offered little sympathy to homeless individuals on the road, deemed "drifters" by social critics.

exploring the attitudes and experiences of those thumbing rides and offering lifts, examining contentious debates about hitchhikers within the media, and tracking the actions of regulatory officials tasked with promoting safety on the nation's roadways."

Ibid, p. 28

By the 1980s desperate and often homeless individuals dominated the hitchhiking ranks, replacing the erstwhile idealistic youths on the road.

Ibid

35. Torrey, Dr. E. Fuller. "Ronald Reagan's Shameful Legacy: Violence, the Homeless, Mental Illness." *Salon.* September 28, 2013. https://www.salon.com/2013/09/29/ ronald_reagans_shameful_legacy_violence_the_homeless_mental_illness/.

Placzek, Jessica. "Did the Emptying of Mental Hospitals Contribute to Homelessness?" *KQED,* December 8, 2016. https://www.kqed.org/news/11209729/ did-the-emptying-of-mental-hospitals-contribute-to-homelessness-here.

The shuttering of mental institutions led to a massive uptick in the homeless population over the years.

36. "Last, through an investigation of how government agencies, including the federal government, the   Federal Bureau of Investigation (FBI), state and local governments, and various police departments, understood and in turn regulated hitchhiking, I show what prompted new laws and how this regulation evolved, confirming   changing public understandings of hitchhiking. Of interest is how police enforced these laws: officers typically ignored enforcement in the case of hitchhikers they deemed worthy, such as clean-cut male college students, while at the same time targeting vagrants, women, and minorities."

Roadside Americans, p16

37. "[C]onstraining Indigenous mobility is a preoccupation of the province of British Columbia."

Morton, Katherine. "Hitchhiking and missing and murdered indigenous women: A critical discourse analysis of billboards on the highway of tears." *Canadian Journal of Sociology/Cahiers canadiens de sociologie* 41, no. 3 (2016): 299-326.

Hitchhiking is described as a form of "contentious mobility." It is quite different from the independence of automobility. Dependence on drivers leads to the dangers (though the dangers in hitching and picking up hitchers is widely overstated in general.)

Contentious Mobilities, p301

38. Highway of Tears docuseries

Real Crime. "Highway Of Tears: The Unsolved Serial Murders Of Aboriginal Women (Full Documentary) | Real Crime." YouTube. July 9, 2022, YouTube Video, 50:24, https://www.youtube.com/watch?v=V3wWjcIc_1M

39. Socio-economic factors are involved in the availability of mobility technologies. ; "social marginalization of Indigenous people in Canada." This ties into "victim construction" and the idea that "wasted lives have no productive purpose within society and are treated as resource drains   and chaos to be managed" (Bauman 2004)

Morton, Katherine. "Hitchhiking and missing and murdered indigenous women: A critical discourse analysis of billboards on the highway of tears." *Canadian Journal of Sociology/Cahiers canadiens de sociologie* 41, no. 3 (2016): 299-326.

Contentious Mobilities   p305

ibid, p306) "Historic constraints on Indigenous mobility are often left out of analyses of contemporary contentious mobility of Indigenous peoples such as hitchhiking." colonization, residential schools program, land seizures and displacement with contemporary mobility issues

40. "Girls don't hitchhike" reads a government-funded billboard on the Highway of Tears, putting the onus on the victims, rather than the victimizers. Beneath the text "girls don't hitchhike" and images of missing and murdered women.

Ibid., 311

41. Tammany Hall was a staple of 1800s corruption in the post-Civil War era. Led by William "Boss" Tweed and the "Tweed Ring" the Tammany Hall political machine engaged in graft and other corrupt practices until an unknown whistleblower

delivered reams of evidence to the *New York Times*. Though many of those involved faced repercussions, the system of bossism would   linger.

Tweed, Boss. Digital history, 2021. https://www.digitalhistory.uh.edu/disp_textbook.cfm?smtID=2&psid=3052.

42. The Tammany system introduced the idea of "honest graft" and its connection to the history of political machines in New Jersey are closely tied to the "bossism" of the Tammany Hall system of "Boss" Tweed.

Seglem, Lee. "New Jersey: The State of Honest Graft." *Asbury Park Press*. Asbury Park Press, January 8, 2020. https://www.app.com/story/opinion/columnists/2020/01/08/new-jersey-state-honest-graft/2832094001/.

43. Tammany Hall managed to survive well into the 20th century. It didn't fully begin to fade away during the administration of New York City mayor Fiorello La Guardia (1934-1945) and was no more by John V. Lindsay's election in 1966.

History. "Tammany Hall." History.com. *A&E* Television Networks, Updated December August 21, 2018. https://www.history.com/topics/us-politics/tammany-hall.

44. Tammany Hall is also responsible in part for the trope of backroom dealings in "smoke-filled rooms" and saloons. Mrs. Ella A. Boole, president of the National Woman's Temperance Union wrote a letter to state presidents of the organization in 1927 regarding this phenomenon:

"Governor Smith has been in politics for 20 years or more. He was born in the city of New York. Since he became a. politician he has been closely identified with Tammany Hall. Tammany Hall has always been regarded as the protector of the saloon in the old days. They not only stood for Sunday opening but many of their meetings were held in back rooms of saloons."

CQ Researcher, Tammany Hall in National Politics

Researcher, CQ. "Tammany Hall in National Politics," May 7, 1927. https://library.cqpress.com/cqresearcher/document.php?id=cqresrre1927050700.

45. Election day street brawls were not uncommon in connection to the Tammany Hall machine. Ballot box stuffing was another common occurrence of the time.

Merwin, Henry Childs. "Tammany Hall." *The Atlantic*, February 1894. https://www.theatlantic.com/magazine/archive/1894/02/tammany-hall/635684/.

46. Malanga, Steven. "The 'Miserable' State," October 9, 2019.   https://www.scribd.com/article/429535970/The-Miserable-State.

47. The Princeton paper describes how vote-rigging in the state of New Jersey often relies on obscurity and confusion of the ballot process.

"New Jersey has a robust Democratic machine. As such, the primary election often supersedes the importance of the general election because winning the primary usually guarantees success in the general election. There are some Republican strongholds in the state, but because there are fewer political players in that space, it is less competitive. In fact, the only two counties in New Jersey that have a balanced ballot design are predominantly Republican."

Journal of Public & International Affairs, Princeton

How New Jersey Political Parties Rig the Ballot."

Ragheb, Suzi A. "How New Jersey Political Parties Rig the Ballot." Princeton University. The Trustees of Princeton University, June 23, 2021. https://jpia. princeton.edu/news/how-new-jersey-political-parties-rig-ballot.

48.   Hutchins, Ryan. 2019. "Convicted Bridgegate Figure Says Christie Managed to 'Escape Justice.'" *Politico*. April 24, 2019. httpps://www.politico.com/states/ new-jersey/story/2019/04/24/former-christie-aide-sentenced-to-13-months-in-bridgegate-case-987943.

49.   New Jersey's one-party state politics depends on "shifting alliances" among various political machines. Despite this, 60 Democratic officials endorsed Chris Christie in 2013 including several notable political machine bosses.

   Moser, Richard. "New Jersey Is a One-Party State." *CounterPunch*, October 2, 2017. https://www.counterpunch.org/2017/10/02/new-jersey-is-a-one-party-state/.

50.   George Norcross leads the "most powerful political family" in New Jersey. A major powerbroker from south Jersey, Norcross is tied in to many major real estate-related deals.

   Solomon, Nancy, and Jeff Pillets. "How the Norcross Political Machine Muscled in on Prime Real Estate in New Jersey's Poorest City." *WNYC*, October 4, 2019. https://www.wnyc.org/story/norcross-political-machine-muscled-prime-real-estate-new-jerseys-poorest-city/.

51.   In the Princeton study "Testing Theories of American Politics: Elites, Interest Groups, and Average Citizens" the researchers found that government is far more responsive to the will and wishes of powerful interests and corporate donors than average citizens. The researchers used policy data from 1981 to 2002 "to empirically determine the state of the U.S. political system."

   "Major Study Finds that the US is an Oligarchy"

   Boren, Zachary Davies. "Major Study Finds the US Is an Oligarchy." Business Insider. *Business Insider*, April 16, 2014. https://www.businessinsider.com/major-study-finds-that-the-us-is-an-oligarchy-2014-4.

52.   Citizens United was a controversial SCOTUS ruling that allowed corporations to make political donations under the guise of such spending being "free speech." This obviously further deepened the divide between average citizens and powerful interests, corporations, lobby groups, and wealthy individuals.

   Lau, Tim. "Citizens United Explained." Brennan Center for Justice, December 12, 2019. httpps://www.brennancenter.org/our-work/research-reports/citizens-united-explained.

53.   "The Tenderloin (or Satan's Circus, as clergy from the city described the   section of New York City from Twenty-third Street to Fifty-seventh, contained   between Tenth Avenue in the west and Fifth Avenue in the east) was New   York City's most popular red-light district. Macy's department store, Pennsylvania Station (New York's busiest train station), Carnegie Hall and Times   Square all resided in the Tenderloin. It was home to an estimated five thousand prostitutes as young as

twelve years old who sold their bodies for a   dollar a turn. The sex industry was so large that entire streets developed their   own specialties as a means to lure in customers. Dance halls on Sixth Avenue showed cancan dancers on stage and, in private booths, explicit sexual   dances. On West Thirty-ninth Street, prostitutes performed fellatio on one   another, to the disgust of many fellow prostitutes but to the admiration of their clients."

Linderoth, Matthew R. *Prohibition on the North Jersey Shore: Gangsters on Vacation.* Arcadia Publishing, 2010.

54.   Even the police officers acted as enforcers for protection rackets. Police Commissioner William McAdoo noted: "The manager of a disorderly house, whether man or woman, does not feel   any sense of security unless someone representing the police authorities   has received money."

ibid., 15

55.   Reformer James A. Bradley owned a brush factory which he used as a gimmick and metaphor for how he would "clean up the   state." During his campaign, he handed out brushes from the New York City brush factory he owned.

Ibid., 23

56.   "Long Branch's main draw for wealthy capitalists was horse racing at

Monmouth Racetrack. The track was so popular that a large iron grandstand   was constructed and claimed national records for attendance. For Bradley,   the threat it posed to Asbury Park and the two other Methodist towns   seemed very real." With no gambling to bring in the big spenders the demographic and socioeconomic make-up of the area swiftly changed.

Ibid

57.   A recurring theme that is famously apparent in the creation of organized crime due to prohibition is the counter-intuitive crime and corruption that arises from these "clean-up" efforts.

"Early on New Jersey Democrats chose to support the working-class factory workers, immigrants and women, making Prohibition out of the question for the Democratic Party of New Jersey. During the campaign, New Jersey Democrat leader James R. Nugent released a damning report. Having   carefully reviewed the correlation of crime and prohibition over forty years in   Ocean Grove, Asbury Park and areas within a one-mile radius, Nugent concluded that controlling people's morality through law did not work."

Ibid., 37

58.   Benjamin Franklin referred to New Jersey as keg or "beer barrel tapped at both ends." (The book, *Gangsters on Vacation,* uses the word keg, as does *Observer* and some other sources have the quote reading "keg" rather than beer barrel. Either way, it does seem to presage the important role New Jersey would have in prohibition and organized crime from that era on.

Novick, Joey. "'a Keg Tapped at Both Ends." Well, It's Time to Tap Back." *Observer.* October 26, 2009. https://observer.com/2009/10/a-keg-tapped-at-both-ends-well-its-time-to-tap-back/.

Soderlund, Jean R. "A Barrel Tapped at Both Ends": New Jersey and Economic Development." *Reviews in American History* 24, no. 4 (1996): 574-578.

59. Just one scandal of its sort during the prohibition era involved a mayor, the chief of police, two local detectives, a New York police sergeant, even a United States customs inspector along with eight   others found guilty of conspiracy.

     Gangsters on Vacation, pg. 137

60. The international nature of organized crime arose in part due to alcohol running from Canada resulting in " a smooth-running, well organized criminal enterprise."

     Humphrey, Matt. "New Book Drinks Deep from B.C.'s History of Rum Running ." *CBCnews*, November 4, 2018. https://www.cbc.ca/news/canada/british-columbia/rum-running-book-1.4887945.

61. Luciano aided Vito Genovese, Bugsy Siegel, Joe Adonis, and Albert Anastasia in clearing the field for what would become known as the Five Families of New York.

     Newark, Tim. *Lucky Luciano: Mafia Murderer and Secret Agent*. Random House, 2011. p. 153

62. Another major hit Luciano is believed to be involved in took out mobsters in Union County at the Elizabeth-Carteret Hotel in Elizabeth, New Jersey.

     Ibid., p. 168

63. Boardwalk Empire's Nucky Thompson is based on Enoch "Nucky" Johnson. The show mixes historical fact and real-life characters and fictional characters.

     Burcky, Adria. "Boardwalk Empire: How the HBO Series Changed Nucky Thompson's History." *CBR*, March 4, 2021. httpps://www.cbr.com/boardwalk-empire-changed-nucky-thompson-history/.

64. Meyer Lansky called Lee Strasberg, who played Hyman Roth in *The Godfather*. "Am I speaking to Hyman Roth," Lansky asked. Strasberg explained he was merely the actor, asking who was calling Lansky expressed he was "disappointed" that he didn't recognize him as he "thought you'd studied my voice."

     Monda, Antonio. "Am I Speaking to Hyman Roth?" *The Common*, November 1, 2014. https://www.thecommononline.org/am-i-speaking-to-hyman-roth/.

     Strasberg says Lansky complained, "You could have made me more sympathetic. After all, I am a grandfather."

     AMC Editors. "Mob Mondays - Five True Mob Stories behind the Godfather: Part II: AMC Talk." *AMC*, June 25, 2016. https://www.amc.com/blogs/mob-mondays-five-true-mob-stories-behind-the-godfather-part-ii--1008812.

65. When killing Gordon failed, Luciano used the feds to take him down. Meyer's brother Jake Lansky personally delivered information regarding Gordon's tax delinquency to Thomas Dewey.

     Newark, Tim. *Lucky Luciano: Mafia Murderer and Secret Agent*. Random House, 2011. p. 171

66. Italian immigrants who might not feel comfortable attempting to get a fair shake out of traditional authorities might take their grievances to the Atlantic-originating organizations that would morph into the modern mafia, most of which had roots in

feudal era secret societies and other earlier existing groups.

Mastrofski, Stephen, and Gary Potter. "Controlling organized crime: A critique of law enforcement policy." *Criminal Justice Policy Review* 2, no. 3 (1987): 269-301.

67. Atlantic City was a seat of organized crime for decades, by May of 1929 over two decades before the Apalachin meeting, the first major mob conference occurred in the area.

PBS. "Gangsters during the Depression." Public Broadcasting Service, 2022. https://www.pbs.org/wgbh/americanexperience/features/dillinger-gangsters-during-depression/.

68. Scribd. "The 'Miserable' State," October 9, 2019. httpps://www.scribd.com/article/429535970/The-Miserable-State.

69. James, Letitia. 2022. "Attorney General James and Governor Hochul File Legal Action in Supreme Court to Block New Jersey from Terminating Waterfront Commission." Ag.ny.gov. March 14, 2022. https://ag.ny.gov/press-release/2022/attorney-general-james-and-governor-hochul-file-legal-action-supreme-court-block.

70. loc. cit. 1950s Congressional inquiries Mafia influence New Jersey

71. Weinberg, D. "Atlantic City (Nj) Takes A Gamble - Can An Organized Law Enforcement Team Defeat Organized Crime?" *Law Enforcement Communications*, 5, No. 3 (1978): 14-17

72. McGeehan, Patrick. "Future of Agency Created to Keep Mob off Docks Now up to Supreme Court." *The New York Times*, March 15, 2022. httpps://www.nytimes.com/2022/03/14/nyregion/mob-docks-agency-supreme-court.html.

73. PolitickerNJ. "Sharpe James Indicted on 33 Counts of Corruption." *Observer*, July 12, 2007. https://observer.com/2007/07/sharpe-james-indicted-on-33-counts-of-corruption/.

74. Malanga, Steven. "The 'Miserable' State," October 9, 20119.

75. "Weinberg devised the specifics of Operation Abscam in conjunction with Agents Fuller and McCarthy. Together they created a fictitious Arab sheikh and a phony shell company for him. With this cover, they met with corrupt businessmen, swindlers, and low-level politicians, until the last year of the operation when the targets became ranking politicians. During these meetings, the fictitious sheikh, played by an undercover FBI agent, and Weinberg, offered the targets money in exchange for political favors."

Hills, Jessica Carolyn. "'Larceny in My Heart': The Abscam Political Scandal, 1978-1983," December 8, 2012. https://etd.auburn.edu/bitstream/handle/10415/3384/Larceny%20In%20My%20Heart.pdf?sequence=2.

76. Camden Errichetti sought a bribe from the phony "Abdul Enterprises" for casino licenses in Atlantic City

Fried, Joseph P. "An Abscam Jury Indicts 2 in Link to Casino Bribe." *The New York Times*, June 19, 1981. httpps://www.nytimes.com/1981/06/19/nyregion/an-abscam-jury-indicts-2-in-link-to-casino-bribe.html.

77. Myron Fuller interview

Fairbanks, Philip. "Interview with Retired FBI Agent Myron Fuller on Abscam & New Jersey Corruption." philfairbanks.com: portfolio, May 10, 2022. https://philfairbanks.com/2022/05/10/interview-with-retired-fbi-agent-myron-fuller-on-abscam-new-jersey-corruption/.

78. Multiple cases involving New Jersey corruption have ties to the Philly mob.

Williams, Jerri. "Episode 027: Bill Grace - Mayor Slayer, Municipal Corruption." Jerri Williams, July 23, 2016. https://jerriwilliams.com/bill-grace-municipal-corruption/.

Williams, Jerri. "Episode 225: Jack Garcia – Undercover Agent, Making Jack Falcone." Jerri Williams, March 3, 2021. https://jerriwilliams.com/episode-225-jack-garcia-undercover-agent-making-jack-falcone/.

United States Attorney's Office. "Fifteen Members and Associates of the Philadelphia Mafia Indicted on Federal Racketeering and Related Charges." The United States Department of Justice, November 23, 2020. https://www.justice.gov/usao-edpa/pr/fifteen-members-and-associates-philadelphia-mafia-indicted-federal-racketeering-and.

79. "I happened to be in the right place (NYC) at the right time (1977) when developing events and factors enabled myself to use informants, wire taps (Title III), undercover operations, searches, etc, as well as backstopping from a VP at Chase Manhattan Bank, a former Department of State employee, and on-demand access to $3.2 Million in cash at CMB in my undercover name."

Fairbanks, Philip. "Interview with Retired FBI Agent Myron Fuller on Abscam & New Jersey Corruption." Phil Fairbanks: portfolio, May 10, 2022. https://philfairbanks.com/2022/05/10/interview-with-retired-fbi-agent-myron-fuller-on-abscam-new-jersey-corruption/.

80. Hannah Arendt's concept of the "Banality of Evil" argues that certain actions that are "terrifyingly normal" within a corrupt bureaucratic state are as evil as hideously sociopathic actions.

White, Thomas. "What Did Hannah Arendt Really Mean by the Banality of Evil?: Aeon Ideas." Aeon Magazine, April 13, 2018. htttps://aeon.co/ideas/what-did-hannah-arendt-really-mean-by-the-banality-of-evil.

It should be noted, however, that despite still being warmly accepted in academic circles, Arendt's opinions on certain topics are far behind the times. Her attitudes on subjects such as race, segregation, and colonialism were far from enlightened. She referred to Swahili as "a kind of a no-language." Denigration and stripping a people of their cultural trappings are a primary tool of the colonizer. This allows certain ethnolinguistic groups to maintain imbalances of power resulting in what lawyer and endangered languages activist, Lino Faelnar, calls "linguistic fascism."

Fairbanks, Philip. "Episode 6: Through the Plastic Screen podcast. "Language, Culture, Education & History with Lino Faelnar." https://www.youtube.com/watch?v=ujBGr2XJIiU

As far as segregation in the South, Arendt's thoughts are quite outdated: "The right to free association, and therefore to discrimination, has greater validity than the principle of equality." Arendt had an affair with the German philosopher Martin Heidegger who would join the Nazi party in 1933. Although at first a German nationalist herself, she was forced to flee Germany with the rise of anti-semitism.

She also wrote of how the "best of German Jewry" were properly set above other ethnicities of Jews in Israel during Adolf Eichmann's trial:

"Everything is organized by the Israeli police force which gives me the creeps. It speaks only Hebrew and looks Arabic. Some downright brutes among them. They obey any order. Outside the courthouse doors the oriental mob, as if one were in Istanbul or some other half-Asiatic country."

Frantzman, Seth J. 2016. "Hannah Arendt, White Supremacist." *The Jerusalem Post |* JPost.com. June 5, 2016. httpps://www.jpost.com/Opinion/Hannah-Arendt-white-supremacist-456007.

Elsewhere Arendt's work exposes blatant racism. Speaking of colonialism in Africa she talks of "human beings … living without the future of a purpose and the past of accomplishment," who are "as incomprehensible as the inmates of a madhouse." Another controversial work on segregation in Little Rock is very telling. She characterizes the children's parents as "social climbers" who aren't concerned with their children's well being "forcing" them to attend school in better funded and equipped districts. In 1964, Ralph Ellison retorted that "she has no conception of what goes on in parents who send children through these lines"

Chapter 3: The Church and the Family

1. *Breaking the Plate Glass Window,* by Reverend Michael Granzen, Ph.D. outlines issues with racism in Union County and relates the story of The Family cop gang.

   Granzen, Michael. *Breaking through the plate glass window–A social ethical study of racial profiling and violent innocence in Elizabeth, New Jersey.* Drew University, 2011.

2. Samuel Clark interview.

   Fairbanks, Philip. "Interview with Police Whistleblower and Author Samuel Clark." Phil Fairbanks: portfolio, May 15, 2022. https://philfairbanks.com/2022/05/15/interview-with-police-whistleblower-and-author-samuel-clark/.

3. Barron, Justine. "Three Years Later: Myths and Conflicts in the Death of Sean Suiter (Part 1 of 3)." The Suiter Files, November 16, 2020. httpps://www.thesuiterfiles.com/post/three-years-later-myths-conflicts-and-casualties-in-the-death-of-sean-suiter-part-1-of-2.

4. But a detective told her, "Just pay attention. You'll find out who's *really* in charge." Officially, stations are run by captains, with the help of an operations staff. At East L.A., Gonzalez discovered, there was a shadow government: a secretive group of sheriff's deputies known as the Banditos." In addition to the sheriff's department gangs, deputy gang "subgroups" are also common.

   Goodyear, Dana. "The L.A. County Sheriff's Deputy-Gang Crisis." The New Yorker, May 30, 2022. https://www.newyorker.com/magazine/2022/06/06/the-la-county-sheriffs-deputy-gang-crisis.

5. Yagman, Stephen. "Rico Will Probe Who's The Real Gang." Los Angeles Times,

August 30, 2000. https://www.latimes.com/archives/la-xpm-2000-aug-30-me-12455-story.html.

6.   Julian Assange: 'We just kept moving'

"It was a private investigator who eventually came and told us about his close relationship with the Anne Hamilton-Byrne *cult.* "

Independent. "Julian Assange: 'We Just Kept Moving'." Independent Digital News and Media, September 23, 2011. https://www.independent.co.uk/arts-entertainment/books/features/julian-assange-we-just-kept-moving-2359423.html.

7.   Niebuhr, Gustav. "'The Family' and Final Harvest." The Washington Post. Wednesday, June 2, 1993. https://www.washingtonpost.com/wp-srv/   national/longterm/cult/children_of_god/child1.htm

8.   Joaquin Phoenix and Rose McGowan Spent Their Early Years in a Religious Cult. Then it Became Infamous Gabrielle Bruney Oct 6, 2019

Bruney, Gabrielle. "Joaquin Phoenix and Rose McGowan Spent Their Early Years in a Religious Cult. Then It Became Infamous." *Esquire*. October 5, 2019. https://www.esquire.com/entertainment/a29374581/children-of-god-cult-joaquin-phoenix-rose-mcgowan/.

9.   River Phoenix admitted in a 1991 interview his greatest regret was having been introduced to sex at age 4.

Hagan, Joe. "Cover Story: Joaquin Phoenix on Joker, Rooney, and River." *Vanity Fair*, October 1, 2019. https://www.vanityfair.com/hollywood/2019/10/joaquin-phoenix-cover-story.

10. Author and reporter Don Lattin wrote a book on the tragic wake of the Family as well as an article in *SF Gate* outlining some of the suicides and overdoses that resulted from years of abuse at the hands of the group.   Deaths in the Family / Common thread of sexual, spiritual abuse among cult defectors who killed themselves Don Lattin, Chronicle Religion Writer Jan. 27, 2005

Lattin, Don. "Deaths in the Family / Common Thread of Sexual, Spiritual Abuse among Cult Defectors Who Killed Themselves." *SFGATE*, January 27, 2005. https://www.sfgate.com/news/article/Deaths-in-the-Family-Common-thread-of-sexual-2702662.php.

11. From a scan of a December 1981 pamphlet from the family: "Techi's first Kiddy Viddy show, 1 year 10 months old. Techi came out from the children's playhouse to perform with her Teddy."

The Family/Children of God. "Techi's Life Story," 1981. http://www.exfamily.org/pubs/misc/techi_scans.shtml.

12. Goodstein, Laurie. "Murder and Suicide Reviving Claims of Child Abuse in Cult." *The New York Times*, January 15, 2005. https://www.nytimes.com/2005/01/15/us/murder-and-suicide-reviving-claims-of-child-abuse-in-cult.html.

13. "Although sex was regarded as a very natural, almost nonchalant occurrence, it too was infused with spiritual meaning. Either sexuality was spiritualized or spirituality was sexualized, whichever way, the intimacy of sexuality was brought into the religious experience. A very particular application of this concept was introduced

later on with the Loving Jesus revelation, which encouraged members to engage in spiritual lovemaking with Jesus, either alone or with a partner."

On Growing Up In the Family and the Freedom of Belief, Daniel Tarpy, paper presented at CESNUR 2011 International Conference

14. Zerby, Karen. "What a Husband, What a Lover." 1996

15. Brocklehurst, Steven. "Children of God Cult Was 'Hell on Earth'." *BBC* News, June 27, 2018. https://www.bbc.com/news/uk-scotland-44613932.

16. Wangerin, Ruth. *The Children of God: A Make-believe Revolution?*. ABC-CLIO, 1993.

17. Report on the Activities of the Children of God." XFamily, September 30, 1974. https://www.xfamily.org/index.php/ Final_Report_on_the_Activities_of_the_Children_of_God.

18. Zerby, Keren. "Spiritual co-director at The Family International." LinkedIn. 2022, *https://www.linkedin.com/in/karenzerby.*

19. COG TFI Survivors. "We, #cogtfisurvivors, are a group of survivors of the extremist cult, the Children of God, more recently known as The Family International."

Facebook. March 13, 2022. https://www.facebook.com/cogtfisurvivors

20. United Church of Canada . "The Apologies." Accessed November 8, 2022. httpps:// united-church.ca/social-action/justice-initiatives/reconciliation-and-indigenous-justice/apologies.

21. Indigenous Corporate Training Inc. "Timeline of the Papal Apology to Residential School Survivors." Indigenous Corporate Training Inc., July 5, 2022. https://www.ictinc.ca/blog/timeline-of-the-papal-apology-to-residential-school-survivors.

22. United Church of Canada . "The Apologies." Accessed November 8, 2022. httpps:// united-church.ca/social-action/justice-initiatives/reconciliation-and-indigenous-justice/apologies.

23. Gardner, Philip. "A Holy or a Broken Hallelujah: The United Church of Canada in the 1960s Decade of Ferment." University of Toronto, 2018. https://tspace.library.utoronto.ca/ bitstream/1807/90362/4/Gardner_Philip_AT_201805_ThD_thesis.pdf

24. Toronto Star. "Minister in Chatham Not Guilty of Sex Assaults." *The Star,* December 4, 2008. httpps://www.thestar.com/news/ontario/2008/12/ 04/minister_in_chatham_not_guilty_of_sex_assaults.html.

25. Beckett. "Settlement Reached with United Church of Canada." Beckett, April 1, 2015. https://beckettinjurylawyers.com/news-and-resources/settlement-reached-united-church-canada.

Duffy, Andrew. "Lawyer's Career Dominated by Clergy Abuse Scandal | *Ottawa Sun,*" May 19, 2016. https://ottawasun.com/2016/05/18/lawyers-career-dominated-by-clergy-abuse-scandal.

26. *Maclean's*. "Welcome to the Complete Maclean's Archive." Maclean's | The Complete Archive, 2022. https://archive.macleans.ca/.

27. Ontario school with history of abuse linked to U.S.-based cult | School of secrets,

Nov 12, 2021

Brown, DeNeen L. "In Canada, a Tougher Stand on Clergy Sex Abuse." The Washington Post. WP Company, April 29, 2002. https://www.washingtonpost. com/archive/politics/2002/04/29/in-canada-a-tougher-stand-on-clergy-sex-abuse/ e2646ec9-9617-4a2a-a8aa-10dec3f7c9e3/.

28.   ibid, McLeans

29.   Government aimed to "elevate the savages" with these abusive residential schools. Only in 1996 did the government appoint a commission to look into the deaths and sexual assaults and physical abuse so many thousands had to face.

Brown, DeNeen L. "In Canada, a Tougher Stand on Clergy Sex Abuse." The *Washington Post.* April 29, 2002. https://www.washingtonpost.com/archive/ politics/2002/04/29/in-canada-a-tougher-stand-on-clergy-sex-abuse/e2646ec9-9617-4a2a-a8aa-10dec3f7c9e3/.

30.   Hinduism Today. "Church's Face Bankruptcy." *Hinduism Today*, March 1, 2001. https://www.hinduismtoday.com/magazine/march-april-2001/2001-03-church-s-face-bankruptcy/.

31.   Turtle Island News. "'United Church to Appeal Liability Ruling over Residential Schools.'" vitacollections.ca, July 8, 1998. httpps://vitacollections.ca/ sixnationsarchive/details.asp?ID=3232959.

Chapter 4: The Early Years

1.   Cook, Steven. "Convicted Child Killer Marybeth Tinning Released." *The Daily Gazette*, August 21, 2018. https://dailygazette.com/2018/08/21/marybeth-tinning-released/.

Chapter 5: Legends, Myths, and Misperceptions

1.   Chen, Angela. "The Armchair Psychologist Who Ticked off YouTube." *The Verge.* April 4, 2019. https://www.theverge.com/2019/4/4/18290795/mental-health-youtube-privacy-rewired-soul-goldwater-rule-psychology-celebrities-science.

2.   "Text of APA's Ethics Annotation Known as 'Goldwater Rule' 7. 3. On occasion psychiatrists are asked for an opinion about an individual who is in the light of public attention or who has disclosed information about himself/herself through public media. In such circumstances, a psychiatrist may share with the public his or her expertise about psychiatric issues in general. However, it is unethical for a psychiatrist to offer a professional opinion unless he or she has conducted an examination and has been granted proper authorization for such a statement."

Levin , Aaron. "Goldwater Rule." Psychiatry.org - Goldwater Rule, 2022. https:// psychiatry.org/news-room/goldwater-rule.

3.   Tattle Life. "Dr. Todd Grande 'Celebrity Psychologist' Diagnosing People He Never Met for Likes& Clicks." Tattle Life, October 17, 2020. httpps://tattle.life/threads/ dr-todd-grande-celebrity-psychologist-diag   nosing-people-he-never-met-for-likes-clicks.10374/.

4.   Reddit. "R/Truecrimediscussion - Does Anyone Else Think Dr Todd Grande (Youtube True Crimer) Needs to Go Away?" reddit, June 29, 2015. https://www. reddit.com/r/TrueCrimeDiscussion/   comments/wm0j40/does_anyone_else_

think_   dr_todd_grande_youtube/.

5.   University of Wilmington has an acceptance rate of 99% PrepScholar. "Wilmington University Requirements for Admission." Wilmington University Admission Requirements, 2022. https://www.prepscholar.com/sat/s/colleges/Wilmington-University-admission-requirements.

Excelsior College has a 100% acceptance rate

Niche. "Explore Excelsior College." Niche, August 18, 2022. https://www.niche.com/colleges/excelsior-college/.

6.   My Problem with Dr. Grande | By Qualified Psychiatrist." YouTube. April 15, 2022, YouTube Video, 21: 58. https://www.youtube.com/watch?v=rT_6hDGv4uk

7.   Det. Johnny Ho claims on the stand that he spoke with Pandina "because of these allegations that Kai put out there" (in Peterson's words). Peterson asks Ho if Kai's claims were "inconsistent" with someone faced with drugged sexual assault.

State of New Jersey v. Caleb McGillvary. Transcript of Grand Jury Hearing. Indictment No. 13-11-00946. pages 105-107

8.   During Peterson's Colloquy, he misrepresents Pandina's expert medical opinion: "From the reports that he [Pandina] has given us, there's absolutely zero signs that there was ever any kind of date rape drug used here, because what he basically says is anyone who is slipped one of these drugs for 10-12 hours is incapacitated. You'd be throwing up. You wouldn't know where you were. You wouldn't be walking around talking to people." So you don't get drugged, allegedly raped, and have no effects whatsoever afterwards. So we don't believe -- the State at this time doesn't believe any of that happened."

In the letter to Liguori in March of 2016, it is admitted not only that Pandina's opinion was misrepresented, but that Pandina wouldn't be able to be called due to the payment from the Galfy estate. Bear in mind, the medical examiner Junaid Shaikh also received a $150,000 payout as per Joseph Galfy's will.

State of New Jersey v. Caleb McGillvary. Transcript of Grand Jury Hearing. Indictment No. 13-11-00946. pages 9-10

9.   GHB, rohypnol, and several other drugs (including the "z-drugs" like zopiclone and eszopiclone) are all classed as DFSA agents. There is no singular "date rape drug." Rather there are several drugs that are commonly used to aid in sexual assault.

Stockham, T. L., and T. P. Rohrig. "The Use of Z-Drugs to Facilitate Sexual Assault." *Forensic Science Review* 22, no. 1 (2010): 61-73.

Use of scopolamine, barbiturates, and other DFSA agents discussed.

Drug Facilitated Sexual Assault   DFC or DFSA is a term used to refer to all forms of nonconsensual activity undertaken when the victim of the activity is profoundly intoxicated.   From: Encyclopedia of Forensic Sciences (Second Edition), 2013

Schwartz, Richard H., Regina Milteer, and Marc A. LeBeau. "Drug-facilitated sexual assault ('date rape')." *Southern medical journal* 93, no. 6 (2000): 558-561.

10.   A study in Norway actually found higher rates of automatism such as sleep-driving in zopiclone users than zolpidem (Ambien). Again, zopiclone results in a metallic

taste similar to what Kai described experiencing.

Poceta, J. Steven. "Zolpidem ingestion, automatisms, and sleep driving: a clinical and legal case series." *Journal of Clinical Sleep Medicine* 7, no. 6 (2011): 632-638.

11. *State of New Jersey v. Caleb McGillvary.* Transcript of Grand Jury Hearing. Indictment No. 13-11-00946. pages 9-10

12. Crime scene photos DSC-0019 and DSC-0013

13. Peterson makes sure to point out that the State does not have to prove, or even provide, any motive.

"Although the State must prove that the defendant acted with – either purposely or knowingly, the State is not required to prove a motive."

State of New Jersey v. Caleb McGillvary. Transcript of Grand Jury Hearing. Indictment No. 13-11-00946. pages 106

14. McNamara p6 22-24 Kai was outside, shared a cigarette with him, he talked about the California incident

page 8:25 "Uhm honestly I think he was under the influence of something [...]."

page 9:1-2 "[...] on and there was a lot of in (inaudible) that I can't really remember cause it was a lot of rambling.

Police interview with John McNamara

15. "As far as this investigation has gone, you're familiar with all of the witness statements, as well as all the reports that have been prepared by various other detectives, law enforcement units, and the doctors. Is that correct?" Peterson asked Ho.

There are only two possibilities here: Ho either knowingly lied or was negligent as his testimony is not consistent with what's laid out in the evidence at hand.

State of New Jersey v. Caleb McGillvary. Transcript of Grand Jury Hearing. Indictment No. 13-11-00946. pages 18

Detective Ho, as we've established, was either negligent in his duties and did not familiarize himself with all the investigative notes and materials before the Grand Jury hearing or he was knowingly and willfully lying. After ensuring Kai could not represent himself pro se, Cito offers to have the Union County Prosecutor's Office oversee the analysis of Galfy's computer. Quite likely to the detriment of Kai.

Case 2:22-cv-04185-MCA Document 1-8 Filed 06/22/22 Page 10 of 13 PageID: 95 August 6, 2019

16. "Oh, because a dream is a personal experience of that deep, dark ground that is the support of our conscious lives, and a myth is the society's dream. The myth is the public dream and the dream is the private myth. If your private myth, your dream, happens to coincide with that of the society, you are in good accord with your group. If it isn't, you've got an adventure in the dark forest ahead of you."

Campbell, Joseph, and Bill Moyers. *The power of myth.* Anchor, 2011.

17. *The American Night,* Jim Morrison includes the unproduced screenplay for HWY: An American Pastoral (Also referred to as The Hitchhiker: An American Pastoral).

Some behind the scenes footage from Paul Ferrara who was involved in the short film's shooting is available on YouTube.

Ferrara, Paul. "MAKING HWY (NEWmusic)." YouTube. 2013, YouTube Video, 6: 50. https://www.youtube.com/watch?v=lj_64K03SlE

18. "Beyond its obvious cultural significance as the only classic film noir directed by a woman (actress Ida Lupino), THE HITCH-HIKER is perhaps better remembered as simply one of the most nightmarish motion pictures of the 1950s. Inspired by the true-life murder spree of Billy Cook, THE HITCH-HIKER is the tension-laden saga of two men on a camping trip (Edmond O'Brien and Frank Lovejoy) who are held captive by a homicidal drifter (William Talman). He forces them, at gunpoint, to embark on a grim joyride across the Mexican desert."

THE HITCH-HIKER. *Kino Lorber - Experience Cinema*, 1953. https://www.kinolorber.com/film/thehitchhikerremastered.

19. Robert Ben Rhoades killed multiple women he picked up on the road. He was known as the "Truck Stop Killer."

Globe Gazette. "Robert Ben Rhoades," October 25, 2022. https://globegazette.com/robert-ben-rhoades/image_526f3ead-402c-5ace-8706-37877567fed3.html.

20. . Ronald James Ward Jr. killed at least 3 women after leaving his home state with jugs of moonshine and heroin-fueled spree of drugs and violence after finding his girlfriend with another man. He is described in some stories as a "drifter."

AP. "Man Convicted of Killing Scotch Plains Woman Dies in Montana Prison." Courier News, April 11, 2014. httpps://www.mycentraljersey.com/story/news/2014/04/11/man-convicted-of-killing-scotch-plains-woman-dies-in-montana-prison/7599909/.

Surles, Taneia. "Hitchhiking Nightmares: These Killers Targeted People Simply Looking for a Lift to Their next Destination." *Front Page Detectives*. October 8, 2021. httpps://www.frontpagedetectives.com/p/hitchhiker-murder-rape-suspect-arrest.

21. Redstall, Victoria. *Serial Killers: Up Close & Very Personal*. p. 76. John Blake Publishing LTD, London, 2011

22. Laverne Pavlinac calls Multnomah County, Sheriff's Department; said she thought her boyfriend John Sosnovske was guilty called anonymously at first; detectives found her story credible, claimed Sosnovske had bragged to friend about killing Bennett; produced supposed note "T. Bennett – Good piece" Sosnovske maintained innocence.

loc. cit. pg. 77

Jesperson suggests police put Pavlinac up to producing a piece of ripped jeans as evidence; "Victoria – how would she know that a piece of the fly area around her jeans was missing if she was not told this by the cops? Only the 'real' killer – ME – and the cops would have known this information so someone must have put it in her head. Why did this not come out in any investigation? Because the Detectives planted a seed in Laverne's head. I beg to say it was more or less something like this: 'Laverne, we are looking for enough evidence for probable cause. If you should find a purse, about this big and possibly a cut-out section of women's jeans fly area resembling a shape like this we can then move forward, arrest John and send him off to prison. What do you say?" Victoria: "what is a matter of official record is that the police took this piece of denim to the crime lab. It didn't match the deceased's jeans. In point of fact, it was a completely different material." Police think Pavlinac is lying or crazy

loc. cit. p. 78

23. Jesperson letter: "Of course they wanted to build a case around the murderer being Sosnovske ... don't you see he was a 'nuisance to law enforcement' and they could quickly close the case. Sosnovske was always in and out of prison for one reason or another. Investigators either hadn't done their homework or they chose to brush this next piece of information under the rug. Hadn't they seen all the reports done on this guy since he'd been out on parole?" Pavlinac had tried to get him sent back to prison "for a variety of bogus reasons." No other leads in the case they were pressured to close it.

loc. cit. p. 79

Graffiti was found by police in a Montana truck stop restroom reading: "I killed Taunja Bennett and two people are on trial for the killing."

loc. cit.pg 81

24. Jesperson police must have been "wetting themselves" over fact that they had screwed up not only allowing him years to continue murdering women but also the embarrassment of wrongfully imprisoning Sosnovske and Pavlinac.

loc cit p. 88

"even though they agreed to give me 30 years, I still wasn't charged with murdering Bennett. It was contingent on me proving that I had killed her." Keeps Ken "Duke" Mensebroten the jailhouse snitch quiet by giving him a body for police to   find to claim to shorten his sentence while he was working on smuggling letters to 7 media sources related to Taunja Bennett's murder. "they were all worried that I held a secret piece of evidence that could prove me to be the real killer. And I did!"

loc cit p. 89

Searchers including Eagle scouts "armed with machetes and clippers" through blackberry bushes

loc cit. p. 90

25. Jesperson to Redstall, "This is why the prison don't want you to interview me because they don't want you to expose the truth. Remember, they are in on the whole cover-up, too. We could bring down the whole of the Multnomah County if you are willing to expose the truth. But be very careful – they may stop you getting in because they read all my letters to you and record all our phone conversations."

loc cit p. 91

26. On April 29, 1994, Phil Stanford, then a journalist at The Oregonian, received a bizarre anonymous letter. The letter writer claimed that they were responsible for the murder of Taunja Bennett but had never murdered before. However, the writer also explained that they had kept murdering and that it had become "real easy" over

time. McAuliffe, Cat. "After Many Twists and Turns, Taunja Bennett's Death Led to the Capture of the 'Happy Face Killer'." Ranker, February 19, 2022. httpps://www.ranker.com/list/keith-hunter-jesperson-facts/cat-mcauliffe.

27. Rachanda Pickle was only 13 years old when she disappeared. As in the case of Jesperson, more murders could have been stopped if not for inaction of the police, ignoring Marlene Gabrielson. Evidence uncovered by the *Oregonian* suggests that John Ackyroyd was responsible for multiple murders and disappearances along Highway 20.

Crombie, Noelle. "Ghosts of Highway 20 - *Oregonlive*," 2022. https://projects.oregonlive.com/ghostsofhighway20/marlene/.

28. ibid

29. *Oregonian* had to fight to unseal records related to Rachanda Pickle during their "cold case" investigation of the Highway 20 murders. Numerous police reports were pored over making connections between various cases now believed to have been committed by Ackyroyd. It all started with a rape report that was never followed up on. An act of neglect that proved to be fatal.

Kristen Hare, "The Oregonian spent years on a story about a serial killer who got away, again and again, with murder"

Hare, Kristen. "The Oregonian Spent Years on a Story about a Serial Killer Who Got Away, Again and Again, with Murder." Poynter, March 8, 2019. https://www.poynter.org/reporting-editing/2019/the-oregonian-spent-years-on-a-story-about-a-serial-killer-who-got-away-again-and-again-with-murder/.

30. ibid

31. The Phantom 309 story dates back to the late 60s in a song by Red Sovine which predates popular CB radio country songs by about a decade.

Iowa 80 Trucking Museum. "Phantom 309." Iowa 80 Trucking Museum, June 29, 2021. https://iowa80truckingmuseum.com/press-release/phan   tom309/.

The Tom Waits song "Big Joe and Phantom 309" is based on the same urban legend as the Sovine song. At least the portion about a trucker who sacrificed his life jackknifing to save a bus full of school children is true if not the repeat apparition of the trucker appearing in the area to this day as in the songs.

Psyne Co. "The True Story behind Phantom 309." Psyne Co., October 17, 2021. https://psyne.co/the-true-story-behind-phantom-309/.

32. Beardsley and Hankey collected various folk tales regarding the Vanishing Hitchhiker. The Vanishing Hitchhiker is not only the name of their paper in California Folklore Quarterly but the title of Professor Brunvands' book on urban legends.

Beardsley, Richard K., and Rosalie Hankey. "The vanishing hitchhiker." *California Folklore Quarterly* 1, no. 4 (1942): 303-335.

33. Jan Harold Brunvands' "1981 study of the intersection of folk legendry and mass communications has become a media event in itself."

Brunvand, Jan Harold. "Reviewed Work: The Vanishing Hitchhiker: American

Urban Legends and Their Meanings." *The Journal of American Folklore The Journal of American Folklore* 96, no. 381. (1983): 356

34. A student documented the "maniac" with the hook hand story in 1971 at the Folklore Archives at the University of California at Berkeley.

Ellis, Bill. ""The Hook" Reconsidered: Problems in Classifying and Interpreting Adolescent Horror Legends." *Folklore* 105, no. 1-2 (1994): 61-75.

35. "Any time you get a drifter and then all of the sudden he's being charged with a homicide, it would be a lack of responsibility for us not to look into that possibility," Romankow said.

6abc. "Kai Arrested in Philadelphia for New Jersey Murder: 6abc Philadelphia." *6abc Philadelphia*, May 17, 2013. https://6abc.com/archive/9105613/.

36. Despite the fact that Kai did not suspect anything untoward occurring after the first night, Judge Kirsch claimed that the fact that Kai returned the second night in lieu of sleeping outside in a dangerous area he had been warned about was a sign that he could not have been assaulted.

Nieto-Munoz, Sophie. "Viral Video Sensation 'Kai the Hitchhiker' Sentenced to 57 Years in Prison for Murder of Lawyer in N.J." *lehighvalleylive*. MenuSubscribe, May 30, 2019. https://www.lehighvalleylive.com/news/2019/05/viral-video-sensation-kai-the-hitchhiker-sentenced-to-57-years-in-prison-for-murder-of-lawyer-in-nj.html?outputType=amp.

37. 310 out of 1000 sexual assaults are reported to police, out of that 310 only 50 reports lead to arrest of which 28 will lead to a felony conviction but only 25 of those perpetrators will be incarcerated meaning only 2.3% of rapists will spend time behind bars.

Reasons for not reporting are manifold: protecting the household or victims from further crimes, retaliation, escalation, belief that the police would not help (sadly, too often the case).

RAINN. "The Criminal Justice System: Statistics." 2022. https://www.rainn.org/statistics/criminal-justice-system.

38. DFSA agents are known to create blackout states that may sometimes be similar to a light sleep. The drugged individual however may come in and out of consciousness and as mentioned previously in the end notes, automatisms such as sleep-driving are not uncommon.

Krasowski, Matthew D. "Drug-Assisted Sexual Assaults." *Critical Issues in Alcohol and Drugs of Abuse Testing (Second Edition)*, 2019.

Schwartz, Richard H., Regina Milteer, and Marc A. LeBeau. "Drug-facilitated sexual assault ('date rape')." *Southern medical journal* 93, no. 6 (2000): 558-561.

39. Traumatic events affect the way that those memories are stored. In addition to this PTSD from traumatic events can affect declarative memory in a broad manner.

Medically reviewed by Nicole Washington, DO, MPH — By Hope Gillette on May 23, 2022

One mechanism for this was only recently discovered in 2015, a rodent study revealed memory subpaths in the brain that are only activated during fear response. In cases like this normal memory processes may be bypassed leading to an entirely new memory network complicating recall.

Gillette, Hope. "Does Trauma Cause Memory Loss?." Psych Central, May 23, 2022. https://psychcentral.com/health/does-trauma-cause-memory-loss.

40. Munoz , Sophie Nieto-. "Viral Video Sensation 'Kai the Hitchhiker' Sentenced to 57 Years in Prison for Murder of Lawyer in N.J." *Star-Ledger*, May 30, 2019. https://www.nj.com/news/2019/05/kai-the-hitchhiker-sentenced-to-57-years-in-prison.html.

41. Pruden, Jana G. "Hitchhiker, Hero, Celebrity, Killer: The Strange Journey of the Man Called Kai." *The Globe and Mail*. June 26, 2020. httpps://www.theglobeandmail.com/canada/article-hitchhiker-hero-celebrity-killer-the-strange-journey-of-the-man/.

42. Grande, Todd. "Kai the Hitchhiker | Analysis of 'Hatchet-Wielding' Personality." YouTube, March 6, 2021. httpps://www.youtube.com/watch?v=XuW1jmxCgjc&feature=youtu.be.

43. "At this early, stage, Plaintiff sufficiently alleges a conspiracy among the individual Moving Defendants to deprive him of his due process rights."

Federal Judge Madame Cox-Arleo ruled that Kai had successfully alleged "that the favorable evidence [suppressed and destroyed in this case] would have produced a different verdict."

Case 2:21-cv-17121-MCA-CLW Document 66 Filed 07/28/22 Page 9 of 17

44. "The gavel of office gets passed in a ceremony last week at the Kiwanis Club of Clark. Kiwanis members serve throughout the community of Clark and are committed to working closely with the Kiwanis Educating Youth Club, known as the KEY Club. From left, Joseph Galfy and Past President, Robert Mega."

Rahway Progress, Vol. 7, No. 64, Thursday October 31, 1996, p. 12 "Club completes elections for international services"

Kochanski, Mega, & Galfy lawfirm where Judge Mega and Galfy were named partners was founded in 1996, the same year that Mega passed on the role of president of the Kiwanis Club to Galfy.

"Kochanski, Mega & Galfy PC - Rahway , NJ - Company Data." n.d. www.dandb.com. Accessed November, 2022. httpps://www.dandb.com/businessdirectory/kochanskimegagalfypc-rahway-nj-12623287.html.

45. The aforementioned "troll army" have been active for years, harassing supporters of Kai and feeding a seemingly neverending stream of disinformation. Denying claims for which factual evidence exists while making claims with nothing to support them. Kavanaugh, Shane Dixon. "The Sad Tale of Kai the Hatchet-Wielding Hitchhiker." *Vocativ*. July 14, 2016. httpps://www.vocativ.com/335097/kai-the-hatchet-wielding-hitchhiker/index.html.

46. Torres, Ella, and John Annese. "Caleb McGillivary, Known as 'Kai the Hitchhiker,' Sentenced to 57 Years in Prison for Killing of New Jersey Lawyer." New York Daily News, May 31, 2019. httpps://www.nydailynews.com/news/crime/

ny-kai-the-hitchhiker-sentenced-for-killing-new-jersey-lawyer-20190530-bcucmqizhffdhhdpy6xuk6zuvu-story.html.

47. "Cito said police found evidence that Galfy had viewed websites with adult content, had passwords for websites on his computer, and that Galfy had contact information for young men on his cellphone. The lawyer said there was also evidence of sexual activity at the house." Later on in the article is the quote from Cito about "something of a sexual nature" occurring at Galfy's home in Clark.

Haydon, Tom. "Accused Killer 'Kai' Acted in Self Defense, Lawyer Says." *Star-Ledger*, March 28, 2017. https://www.nj.com/union/2017/03/accused_murderer_kai_acted_in_self-defense_against.html.

There were two computers in Galfy's home. Pornographic websites and contact information for young men were found on Galfy's devices. Kai wanted a forensics expert to look at the computers, but Cito let the judge know they had "worked something out, Your Honor." In fact, Cito claimed, "it's actually even better, because Detective Ho and myself will review the computer, we'll come up with an itemization and a summary of the data we're going -- that I'm inquiring about and so that way it's an agreement between the two of us as to actually what's on the computer and we can work out a stipulation if I'm going to use that stuff."

Case 2:22-cv-04185-MCA Document 1-8 Filed 06/22/22 Page 10 of 13 PageID: 95 August 6, 2019

48. Wavywebsurf. "-New (Corrected) Video." Twitter, October 20, 2018. httpps://twitter.com/wavywebsurf/status/1053434834922692608.

49. metalslut episode 21, "Kai and Mo go at it without a guest, and touch on their mutual run-in with Kai "the Hatchet Weilding Hitchhiker". Other topics include crystal meth and weed dispensaries"

"Metalslut." via fyyd: Podcast, Search, Engine. Accessed November 15, 2022. https://fyyd.de/podcast/metalslut/12.

50. httpps://www.tiktok.com/@xanxotic/video/6946597641413315845

51. Tharrett, Matthew. "Slain NJ Attorney Joseph Galfy Could Be Victim of 'Intimate Partner Violence Homicide.'" *Queerty*, May 18, 2013. https://www.queerty.com/slain-nj-attorney-joseph-galfy-could-be-victim-of-intimate-partner-violence-homicide-20130517.

52. A "sexual encounter gone violent" is one way to put "drug-facilitated sexual assault" certainly, but perhaps not the most accurate or responsible way.

Salo, Jackie. "Murder Trial for 'Kai the Hatchet-Wielding Hitchhiker' Underway." *New York Post.* April 9, 2019. https://nypost.com/2019/04/09/murder-trial-for-kai-the-hatchet-wielding-hitchhiker-underway/.

53. "A man accused of killing a 73-year-old Clark lawyer in his home testified Wednesday that he was victim of 'date rape' by the attorney, and that he beat the older man to fend off a sexual assault." Remember that use of date rape drugs does not imply a *date* rape. For this reason, we use the scientific term DFSA rather than "date rape" and DFSA agent rather than "date rape drug."

Haydon, Tom. "Combative 'Kai the Hitchhiker' Takes the Stand in Clark Murder

Case." *TAPintoClark*, April 17, 2019. htttps://www.tapinto.net/towns/clark/sections/law-and-justice/articles/combative-kai-the-hitchhiker-takes-the-stand-in-clark-murder-case.

54. Thompson eventually admitted that when he wrote of a "rumor" that presidential candidate Ed Muskie was under the influence of African psychedelic drug ibogaine he was referring the rumor he had started himself.

Tomoski, M. "Hunter S. Thompson Once Spread a Rumor of a Presidential Candidate's Drug Addiction." *The Plaid Zebra*, May 10, 2016. https://theplaidzebra.com/hunter-s-thompson-spread-rumor-presidential-candidates-drug-addiction-taken-seriously/.

55. Fairbanks, Philip. "Hey @Philstilton You Wanna Explain Why You Literally Made up Lies and Pass Them off as the Truth, or Nah?" Twitter. Twitter, June 14, 2022. https://twitter.com/kafkaguy/status/1536521738124550144.

Chapter 6: Something Rotten In the Garden State

1. Not only was the science behind DFSA agents misrepresented, but it seems as if the prosecution is trying to oversimplify the multitude of actions and effects of various drugs that have been used to facilitate sexual assault. "Dr. Pandina opined that the effects of the date rape drug typically last eight to ten hours after ingestion."

Not only did Pandina claim that "acute" effects lasted a few hours with some agents, but the prosecution seems to make a claim there is only one type of "date rape drug" with one type of effects.

State of New Jersey v. Caleb McGillvary. Transcript of Grand Jury Hearing. Indictment No. 13-11-00946. pages 106

2. The bitter aftertaste resulting from zopiclone and eszopiclone is well documented.

Yoshida, Miyako, Honami Kojima, Atsushi Uda, Tamami Haraguchi, Minoru Ozeki, Ikuo Kawasaki, Kazuhiro Yamamoto, Ikuko Yano, Midori Hirai, and Takahiro Uchida. "Bitterness-masking effects of different beverages on zopiclone and eszopiclone tablets." *Chemical and Pharmaceutical Bulletin* 67, no. 5 (2019): 404-409.

3. Anthes, Emily. "Widely Used Autism Drug Carries Heavy Risks for Children." Scientific American, May 8, 2014. https://www.scientificamerican.com/article/widely-used-autism-drug-carries-heavy-risks-for-children/.

4. . AHRP. "Biederman J & J Risperdal Documents." Alliance for Human Research Protection, November 25, 2008. htttps://ahrp.org/biederman-j-j-risperdal-documents-2/.

5. Torrejon, Rodrigo. "About 1.6 Tons of Cocaine Seized at Port Newark, Largest Drug Bust in 25 Years." North Jersey Media Group, March 11, 2019. https://www.northjersey.com/story/news/ new-jersey/2019/03/11/1-6-tons-cocaine-seized-port-newark-largest-bust-25-years/3128185002/.

6. The United States Department of Justice. "Johnson & Johnson to Pay More than $2.2 Billion to Resolve Criminal and Civil Investigations." The United States Department of Justice, October 22, 2014. htttps://www.justice.gov/opa/pr/johnson-johnson-pay-more-22-billion-resolve-criminal-and-civil-investigations.

7.   Harris, Gardiner. "Research Center Tied to Drug Company." *The New York Times*, November 24, 2008. https://www.nytimes.com/2008/11/25/   health/25psych. html.

8.   "Working closely with the Union County Board of Chosen Freeholders, the Union County Improvement Authority and the Department of Children and Families, Mr. Romankow was the driving force for new program designs, public grant writing, and construction of a new state-of-the-art 11,000 square-foot Child Advocacy Center, dedicated on October 3, 2012. The Center housed 26 full time staff, including investigators from the Prosecutor's Office, Division of Child Protection and Permanency, mental health staff from Trinitas Regional Medical Center and nursing staff from Runnells Specialized Hospital of Union County."

     Romankow, Theodore J. "Ted Romankow - Certified Civil Trial Attorney New Jersey." Javerbaum Wurgaft Hicks Kahn Wikstrom & Sinins, P.C., May 10, 2021. https://www.javerbaumwurgaft.com/attorney/theodore-romankow/.

9.   Haydon, Tom. "Restraint Contributed to Union County Inmate's Death, Authorities Say." *Star-Ledger*, June 18, 2014. httpps://www.nj.com/union/2014/06/ restraint_in_union_county_jail_contributed_to_inmate_ death_authorities_say_ mans_mother_claims_he_was.html.

10. *Caleb L. McGillivary v. James Galfy et al.* 2-21-cv-17121-MCA-CLW, Document 51-2. March 3, 2022

11. UMDNJ had to pay $8.3 million after it was revealed the extent of kickbacks being funneled through the university.

     Ryan, Joe. "UMDNJ to Pay $8.3 Million to Settle Kickbacks Case." *Star-Ledger*. October 1, 2009. https://www.nj.com/news/2009/09/umdnj_to_pay_83_million_ to_set.html.

12. Yale and Princeton donation diversion scandals prove that even the Ivy League isn't immune to this type of behavior.

     Muskus, Jeff. "Donors' Suit Charges Princeton with Fraud." *Yale Daily News*, October 28, 2004. https://yaledailynews.com/blog/2004/10/28/donors-suit-charges- princeton-with-fraud.

13. US Department of Justice. "New Jersey Hospital to Pay $3 Million to Resolve Allegations of Medicare Fraud." The United States Department of Justice, November 18, 2009. https://www.justice.gov/opa/pr/new-jersey-hospital-pay-3- million-resolve-allegations-medicare-fraud.

14. Pillets, Jeff, and Nancy Solomon. "Investigators Hit Norcross Hospital with Fraud Allegation in New Jersey Tax Break Program." *WNYC*, June 18, 2019. https://www. wnyc.org/story/investiagators-fraud-allegation-norcross-hospital-nj-tax-break/.

15. Redden, Elizabeth. "Proposed Settlement Reached in Sham University Case." Proposed settlement reached in sham university case, January 28, 2022. https:// www.insidehighered.com/news/2022/01/28/pro posed-settlement-reached-sham- university-case.

16. Snyder, Susan, and Craig R McCoy. "Rutgers Business School Accused of Rankings Fraud, Hiring Own Grads in Temp Jobs to Boost Its Scores." *The Philadelphia*

Inquirer, April 22, 2022. httpps://www.inquirer.com/news/rutgers-college-rankings-temple-lawsuits-20220422.html.

17. Shea, Kevin. "Ex-Rutgers Cancer Doc Ordered to Start Serving Jail Term." *Star-Ledger,* January 27, 2022. htttps://www.nj.com/middlesex/2022/01/ex-rutgers-cancer-doc-ordered-to-start-serving-jail-term.html.

18. "The fact that some of the university's most prominent doctors now stand accused of taking part in an illegal scheme that involved life-or-death medical decisions is likely to further tarnish the school's image at a time when state officials are deciding whether to merge the institution with Rutgers University and Robert Wood Johnson University Hospital."

    Kocieniewski, David. "Latest Twist in a Scandal Hits a Medical School When It's Down." *The New York Times*, November 24, 2006. https://www.nytimes.com/2006/11/24/nyregion/24hosp.html.

19. Peterson, Iver. "In Camden, Another Mayor Is Indicted on Corruption Charges." *The New York Times*. March 31, 2000. htttps://www.nytimes.com/2000/03/31/nyregion/in-camden-another-mayor-is-indicted-on-corruption-charges.html?pagewanted=all&src=pm.

20. Opposite of the situation in Camden, Romankow resisted state oversight in affairs of Union County.

    Maciag, Mike. "Why Camden, N.J., the Murder Capital of the Country, Dis banded Its Police Force." Governing, May 21, 2014. https://www.gov erning.com/topics/public-justice-safety/gov-camden-disbands-police-force-for-new-department.html.

21. Shaikh was faculty at NJMS-UMDNJ, a university with a recent history of donation fraud.

    Sherman, Ted. "UMDNJ Whistleblower Cases Cost Rutgers Nearly $2m in Settlements." *Star-Ledger*, April 26, 2015. htttps://www.nj.com/news/2015/04/umdnj_whistleblower_cases_cost_rutgers_nearly_2m_i.html.

22. Bryant would be sentenced to four years in prison for his part in political corruption part of which was connected to the "low-show" job at UMDNJ at the same time as he was using his position to try to secure $11 million in state funding for the school.

    Lu, Adrienne, and Matt Katz. "Wayne Bryant, Imprisoned for N.J. Corruption, Indicted on Unrelated Federal Fraud Charges." The Philadelphia In quirer, September 28, 2010. https://www.inquirer.com/philly/news/homepage/20100928_Wayne_Bryant__imprisoned_for_N_J__corruption__indicted_on_unrelated_federal_fraud_charges.html.

23. St. Barnabas (RJWBarnabas) was made to pay a jaw-dropping $265M after being caught out in massive Medicare overbilling scam.

    Fierce Healthcare. "St. Barnabas to Pay $265m for Medicare Fraud." Fierce Healthcare, June 15, 2006. https://www.fiercehealthcare.com/health care/st-barnabas-to-pay-265m-for-medicare-fraud.

    FTC Bureau of Competition Director Holly Vedova called them out by name in June 2022.

Federal Trade Commission. "Statement of Bureau of Competition Director Holly Vedova Regarding the Decision of Utah Healthcare Competi tors HCA Healthcare and Steward Health Care System to Abandon Their Proposed Merger." Federal Trade Commission, June 16, 2022. htttps://www.ftc.gov/news-events/news/press-releases/2022/06/state ment-bureau-competition-director-holly-vedova-regarding-decision-utah-healthcare-competitors.

24. Moran , Tom. "Who Needs Voters? the Bosses Choose Phil Murphy: Moran." nj, October 9, 2016. htttps://www.nj.com/opinion/2016/10/ who_needs_voters_the_bosses_choose_phil_murphy_mor.html.

25. A single donation of $750k was made to the PAC that Murphy's wife sits on the board of.

Balcerzak , Ashley and, and Charles Stile. "Njea Donates $750,000 to Another Political Dark Money Group Tied to Phil Murphy." North Jersey Me dia Group, June 22, 2022. https://www.northjersey.com/story/news/2022/06/22/nj-governor-phil-murphy-dark-money-group-njea-dona tion/7697947001/.

Friedman, Matt. "Murphy's Non-Profit: Will We Ever Know the Donors?" POLITICO, February 15, 2022. https://www.politico.com/newslet ters/new-jersey-playbook/2022/02/15/murphys-non-profit-will-we-ever-know-the-donors-00008882.

26. Friedman, Matt. "Phil Murphy Took on New Jersey's Democratic Machine. Now He Needs It to Win." POLITICO, May 31, 2021. htttps://www.politico.com/news/2021/05/31/phily-murphy-democrats-491359.

27. Bridget Kelley and Bill Baroni went to trial over the infamous "time for some traffic problems" email.

Porter, David. "'Time for Some Traffic Problems in Fort Lee': Witness in GWB Trial Recounts Getting Key Email." NBC New York, September 26, 2016. https://www.nbcnewyork.com/news/local/david-wildstein-george-washington-bridge-lane-closure-trial-port-authority-chris-christie/1312824/.

28. : Romankow argued against putting Union County prosecutors under Attorney General guidance which would save counties $400 million annually. Romankow argued that it would be better to get rid of county police departments to save money.

Peyton, Paul J. "Romankow Opposes Moving County Prosecutors to AG Budget." *Westfield Leader.* June 17, 2010.

Barr, Lauren. S. "Westfield Council Adjusts Meeting Schedule, Renews Licenses." Westfield Leader. June 17, 2010, https://www.goleader.com/10jun17/10jun17.pdf

29. Baruch College. "Weissman School of Arts and Sciences." Baruch College, 2022. http://www.baruch.cuny.edu/wsas/academics/ history/bmurphy.htm.

30. Weil, Jonathan. "Contest for Funniest New Jersey Joke Has a Winner." *Bloomberg,* March 23, 2012. httpp://www.bloomberg.com/news/ articles/2012-03-22/contest-for-funniest-new-jersey-joke-has-a-winner.

31. "Controversial Union County-Funded Newsletter Has Been Nice to Union County Democrats: The Auditor." *Star-Ledger*, January 25, 2015.

32. 2010 was just one of a handful of years (for the years that are available/that taxes were filed by the Clark PBA) that Joseph Teston was listed as secretary of the Clark PBA. Considering he was a long-time officer of the organization it's somewhat hypocritical of them to call out the mayor while ignoring high-ranking Clark officers they are certainly familiar with.

2007 Form 990 for New Jersey State Policemens Benevolent Association – Clark PBA Local 125

33. Dincer, Oguzhan, and Michael Johnston. "Measuring Illegal and Legal Corruption in American States: Some Results from the Corruption in America Survey." Edmond & Lily Safra Center for Ethics, December 1, 2014. https://ethics.harvard.edu/blog/measuring-illegal-and-legal-corruption-american-states-some-results-safra.

34. Kusnetz, Nicholas. "How Did New Jersey Rank Tops in Integrity?" Center for Public Integrity, May 1, 2015. httpps://publicintegrity.org/politics/state-politics/how-did-new-jersey-rank-tops-in-integrity/.

35. Chris Christie would see that the ethics committee that would oversee the Bridgegate scandal investigation was full of friendlies. Interesting to see that they didn't make an announcement, merely listing the name of Susana Espasa Guerrero as executive director on the website.

Magyar, Mark J. "Christie Loyalist to Run Ethics Panel That Would Get Bridgegate Complaint." *WNYC*, January 29, 2014. https://www.wnyc.org/story/christie-loyalist-run-ethics-panel-would-get-bridgegate-complaints/.

36. The state troopers involved in the investigation already were considering shutting it down due to potential "political involvements."

Alonzo, Annabelle. "Police Corruption: Officials from New Jersey State Police Buried Corruption Probe Lodged in 2017." *Latin Times*, June 17, 2020. https://www.latintimes.com/police-corruption-officials-new-jersey-state-police-buried-corruption-probe-lodged-459432.

37. Rys, Richard. "'They Have No Choice.'" *Philadelphia Magazine*, May 15, 2006. https://www.phillymag.com/news/2006/05/15/they-have-no-choice/.

38. Stoolmacher, Irwin. "A Progressive Perspective: Blatant Bossism Still Rampant in New Jersey ." Trentonian, January 16, 2022. httpps://www.trentonian.com/2022/01/16/a-progressive-perspective-blatant-bossism-still-rampant-in-new-jersey/.

39. Halbfinger, David M. "44 Charged by U.S. in New Jersey Corruption Sweep." The New York Times, July 23, 2009. httpps://www.nytimes.com/2009/07/24/nyregion/24jersey.html.

40. Rosenberg, Amy S. "How New Jersey Power Brokers Bankrolled the Election of Atlantic City Mayor Frank Gilliam." *Inquirer*, December 21, 2018. httpps://www.inquirer.com/news/new-jersey/atlantic-city-mayor-frank-gilliam-fbi-raid-campaign-finance-new-jersey-20181221.html.

41. Sullivan , S.P. "Mayors under Indictment: A Long Jersey Tradition." nj, March 11, 2017. https://www.nj.com/politics/2017/03/   mayors_under_indictment_a_long_

jersey_tradition.html.

42. Roberts, Sam. "Nicky Scarfo, Mob Boss Who Plundered Atlantic City in the '80s, Dies at 87." *The New York Times,* January 17, 2017. httpps://www.nytimes.com/2017/01/17/nyregion/nicky-scarfo-mob-boss-who-plundered-atlantic-city-in-the-80s-dies-at-87.html.

43. The "Miserable" State, Manhattan Institute

44. $10,000 in a coffee cup isn't nearly as sophisticated as Hague's specially designed bribe delivery box.

Gold, Michael. "$10,000 In a Coffee Cup: 8 Swept up in N.J. Political Corruption Cases." *The New York Times,* December 24, 2019. https://www.nytimes.com/2019/12/24/nyregion/new-jersey-corruption-charges.html.

45. Mansnerus, Laura. "U.S. Charges Essex Leader with Extortion." *The New York Times,* October 29, 2002. https://www.nytimes.com/2002/10/29/

nyregion/us-charges-essex-leader-with-extortion.html.

46. Mansnerus, Laura. "Essex County Executive Is Convicted of Extortion." *The New York Times,* October 29, 2002. httpps://www.nytimes.com/1994/02/22/nyregion/essex-county-executive-is-convicted-of-extortion.html.

47. Staff, Reuters. "Former Newark Mayor Convicted of Fraud." Reuters, April 17, 2008. https://www.reuters.com/article/us-crime-newark-james-idUSN1647165420080416.

48. Coniglio would use his political position to funnel money to Hackensack University Medical Center in exchange for a $5,000 per month "consulting" sinecure.

Associated Press. "Former State Sen. Joseph Coniglio Is Freed from Prison." March 26, 2011. https://www.nj.com/news/2011/03/former_state_sen_joseph_conigl_3.html.

49. Friedman, Matt. "Bribery Could Soon Be Charged as Bribery in N.J." POLITICO, March 18, 2022. https://www.politico.com/newsletters/ new-jersey-playbook/2022/03/18/bribery-could-soon-be-charged-as-bribery-in-n-j-00018383.

50. Mayor Sal Bonaccorso, Police Chief Pedro Matos, and Internal Affairs Sgt. Joseph Teston (the former secretary of the Clark PBA) were caught using racist slurs, including the n-word, on recording.

"A Culture of Racist Corruption in Clark Township: Editorial." *Star-Ledger,* April 4, 2022. https://www.nj.com/opinion/2022/04/a-culture-of-racist-corruption-in-clark-township-editorial.html.

Chapter 7: Galfy Country

1. The DeCavalcante's are the only New Jersey-based mafia family.

Repetto, Thomas. *Bringing down the Mob: The War against the American Mafia,* page 126.

Remnick, David. "Is This the End of Rico?" *The New Yorker,* March 25, 2001. https://www.newyorker.com/magazine/2001/04/02/is-this-the-end-of-rico.

2. Tarrazi, Alexis. "2 Union County Decavalcante Crime Family Members Admit

Selling Cocaine." Westfield, NJ. *Patch,* April 4, 2017. htttps://patch.com/new-jersey/westfield/2-union-county-decavalcante-crime-family-members-admit-selling-cocaine.

3. There were reportedly around 500,000 Colombians in Jackson Heights, Queens. One of the highest concentrations at the time in any city outside of Bogota. The Hudson County-Elizabeth area also had a high percentage of Colombians at the time the area was known as a large distribution center for cocaine.

    Kofoed, Karen. "Miami-New York Colombian connection keeps agents busy," *Courier-Post,* Apr. 6, 1986. p. 10

4. Authorities estimated 500 kilograms of cocaine ran through the stash house in Passaic between March and November of 1985.

    Wright, Chapin. "7 Colombians indicted in $500M cocaine ring." *The Record,* Sunday, April 6, 1986. A-53

    By 1989, news reports claimed that cocaine had become so plentiful in the region that "Colombian drug traffickers have begun selling to dealers outside their ethnic group." Previously it had been believed that Hispanic drug dealers who were primarily trafficking in it were introducing it through their own South American connections.

    Lally, Robin and Alan D. Abbey. "Police can't dismiss common thread in drug war." *Daily Record,* Morris County, N.J. Sunday, December 3, 1989. A9

    A car repair shop in Paterson, New Jersey was found to be a major "stash house" and headquarters of a drug ring. A raid returned 99 one-kilo packages of cocaine, $22,000 in cash and two loaded handguns.

    AP. "Record N.J. raid nets $100M in 'coke.'" *The Courier News.* November 23, 1985, A1

    Below is just a small selection of stories involving cocaine being distributed through New Jersey in discreetly altered vehicles with secret panels or hidden compartments:

    Torrejan, Rodrigo. "Two Paterson men charged with trying to distribute cocaine." *The Herald-News.* March 8, 2019. L7.

    Sampson, Peter J. "2 held in cocaine operation." *The Record.* May 4, 2012. L3

    "Drug trial to hear key U.S. witness." *Courier-Post.* September 5, 1979. 5A

    "Three charged with cocaine possession." *Asbury Park Press.* May 16, 1983. page 4.

    Associated Press. "7 held after 22 pounds of cocaine found in car." *Asbury Park Press.* October 7, 1986. Page 6

5. Torrejon, Rodrigo. "About 1.6 Tons of Cocaine Seized at Port Newark, Largest Drug Bust in 25 Years." North Jersey Media Group, March 11, 2019. https://www.northjersey.com/story/   news/new-jersey/2019/03/11/1-6-tons-cocaine-seized-port-newark-largest-bust-25-years/3128185002/.

6. Madrigal, Irene. "Top 10 Secrets of the Port Newark-Elizabeth Marine Terminal." Untapped New York, July 12, 2021. htttps://untappedcities.com/2021/07/12/secrets-of-port-newark/.

7. Troncone, Tom. "Six Union County Men Charged in 'Largest Mob Takedown in

U.S. History'." Clark-Garwood, NJ *Patch,* January 21, 2011. https://patch.com/new-jersey/clark/six-union-county-men-charged-with-extorting-port-workfcc9a1c778.

8.   Cryan has made multiple public statements making his opinion on the Waterfront Commission clear. On Nov 22, 2021, for instance, Joe Cryan tweeted: "It is a big day for the Port of Elizabeth & all the ports in our area. The Supreme Court just turned down the Waterfront Commission's appeal of the decision to allow our state to leave the compact.

The Waterfront Commission has delayed employee hiring & has become an obstacle to economic progress at the Port. This decision is a really big deal, especially for the 20th District. Congrats to all who made this possible."

Cryan, Joe. "It Is a Big Day for the Port of Elizabeth & All the Ports in Our Area. The Supreme Court Just Turned down the Waterfront Commission's Appeal of the Decision to Allow Our State to Leave the Compact." Twitter, November 22, 2021. https://twitter.com/SenatorJoeCryan/status/1462801744036048913.

9.   Sullivan Ronald. "Democrats Say Hughes Was Warned on DeVita's Alleged Ties to Mafia in 1966; Sills Used Data of State Police Union County Prosecutor Also Protested When Judge Was Aide." *The New York Times,* December 18, 1969. httpps://www.nytimes.com/1969/12/18/archives/democrats-say-hughes-was-warned-on-devitas-alleged-ties-to-mafia-in.html.

10.   Paterson, Bruce. "Letter: Union County Watchdog Eyes NJ Government 'Corruption' in Real Time." *TAPintoWestfield,* March 18, 2022. httpps://www.tapinto.net/towns/westfield/ sections/government/articles/letter-union-county-watchdog-eyes-nj-government-corruption-in-real-time.

11.   No public bidding on a $123.8 million dollar government complex in Elizabeth, New Jersey. The project manager for the Union County Improvement Authority was also the county's finance director and also recommended the architects and construction manager for the project.

Sherman, Ted. "Was Politics in Play When Public Bidding Laws Were Cast aside for a $123.8m Project?" *Star-Ledger,* December 13, 2021. httpps://www.nj.com/politics/2021/12/an-inside-game.html.

12 . Reporters Committee for Freedom of the Press. "New Jersey Blogger Considered a Journalist under State Shield Law." The Reporters Committee for Freedom of the Press, April 16, 2013. httpps://www.rcfp.org/new-jersey-blogger-considered-journalist-under-state-shield-law/.

13.   Chronicle, Cranford. "Union County Opens New Child Advocacy Center in Elizabeth." nj, October 4, 2012. httpps://www.nj.com/cranford/2012/10/ union_county_opens_new_child_a.html.

The United States Department of Justice. "New Jersey Hospital to Pay $3 Million to Resolve Allegations of Medicare Fraud." The United States Department of Justice, November 18, 2009. https://www.justice.gov/opa/pr/new-jersey-hospital-pay-3-million-resolve-allegations-medicare-fraud.

14.   Haydon, Tom. "Judge Rules Union County Blogger Is Protected by the State's Shield Law." nj, April 12, 2013. httpps://www.nj.com/union/2013/04/ union_county_blogger_scores_vi.html.

15. Smith, Alicia. "Two Counties Were Trying to Violate the Public Bidding Laws in New Jersey. Now the Legislature May Make It Legal." List23, March 2, 2022. https://list23.com/724379-two-counties-were-trying-to-violate-the-public-bidding-laws-in-new-jersey-now-the-legislature-may-ma/.

16. Senate bill s-1714 would allow county Improvement Authorities to circumvent the Local Public Contract Laws (LPCL) that are designed to keep bidding open, fair, and transparent. Scutari and Sarlo both would benefit from the bill. Scutari, in addition to the no-show job scandal, faced an investigation over a 6 figure amount stolen from Linden City when he was prosecutor there.

17. Paterson, Bruce. "Letter: Union County Watchdog Eyes NJ Government 'Corruption' in Real Time." *TAPinto Westfield*, March 18, 222AD. httpps://www.tapinto.net/towns/westfield/ sections/government/articles/letter-union-county-watchdog-eyes-nj-government-corruption-in-real-time.

As of this writing, Scutari is still "under the microscope" not only for the no-show but also for civil rights violations, malicious prosecution, and section 1983 claims.

Toutant, Charles. "NJ Sen. Nicholas Scutari under Microscope for Alleged Absences as Prosecutor." *New Jersey Law Journal*, August 9, 2022. https://www.law.com/njlawjournal/2022/08/09/n-j-sen-nicholas-scutari-under-microscope-for-alleged-absences-as-prosecutor/.

18. Munoz, Sophie Nieto. "Progressive Activists Call for Investigation into Senator for Alleged 'No-Show Job'." *New Jersey Monitor*, August 13, 2021. https://newjerseymonitor.com/2021/08/13/progressive-activists-call-for-investigation-into-senator-for-alleged-no-show-job/.

19. Paterson, Bruce. "Letter: Union County Watchdog Eyes NJ Government 'Corruption' in Real Time." *TAPinto Westfield*, March 18, 2022. httpps://www.tapinto.net/towns/westfield/ sections/government/articles/letter-union-county-watchdog-eyes-nj-government-corruption-in-real-time.

20. Lines 21 through 25 of page 9 of the James Galfy interview with Officer Harrison has Galfy admitting he was sued in the police department. The two cases I found involve harassment and discrimination cases. Galfy and others are named, but the Chief of Police is conspicuously not.

JG: "We, we've met each other you know from time to time in the office, I'd come in and we, we... he did all my legal work so you know my closings uhm when I was in the police department he did all my, all my... you know I had deep pockets and got sued for everything... (inaudible) you get sued for everything so... so he handled all of my civil suits uhm but it was, that was pretty much it..."

21. Renna, Tina. "Renna Is a Journalist – Prosecutor Romankow's Political Vendetta Fails." County Watchers, April 12, 2013. httpps://countywatchers.wordpress.com/2013/04/12/renna-is-a-journalist-prosecutor-romankows-political-vendetta-fails/.

22. Kilroy, Carly. "Details about Union County's 'Generatorgate' Revealed, Reports Say." Westfield, NJ *Patch*, May 28, 2014. httpps://patch.com/new-jersey/westfield/details-about-union-countys-generatorgate-revealed-reports-say_6b0a4279.

23. Novak, Steve. "'Generator-Gate' Documents Revealed: 3 Things They Tell Us."

lehighvalleylive, May 18, 2016. htttps://www.lehighvalleylive.com/warren-county/2016/05/generator-gate_3_things_reveal.html.

24. County officials tried to keep the total amount (over $1 million) of unaccounted funds the county was on the hook for.

    Hutchins, Ryan. "Union County MusicFest Organizers Lost Track of Concert Money." *Star-Ledger*, August 26, 2011. https://www.nj.com/news/2011/08/union_county_musicfest_organiz.html.

25. "New Jersey applies its shield law liberally, and it shouldn't hinge on whether someone is a professional, nonpartisan, or even reliable journalist. It's a functional test: Does Renna gather information that's in the public interest and publish it? Yes. What's at issue here is whether she's connected to the news media."

    Board, Star-Ledger Editorial. "Don't Force Union County Watchdog to Reveal Her Sources: Editorial." *Star-Ledger*, January 31, 2013. https://www.nj.com/njv_editorial_page/2013/01/dont_force_union_county_watchd.html.

26. Neuhauser, Alan. "Union County Prosecutor: Mismanagement, but No Criminal Activity, by MusicFest Organizers." New Providence-Berkeley Heights, NJ *Patch*, August 25, 2011. https://patch.com/new-jersey/newprovidence/union-county-prosecutor-mismanagement-but-no-criminal51bceeb51a.

27. In McMinnville, Tennessee violations of sunshine laws are a regular occurrence. Backyard barbecue politicking is also not unheard of, so Romankow's claims that meetings that county officials provide meals for shouldn't be considered "open meetings" seems like a potential cop-out.

    Rubin, Ann R. "Meals Provided to Freeholders Prior to Meetings and the Open Public Meetings Act." Union County Prosecutor's Office. February 6, 2009.

28. Baxter, Christopher. "Secret Files Reveal How Pay-to-Play Works in N.J." *Star-Ledger*, June 23, 2013. htttps://www.nj.com/politics/2013/06/secret_files_reveal_how_pay-to-play_works_in_nj.html.

29. Baxter, Christopher. "Secret Files Reveal How Pay-to-Play Works in N.J." *Star-Ledger*, June 23, 2013. https://www.nj.com/politics/2013/06/secret_files_reveal_how_pay-to-play_works_in_nj.html.

30. Ingle, Bob and Sandy McClure. *The Soprano State: New Jersey's Culture of Corruption*. 2010, p135

31. The Auditor. "Controversial Union County-Funded Newsletter Has Been Nice to Union County Democrats: ." nj, January 25, 2015. htttps://www.nj.com/politics/2015/01/controversial_union_county-funded_newsletter_has_b.html.

32. "Keywood Strategies is uniquely qualified to assist your business through the maze of New Jersey politics. With 562 municipalities, 21 counties and the strongest form of State government in the United States, New Jersey is unlike any other state in the nation. From 'home rule,' to major elections every year, navigating New Jersey politics and government requires experience and knowledge.

    Throughout their careers, Keywood Strategies partners George and Angie Devanney have worked with several of New Jersey's most influential elected officials, including mayors, county officials, legislators and governors, among them current

NJ State Senate President Nick Scutari. During Senator Scutari's time as Union County Freeholder Director, George served as Union County Manager, while Angie served as Scutari's Director of Constituent Services. In 2018, George and Angie served on an exclusive campaign committee that guided the election of Senator Scutari to the Union County Democratic Chairmanship. George has also served as the Democratic Chairman of Berkeley Heights since 2013."

Strategies, Keywood. Keywood Strategies: About the company, November 11, 2022. http://www.keywoodstrategies.com/about.php.

33. Sherman, Ted. "Was Politics in Play When Public Bidding Laws Were Cast aside for a $123.8m Project?" *Star-Ledger*, December 13, 2021. httpps://www.nj.com/politics/2021/12/an-inside-game.html.

34. Star-Ledger. "Freeholders and Free Speech in Union County." *Star-Ledger*, August 20, 2009. https://www.nj.com/njv_editorial_page/2009/08/ freeholders_and_free_speech_in.html.

35. Gold, Michael. "$10,000 In a Coffee Cup: 8 Swept up in N.J. Political Corruption Cases." *The New York Times*, December 24, 2019. httpps://www.nytimes.com/2019/12/24/nyregion/new-jersey-corruption-charges.html.

36. Office of The Attorney General. "AG Grewal Announces Criminal Charges Against Five Public Officials and Political Candidates in Major Corruption Investigation." State of New Jersey, December 19, 2019. httpps://www.nj.gov/oag/newsreleases19/pr20191219a.html.

37. As with MusicFest, GeneratorGate, and Cernadas Jr. helping out his mob-affiliated father avoid legal trouble, the Devanney situation reveals how reticent Romankow's office was regarding investigating or censuring their favored friends.

Renna, Tina. "December 2012." countywatchers, 2022. https://countywatchers.wordpress.com/2012/12/.

"The group investigates the county by obtaining public records, asking questions at Freeholder meetings and talking to sources inside the county. Tina, along with her colleagues John Bury and Jim Buettner, analyze what they find and report about it on their blog countywatchers.com.

In the past, the group has sent their findings of malfeasance to law enforcement only to find that instead of pursuing criminal charges the perpetrators were protected. For instance, after the County Watchers showed evidence that there was possibly tens of thousands of dollars of cash missing from the county 2010 Musicfest event, Romankow was forced by the State Attorney General to investigate. He wrote a scathing report and stated that the event was mismanaged, implementing County Manager George Devanney, Senator Raymond Lesniak's nephew, but stopped short of conducting a criminal investigation. Devanney was allowed to retire days before the report was released and Romankow and his first assistant went on to attend Devanney's retirement party.

Another example of the politically connected being protected happened in 2012. The County Watchers issued a report about county chain saws that were taken from county property and pawned off. The suspect, in this case, was identified as Patrick Scanlon Jr., step-son of Freeholder Deborah Scanlon. Patrick, who was on probation, left the county payroll after the County Watchers published their findings, and was put on the Township of Union's payroll the following month. After a year-long investigation, the Union County police closed the case without seeking any criminal charges."

Renna, Joe. "Of Course She's A Journalist." Renna Media. 2005, https://www. rennamedia.com/wp-content/uploads/ 2016/11/AAPApr13.pdf.

38. Friedman, Matt. "New Jersey Inquiry Examined Payments to Top Democratic Aide." *POLITICO*, March 11, 2022. https://www.politico.com/news/2022/03/11/ state-probe-sean-caddle-political-groups-00016135.

39. Friedman, Matt. "New Jersey Political Consultant Sean Caddle Pleads Guilty in Murder-for-Hire Plot." *POLITICO*, January 25, 2022. https://www.politico.com/ news/2022/01/25/sean-caddle-pleads-guilty-murder-00002119.

40. Balcerzak, Ashley and Steve Janoski. "Complete Coverage, Timeline for Murder-for-Hire Case That Has NJ Political World Abuzz." North Jersey Media Group, March 30, 2022. https://www.northjersey.com/story/news/2022/03/30/nj-murder-for-hire-case-political-agent-sean-caddle/9459162002/.

41. Harris, Vashti, and Riley Yates. "Clark Residents Continue to Call for Mayor to Resign over Racist and Sexist Remarks." *Star-Ledger*, May 3, 2022. httpps://www. nj.com/news/2022/05/clark-residents-continue-to-call-for-mayor-to-resign-over-racist-and-sexist-remarks.html.

42. Prosecutors office and Attorney General's office helped shield the racist cops and politicians for years. Officials falsified records to hurt the whistleblower's career for "crossing the blue line."

Yates, Riley, and S.P. Sullivan. "Criticism Mounts of Clark Mayor, Police Officials Allegedly Recorded Using Racial Slurs." *Star-Ledger*, April 5, 2022. https://www. nj.com/news/2022/04/criticism-builds-of-clark-mayor-police-officials-allegedly-caught-using-racial-slurs.html.

43. Fox, Joey. "Clark PBA Calls for Bonaccorso's Resignation Following Racial Slur Scandal." *New Jersey Globe*, April 22, 2022. httpps://newjerseyglobe.com/local/clark-pba-calls-for-bonaccorsos-resignation-following-racial-slur-scandal/.

Chapter 8: On The Waterfront

1. Jackman, Tom. "New York Mafia Still Active, but Flashy 'Mob Hits' Decline as Witnesses Flip and Law Hits Harder." The Washington Post, March 15, 2019. httpps://www.washingtonpost.com/crime-law/2019/03/15/new-york-mafia-still-active-flashy-mob-hits-decline-witnesses-flip-law-hits-harder/.

2. After denying the existence of organized crime since the 30s, the FBI could no longer do so after the Apalachin meeting.

Jackman, Tom. "New York Mafia Still Active, but Flashy 'Mob Hits' Decline as Witnesses Flip and Law Hits Harder." *The Washington Post*, March 15, 2019. https:// www.washingtonpost.com/crime-law/2019/03/15/new-york-mafia-still-active-flashy-mob-hits-decline-witnesses-flip-law-hits-harder/.

3. Solomon, Nancy. "New Jersey Party Bosses Try to Fend off Progressive Reformers." *Gothamist*, March 13, 2019. httpps://gothamist.com/news/new-jersey-party-bosses-

try-fend-progressive-reformers.

4. Pizarro, Max. "At Union County Breakfast, Sweeney v. Murphy v. Lesniak." *Observer,* October 29, 2014. httpps://observer.com/2014/10/at-union-county-breakfast-sweeney-v-murphy-v-lesniak/.

5. Murphy, Sean. "'An Underworld Syndicate': Malcolm Johnson's 'On the Waterfront' Articles'." The Pulitzer Prizes, 2022. https://www.pulitzer.org/article/underworld-syndicate-malcolm-johnsons-waterfront-articles.

6. Woodard, Fletch. *Fletch. Woodard: his fights with those bad, bad town boys, a drive for the life of a human being! the accusation, arrest, imprisonment and trials of himself and the Flynns, charged with the murder of Enoch Cooksey.* Facsimile edition. McMinnville, Tenn.: Art Emporium, 2001

7. Chaffin, Joshua. "On the Waterfront: The Political Fight over Organised Crime at the Port of New York." *Financial Times,* May 26, 2022. https://www.ft.com/content/f2d12689-411c-4bbd-a475-4c8254568ee4.

8. McShane, Larry. "Waterfront Corrupt: Probe Finds Execs Wasted Anti-Terror Cash, Surfed for Porn, Misused Boats." *New York Daily News,* August 12, 2009. httpps://www.nydailynews.com/news/waterfront-corrupt-probe-finds-execs-wasted-anti-terror-cash-surfed-porn-misused-boats-article-1.400652.

9. New York State. "Waterfront Commission Plagued by Abuse and Corruption." Office of the Inspector General, August 11, 2009. httpps://ig.ny.gov/news/waterfront-commission-plagued-abuse-and-corruption.

10. Blumenthal, Ralph. "Corruption Found at Waterfront Watchdog." *The New York Times,* August 11, 2009. https://www.nytimes.com/2009/08/12/nyregion/12waterfront.html

11. Blumenthal, Ralph. "Corruption Found at Waterfront Watchdog." *The New York Times,* August 11, 2009. https://www.nytimes.com/2009/08/12/nyregion/12waterfront.html

12. McShane, Larry. "Waterfront Corrupt: Probe Finds Execs Wasted Anti-Terror Cash, Surfed for Porn, Misused Boats." *New York Daily News,* January 11, 2019. httpps://www.nydailynews.com/news/waterfront-corrupt-probe-finds-execs-wasted-anti-terror-cash-surfed-porn-misused-boats-article-1.400652.

13. The United States Department of Justice. "Genovese Organized Crime Family Soldier Sentenced to 41 Months in Prison for Racketeering Conspiracy." The United States Department of Justice, April 17, 2015. https://www.justice.gov/usao-nj/pr/genovese-organized-crime-family-soldier-sentenced-41-months-prison-racketeering.

14. Renna, Tina. "Union County's First Assistant Prosecutor Named in Report 'Waterfront Commission Plagued by Abuse and Corruption.'" countywatchers, August 11, 2010. httpps://countywatchers.wordpress.com/2010/08/11/union-countys-first-assistant-prosecutor-named-in-waterfront-commission-investigation/.

15. In addition to kickbacks for years, Cernadas was found to be involved in corruption related to union funds being siphoned into a pharmaceutical company owned by

organized crime.

Sherman, Ted. "Ex-Longshoremen's Union Official Is Indicted on Waterfront Corruption Charges." *Star-Ledger,* December 16, 2010. https://www.nj.com/news/2010/12/ex-longshoremen_union_official.html.

16. Wallye. "Hackett's Lawyer Was No Temple Houston." *Observer,* January 24, 2009. https://observer.com/2009/01/hacketts-lawyer-was-no-temple-houston/.

17. Whelan, Jeff S. "Ex-Kingpin Lynch Seeks Early Release." *Star-Ledger,* September 4, 2008. httpps://www.nj.com/news/ledger/topstories/2008/   09/exkingpin_lynch_seeks_early_re.html.

18. "In sometime opposition to the Norcross gang is Union County's Sen. Ray Lesniak, who convinced McGreevey not to quit in time to hold a special election, as Lynch and Norcross had wanted. Lesniak said of the struggle with the duo, 'It was an eye-opener to me and demonstrated that we (party bosses) have way too much power.' That's right, he said 'we.' Lesniak, known for an oversized ego, confessed, Union County is in the north just below Essex and Hudson counties."

     Ingle, Bob and Sandy McClure. *The Soprano State: New Jersey's Culture of Corruption.* 2010, p135

19. Office of the Inspector General. "Waterfront Commission Plagued by Abuse and Corruption." New York State, August 11, 2009. httpps://ig.ny.gov/news/waterfront-commission-plagued-abuse-and-corruption.

20. Waterfront Commission of new york harbor (*WCNYH*). "Snitches Get Stitches." Accessed November 15, 2022. httpps://www.wcnyh.gov/newspage361.html.

21. Pizarro, Max, And Timothy J. Carroll. "Waterfront Commission Argues Busts Prove Effectiveness but Lesniak Not Sold – Yet." *Observer,* January 21, 2011. https://observer.com/2011/01/waterfront-commission-argues-busts-prove-effectiveness-but-lesniak-not-sold-yet/.

22. Leonardis presented a dockworker's cargo hook at a legislative meeting the previous fall, proclaiming: "As this hook has outlived its usefulness, I think so has the Waterfront Commission."

     Bonney, Joseph. "Whacked on the Waterfront." Whacked on the Waterfront | JOC.com, January 31, 2011. httpps://www.joc.com/maritime-news/whacked-waterfront_20110131.html.

23. Largest mob takedown to date.   Staff, Star-Ledger. "More than 120 Members of Organized Crime Families Are Arrested in Massive Sweep." *Star-Ledger,* January 21, 2011. httpps://www.nj.com/news/2011/01/   more_than_120_members_of_organ.html.

24. Considine, Bob. 2011. "The Jersey Mob 2.0." *Star-Ledger.* February 17, 2011. https://www.nj.com/inside-jersey/2011/02/   the_jersey_mob_20.html.

25. Porter, David. "15 Charged in N.J. as Part of Mob Takedown." *New Jersey Herald,* January 20, 2011. httpps://www.njherald.com/story/news/2011/01/21/15-charged-in-n-j/3974217007/.

26. Berger, Paul, and Jess Bravin. "New York Asks Supreme Court to Stop New Jersey from Leaving Crime-Fighting Agency." *The Wall Street Journal,* March 14, 2022.

https://www.wsj.com/articles/new-york-asks-supreme-court-to-stop-new-jersey-from-leaving-crime-fighting-a   gency-11647297216. \

27. Justia Law. "New Jersey v. New York, 283 U.S. 336 (1931)." Justia Law, May 4, 1931. https://supreme.justia.com/cases/federal/us/283/336/.

28. Lesniak, Raymond. "Raymond Lesniak: Settling Scores." *New Jersey Globe*, April 21, 2022. httpps://newjerseyglobe.com/legislature/raymond-lesniak-settling-scores/.

29. Friedman, Matt. "How One Election Left This Powerful Democratic Organization Fighting to Survive." *POLITICO*, November 17, 2021. httpps://www.politico.com/news/2021/11/17/south-jersey-democrats-norcross-522737.

30. Former International Longshoreman's Association (ILA) Local 1235 President Albert Cernadas Sr. of Union gave $750 to Assembly Majority Leader Joe Cryan (D-Union Twp.). Cryan hails from Lesniak's Union County legislative district in 2004. He gave $2,000 to state Sen. Ronald L. Rice (D-Newark) in 2005, according to the state Election Law Enforcement Commission (ELEC).

     Cernadas Sr. is the father of Union County prosecutor Albert Cernadas Jr. Cernadas Sr. also gave $150 to Cryan in 2005 and $500 to Rice in 1999.

     Pizarro, Max, and Timothy J. Carroll. 2011. "Waterfront Commission Argues Busts Prove Effectiveness but Lesniak Not Sold – Yet." *Observer.* January 21, 2011. https://observer.com/2011/01/waterfront-commission-argues-busts-prove-effectiveness-but-lesniak-not-sold-yet/.

31. Racioppi, Dustin. "Dr. Salomon Melgen, Who Stood Trial with Sen. Bob Menendez, Gets Clemency from Trump." North Jersey Media Group, January 20, 2021. https://www.northjersey.com/story/news/new-jersey/2021/01/20/salomon-melgen-friend-bob-menendez-pardoned-president-trump/4210560001/.

32. Justia Law. "United States v. Cryan, 490 F. Supp. 1234 (D.N.J. 1980)." Justia Law, May 22, 1980. https://law.justia.com/cases/federal/   district-courts/FSupp/490/1234/1905133/.

33. FBI Undercover Operations: Hearings before the subcommittee on civil and constitutional rights of the committee on the judiciary House of Representatives Ninety-Seventh Congress, Second Session, pg 1006.

34. Bichao, Sergio. "Union President from Hunterdon Gets 2 Years for Mafia Extortion." *Courier News*, December 10, 2014. httpps://www.mycentraljersey.com/story/news/   crime/jersey-mayhem/2014/12/10/union-president-hunterdon-gets-years-mafia-extortion/20203365/.

35. Sherman, Ted. "Ex-Longshoremen's Union Official Is Indicted on Waterfront Corruption Charges." *Star-Ledger*, December 16, 2010. https://www.nj.com/news/2010/12/ex-longshoremen_union_official.html.

36. The $52,000 was to go to Ruiz, union members told the authorities. Sherman, Ted. "Ex-Longshoremen's Union Official Is Indicted on Waterfront Corruption Charges." *Star-Ledger*, December 16, 2010. httpps://www.nj.com/news/2010/12/ex-longshoremen_union_official.html.

37. Aulisi would be sentenced to 18 months.

     Bonney, Joseph. "Ex-Ila Official Gets 18 Months for Extortion." Ex-ILA official gets 18 months for extortion | JOC.com, October 9, 2014. https://www.joc.com/port-news/longshoreman-labor/international-longshoremen%E2%80%99s-association/ex-ila-official-gets-18-months-extortion_20141009.html.

38. Renna, Tina. "Union County's First Assistant Prosecutor Named in Waterfront Commission Investigation." County Watchers, August 11, 2010. https://countywatchers.wordpress.com/2010/08/11/union- countys-first-assistant-prosecutor-named-in-waterfront-commission- investigation/

39. Mansnerus, Laura. 2003. "McGreevey Trip to Puerto Rico Is Criticized." *The New York Times*, July 22, 2003, sec. New York. httpps://www.nytimes.com/2003/07/22/nyregion/mcgreevey-trip-to-puerto-rico-is-criticized.html.

40. "Sixty years after On the Waterfront (filmed in and based on the Hoboken docks) made New Jersey's mob-connected union bosses and crime-fighting waterfront commission national viewing, the scenario continues. A Genovese crime family soldier and two crime family associates, including a former president of the International Longshoremen's Association, pleaded guilty to a scheme that for three decades used violence and threats to extort Christmas-time tribute payments from dock workers, according to federal prosecutors. Genovese family soldier Stephen Depiro and two Genovese family associates, Albert Cernadas, former president of ILA Local 1235, and Nunzio LaGrasso, former vice president of ILA Local 1478, pleaded guilty to racketeering conspiracy. Since 2005, Depiro managed the Genovese family's control over the New Jersey waterfront, according to the feds. In addition to conspiring to collect the tribute payments, Depiro controlled a sports betting operation, the feds said. The racketeering charges could land the three in prison for up to 20 years. In the long-running federal case, Thomas Leonardis, former president of ILA Local 1235, was sentenced to a year and 10 months in jail after admitting that he conspired to extort the tribute payments from longshoremen on the New Jersey piers. Other longshoremen have been sentenced in the case. Federal and state prosecutors have continually thanked the Waterfront Commission of New York Harbor for its help, even as Sen. Ray Lesniak is looking to end New Jersey's role in the commission because he says things have changed, and it is no longer needed."

The Soprano State. "Update 14." https://www.thesopranostate.com/update14.htm

41. Frassinelli, Mike. 2009. "Angelo Prisco, Reputed N.J. Mobster, Convicted in Cousin's Murder." *Star-Ledger.* April 28, 2009. httpps://www.nj.com/news/2009/04/reputed_mobster_angelo_prisco.html.

42. ABC7. 2011. "Mob Arrests Raise Issues of Crime, Security between Port Newark and Newark Airport | *ABC7 San Francisco* | Abc7news.com." ABC7 San Francisco. February 14, 2011. httpps://abc7news.com/archive/7956130/.

43. "Retired Trooper Writes about Fighting the Mob." *Daily Record.* March 18, 2017. httpps://www.dailyrecord.com/story/news/   local/2017/03/18/retired-trooper-writes-fighting-mob/   99322020/.

44. Under the "About" tab on Buccino's LinkedIn profile: "Retiring after 51 years in law enforcement. NJSP, SCI, DCJ and Union County Prosecutor's Office. Can't retire, head full of knowledge, expertise, and plenty of energy. President of Corporate Integrity Consultant Company specializing in due diligence and background

investigations."

Buccino, Robert. LinkedIn. https://www.linkedin.com/in/robert-buccino-27427319/

45. Private communication.

46. "Organized Crime Module 1 Key Issues: Similarities & Differences." www.unodc. org. htttps://www.unodc.org/e4j/zh/ organized-crime/module-1/key-issues/ similarities-and-differences.html.

47. "KKR Appoints General David Petraeus Chairman of KKR Global Institute." 2013. Www.businesswire.com. May 30, 2013. htttps://www.businesswire.com/ news/ home/20130530005466/en/KKR-Appoints-General-David-Petraeus-Chairman-of-KKR-Global-Institute.

48. "Among other activities, KKR buys companies and reorganizes them to make them profitable. It manages investments for pension funds of the SEIU, a union with an estimated 2 million members, many in low-wage jobs, such as office cleaning and nursing assistance.

    "SEIU local and national pension funds made up more than 30% of KKR's 2006 Fund, one of several investment funds in the firm's portfolio."

    Furchtgott-Roth, Diana. 2008. "Https://Www.nysun.com/." *The New York Sun.* July 8, 2008. https://www.nysun.com/article/opinion-holding-up-a-mirror-to-the-seiu.

    Andrew Stern, President Emeritus of the Service Employees International Union (SEIU) is also a member of KKR's Sustainability Expert Advisory Council.

    KKR. 2022. "The Three E's of Shared Ownership: Engaging, Empowering, and Elevating Workers." KKR. September 21, 2022. https://www.kkr.com/global-perspectives/kkr-blog/three-e %E2%80%99s-shared-ownership-engaging-empowering-and-elevating-workers.

49. Bulos, Nabih. 2016. "In Syria, Militias Armed by the Pentagon Fight Those Armed by the CIA." *Los Angeles Times.* March 27, 2016. htttps://www.latimes.com/world/ middleeast/la-fg-cia-pentagon-isis-20160327-story.html.

    Mazzetti, Mark, and Ali Younes. 2016. "C.I.A. Arms for Syrian Rebels Supplied Black Market, Officials Say (Published 2016)." *The New York Times,* June 26, 2016, sec. World. htttps://www.nytimes.com/2016/06/27/world/middleeast/cia-arms-for-syrian-rebels-supplied-black-market-officials-say.html.

50. KKR was one of the groups that helped fund Operation Timber Sycamore. Around 1/3 of KKR's investments included pension funds such as SEIU.

    Zuesse, Eric. 2018. "Who Was Secretly behind America's Invading and Occupying Syria?" *Countercurrents.org.* December 27, 2018. htttps://countercurrents. org/2018/12/who-was-secretly-behind-americas-invading-and-occupying-syria/.

51. Inspector General Investigation, 8/11/2009, Jon S. Corzine. htttps://www.wcnyh. gov/news/IG Investigation_8-11-2009.pdf.

Chapter 9: Code of Silence in the House of Horrors

1. Atmonavage, Joe. "No Timeline Set for Closing N.J.'s Troubled Women's Prison,

Doc Head Says." *Star-Ledger*, May 11, 2022. httpps://www.nj.com/news/2022/05/no-timeline-for-closing-njs-troubled-womens-prison-doc-head-says.html.

2. Sullivan, S.P. "Sexual Abuse of Inmates at N.J. Women's Prison Is an 'Open Secret,' Federal Inquiry Finds." *Star-Ledger*, April 14, 2020. httpps://www.nj.com/coronavirus/2020/04/sexual-abuse-of-inmates-at-nj-womens-prison-is-an-open-secret-federal-inquiry-finds.html.

3. "Collins v. Union County Jail: Supreme Court of New Jersey: 07-15-1997: Www.anylaw.com." anylaw, July 15, 1997. httpps://www.anylaw.com/case/collins-v-union-county-jail/supreme-court-of-new-jersey/07-14-1997/dbh2TmYBTlTomsSBxNGL.

4. "Crossing the Thin Blue Line: Protecting Law Enforcement Officers Who Blow the Whistle Ann C. Hodges Professor of Law Emerita at the University of Richmond and Justin Pugh Law Clerk, Circuit Court for the City of Portsmouth, Virginia. "Law enforcement makes headline news for shootings of unarmed civilians, departmental corruption, and abuse of suspects and witnesses. Also well-documented is the code of silence, the thin blue line, which discourages officers from reporting improper and unlawful conduct by fellow officers."

    Hodges, Ann C., and Justin Pugh. "Crossing the Thin Blue Line: Protecting Law Enforcement Officers Who Blow the Whistle." *UC Davis L. Rev. Online* 52 (2018): 1.

5. The term originates from Edinburgh murderer of the surname Burke. Burke's accomplice turned state's witness so in addition to using the term "burke/burked" to mean strangle it is also "applied to any project that is quietly stopped or stifled—as 'the question has been BURKED.'"

    "Australian Slang ~ Local Lingo." Australian Slang and Unique Phrases. Ac cessed November 15, 2022. https://www.freesettlerorfelon.com/aus   tralian_slang.html.

6. Vazquez,U.S.D.J.,John Micheal. "Mesadieu v. City of Elizabeth, D.N.J., Judgment, Law, ." https://www.casemine.com, September 7, 2017. httpps://www.casemine.com/judgement/   us/59b8de59add7b044ef8f67ad.

    Mesadieu v. City of Elizabeth: In this case, Elizabeth Chief of Police Jim Cosgrove is also named as being one of the Union County officials who suppressed knowledge of racial profiling. Cosgrove, like Bonaccorso in Clark would be forced down due to egregious racist and sexist language.

    Julie Daurio Producer. "Getting Rid of Elizabeth's Police Director Should Just Be the Beginning of Change, Activist Says." *Star-Ledger*, May 1, 2019. httpps://www.nj.com/opinion/2019/05/getting-rid-of-eliza   beths-police-director-should-just-be-the-beginning-of-change-ac   tivist-says.html.

7. Martini, Willliam. "Espinosa v. County of Union, 2005 WL 2089916: D.N.J., Judgment, Law." https://www.casemine.com, August 30, 2005. https://www.casemine.com/judgement/

    us/5914b608add7b04934776666.

8. Hedges, Chris. "Blue Shadows -- a Special Report.; Suspicions Swirl around New

Jersey Police Clique." *The New York Times*, May 13, 2000. httpps://www.nytimes.com/2000/05/13/nyregion/blue-shadows-a-special-report-suspicions-swirl-around-new-jersey-police-clique.html.

9. "A secret grand jury report in 1998 said that nearly *one-fifth of the 370-member Elizabeth force* belonged to the Family. Officers on the police force testified under oath that the group led by the day shift commander Lieutenant Szpond conducted bizarre initiations and rites of entrance – and held threatening excommunication rituals for those who resisted racist codes of behavior. In several criminal prosecutions and internal department inquiries, members of the Family were accused of threatening Black and Hispanic/Latinx officers, controlling promotions and overtime, pervasive racial profiling, brutality and planting drugs on Blacks and Hispanic/Latinx men. One apparent member of the Family, Mary Rabadeau, served as Elizabeth police director and was later promoted to chief of the New Jersey Transit Police Department."

    Physical abuse, false arrest, often inspired by racism were hallmarks of "The Family." The 2000 article from New York Times pointed out that at the time the entire department had only four Hispanic officers and no black officers among the 60 or so "superior officers."

    Granzen, Michael. *Breaking Through the Plate Glass Window*, p. 193-194

10. loc. cit.

11. loc. cit.

12. Clark, Samuel. *Total Misconduct: a factual account of police and political corruption.* 2005

13. Hedges, Chris. "BLUE SHADOWS – A Special Report.; Suspicions Swirl Around New Jersey Police Clique," https://www.nytimes.com/2000/05/13/nyregion/blue-shadows-a-special-report-suspicions-swirl-around-new-jersey-police-clique.html

14. Yates, Riley, and S.P. Sullivan . "Clark Has a History of Payouts to Police Officers Who Recorded Their Bosses' Alleged Misdeeds." *Star-Ledger*, May 3, 2022. https://www.nj.com/news/2022/05/clark-has-a-history-of-payouts-to-police-officers-who-recorded-their-bosses-alleged-misdeeds.html.

15. Granzen, Michael. *Breaking Through the Plate Glass Window*

16. Granzen, Michael. *Breaking Through the Plate Glass Window* p. 129-130

17. O'Connor, Julie. "Elizabeth Police Sergeant Will Keep $600K Award from Whistle Blower Lawsuit." *Star-Ledger*, December 30, 2009. httpps://www.nj.com/news/2009/12/   elizabeth_police_sergeant_will.html.

18. Justia Law. "John Guslavage V. the City of Elizabeth." Justia Law, March 23, 2009. https://law.justia.com/cases/new-jersey/appellate-division-unpublished/2009/a2408-06-opn.html.

19. U.S. District Judge Gary A. Feess ruled in 2001, after presiding over about a hundred federal police corruption lawsuits that the city's police department could be sued as a racketeering enterprise.

    ABC News. "Judge: LAPD Can Be Sued as Racketeering Enterprise." Accessed November 2022. https://abcnews.go.com/US/story?   id=93521&page=1.

20. Rowan, Michael. "Leaving No Stone Unturned: Using RICO as a Remedy for Police Misconduct." *Fla. St. UL Rev.* 31 (2003): 231.

21. Rickman, Rick. "Sex on Duty? Driving Drunk? White Cops in Union County, NJ Got a Pass, Lawsuit Says." New Jersey 101.5, August 2, 2022. https://nj1015.com/sex-on-duty-driving-drunk-white-cops-in-union-county-nj-got-a-pass-lawsuit-says/.

22. Hughes, Andrea Crowley. "Lawsuit Claims Union County Police 'Old Boys Club' Members Get Pass on Misconduct." *TAPinto*, August 6, 2022. https://www.tapinto.net/towns/westfield/sections/union-county-news/articles/lawsuit-claims-union-county-police-old-boys-club-members-get-pass-on-misconduct.

23. Kadosh, Matt. "9 Cops in Union County among 389 in State AG's 2021 'Major Discipline' Report." *TAPinto*, March 3, 2022. https://www.tapinto.net/towns/westfield/sections/union-county-news/articles/9-cops-in-union-county-among-389-in-state-ag-s-2021-major-discipline-report.

24. httpps://www.tapinto.net/towns/westfield/sections/union-county-news/articles/lawsuit-claims-union-county-police-old-boys-club-members-get-pass-on-misconduct

25. httpps://www.tapinto.net/towns/westfield/sections/union-county-news/articles/9-cops-in-union-county-among-389-in-state-ag-s-2021-major-discipline-report

26. Justia Law. "Angela Hoag v. Commissioner Devon Brown, New Jersey Department of Corrections, Et Al.." Justia Law, September 25, 2007. httpps://law.justia.com/cases/new-jersey/appellate-division-published/2007/a5537-05-opn.html.

27. Justia Law. "Conrad J. Benedetto v. Marlena Russo." Justia Law, June 4, 2018. https://law.justia.com/cases/new-jersey/appellate-division-unpublished/2018/a2514-16.html.

     Justia Law. "Angela Hoag v. Commissioner Devon Brown, New Jersey Department of Corrections, Et Al.." Justia Law, September 25, 2007.

28. *In the Matter of Augustin Alvarez*, Union County, Department of Corrections, CSC DKT. No. 2021-1692 OAL DKT. NO. CSV 04718-   21, Final Administrative Action of the Civil Service Commission, June 20, 2022 https://nj.gov/csc/about/meetings/decisions/pdf/2022/6-15-22/A002%20ALVAREZ%20AUGUSTIN.PDF

29. Commission of Investigation. "The Changing Face of ORGANIZED CRIME IN NEW JERSEY: A Status Report." State of New Jersey, May, 2004.

30. Atmonavage | NJ Advance Media for NJ.com, Joe, and Blake Nelson . "7 Inmates Committed Suicide at N.J. Jail and Staff Failed to Provide Help, Federal Investigators Say." *Star-Ledger*, January 14, 2021. httpps://www.nj.com/news/2021/01/7-inmates-committed-suicide-at-nj-jail-where-feds-allege-staff-failed-to-provide-help.html.

     Three correctional officers were charged in the deaths of two inmates from suicide.

31. Everett, Rebecca. "No Jail for Officer Accused of Fudging Records When Inmate Killed Himself." *Star-Ledger*, April 6, 2018. httpps://www.nj.com/cumberland/2018/04/no_jail_for_guard_accused_of_fudging_records_when.html.

Chapter 10: Defense for the Prosecution

1. Appellate Division, July 25, 2019, A-004519-18,

2. Unnecessary infliction of pain is, in essence, "cruel and unusual punishment."

   Luise, Maria A. "Solitary confinement: Legal and psychological considerations." *New Eng. J. on Crim. & Civ. Confinement* 15 (1989): 301.

   Gallagher, Shaun. "The cruel and unusual phenomenology of solitary confinement." *Frontiers in Psychology* 5 (2014): 585.

   Lack of interaction and intersubjectivity has detrimental effects on the psychological state that can extend to physical manifestations such as motor disruptions and "extensive and serious disruptions of experience."

   8th amendment claims aren't the only arguments against prolonged solitary confinement.

   This Note argues that this right to be treated with dignity— even if only a background norm—has the potential to exist outside the purview of the Eighth Amendment and may conceptually live within those substantive liberty guarantees inherent in the Due Process Clause. By breaking from traditional notions of how solitary confinement might be categorically challenged (i.e., on Eighth Amendment grounds), this Note hopes to spark conversation in the legal community regarding an alternative theory to challenging the indignity of solitary confinement.

   Scientific American. "Solitary Confinement Is Cruel and Ineffective." *Scien-tific American*, August 1, 2013. https://www.scientificamerican.com/article/solitary-confinement-cruel-ineffective-unusual/.

3. McGillivary, Caleb "Kai the Hitchhiker." Facebook

   https://www.facebook.com/yodhehwawheh/posts/pfbid0RfMACzgNMv4r6hgee 5n4wbFqYCSXwkZV5dmevN2B1TxTbaM7pN54JhUKJGAemtBTl

4. Haydon, Tom. "Union County Prosecutor Calls It Quits after 11 Years." *Star-Ledger*, May 16, 2013. https://www.nj.com/union/2013/05/union_county_prosecutor_calls. html.

   Zalot, Morgan, Brian X. McCrone, and Sam Wood. "'Kai the Hitchhiker' Arrested at Center City Bus Depot for NJ Murder." *Inquirer*, May 16, 2013. https://www.inquirer.com/philly/news/Kai_the_Hitchhiker_an_internet_sensation_wanted_for_murder_in_NJ.html.

   Haydon, Tom. "Accused Murderer 'Kai the Hitchhiker' Wages Legal Fight from Jail." *Star-Ledger*, March 7, 2016. https://www.nj.com/union/2016/03/accused_of_murder_kai_the_hitchhiker_wages_legal_f.html.

5. Haydon, Tom. "3 Years and Counting; No Trial Yet for YouTube Star." *Star-Ledger*, May 12, 2016.

6. Detective Edward Suter's report from July 17, 2013, notes that Detective Ho delivered items to be processed for latent prints on Thursday, June 27, 2013. The items were "assorted beer & wine bottles, a stem glass and coffee mugs." The items were "rinsed with fresh water" and "allowed to air dry" after being fumed with cyanoacrylate and fluorescent dye. No toxicology tests on any residue or analysis to

determine presence of DFSA agents were done.

Suter, Edward. Supplementary Investigative Report, July 17, 2013.

7. Union County Prosecutor's Office Forensic Laboratory, Lab#: L 13-2765 Report Number 2

8. Peterson attempts a bait and switch. "There was a rape kit done on Joe. No semen was found. No semen has been found on any of the bedsheets."

First off, why would you run a rape kit on the alleged rapist? Secondly, the hairs mashed into the mattress and the urine stain on the floor corroborate Kai's claims he was not assaulted *on* the bed at all. Not to mention the fact that investigative reports do note semen (and "unidentified blood") on Galfy's penis at the time of his death.

State of New Jersey v. Caleb McGillvary. Transcript of Grand Jury Hearing. Indictment No. 13-11-00946. page 7

Also a "minor DNA type" was found indicating a "sperm fraction of the interior front of [Galfy's] underwear."

Union County Prosecutor's Office Forensic Laboratory. Lab#: L 13-2765 Report Number 2. Page 4

"When you do rape kits, you will photograph the individual's body or at least make a diagram to show where injuries may be, including rug burns, which [Appellant] has said he had rug burns on his lower back. Either photographs or a diagram would have revealed that and neither was done." [15T15-23 to 16-3]

Ho even admitted that a "rape kit could have been done on [Apellant]" [13T103-1 to 3] as testing can be done within five days and Kai was apprehended and interrogated by Ho four days later.

Case 2:22-cv-04185-MCA Document 1-9 Filed 06/22/22 Page 55 of 87 PageID: 153

9. Rape or other serious bodily harm are grounds for self-defense. Kai was unable to easily retreat with Galfy above him and he had been drugged to make resisting more difficult. Since he was physically helpless or incapacitated this would qualify as aggravated sexual assault which meets the definition of "serious bodily harm" as per N.J.S.A. 2c:3-4.

Tharney, Laura C., and Samuel M. Silver. "Legislation and Law Revision Commissions: One Option for the Management and Maintenance of Ever-Increasing Bodies of Statutory Law." *Seton Hall Legis. J.* 41 (2016): 329.

"bodily harm which creates a substantial risk of death or which causes serious, permanent disfigurement or protracted loss or impairment of the function of any bodily member or organ or which results from aggravated sexual assault or sexual assault."

Justia Law. "2013 New Jersey Revised Statutes :: Title 2C - The New Jersey Code of Criminal Justice :: Section 2C:3-11 - Definitions." Justia Law, 2022. https://law.justia.com/codes/new-jersey/2013/title-2c/sect ion-2c-3-11.

Federal and State precedent require prosecutors disclose exculpatory and impeachment evidence to defense counsel. The United States Supreme Court in Brady v. Maryland, 373 U.S.

83, 87 (1963), held "suppression by the prosecution of evidence favorable to an accused . . . violates due process where the evidence is material either to guilt or to punishment, irrespective of the good faith or bad faith of the prosecution."

ATTORNEY GENERAL LAW ENFORCEMENT DIRECTIVE NO. 2019-6, Gurbir S. Grewal, Attorney General. "Directive Establishing County Policies to Comply with Brady v. Maryland   and Giglio v. United States," December 4. 2019, https://www.nj.gov/oag/dcj/agguide/directives/ag-Directive-2019-6.pdf

10. "In New Jersey, there are four elements to spoliation: (1) the evidence must be within a party's control; (2) an actual suppression or withholding; (3) of relevant evidence; (4) where it was reasonably foreseeable that the evidence would be discoverable."

"New Jersey District Court Approves Spoliation Sanction for Plaintiff's Deactivation of Facebook Account." n.d. Www.grsm.com. Accessed November 29, 2022. https://www.grsm.com/publications/2013/new-jersey-district-court-approves-spoliation-sanction-for-plaintiff-s-deactivation-of-facebook-account.

11. *James Galfy vs. Detective Terrance Harrison* (Transcript of James Galfy, 13001703, May 13, 2013)

12. Photographs entered into evidence (DSC-0019 and DSC-0013) clearly show that the short hairs belonging to Kai are in the *vertical* side of the mattress, not on top. Crime scene photo DSC-0270 shows the urine stain on the floor which also lends credence to Kai's narrative regarding his location when he woke up during the assault.

13. Joe McNamara (page 6, lines 22-24) told police that Kai was outside, shared a cigarette with him, and he talked about the California incident

page 8:25 "Uhm honestly I think he was under the influence of something."

page 9:1-2 "on and there was a lot of in (inaudible) that I can't really remember cause it was a lot of rambling."

Police interview with John McNamara

14. "At this early, stage, Plaintiff sufficiently alleges a conspiracy among the individual Moving Defendants to deprive him of his due process rights."

"Dr. Pandina's testimony, if offered at trial, would have allowed Plaintiff to prove intoxication by clear and convincing evidence, and thus would have changed the outcome of the trial."

Case 2:21-cv-17121-MCA-CLW Document 66 Filed 07/28/22 Pages 9-10 of 17 PageID: 1005

15. There is a three-year statute of limitations on title 1983 claims of destruction of evidence by a prosecutor, but the clock doesn't start until the initial sentence has been vacated.

Soronen, Lisa. "The NCSL Blog." SCOTUS Case: Statute of Limitations on Fabricated Evidence > National Conference of State Legislatures, 2022. https://

www.ncsl.org/blog/2019/01/28/scotus-case-statute-of-limitations-on-fabricated-evidence.aspx.

16. Letter to Peter Liguori from UC Prosecutor Grace Park. State v. Caleb McGillvary, Indictment No.: 13-11-00946-I, March 23, 2016.

17. NJSA 2c:3-4

18. archive.ph. "One More Step." archive.ph, 2022. httpps://archive.fo/o/AQoeR/www.qxmagazine.com/ 2011/05/nightmare-on-cleveland-street/.

19. Fairbanks, Philip. "Kai the Hitchhiker Uncovers Potential Pedophile Ring & Cover up in New Jersey." Phil Fairbanks: portfolio, February 24, 2022. https://philfairbanks.com/2022/02/24/kai-the-hitchhiker-uncovers-potential-pedophile-ring-cover-up-in-new-jersey/.

20. Justia Law. "In the Matter of James F. Boylan, an Attorney at Law." Justia Law, January 28, 2000. httpps://law.justia.com/cases/new-jersey/supreme-court/2000/d-258-98-opn.html.

21. Kirsch admitted he had spoke to the jury pool previously (page 3, lines 5-11).

5 (In unison) Good morning.

6 THE COURT: Some of you I've said this to

7 when we were in Judge Cassidy's courtroom and some I

8 did not, in the jury administration room, so, now I'm

9 going to say this. I'm going to give you your first

10 instruction, and that is from this moment on you may

11 not talk to any other person about this case.

On page 59 of the April 2nd, 2019 Jury Selection transcript one prospective male juror mentioned that Nick Scutari, the Union County political luminary who comes up multiple times in this book was her neighbor. She also mentions that she knows then-Sheriff Cryan. The judge refers to Scutari, the no-show prosecutor who attempted to circumvent LPCL's put in place to prevent bid-rigging was a "nice man" on page 60.

On page 49 a potential juror when asked if they knew anyone who works with the prosecutors, Juror No. 0353 admits her brother-in-law works in the evidence locker. They are not dismissed as a result. Another knew a former chief of detectives. Multiple other jurors note their connection to law enforcement. "The fact that you know somebody or related to somebody or yourself are e engaged in law enforcement doesn't mean that you can't be a fair and impartial juror. Okay?"

On pages 64 and 65 it's made clear that even knowing investigators who were involved in the investigation of Kai's case aren't excluded. Officers Acabou, Meehan, Mirabile, and DeAquino were among those named by potential jurors who were connected to the case in question.

Page 94, the judge makes a joke about having no "financial interest" in a program he recommends. The Juror responds, "Yeah. Just like the cafeteria." "Just like the cafeteria," the judge responds.

On page 97, one juror who is married to someone in law enforcement in the area admits her connection may bias her belief toward law enforcement statements and is not dismissed as a result: "Oh, well, my brother-in-law is pretty -- a very good friend of mine, and I do take his word in law enforcement like the question that's going to come up. So, I might be impartial towards law enforcement, and believe them more -- not believe them, but trust that they say the truth."

Pages 101 through 104 have the judge requesting a sidebar with one potential juror who has admitted they "have a close personal relationship with somebody who is involved in law enforcement and that you believe it might affect your fairness and impartiality." Kirsch walks him through various scenarios where a law enforcement officer might be mistaken about something despite swearing under oath. When asked if he could evaluate without pre-judging, the juror responds they "probable [sic] could."

The juror goes on, explaining his inability to remain unbiased: "I'm around police officers a lot, and I just tend to, I guess, over trust maybe, or maybe I have more of a trusting person -- I don't know what it is, but I don't know."

One woman admitted she couldn't "put aside" her son's unfair treatment, being set up on felony charges. Unlike with potential jurors who admit they take any word out of a cop's mouth as gospel she is swiftly dismissed (pages 161-162).

Pages 198-199 a man discloses that his wife is a social worker and he works at a private school and that, as a result, he is sensitive to crimes involving molestation or sexual assault. The judge asks if Kai's assault allegations are "too close to home for you?" The potential juror notes that he couldn't know without having details about the situation. When he brings up (page 200) that some "have had to go directly to trial" while others "that have – just lack of evidence" he is dismissed.

From page 213 Line 4 to page 220 Line 3, we have a female juror whose friend was sexually assaulted initially seated, then dismissed the next day (cf. 4/3/19 150 L1 - P151 L6). Page 226, Juror 067 mentions a family member confiding they had been raped. They were excluded the next day (cf. 4/3/19 P6 L2-4).

Prospective jurors are dismissed for the day on page 248. Just over 2 minutes are off the record. A sidebar begins, Juror No. 0592 brings up the judge "forgot to ask me" a question. They were "nervous" so they didn't bring it up but "thought that it might be relevant." They bring up the fact that they had a friend who was killed outside a bar "and it went to a murder trial." The judge asks (page 249) if he feels justice was served. "No, they found him not guilty. It was very hard for the family and everything." The judge acknowledges the potential juror's "personal pain" reminding him it was "[u]nfortunate -- but you understand that this has nothing to do with the case?" "Sure," the potential juror replies. The judge simply answers, "Okay. We'll see you tomorrow."

The next day's proceedings are listed in the April 3rd, 2019 transcript. On page 6, the woman whose family member had been raped was dismissed. Page 37, Juror No. 0813 opens up about how she was molested from the ages of six to ten. "Talk quieter," the judge tells her. Inexplicably, the assault survivor apologizes for the exchange. "Oh, I'm sorry. Any discussions about are like a trigger for me." She admits she would not be able to be "impartial" regarding "discussions on sexual assault." The judge thanks her for her honesty and patience and dismisses her.

On page 76, beginning on line 13, the judge asks a Hispanic woman if she could "set aside" her emotions regarding a family member having been assaulted sexually. Note that in cases where a potential juror admits their bias in favor of law enforcement, or their potential desire for vengeance in a murder trial the judge uses the gentler "impartial and fair" standard rather than asking them to "put aside" powerful emotional triggers like child molestation or rape inflicted on themselves or their loved ones.

On page 79 a man admits he thinks law enforcement is "more likely than not" to be honest and truthful in their statements. Instead of being asked if he can "set aside" his pro-cop bias, he's simply asked, "Would you make for a fair juror in this case?" "I think so," he responds.

This goes on for a few pages, on page 83 the judge claims his "view regarding the testimony of law enforcement" regarding the infallibility of police, is "not uncommon." "Actually," the judge goes on, "we get -- there -- there is no common answer. There's folks who have a very strong opinion that disbelieve police, and then there are those on the other side who believe what a law enforcement officer says. The -- the question really tries to determine whether you will prejudge somebody's testimony simply because of what they do for a living and, so, while you are entitled to your view, you're not entitled to predispose somebody simply because of what they do, and that -- you know, I don't know what your religious affiliation is, but if somebody were to come in with a -- clearly as a member of the clergy, you would have to evaluate him or her based on their body language, what they say, how they say it --. "Yup," the juror responds to the judge's nearly impressive soliloquy of rehabilitation efforts. As we saw with another juror, the judge has to pose hypotheticals where a law enforcement officer could be completely honest but still "mistaken."

On page 156, a Black woman says she "just feel[s] like anybody who molested or raped someone should be killed." She is obviously dismissed without being asked anything about "impartial" or "fair" treatment. No backbending exercises like we saw with jurors who admit they trust police officers to a fault.

Kai pointed out a few other sections where the judge's classism is on display. If you pore over the few hundred pages of Voir Dire (available online at bit.ly/kaidocs) you will easily note the trends. This note, despite being multiple pages, is actually quite abridged.

22.   Kai pointed out the impossibility of Judge Kirsch's claims regarding his location. If Judge Kirsch had allowed audio and video recordings of the court to be entered into evidence, he might have proved this. Unfortunately like the "unidentified blood" that was never tested, the lack of a rape kit on Kai, the rag that was never tested, the video of someone removing what may be evidence from the scene and so much more, anything that could prove Kai's claims is not examined. Judge Kirsch bemoans Kai's "never-ending series of unsupported allegations." As you may recall, Kai's allegations have been ruled by a federal judge to be founded. He was a victim of a conspiracy to deny him due process.

"Dim the lights, folks. I'm going to move so I can see the screen closer."

Clerk of the Appellate Division, July 25, 2019, A-004519-18, p. 61 11-12

THE COURT: I'm watching Mr. McGillvary and the sheriff's officers from my perch on the bench. That is a patent falsehood. It was never raised to the Court and this is yet another last second desperate attempt to malign and disparage and blame others.

Kai: Objection.

COURT: Which is very consistent with Mr. McGillvary's -- Kai: Move for an evidentiary hearing on the video and audio of that statement. COURT: --never-ending series of unsupported allegations.

Appellate Division, July 25, 2019, A-004519-18, p. 53 16-25

23. "Ok I'm securing the house and I understand that somebody might break in. I need to know should I be concerned about that." Harrison, the police interviewer responds that the sheriffs will be there a while and that he would inform him "as soon as we're out of here." This would provide perfect cover for someone to remove items as witnessed in the ABC7NY video that was pulled and not allowed to be entered into evidence.

This is found on page 21, lines 12-15

Transcript of James Galfy. Docket/Case: 13001703, May 13, 2013. Detective Terrance Harrison, transcribed June 17, 2016.

Cito refers to a photograph that shows "a gentleman leaving the house with a bag[.]" There is yellow crime scene tape around the house currently and a man with a bag is clearly leaving said active crime scene. Cito asks to enter the photos into evidence. Judge Kirsch calls the lawyers to a sidebar and asks to see the photographs. Kirsch argues the photos can not be "authenticated."

"How do we know when they were taken, who took them? You could ask the sergeant [Gardner] if she took them, well, then she can authenticate them. They're not self-authenticating."

Cito argues that they are "because they are photographs of the location. She observed it. Clark police are here." The judge asks Cito to talk "a little quieter" at this point. Cito points out that the crime scene was only blocked off for two days, narrowing down the time it could have been taken. Further narrowing it down seeing as Clark Police were currently on the scene.

The judge makes the preposterous claim that you can not tell "what month or what year" it was taken and that the witness was not "competent to testify to that."

Case 2:22-cv-04185-MCA Document 1-12 Filed 06/22/22 Page 4-6 of 7 PageID: 298-300

24. ABC7NY had a video segment that featured the scene outside Galfy's Starlite Drive home. An unidentified person is seen with a bag. Considering some of the items that were cataloged but then never tested, it's not entirely implausible that evidence could have been removed. Unfortunately, we can not be certain of the identity of the person. The judge wouldn't allow stills from the video to be entered into evidence and ABC7NY removed the video. When I contacted them they said I would have to subpoena them for the material.

"The ABC 7 News New York Video showing the breach of the Crime scene, as indicated in the April 9, 2019 transcript in the matter of 'State of New Jersey v. Caleb L. McGillvary'"

Caleb L. McGillivary, Plaintiff v. James Galfy et al., Defendant. Civil Docket No. 2:21-CV-17121-MCA-CLW,

25. Crime scene photos DSC-0019 and DSC-0013 (see chapter 12 for image)

26. It is difficult to test for GHB (in blood or urine) due to the short window of detection and potential inaccuracy.

Kintz, Pascal, Vincent Cirimele, Carole Jamey, and Bertrand Ludes. 2003. "Testing for GHB in Hair by GC/MS/MS after a Single Exposure. Application to Document Sexual Assault." *Journal of Forensic Sciences* 48 (1): 195–200. httpps://pubmed.ncbi.nlm.nih.gov/12570228/.

27. Cito speaks of how the carpet and fibers were negligently not tested. He incorrectly implies, however, that carpets can not be tested for drugs.

"The Last thing is the carpet or the carpet fibers. That whole area should have either been cut out or, at least, preserved or the fibers preserved to determine the combination of whose DNA was in the fluid, was it blood, was it urine, was it semen and that would have, at least, confirmeed what type of assault or what actually occurred, especially if there was semen in the carpeting. Also, if there was urine in the carpeting, that would determine that it was my client's and it would have confirmed his position that he did urinate at the time and that Mr. Galfy had ejaculated in that area.

My client is also noting that it could also be tested for drugs, but I am not sure how you can test fibers for drugs."

Clerk of the Appellate Division, July 25, 2019, A-004519-18

An oddly rolled paper napkin in the trash can was photographed at the crime scene [DA 107, 110] (quite possibly an improvised paper funnel that has come unrolled. It could have been used to put crushed pills or powders in the glass of beer he gave Kai). No analysis was done on any of the items. No testing was done on carpet fibers [DA 4-13] which could have been tested to see if it contained any drug residue.

28. J West , Matthew, and Michael J Went. "The Spectroscopic Detection of Drugs of Abuse on Textile Fibres after Recovery with Adhesive Lifters." *Forensic science international*, May 23, 2009. httpps://pubmed.ncbi.nlm.nih.gov/19464829/.

Harper, Lane, Jeff Powell, and Em M Pijl. "An Overview of Forensic Drug Testing Methods and Their Suitability for Harm Reduction Point-of-Care Services." *Harm reduction journal*, July 31, 2017. https://www.ncbi.nlm.nih.gov/pmc/articles/PMC5537996/.

29. Prosecutor Park wrote to Liguori in March 2016. In the letter, the prosecutor explains to Kai's then-public defender that she reviewed a portion of the grand jury transcript with Dr. Pandina. Pandina "clarified" the effects of date rape drugs and their detection (Ho and Peterson had previously misrepresented the science as per Pandina). Pandina also admitted to Park "that within the last year his research institute at Rutgers University, (The Center for Alcohol Studies), unexpectedly

received charitable funds from the Estate of Joseph Galfy, (the victim in this case), meant to further the research of his team. Although Dr. Pandina reports never knowing or meeting with Mr. Galfy, this presents a conflict of interest if the State were to call Dr. Pandina as an expert in any matters regarding this case. Therefore, the State will not be able to use Dr. Pandina as a witness in this case."

Letter to Peter Liguori from UC Prosecutor Grace Park. State v. Caleb McGill vary, Indictment No.: 13-11-00946-I, March 23, 2016.

30. In 2022, Kai sought discovery for several things. Among them, financial records. Already, the will and testament had resulted in major revelations. Kai found that $150,000 checks had been cut to Pandina and Shaikh's programs at the universities they were employed by. Kai also sought further information about the untraceable assets (specifically "currency, coins or ingots of gold or other precious metals, and commodities" as mentioned in the will itself) of Galfy/the Galfy estate.

"The check issued on April 28, 2015 from Account # 38103463625, Bank # 02120033; in the amount of $150,000.00; to the workplace of Robert Pandina: was the 1075th check issued from the financial account of the Estate; from July 3, 2013 until April 28, 2015. It was personally signed by James Galfy, making it an illegal benefit as defined by N.J.S.A. 2C:28 et seq. It was endorsed on May 22, 2015, making it an illegal act of witness tampering as defined by N.J.S.A. 2C:28-5(c). These facts were fraudulently concealed from plaintiff until February 20, 2022. Plaintiff could not possibly have discovered these documents despite every diligent effort, until February 20, 2022."

Caleb L. McGillivary v. James Galfy et al. 2-21-cv-17121-MCA-CLW, Document 51-2. March 3, 2022

31. The court, at defense's request, asked the jury to find Kai "guilty, period. [...] 'Unless you believe the defendant lawfully acted in self-defense as defined and explained herein on pages 18 to 20.' Period. Acceptable, Mr. Peterson?" Peterson and Cito are both agreeable. Cito mentions Kai wants him "to not present to the jury the defense of involuntarily intoxication." "On what grounds?" asks Kirsch.

Clerk of the Appellate Division, July 25, 2019, A-004519-18, p. 13

32. NJSA 2C:2-8. "Intoxication a. Except as provided in subsection d. of this section, intoxication of the actor is not a defense unless it negatives an element of the offense." In this case, since proving intoxication against his will would prove self defense negating the murder charge proving intoxication was a primary element to Kai's case.

33. In criminal law the burden of proof is "beyond a reasonable doubt" which is far higher than the "clear and convincing evidence" required in will disputes, far more than the "preponderance of evidence" needed in most civil cases (much of which, in Kai's case is shared in this book and the supplement volume).

Legal Information Institute. "Burden of Proof." Legal Information Institute, 2022. https://www.law.cornell.edu/wex/burden_of_proof.

34. "Clear and convincing evidence is that which produces in your mind a firm belief or conviction as to the truth of the facts sought to be proven and is evidence so clear, direct, weighty and convincing as to enable you to come to a clear conviction

without hesitancy of the truth of the particular facts in issue."

Coming up with "clear and convincing proof" of his involuntary intoxication was impossible thanks to the faulty investigation procedure and loss, destruction, or uncollected evidence.

Clerk of the Appellate Division, July 25, 2019, A-004519-18, page 103

35.   "As far as manifest injustices go, this rings together with trial by water or a witch who was thrown into a drowning pool, and if she sank and drowned she was innocent, but if she floated she was put to death for being a witch.

And I think it's important that the Court take into consideration the tens of thousands of people who I've met who now question why didn't Kai hurt us? The hundreds of people that I've stayed with, who now question, why didn't Kai hurt us? Because this trial didn't answer those questions. But my character does. My character for helping people is why people were safe with me. My people for protecting -- my character for protecting people is why people are safe with me. My character for pursuing justice is why people still trust me, because I'm still innocent, and I'm still telling the truth, and despite the treachery of my former counsel and despite the misconduct of the malicious prosecution, and despite the bias of the cronies on the bench, I will overturn your false conviction, and your worthless sentence. This has been nothing but a sham trial, and you have railroaded an innocent man, shame on you."

Clerk of the Appellate Division, July 25, 2019, A-004519-18, page 51

36.   CBS News. "Citing Excessive Media Coverage, Lawyer for Chelsea Bombing Suspect Asks for Change of Venue." *CBS News*, March 25, 2017. https://www.cbsnews.com/newyork/news/chelsea-bombing-change-of-venue/.

37.   Zapotosky, Matt. "New York Bombing Suspect Makes First Court Appearance." *The Washington Post*, October 13, 2016. htppps://www.washingtonpost.com/world/national-security/new-york-bombing-suspect-makes-first-court-appearance/2016/10/13/73b4e514-90bf-11e6-a6a3-d50061aa9fae_story.html.

38.   The United States Department of Justice. "Chelsea Bomber Ahmad Khan Rahimi Convicted for Executing September 2016 Bombing in New York City." The United States Department of Justice, October 16, 2017. https://www.justice.gov/opa/pr/chelsea-bomber-ahmad-khan-rahimi-convicted-executing-september-2016-bombing-new-york-city.

39.   Chi'en, Arthur. "Video Evidence in Ahmad Khan Rahimi Trial." *FOX 5 New York*, November 1, 2019. https://www.fox5ny.com/news/video-evidence-in-ahmad-khan-rahimi-trial.

40.   Fairbanks, Philip. "Defense for the Prosecution: The Trial of Kai The Hitchhiker." Phil Fairbanks: portfolio, April 9, 2021. htppps://philfairbanks.com/2021/04/09/defense-for-the-prosecution-the-trial-of-kai-the-hitchhiker/.

41.   The judge brought up Kai's statement, characterizing it as "another outburst, an unrestrained outburst."

"This is a kangaroo court. Why don't you put on your pointy hats and burn a cross out front, you're trying to lynch me."

Clerk of the Appellate Division, July 25, 2019, A-004519-18, p. 52, 15-21

42. "Sovereign immunity was derived from British common law doctrine based on the idea that the King could do no wrong. In the United States, sovereign immunity typically applies to the federal government and state government, but not to municipalities. Federal and state governments, however, have the ability to waive their sovereign immunity. The federal government did this when it passed the Federal Tort Claims Act, which waived federal immunity for numerous types of torts claims."

Legal Information Institute. "Sovereign Immunity." Legal Information Insti tute, 2022. https://www.law.cornell.edu/wex/sovereign_immunity.

43. Kai the Hitchhiker. "Kai the Hatchet-Wielding Hitchhiker Juggling in Jail." YouTube. 2022, 0: 58, https://www.youtube.com/c/KaitheHitchhikerforreal

44. Kai the Hitchhiker's Blog. "You've got to see this, it's The Best Interview EVER." Facebook. September 20, 2021. httpps://web.facebook.com/kai.hitchhiker.blog?_rdc=1&_rdr

Chapter 11: A Slap on the Wrist

1. "The third and final trial of Oscar Wilde saw him tried for acts of 'gross indecency' of the type he was accusing the Marquess of Queensbury and enacted upon Queensbury's son. Over 120 cases of gross indecency of this type had been tried at the Old Bailey and Wilde's was extraordinarily unusual as far as severity. Was Wilde being especially punished for his role in absconding client lists from Cleveland Street? Had Wilde crossed some invisible line, not through his outrageous behavior, but through threatening to uncover the salacious and outrageous behavior of others, including those in the court?

"According to records from the Old Bailey Courthouse, Wilde was being extorted. Surely, many Lords were as well. The Cleveland Street Scandal was the Franklin Cover-Up of its day and would not have been broke in the first place had not a frightened messenger boy admitted the sex work cover operations when discovered with an inordinate amount of change in his pocket. 4 schillings at the time would have been several weeks earnings and the police were investigating "a theft" at the time, so thanks to self-preservation the brothel was finally closed. Wilde was not being extorted by a rent boy however. Wilde was in fact 'protecting himself' vis a vis certain "stolen items." Is it possible certain "stolen items" could have (as they finally did in the 70s) implicate persons such as the 'Honorable Hamilton Cuffe,' who would prosecute Wilde in 1895 as Director of Public Prosecutions.

"In The Picture of Dorian Gray, Wilde would seem to allude to the actions of the Ripper murderer and the Cleveland Street Scandal. Both Arthur Conan Doyle and Oscar Wilde were even approached to write about the Ripper killings. The killings ended after the suicide of John Pruitt, an Oxford colleague of Wilde's. Wilde didn't believe the current official story that Pruitt was the murderer, pointing out that he was a lawyer, not a doctor as the Metropolitan Police Criminal Investigation Department had claimed. Wilde also pointed out that Pruitt's suicide was more likely precipitated by the discovery of a relationship he had with a schoolboy that had just been found out."

Fairbanks, Philip *Pedogate Primer: the politics of pedophilia.* 12-13.

2. Bender, Bryan. "Pentagon Vows Action on Porn Cases." *Boston.com*, January 8, 2011. http://archive.boston.com/news/nation/washington/articles/2011/01/08/pentagon_vows_action_on_porn_cases/.

3. CRS. "All Info - S.1413 - 116th Congress (2019-2020): End Network Abuse Act ," May 9, 2019. httpps://www.congress.gov/bill/116th-congress/senate-bill/1413/all-info.

4. Ed Buck was a powerful and wealthy political donor. His status and connection to major local, state, and federal politicians were likely one reason he escaped justice despite murdering multiple black men for his own sick, sexual pleasure via forcible overdose. Buck would drug his victims with GHB without their knowledge, combining that with heavy doses of methamphetamines.

    Finnegan, Michael & Hailey Branson-Potts. "Ed Buck Convicted in Meth Overdose Deaths of Gemmel Moore and Timothy Dean." *Los Angeles Times*, 27 July 2021, www.latimes.com/california/story/2021-07-27/ed-buck-convicted-methamphetamine-overdose-deaths. Accessed 14 July 2022.

5. The Canadian Press Staff. "Fashion Mogul Peter Nygard Waives Right to Bail Hearing in Quebec Sex Crime Case." *Montreal*, 14 July 2022, montreal.ctvnews.ca/fashion-mogul-peter-nygard-waives-right-to-bail-hearing-in-quebec-sex-crime-case-1.5987797. Accessed 29 Nov. 2022

6. *Prudential Property & Cas. Ins. Co. v Boylan* 307 NJ Super 162 (App Div 1997)

7. Boylan coached coerced women, traded sexual favors for leniency in court, and defrauded the city.

    Findlaw. "Findlaw's Supreme Court of New Jersey Case and Opinions." Find law, January 28, 2000. https://caselaw.findlaw.com/nj-supreme-court/1417417.html.

    Justia Law. "United States v. Boylan, 5 F. Supp. 2d 274 (D.N.J. 1998)." Justia Law, May 8, 1998. https://law.justia.com/cases/federal/district-courts/FSupp2/5/274/2341583/.

8. Judge Roman Montez and his actions were brought to my attention by one of my anonymous sources.

    Eustachewich, Lia. "NJ Judge Reprimanded for Sexual Relationship with Stripper." *New York Post*, May 24, 2014. https://nypost.com/2014/05/24/nj-judge-reprimanded-for-sexual-relationship-with-strip per/.

9. The New York Times. "Ex-Judge Gets Jail Term for Seeking Sex Favors." *The New York Times*, May 9, 1998. httpps://www.nytimes.com/1998/05/09/nyregion/metro-news-briefs-new-jersey-ex-judge-gets-jail-term-for-seeking-sex-favors.html.

    Findlaw. "Findlaw's Supreme Court of New Jersey Case and Opinions." Find law, January 28, 2000. https://caselaw.findlaw.com/nj-supreme-court/1417417.html.

10. Irenas, Joseph E. "Parkin v. United States." Legal research tools from Casetext, October 15, 2012. https://casetext.com/case/parkin-v-united-states-1.

11. *Parkin v. United States*, No. 12-4081, (3d Cir. 2014)

    "Digital Repository - Villanova University Charles Widger School of Law." January 4, 2009. https://digitalcommons.law.villanova.edu/.

12. *Angelo M. Perrucci vs. An Attorney at Law* (Supreme Court of New Jersey, Docket No. DRB 21-032, August 25, 2021)

13. "See, e.g., In re Quatrella, 237 N.J. 402 (2019) (attorney convicted of conspiracy to commit wire fraud after taking part in a scheme to defraud life insurance providers via three stranger-originated life insurance policies; the victims affected by the crimes lost $2,700,000 and the intended loss to the insurance providers would have exceeded $14,000,000);"

   Supreme Court of New Jersey, Disciplinary Review Board. Docket No. DRB 20-081. District Docket No. XIV-2017-0669E

   https://drblookupportal.judiciary.state.nj.us/DocumentHandler.ashx?document_id=1138879

14. Raymond Hall interview:

   "Yeah. I mean, so sometimes it's hard to really figure out, I mean, sometimes if you got a public official who you know how much money they make and they're living above their means. If they're making, whatever, say a part-time legislator, like the state of Maryland is. Say you're making 50 grand, but you have $300,000 car or whatever it is, living above your means is one thing. You hear of like different things that these public officials have, like I said before, like gambling or another relationship somewhere where they're hiding it from their wife or husband but sometimes these public officials, if they're not taking much, you might not see any of that.

   Say they're taking a thousand bucks or 5,000 bucks or something like that. You might not see as much as if somebody's taking more [25:14 inaudible]. But I think you just kind of stay on top of them as much as you can and just do as much research, figure out the issues that they are for and everything. Maybe they have, for whatever odd reason they support this development or they support this type of zoning or whatever, and then you scratch your head, like, why are they only ones that are supported and all of a sudden they have a relationship with that business man? And then all a sudden, it'll still be hard for the public to find out if they're getting bribed or not. But that's something that the FBI can look into too, if there are strong enough allegations, so it could be just picking through, with what they approve and not approve with the local state level. Like I said they're living above their means, stuff like that. It is kind of hard to pick it out sometimes, but sometimes there are indicators like what I mentioned." […] "Real quick, the classic kind of like Money too is because it's harder to trace, obviously. Something that is very traceable. So yeah, if somebody just gives you a handshake with $5,000, $10,000 or in a coffee mug or whatever, it is harder to trace. And also obviously there's a lot of different Supreme Court rulings that's out there, where it's even harder sometimes because sometimes it might not be a straight up drive. It might be some kind of gratuity. I'll leave that to the prosecutors to figure it out. But some people disguise these things that's consulting work or something like that, which, if you're a government employee, you're not doing consulting work."

15. Evan Katzman: "Respondent unequivocally should be disbarred. He solicited high school-aged girls for sex in exchange for money. He showed no remorse for his behavior at trial; rather, he claimed that the children seemed older than they actually

were. The court found respondent's attempts in this regard to be untenable and absurd."

In re Katzman, Docket No. DRB 18-365, 10 (N.J. Jun. 4, 2019)

16. Brian P. Meehan: "BRIAN P. MEEHAN of BERWYN, PENNSYLVANIA, who was admitted to the bar of this State in 1988, having been convicted following a plea of no contest in the Court of Common Pleas, First Judicial District of Pennsylvania to Statutory Sexual Assault: 11 years or older, in violation of 18 Pa.C.S. § 3122.1.(B); Corruption of Minors–Defendant Age 18 or Above, in violation of 18 Pa.C.S. § 6301(A)(1)(ii) ; and Promoting Prostitution—Own House of Prostitution/or/Business, in violation of 18 Pa.C.S. § 5902(B)(1) ;"

In re Brian P. Meehan, 182 A.3d 937, (N.J. 2018)

17. Jeffrey Toman was disbarred for not appearing in his own defense, rather than for preying on minors. "And Jeffrey Toman having failed to appear on the Order directing him to show cause why he should not be disbarred or otherwise disciplined; "

In re Toman, D-85, (N.J. Apr. 23, 2019)

18. Andrew Michael Carroll, while acting as a public defender, engaged in an inappropriate sexual relationship with a client. The client in question was accused of child abuse:

"Respondent earned admission to the Pennsylvania bar in 2003 and the New Jersey bar in 2004. At the relevant times, he was employed as an Assistant Public Defender with the Office of Parental Representation in Trenton, New Jersey. He has no history of discipline, but is currently administratively suspended in Pennsylvania. Respondent now engages in the private practice of law.

Respondent and the OAE entered into a disciplinary stipulation, dated January 31, 2017, which sets forth the following facts in support of respondent's admitted ethics violations.

In October 2015, in the normal course of his employment at the Office of the Public Defender (OPD), respondent was appointed to defend L.S. against allegations that she had abused her minor son. The Division of Child Protection and Permanency (DCPP) alleged that L.S., an alcoholic, had gotten drunk and passed out while caring for him. Due to L.S.'s struggles with alcoholism, her son was placed in the custody of his maternal grandmother. The DCPP sought to curtail L.S.'s parenting time and implement supervised visitation.

On October 30, 2015, after representing L.S. at an Order to Show Cause in family court, represent offered to drive her home; the weather was inclement due to Hurricane Patricia. L.S. declined respondent's offer, but, shortly thereafter, she and respondent began texting each other, including messages that were sexual in nature. On the day before Thanksgiving, respondent and L.S. consummated a sexual relationship."

In re Carroll, Docket No. DRB 17-049, 2-3 (N.J. Aug. 22, 2017)

19. In most cases, if a predator is disbarred they were found guilty in federal court. Tobin G. Nilsen is no exception.

"Over a three-week period, respondent sent photos of himself to the mother, and explained how she could access child pornography on the internet in order to acclimate her daughter to the notion of engaging in sex with him. He also described the sex acts in which he wanted to engage with the mother and daughter. At some point, respondent and the mother spoke on the phone to arrange a specific date for him to meet with her and her daughter.

Eventually, respondent purchased an airline ticket to travel from New Jersey to Atlanta. Respondent never made it to the airport, however, because, prior to his scheduled flight, he was arrested by law enforcement officers in New Jersey for soliciting a different putative mother/daughter pair for sex (discussed below)."

In re Nilsen, Docket No. DRB 16-222, 3-4 (N.J. Feb. 23, 2017)

20. Todd C. Sicklinger was a repeat offender. Multiple instances, often involving flashing (public nudity), public masturbation in various locations, and lewd behavior in public places. In one instance, Sicklinger was observed by an officer with his hands down his pants "stroking his penis as he was walking through the lot." When asked for his identification, Sicklinger's response was "[F***] You I will fight you now." The officer told Sicklinger "to relax and keep his voice down." At this point, the officer also "observed that Mr. Sicklinger's penis was still erect."

In re Sicklinger, District Docket No. XIV-2010-0580E (N.J. Nov. 2, 2016)

21. "High-Profile Florida lawyer" John Rex Powell had already been found guilty for his abuse of an Australian boy. He was found to be involved in a pedophile ring that spanned the globe.

Mitchell, Peter. "US lawyer faces jail for abusing Aust boy," *Sydney Morning Herald,* March 10, 2014

Despite this, he was still admitted to the bar in New Jersey until 2016. Perhaps because the case received federal attention, he "tendered his consent to disbarment as an attorney at law of the State of New Jersey" in March of 2016.

In re Powell, 131 A.3d 955, (N.J. 2016)

22. David J. Witherspoon:

"But even a conviction for a sexual offense has not always resulted in an attorney's disbarment. For example, in a matter involving an attorney who admitted, as part of a guilty plea to second-degree sexual assault, see N.J.S.A. 2C:14-2b, that he had "purposely touched the buttocks of a ten-year-old boy who was visiting [his] son," we concluded that a three-year period of suspension was the appropriate discipline. In re Herman, 108 N.J. 66, 67, 71 (1987). In reaching that conclusion, we agreed with the DRB that although the crime did not directly involve respondent's practice of law, it adversely reflected on his fitness to practice, id. at 69-70 (quoting from DRB recommendation), and we concluded that it also violated his duty to adhere to the high standards of conduct expected of members of our profession, id. at 70. Of particular note, we recognized, as a relevant consideration, the impact that respondent's conduct had on the victim. Id. at 69-70. As reported by the DRB, "[t]his was a serious crime of moral turpitude involving a child of tender years. The young victim required weeks of counseling, but a traumatic event such as this will long leave its scar on the victim." Id. at 69. In mitigation, we noted that respondent had an unblemished disciplinary history, had cooperated with the police, and had ceased practicing, effectively accepting a voluntary suspension, almost immediately after his arrest. Id. at 69-70. We therefore imposed a three-year suspension, retroactive to the date when the voluntary suspension had begun. Id. At 70."

In re: David J. Witherspoon (N.J. July 29, 2010)

23. William S. Wolfson, another repeat offender, had a nasty habit of groping women.

"On December 19, 2002 respondent pleaded guilty to a one-count accusation charging him with criminal sexual contact. During the plea hearing, respondent admitted that on August 22, 2002, he had touched the breast of a female employee at his doctor's office while he was receiving a medical test. Respondent further admitted that his conduct was intentional and that his purpose was his own sexual gratification. On December 3, 2002, respondent gave a statement to the Hunterdon County Prosecutor's Office in which he revealed that over a period of three to fo~ years, he had touched six female employees at his doctor's office between ten and fifteen times. According to respondent's statement, he could recall the details of only two ~f these incidents. Respondent admitted that, on those two occasions, he had "cupped" the breast of female staff for his own sexual gratification. Respondent stated that both victims had looked upset as a result of his conduct and that during other incidents that he could not specifically recall, the victims had pushed his hand away, told him to stop, or had walked out of the examining room."

In the matter of William F. Wolfson. Disciplinary Review Board, Docket No. DRB 03-205

24. James W. Kennedy was caught downloading tens of thousands of child sexual abuse images. He received a six months suspension (his charges were in New Jersey, not federal). He would be temporarily suspended years later for failure to cooperate with an ethics investigation and again temporarily for "failure to comply with a fee arbitration determination."

Respondent was admitted to the New Jersey and New York bars in 1983. Effective October 13, 2003, he was suspended for six months after pleading guilty in the Superior Court of New Jersey to one count of fourth-degree child endangerment (N.J.S.A. 2C:24-4(b)(5)). Respondent had downloaded, from the internet, 20,000 to 30,000 images of children, some under the age of sixteen, engaged in sexual acts. In re Kennedy, 177 N.J. 517 (2003). Respondent was reinstated on May 4, 2004. In re Kennedy, 179 N.J. 532 (2004).

On December 9, 2015, respondent was temporarily suspended for failure to cooperate with an ethics investigation. He remains suspended to date. In re Kennedy, 223 N.J. 398 (2015).

Effective March 31, 2017, the Court again temporarily suspended respondent, this time for failure to comply with a fee arbitration determination in the Lepre matter, discussed below. In re Kennedy, 228 N.J. 336 (2017). I. The Brown Matter (DRB 17-027 — District Docket No. IIIA-2015-0003E)

In re Kennedy, Docket No. DRB 17-027, 2-3 (N.J. Jul. 28, 2017)

25. Despite claims that sexual crimes are taken seriously in disbarment procedures when the case doesn't rise to the federal level they are often defended by the Office of

Attorney Ethics, and New Jersey Supreme Court.

"There is no question that respondent improperly touched a minor. However, in determining the quantum of discipline, we took into account respondent's youth, his immaturity, as documented by his therapist, his obvious remorse, the aberrational nature of his conduct, the fact that his actions were not related to the practice of law and the fact that respondent has recognized his lack of maturity and judgment and has sought treatment. We have also considered the letters and affidavit from respondent's friends and his former and current employers attesting to his good character."

In re Salvatore J. Maiorino. October 31, 2002

26. Terry G. Tucker "was reprimanded" for making unwanted sexual advances to a bankruptcy client.

Poritz, Hon. Deborah T., Chief Justice Supreme Court of New Jersey and David E. Johnson, Jr. Director Office of Attorney Ethics. 2002 State of the Attorney Discipline System Report. May 20, 2003, http://cafr1.com/Court/ALL_1995-2008/COURT/NJ/ATTORN1.pdf

27. James L. Peck, IV was temporarily suspended after he "pleaded guilty to one count of knowingly and willfully possessing child pornography in violation of 18 *U.S.C.A* 2252(a)(4)(B)."

In re Peck, 170 N.J. 4 782 A.2d 919, Oct. 25, 2001

28. Donald M. Ferraiolo is another instance where sexual crimes against children aren't deemed heinous enough to result in disbarment. Ferraiolo was suspended despite attempting to pick up a preteen boy online.

"This Court suspended an attorney for one year, when the attorney attempted to meet a minor after engaging in illicit online conversations. *In re Ferraiolo* , 170 *N.J.* 600, 790 *A* .2d 883 (2002). There, the attorney entered an Internet chat room to communicate with a person he believed to be a child. He discussed sexual acts that he wished to engage the minor in and sent the minor boy two nude photos respondent claimed were of himself. He then arranged a meeting with the boy, appeared at the location, and was subsequently arrested by an undercover officer, who had been posing as the minor. The attorney admitted that he frequented Internet chat rooms that introduced older men to younger boys and had previously arranged to meet a boy for the purpose of engaging in sexual acts, but had never actually met with the boy. The DRB highlighted the attorney's favorable prognosis provided by psychological reports, his unblemished legal career, and letters from friends and family attesting to his otherwise good character. The DRB recommended a one-year suspension, which this Court ordered. *See also In re Ruddy* , 130 *N.J.* 85, 86, 612 *A* .2d 949 (1992) (suspending respondent for two years after he sexually molested several pre-teenage boys)."

In re Legato, 229 N.J. 173, 184 (N.J. 2017)

29. Gerard Gilligan

See In re Gilligan, 147 N.J. 268 (1997) (reprimand for attorney convicted of lewdness when he exposed and fondled his genitals for sexual gratification in front of three individuals, two of whom were children under the age of thirteen); In re

Pierce, 139 N.J. 533 (1995) (reprimand; attorney convicted of lewdness after he exposed his genitals to a twelve-year-old girl);

In re Gillen, Docket No. DRB 16-269, 8-9 (N.J. Apr. 25, 2017)

30. Ty Hyderally "argued for equal pay for women," defended a councilman embroiled in a sexual harassment suit. He was suspended in after being convicted of assaulting his girlfriend "and slamming her into a wall" when she tried leaving his condo during an argument in 2015.

Pries, Allison. "Lawyer who fought for equal pay for women suspended after assaulting his girlfriend," *Star-Ledger*, Aug. 29, 20181221

31. In 1999, respondent was reprimanded, on a motion for reciprocal discipline, based on a two-year suspension imposed by the Judge Advocate General (JAG). The JAG suspended respondent for committing a criminal act that reflected adversely on his honesty, trustworthiness, or fitness to practice as a judge advocate. Specifically, the JAG found that, while in the Navy, respondent had made sexual advances to at least two women who were his legal aid clients, conduct comparable to RPC 8.4(d) (conduct prejudicial to the administration of justice). In re Hyderallly, 162 N.J. 95 (1999).

In re Hyderally, Docket No. 17-228, 2 (N.J. Dec. 20, 2017)

32. Pristin, Terry. "Jail Rape Victim Can Sue." *The New York Times,* July 16, 1997. https://www.nytimes.com/1997/07/16/nyregion/jail-rape-victim-can-sue.html.

33. With assemblyman Neil M. Cohen, we see mention of the "bright-line rule:"

We now sanction respondent to an indeterminate suspension from the practice of law, pursuant to Rule 1:20–15A(a)(2). We caution that while we do not establish a bright-line rule requiring disbarment in all cases involving sexual offenses against children, in the future, convictions in egregious cases involving child pornography may result in disbarment of attorneys who commit these offenses, in light of society's increasing recognition of the harm done to the victims of those offenses.

In re: Neil M. Cohen. October 23, 2014, https://caselaw.findlaw.com/nj-supreme-court/1681590.html.

34. The matter of In Re Cohen 204 NJ 588 (2011)

Findlaw. "Findlaw's Supreme Court of New Jersey Case and Opinions." Findlaw, October 23, 2014. https://caselaw.findlaw.com/nj-supreme-court/1681590.html.

35. If you check the link cited for Cohen's career history at Wikipedia, you'll find that the page has been pulled from the internet. A version from 2009 is still available at the Internet Archive.

https://web.archive.org/web/20091020064816/http://www.njleg.state.nj.us/members/BIO.asp?Leg=62

36. Spoto , MaryAnn. "Ex-Assemblyman Neil Cohen Admits Viewing Child Porn, but Pleads Not Guilty to Charges." *Star-Ledger*, March 10, 2009. htttps://www.nj.com/news/2009/03/exassemblyman_neil_cohen_admit.html.

37. ibid

38. Margolin, Josh. "Assemblyman Neil Cohen under Child Porn Investigation." *Star-*

Ledger, July 25, 2008. httpps://www.nj.com/news/2008/07/   assemblyman_ neil_cohen_investi.html.

39.   "One suggestion for politics watchers: keep an eye on State Senator Nia Gill, who is also Assemblyman Neil Cohen's longtime law partner. The word is that Gill's role in the investigation – as an advisor to Cohen – may have created a huge conflict with the state Attorney General's office. Gill probably had trouble with the A.G.'s office before the Cohen problem, but sources suggest that is has become exponentially worse over the last few days."

"Was There Anything on Cohen's Law Office Computer?" 2008. *Observer.* July 25, 2008. https://observer.com/2008/07/was-there-anything-on-cohens-law-office-computer/.

40.   Chang, David, and Ted Greenberg. "NJ Man Accused of Possessing and Distributing Child Pornography." *NBC10 Philadelphia,* June 15, 2022. httpps://www.nbcphiladelphia.com/news/local/nj-man-accused-of-possessing-and-distributing-child-pornography/3402439/.

41.   WCBS Newsradio 880. "NJ High School Teacher, 72, Accused of Repeated Sexual Contact with Student, 14." NJ teacher accused of sexual contact with 14-year-old, January 31, 2022.

42.   Burak had been "temporarily suspended from the practice of law since April 24, 2008, be disbarred based on respondent's plea of guilty in the United States District Court for the District of New Jersey to possession of child pornography" initially. This is the rare case where a lawyer who had not been busted by federal authorities actually lost their privilege to practice law.

In re Burak, 33 A.3d 517, (N.J. 2012)

This may have had something to do with the fact that the material Burak was downloading was "particularly unsettling" and violent:

We found particularly unsettling the fact that several of the images portrayed children engaged in sadistic or masochistic conduct or other depictions of violence, such as bondage.

In the Matter of Neil M. Cohen. June 24, 2014, https://law.justia.com/cases/new-jersey/supreme-court/2014/d-50-13.html

43.   Steven C. Cunningham

"During September and October 2004, on three separate occasions, respondent engaged an individual, whom he believed to be a twelve year-old boy, in internet "chat."2 The child was actually a Passaic County detective posing as a twelve year-old boy, in an undercover internet operation. Respondent conducted the illicit communications from his home computer in Jersey City, through his America Online internet account. During two of the conversations, respondent described, in lurid detail, certain sexual acts that he hoped to perform the boy. He also described sex acts that he hoped to teach the boy to perform on him, inviting the child to "get together in New York"

In the matter of Steven C. Cunningham, Disciplinary Review board, Docket No. DRB 06-250, District Docket No. XIV-06-041E

In re: Neil M. Cohen also cites the case *In re Sosnowski*, 197 N.J. 23, 961 A.2d 697 (2008). The Supreme Court of New Jersey admits that "[f]or cases involving possession of child pornography, the discipline imposed has ranged from a six-month suspension to disbarment." The court mentions the Burak case meriting actual disbarment. With Cohen, Burak, Sosnowski and several others who received more than a slap on the wrist suspension and being sentenced to therapy the fact that FBI or other federal involvement made the story too big to cover up could be another factor.

44. *In re Sosnowski*, 197 N.J. 23, 961 A.2d 697 (2008). The attorney admitted to possessing sixty-seven images of child pornography and eight sexually explicit video files of children engaging in sexual acts and exposing their genitals. In addition, the attorney had placed hidden cameras in a child's bathroom and bedroom. He was sentenced to thirty-seven months in prison, with five years of supervised release, and was ordered to pay a $100 assessment.

45. *In re: Charles P. Wright*, December 3, 1997.

46. *Matter of X*, 120 N.J. 459 (1990):

   "Occasionally a case arises with facts so egregious that although tragic, they cry out for disbarment. This is such a case. Respondent was admitted to the New Jersey bar in 1967. On July 20, 1988, he was charged in a twenty-eight-count indictment with five counts of aggravated sexual assault in violation of N.J.S.A. 2C:14-2, eight counts of sexual assault in violation of N.J.S.A. 2C:14-2, five counts of attempted sexual assault in violation of N.J.S.A. 2C:5-1 and N.J.S.A. 2C:14-2, seven counts of criminal sexual contact in violation of N.J.S.A. 2C:14-2 and 14-3, and three counts of endangering the welfare of children in violation of N.J.S.A. 2C:24-4. The charges related to numerous incidents occurring between 1980 and 1988, in which respondent engaged in various sexual acts with his three daughters."

47. Steve Allen Herman

   "Several times between May 1, and July 31, 1984 respondent, 44, purposely touched the buttocks of a ten-year-old boy who was visiting respondent's son in *68 respondent's home. Respondent either touched the buttocks from the outside of the boy's clothing or would insert his hand inside the boy's pants. Respondent was arrested on September 16, 1984. On March 1, 1985 he pleaded guilty to a Mercer County accusation which charged him with committing sexual assault, contrary to N.J.S.A. 2C:14-2b. This law provides that a person is guilty of sexual assault if he commits an act of sexual contact with a victim who is less than 13 years old and the actor is at least 4 years older than the victim. As part of the plea agreement, the State recommended dismissal of other complaints charging respondent with similar conduct with about five different boys. The State also agreed that no charges would be filed against respondent as a result of a then pending investigation involving one or two other boys. Pursuant to N.J.S.A. 2C:47-1 respondent was referred to the Adult Diagnostic and Treatment Center for examination. The examination revealed that respondent's conduct qualified him to be sentenced under the purview of the State Sex Offender Act in that there had been a pattern of repetitive, compulsive behavior. Under this Act, a court could sentence a defendent to the Diagnostic Center for a program of specialized treatment for his mental condition. Respondent was sentenced on June 14, 1985. The court was informed respondent had been undergoing counseling since the time of the incident and it would continue. Although there is a presumption of imprisonment for conviction of a second degree crime, N.J.S.A. 2C:44-1d, the court placed respondent on three years probation with the condition that counseling be continued, and the counselor file a report with the probation department every 90 days."

Matter of Herman, 108 N.J. 66 (1987)

48. "That statute provides that any person who 'engages in sexual conduct which would impair or debauch the morals of . . . a child under the age of 16 is guilty of a crime of the third degree.' For the reasons expressed below, we determine that a two-year suspension and conditions are appropriate."

In the matter of Roger Paul Frye, Supreme Court of New Jersey, Disciplinary Review Board, Docket No. DRB 13-221, District Docket No. XIV-2011-0258E. https:// drblookupportal.judiciary.state.nj.us/ DocumentHandler.ashx?document_ id=1048716

49. The article on Neil M. Cohen from Wikipedia (December grab from Internet Archive below) has seven links to stories about Cohen that have been pulled and return an error message or some completely different story. The access date listed below is as per the Wikipedia citations. The majority of the stories about Cohen's sex crimes that were initially cited in the Wikipedia entry have been scrubbed from the net.

McAlpin, John P. (July 24, 2008). "Lawmaker investigated for child porn, sources say". *The Record.* Bergen, New Jersey: Gannett Company. Retrieved July 24, 2008. Margolin, Josh; Schwaneberg, Robert (July 24, 2008). "Assemblyman Neil Cohen under child porn investigation". *The Star-Ledger.* Newark, New Jersey. Retrieved July 25, 2008.

Friedman, Matt (July 24, 2008). "Cohen under investigation for child pornography". *PolitickerNJ.* New York City: Observer Media. Retrieved July 25, 2008.

Young, Elise (July 28, 2008). "Cohen resigns following porn discovery". The Record. Bergen, New Jersey: Gannett Company. Retrieved July 28, 2008.

Friedman, Matt (July 28, 2008). "Cohen Resigns". *PolitickerNJ.* New York City: Observer Media. Retrieved July 28, 2008.

"Dems choose Cohen's successor". *The Press of Atlantic City.* Pleasantville, New Jersey: BH Media Group Holdings. August 21, 2008. Retrieved July 15, 2010.

Toutant, Charles (April 13, 2010). "N.J. Lawyer Pleads Guilty to Child Pornography Charge". *New Jersey Law Journal.* New York City: ALM Media LLC. Retrieved December 20, 2018.

"Inmate locator". New Jersey Department of Corrections. Archived from the original on April 2, 2015. Retrieved January 17, 2012

Former New Jersey Assemblyman Neil M. Cohen Faces New Child Pornography Charge in Connection With Computer in Law Office Office of the New Jersey Attorney General, Anne Milgram.

https://web.archive.org/web/20221210025601/https://en.wikipedia.org/wiki/ Neil_M._Cohen

50. In Re Haldusiewicz 185 NJ 278 (2005)) involves a deputy attorney general who, like assemblyman Cohen was downloading child abuse images from his government office. He was sentenced to three years probation and a $1,500 fine.

In the matter of Frank L. Armour, Supreme Court of New Jersey, Disciplinary Review Board, Docket No. DRB 06-178, District Docket No. XIV-05-517E

51. NPR. "'Chasing Cosby' Author Says Covering the Cosby Case Was a Journey of Disillusionment." *NPR,* June 22, 2019. httpps://www.npr.org/transcripts/734570435.

52. Manning , Peter. "How 'Access Journalism' Is Threatening Investigative Journalism." The Conversation, December 20, 2018. https://theconversation.com/how-access-journalism-is-threatening-investigative-journalism-108831.

53. S.I. Syzmanski "terminated the examination because of the volume of suspected child pornography found, but stated that if the examination was continued more would be found."

"Attorney Joseph J. Haldusiewicz of Newark, NJ: Convicted Pervert." Ac   cessed November 15, 2022. http://www.noethics.net/News/index.php?   option=com_cont ent&view=article&id=2554:attorney-joseph-j-hal   dusiewicz-of-newark-nj-convicted-pervert-&Itemid=101.

54. *In the Matter of Joseph L. Haldusiewicz,* June 2005

55. "Second, although disciplinary cases are fact sensitive and must be decided on a case by case basis, possession, of child pornography is a very serious offense that, absent special circumstances, should be met with a long-term suspension. In our view, the six-month suspension imposed by the majority is insufficient."

Minority Opinion Haldusiewicz

56. Fink was arrested on child pornography charges in Delaware in May of 2000. In 2002 he was found guilty of 30 felony counts. This is a single example out of multiple cases where a lawyer who was disbarred in another state for child sex related crimes found a home in the New Jersey Bar. The court ruled in favor of a two-year suspension at the time. One member of the court argued that Fink should be prohibited from applying for reinstatement in New Jersey until or unless he was reappointed in Delaware. One voted recommending his disbarment and three abstained from voting.

In the matter of Kenneth E. Fink, Supreme Court of New Jersey, Disciplinary Review Board, Docket No. DRB 04-014

57. Rosanelli would also only receive a suspension for downloading child abuse materials. In a sadly ironic turn, the Office of Attorney Ethics took more issue with him failing to file an affidavit in his defense. OAE felt this "paint[ed] a very clear picture of an attorney who continues to 'thumb his nose' at the disciplinary system."

In Re Rosanelli 176 NJ 275 (2003).

58. Legacy.com. "Donald S. Rosanelli Esq's Obituary (2015) The Washington Post." Legacy.com, December 12, 2015. httpps://www.legacy.com/us/obituaries/washingtonpost/name/donald-rosanelli-obituary?id=6059897.

59. *In the Matter of Donald S. ROSANELLI, an Attorney at Law* (Attorney No.

030491981). Supreme Court of New Jersey, March 29, 2004.

60. New York Times. "How Democrats See the World." The New York Times, February 19, 2004. https://www.nytimes.com/2004/02/19/opinion/   1-how-democrats-see-the-world-457485.html.

60. *In Re Armour,* 192 N.J. 218: N.J.,

61. Ruddy used his position as a "volunteer athletic coach" to procure multiple preteen victims.

In Re Ruddy 130 NJ 85 (1992), Disciplinary Review Board docket no. DRB 91-391

62. Cunningham received treatment at the Adult Diagnostic and Treatment Center in Avenel, New Jersey. In the matter of Regan Clair Kenyon, Jr. Supreme Court of New Jersey, Disciplinary Review Board, Docket No. DRB 15-351, District Docket No. XIV-2011-0641E

63. "The charges included in the three-count complaint can be summarized briefly. Count One charged respondent David Witherspoon with sexual harassment, sexual discrimination and conflicts of interest, in violation of *RPC* 1.7(a)(2), *RPC* 4.4, *RPC* 8.4(d), and *RPC* 8.4(g). Count Two charged respondent with practicing law while ineligible based on respondent's failure to pay the required annual assessment to the Lawyers' Fund for Client Protection, in violation of *RPC* 5.5(a)(1) and *RPC* 8.4(d)."

In re Witherspoon, 203 N.J. 343, 345 (N.J. 2010)

64. "JUSTICE TIMPONE delivered the opinion of the Court. These consolidated matters involve attorneys, with no previous disciplinary history, who pled guilty to sex offenses in which their intended victims were children ranging in ages from nine to twelve. Respondents Mark G. Legato and Regan C. Kenyon, Jr., each pled guilty to third-degree attempted endangering the welfare of a child. Respondent Alexander D. Walter pled guilty to third-degree endangering the welfare of a child. Each respondent was sentenced to parole supervision for life (PSL), N.J.S.A. 2C:43–6.4, and subjected to the registration requirements of Megan's Law, N.J.S.A. 2C:7–1 to –11. Under Megan's Law, the respondents must, among other requirements, register their addresses, provide community notification, and submit to Internet registration. PSL subjects the respondents to supervision by the Division of Parole for at least fifteen years and to conditions such as counseling and limited Internet access and use."

In re Legato, 229 N.J. 173, (N.J. 2017)

65. "The Supreme Court of New Jersey held that a suspension from the practice of law for a period of one year was the appropriate discipline for an attorney who pled guilty in the Superior Court of New Jersey, Law Division, Bergen County to a one-count accusation charging him with "attempted endangering [of] the welfare of a child," in violation of N.J.S.A. 2C:5-1 and N.J.S.A. 2C:24-4. The respondent's offense involved communicating on several occasions, via an Internet chat room, with "Jay," who respondent believed was a 14 year old boy. Respondent told Jay that he wanted to take him to respondent's home to engage in numerous sexual acts, some of which were explicitly stated. The respondent was arrested when he appeared for the meeting with Jay."

Poritz, Hon. Deborah T., Chief Justice Supreme Court of New Jersey and David

E. Johnson, Jr. Director Office of Attorney Ethics. 2002 State of the Attorney Discipline System Report. May 20, 2003,

66.   Gernert also got away with a suspension.

Matter of Gernert. January 16, 1997.

He sexually assaulted multiple children between the ages of 6 and 12 in multiple municipalities.

"Schuylkill man faces child rape charges ** Shenandoah resident faces 39 counts. Police seek other victims." *The Morning Call,* Jan. 14, 2003, https://www.mcall.com/news/mc-xpm-2003-01-15-3459644-story.html

67.   Rickman, Rick. "No Prison Time for Child Molester from One of the NJ Shore's Wealthiest Families." New Jersey 101.5, August 10, 2022. httpps://nj1015.com/hal-sitt-deal-nj/.

68.   Brosnan, Erica. New York City Breaking News, Today's News | WCBS NewsRadio 880, February 1, 2022   https://www.audacy.com/wcbs880/news.

69.   Coleman, Chris. "Teacher with Salem County Special Services School District Facing Child Porn-Related Charges." WPG Talk Radio 95.5 FM, August 9, 2022. https://wpgtalkradio.com/teacher-with-salem-county-nj-special-services-school-district-facing-child-porn-related-charges/.

70.   United States Department of Justice. "Union County, New Jersey, Youth Organization Leader Charged with Possessing Images of Child Sexual Abuse." The United States Department of Justice, November 14, 2018. https://www.justice.gov/usao-nj/pr/union-county-new-jersey-woman-admits-role-2-million-debt-payoff-scheme.

71.   Everett, Rebecca. "Which 11 N.J. Cities Have the Most Sex Offenders and Why?" *Star-Ledger*, March 17, 2018. httpps://www.nj.com/news/2018/03/which_cities_have_the_most_sex_offenders_and_why.html.

Chapter 12: Nightmare on Skylite Drive

1.   Watson, Catherine. "Testimony Continues on Proposed Expansion of West field Stop & Shop." *Westernfield Leader.* May 16, 2013, https://www.goleader.com/13may16/13may16.pdf.

2.   Romankow and Galfy both associated with the American Legion and other veteran's groups and appeared at local Memorial Day Parades. Romankow offered the Memorial Prayer for the Memorial Day Parade in May 2019.

Rybolt, Barbara. "Berkeley Heights Honors the Fallen With a Memorial Day Parade and Ceremony," *TAPintoBerkeleyHeights,* May 27, 2019. httpps://www.tapinto.net/towns/berkeley-heights/sections/giving-back/articles/berkeley-heights-honors-the-fallen-with-a-memorial-day-parade-and-ceremony

"The three men raising the Stars and Stripes over the new Veterans Memorial Park in Berkeley Heights are from three different generations and have three very different life experiences.

Ted Romankow, a very youthful 75, was the Union County prosecutor for 11 years and is a former Berkeley Heights mayor." Di Ionno, Mark. NJ Advance Media.

"Citizens' Efforts Honor Vets in Time for Memorial Day | Di Ionno." Nj. May 25, 2016. httpps://www.nj.com/news/2016/05/ citizens_efforts_honor_vets_in_ time_for_memorial_d.html.

Galfy was a member of American Legion Post 328. He was personally "honored" on May 26, 2014 during the Clark Memorial Day parade in Union County.

Clark Monthly NJ. "Clark Memorial Day Parade," May 14, 2014. httpps://www. rennamedia.com/wp-content/ uploads/2014/05/ClkMay14.pdf

3. p16:11-12 "And initially he was living there uhm and there was an issue with some kind of a vagrant guy who robbed him when he was down there."

    p18:20-22 Galfy's brother describes him as "a very private individual when it came to his personal life and even Andy and I were talking while we were out there and it's amazing how little we know about what he did [...]."

    p21:12 James Galfy announces he will be "securing the house." Transcript of James Galfy. Docket/Case: 13001703, May 13, 2013. Detective Terrance Harrison, transcribed June 17, 2016

4. Neptune Society. "Norman Springer Obituary." Neptune Cremation Service, March 21, 2022. https://obituaries.neptunesociety.com/obituaries/las-vegas-nv/norman-springer-10667644.

5. Judge Robert Mega and Joseph Galfy were former partners at Kochanski, Mega and Galfy.

    "Kochanski, Mega & Galfy PC - Rahway , NJ - Company Data." https://www. dandb.com/businessdirectory/kochanskimegagalfypc-rahway-nj-12623287.html.

    Radaris lists Mega as an "associate" of Galfy.

    "Joseph J Galfy from 46 Starlite Dr, Clark, NJ 07066 - Radaris." n.d. Radaris.com. Accessed November 30, 2022. httpps://radaris.com/Joseph-Galfy/1187510223.

    Mega was saved as contact no. 18 in Galfy's phone.

    NJ.com, Tom Haydon | NJ Advance Media for. 2016. "3 Years and Counting; No Trial yet for YouTube Star." Nj. May 12, 2016. https://www.nj.com/ union/2016/05/ kai_the_hitchhiker_wages_legal_battle_from_jail_fi.html.

    Mega and Galfy were also connected through their membership in the Kiwanis club as will be discussed in the following note.

6. Galfy is listed as a chairman of an event for the Kiwanis involving youth.

    Rahway News Record/Clark Patriot. "Sporting Donation," p. 5, July 16, 1987. httpp:// www.digifind-it.com/rahway/data/news-record/1987/1987-07-16.pdf

7. Kochanski, Baron & Galfy was founded in 1989. Andy Baron, another named partner, was one of the few people James Galfy mentioned as knowing his brother well. https://www.buzzfile.com/business/Kochanski-Baron.And.Galfy-PC-732-382-5070

    https://www.linkedin.com/in/andy-baron-3601b5b

8. Kennedy, Marina. "Review: Luciano's Ristorante in Rahway NJ for Italian Food Lovers and Many More." BroadwayWorld.com, April 5, 2021. httpps://www.

broadwayworld.com/bwwfood-wine/article/BWW-Review-LUCIANOS-RISTORANTE-in-Rahway-NJ-for-Italian-Food-Lovers-and-Many-More-20210405.

9. "In other testimony Tuesday, Dr. Sandy Wang, a cardiologist, said he and his partner had treated Galfy since 1988 until April 2013. Wang listed more than eight medications and vitamins that Galfy took, including prescription drugs for heart and blood pressure, as well as Cialis for erectile dysfunction. Wang said it was unlikely that the dosages of medications Galfy received could have caused him to pass-out."

    Haydon, Tom. 2019. "Jurors Hear Recording of Kai the Hitchhiker Claiming Clark Lawyer 'Raped Me.'" *TAPinto.* April 16, 2019. httpps://www.tapinto.net/towns/clark/sections/law-and-justice/articles/jurors-hear-recording-of-kai-the-hitchhiker-claiming-clark-lawyer-raped-me-aa10ed0e-8896-4208-a451-2082c28cefc8.

10. Cialis and stimulants are often coingested in cases of "pnp" or "chemsex."

    "Sexualized Drug Use (Chemsex and Methamphetamine) and Men Who Have Sex with Men | the Ontario HIV Treatment Network." 2019. Ohtn.on.ca. May 28, 2019. https://www.ohtn.on.ca/sexualized-drug-use-chemsex-and-methamphetamine-and-men-who-have-sex-with-men/.

11. Dothée, Nick. 2020. "Opinion | 'Chemsex' Culture Almost Killed Me. This Is How I Survived." *NBC News.* February 29, 2020. httpps://www.nbcnews.com/think/opinion/gay-chemsex-culture-hollywood-almost-killed-me-how-i-survived-ncna1144576.

12. Ed Buck's "'Party and Play' fetish" combined with his near untouchable status due to political connections allowed him to murder multiple Black men over the course of years.

    Finnegan, Michael, and Hailey Branson-Potts. 2021. "Graphic Videos, Victims Lay Bare the Horror of Ed Buck's Deadly 'Party and Play' Fetish." *Los Angeles Times.* July 22, 2021. httpps://www.latimes.com/california/story/2021-07-22/ed-buck-methamphetamine-fatal-overdose-trial.

13. The Grand Jury transcript features multiple references to "securing the house."

14. Haydon, Tom, and Tomas Dinges. 2013. "Authorities Rule Death of 73-Year-Old Clark Lawyer a Homicide." *Star-Ledger.* May 15, 2013. httpps://www.nj.com/union/2013/05/   clark_mans_death_ruled_a_homic.html.

15. Kai had planned to visit Kim Conley.

    "Defendant's last phone contact was with Kimberly

    Conley-Burns. She testified at trial that she contacted defendant on Facebook, as he was an internet personality, informing him that if he were ever in New Jersey, she could find him a place to stay. On Saturday, May 11, the day before the murder, defendant told Conley-Burns that he had met a man in Times Square who drove him to New Jersey, and was planning to stay in Newark, which defendant mistakenly believed was where the victim lived. Defendant mentioned that the person was older, his name was Joe, and that he was a lawyer.

    "In a voicemail and text exchange, Conley-Burns warned defendant that Newark was dangerous and that he needed to be careful. He responded that he had found someone: 'a good person who put [him] up for the night.'

"Defendant and Conley-Burns planned to meet in Asbury Park on May 12, which was Mother's Day. Because of a family brunch, Conley-Burns did not appear when defendant arrived that morning, so they changed their plan, agreeing to go to Philadelphia the following day. Defendant texted Conley-Burns that he had 'to head up to Newark.'"

STATE OF NEW JERSEY, Plaintiff-Respondent, v. CALEB L. MCGILLVARY, Defendant-Appellant. A-4519-18. p. 2, August 4, 2021.

16. In Kai's interview with Detective Ho and during his testimony on the witness stand, he testified that Galfy was insistent on parking away from neighbors' view. In Harrison's interview with James Galfy, he remarks how even business associate and friend of Galfy's, Andy Baron, knew very little about his guarded, private life.

17. Thailand, one of Galfy's favorite vacation spots has long been a hub of child sex trafficking.

Rojanaphruk, Pravit, and Senior Staff Writer. 2019. "Thailand Still Hub of Global Sex Trafficking Rings: UN." Khaosod English. August 16, 2019. https://www.khaosodenglish.com/news/2019/08/16/thailand-still-hub-of-global-sex-trafficking-rings-un/.

18. Former mayor of Clark, Robert Ellenport, notes that Bali was one of Galfy's favorite vacation spots.

Associated Press. 2013. "Coffee Run Leads to Hatchet Hitchhiker Arrest." *Sarasota Herald-Tribune.* May 18, 2013. httpps://www.heraldtribune.com/story/news/2013/05/18/coffee-run-leads-to-hatchet-hitchhiker-arrest/29172788007/.

As for facts like Galfy's story of a young male friend who would become frequently intoxicated with him, his favorite vacation spot being Thailand a hub of child sex trafficking, for instance. "Even if relevant, 'evidence may be excluded if its probative value is substantially outweighed by the risk of. . . undue prejudice, confusion of issues, or misleading the jury."

Confusion of issues and misleading the jury weren't a problem when it served the state's argument though. Hence bait and switch regarding analysis on the mugs when no toxicology screen had been done and any analysis was after they'd been rinsed after being removed from the dishwasher.

Case 2:22-cv-04185-MCA Document 1-10 Filed 06/22/22 Pages 58, 60 of 101 PageIDs: 243, 245

19. "Zopiclone exhibits an adverse–effect profile characterized by poor quality of awakening, drowsiness, tiredness, nightmares, and a dry or bitter taste in the mouth."

Monti, J. M. 2017. "Pharmacotherapeutic Principles for Hypnotic Medications⊠." *ScienceDirect.* Elsevier. January 1, 2017. httpps://www.sciencedirect.com/science/article/pii/B9780128093245009718.

20. Canadian pharmacies and other grey market sources created a wild west situation online. Various pharmaceutical drugs and analogues of controlled substances flooded the online market through the 2010s.

Fittler, Andras, Gergely Bősze, and Lajos Botz. "Evaluating Aspects of Online Medication Safety in Long-Term Follow-up of 136 Internet Pharma   cies: Illegal Rogue Online Pharmacies Flourish and Are Long-Lived." Journal of medical Internet research, September 10, 2013. https://www.ncbi.nlm.nih.gov/pmc/articles/PMC3785996/.

21. "Could you help me out with this? I've never used one of these before." This claim, by the way, is disproved by Galfy's financial records, specifically a purchase from two weeks earlier from the same machine.

    Clerk of the Appellate Division, July 25, 2019, A-004519-18

22. McNamara mentions the tattoo on Kai's cheek being very visible after he had cut his hair.

    Police interview with John McNamara

23. The glasses and mugs that Kai alleges were drugged were found in a dishwasher as seen in crime scene photo (crime scene photo marked da 114). They were ordered to be rinsed and allowed to air dry before any tests were done.

    Supplementary Investigation Report. UCPO # 13-000083, Case Number 13-1093-5. May 17, 2013

    Some time between the first investigative reports on the 13th of May 2013 and Gardner's report from the 15th evidence related to Kai's claim of being drugged was destroyed.

    "From the kitchen we collected a BMW travel mug that was in the sink, and two coffee mugs that were in the drying rack next to the sink (items 67-69). Several glasses were observed in the kitchen's dishwasher, but there was evidence that the washer had been run and we did not collect them."

    Case 2:22-cv-04185-MCA Document 1-11 Filed 06/22/22 Page 5 of 8 PageID: 291

    Blood that was found on Galfy's penis was not tested to determine whether it was Kai's. In addition, a rape kit was run on Galfy which may have confused members of the jury.

    Union County Prosecutor's Office Forensic Laboratory, Lab#: L 13-2765 Report Number 2

24. At the Grand Jury, Peterson claimed that Shaikh said it didn't appear to have taken long. No motive was provided but also the contradictory claims that it was a vicious, premeditated act and also that the area was left clean and orderly denoting a short struggle.

    State of New Jersey v. Caleb McGillvary. Transcript of Grand Jury Hearing. Indictment No. 13-11-00946, page 44.

    The room was "clean and orderly" suggesting no long tussle from on equal footing as if Kai and Galfy were both vertical the pudgy lawyer's body would have knocked things out of place and into disarray. Detective Robert B. Henderson told the officers what to collect [DA 20]. They took the bedding despite Kai explaining the assault took place on the ground. They did not test the carpet where urine stains could have contained evidence of forcible intoxication. The possible paper funnel was not collected or analyzed and even the glasses were "rinsed clean" before any tests were run on them.

Case 2:22-cv-04185-MCA Document 1-7 Filed 06/22/22 Page 13 of 25 PageID: 73

25. Galfy's will lists "currency, coins or ingots of gold and other precious metals." Nothing of value belonging to Galfy was listed as stolen. In addition, gold and coins are a fairly untraceable form of currency.

Case 2:21-cv-17121-MCA-CLW Document 51-2 Filed 03/03/22 Page 3 of 6 PageID: 806

26. There were "some kind of blood tracks" in the hall outside of Galfy's bedroom.

State of New Jersey v. Caleb McGillvary. Transcript of Grand Jury Hearing. Indictment No. 13-11-00946, page 29.

27. No bruising on the neck according to the Grand Jury, bruises were found on the chest as well as "some kind of grab marks."

State of New Jersey v. Caleb McGillvary. Transcript of Grand Jury Hearing. Indictment No. 13-11-00946, pages 44, 50.

28. Galfy's neck was broken in what Dr. Shaikh claimed was a "crushing-type fracture." Shaikh, in addition to being mysteriously named in Galfy's will, was the medical examiner who performed Galfy's autopsy.

State of New Jersey v. Caleb McGillvary. Transcript of Grand Jury Hearing. Indictment No. 13-11-00946

Autopsy Report. U.C.S.O. Case Number 13-1093-1

29. It is mentioned that blood and semen were found on Galfy. "No further analysis was conducted" due to the low number of spermatozoa (likely a result of being in his 70s).

Union County Prosecutor's Office Forensic Laboratory, Lab#: L 13-2765 Report Number 2

"The following additional evidence item was received by Carmen Malanga on November 20, 2013 from Terrance Harrison of the Union County Prosecutor's Office.

003 blue towel, analysis: serological analysis on items 3, 14, 16, 39, 41, 72, 75, 98 through 100, 109, 119, and 122) for the presence of biological materials. Galfy's oral swab and anal swab were negative for semen but his underwear and penis were not.

UCPO Evidence Submittal Form: UCPO-13-000083; 13-1093-8 6/27/13 - 1355hrs, Ho, Detective Johnny

Galfy "can not be excluded as a possible source of the DNA" found on the blue towel. Kai is. "A minor DNA type at the D2S1338 genetic marker was detected for the sperm fraction of the interior front of the underwear (Item 109A SP). Due to limited genetic information, no conclusions can be reached regarding the possible sources of the minor type." Galfy is excluded from a "partial DNA profile" taken from the stained area of a left shoe (Item 119A). Kai "cannot be excluded as a possible source of the DNA" here.

UCPO Forensic Lab Report 2 page 4 of 7

Penis and external genital smears of Joseph Galfy returned "Intact spermatozoa and acrosomal heads seen."

Galfy, Joseph. Case No. 20-13-0421. D.O.D. 5/13/2013. Histopathology Report

30. *State of New Jersey v. Caleb McGillvary.* Transcript of Grand Jury Hearing. Indictment No. 13-11-00946

31. Çam, Deniz. 2019. "How a Du Pont Heir Avoided Jail Time for a Heinous Crime." *Forbes.* June 14, 2019. httpps://www.forbes.com/sites/denizcam/2019/06/14/how-a-du-pont-heir-avoided-jail-time-for-a-heinous-crime/.

32. State of New Jersey v. Caleb McGillvary. Transcript of Grand Jury Hearing. Indictment No. 13-11-00946, page 87.

33. Zezima, Katie. 2013. "Coffee Run Ends 'Hatchet-Wielding Hitchhiker's Run." *NBC10 Philadelphia.* May 17, 2013. httpps://www.nbcphiladelphia.com/news/local/phi-kai-arrest-jail/2088911/.

33. Judge Regina's "voluminous opinion" (as Judge Kirsch referred to it) denying Kai's motion to dismiss indictment featured blatant victim-blaming logic related to a picture Kai posed for with someone where he was smiling. "Defendant's conduct after the alleged sexual assault [...] is inconsistent with his claim that Galfy drugged him and attempted to rape him." [DA 70-71 P22-23] This is identical to the sort of justifications that rapists and other predators have used for years.

Case 2:22-cv-04185-MCA Document 1-7 Filed 06/22/22 Page 13 of 25 PageID: 73

Speaking of victim-blaming, Judge Kirsch carried the torch for Caulfield during the trial when he claimed Kai was responsible for not being given a rape kit, despite Peterson, Ho, and other UCPO investigators being aware of "signs of a sexual assault:"

"The failure of the State to administer a rape kit falls exclusively and entirely on Mr. McGillvary and his actions and inactions." [15T42-5 to 9].

Case 2:22-cv-04185-MCA Document 1-9 Filed 06/22/22 Page 56 of 87 PageID: 154

The state also tried to claim that Kai could not have been judged by virtue of his "remarkable memory as to extraordinary details." The science of traumatic memory is a complex thing. During traumatic events, some details may be detailed and easily accessible while others may be erroneous or entirely absent. Case 2:22-cv-04185-MCA Document 1-10 Filed 06/22/22 Page 53 of 101 PageID: 238

Gardner notes being called by Detective Henderson of UCPO and asked to return to Galfy's Clark residence. He and Sgt. Krill did so, meeting Henderson who explained "a suspect ha[d] been developed." It's also noted at this point that "through their investigation the UCPO developed information that a sexual assault may have occurred in the house. He requested we collect the bottles located in the garbage can in the garage, any cups or glasses in the kitchen, the bedding in the spare bedroom as well as any pill bottles in the house."

Gardner, Adrian. Supplementary Investigation Report, Case Number 13-1093-2.

5/17/13

Gardner admits she was asked "to collect the bottles from the garage and the pill bottles." [10T156-16 to 19] but admits that the bottles in the refrigerator "were not collected."

Case 2:22-cv-04185-MCA Document 1-9 Filed 06/22/22 Page 70 of 87 PageID: 168

34. "When you do rape kits, you will photograph the individual's body or at least make a diagram to show where injuries may be, including rug burns, which [Appellant] has said he had rug burns on his lower back. Either photographs or a diagram would have revealed that and neither was done." [15T15-23 to 16-3]

Ho even admitted that a "rape kit could have been done on [Apellant]" [13T103-1 to 3] as testing can be done within five days and Kai was apprehended and interrogated by Ho four days later.

Case 2:22-cv-04185-MCA Document 1-9 Filed 06/22/22 Page 55 of 87 PageID: 153

35. loc. cit.

36. CCTV footage of Kai cutting his hair at the train station, like so much other vital evidence that could have corroborated his claims, was unavailable due to "technical issues" according to Det. Michael Fong:

"Additional footage of McGillivary was sought for trip heading south. Asbury Park Police was contacted again at the beginning of June 2013, however due to a technical issue, their standard thirty day retention was interrupted and no video of May 13, 2013 could be viewed."

Case 2:22-cv-04185-MCA Document 1-18 Filed 06/22/22 Page 3 of 8 PageID: 325

Chapter 13: Two Sets of Laws

1. Person (legal definition). "The term "person" is defined in 18 U.S.C. § 2510(6) to mean any individual person as well as natural and legal entities. It specifically includes United States and state agents. According to the legislative history, "(o)nly the governmental units themselves are excluded." S.Rep. No. 1097, 90th Cong., 2d Sess. 90 (1968)."

"1048. Definition—'Person.'" 2015. Www.justice.gov. February 19, 2015. httpps://www.justice.gov/archives/jm/criminal-resource-manual-1048-definition-person.

2. Natural person definition: "A living, breathing human being, as opposed to a legal entity such as a corporation. Different rules and protections apply to natural persons and corporations, such as the Fifth Amendment right against self-incrimination, which applies only to natural persons."

"Natural Person Definition." Www.nolo.com. httpps://www.nolo.com/dictionary/natural-person-term.html.

3. Philip Fairbanks: I was going to ask, first off, now, you were with the Newark Police Department. New Jersey has kind of got a reputation when it comes to graft and corruption that goes back to the 19th century really, at least. But do you believe

that New Jersey is uniquely corrupt or is it a different flavor of corruption or more flamboyant, or is it just more out in the open, or is this something that happens pretty much in any state wherever?

Samuel Clark: Yes. Yes, it does. I was involved in some meeting with some people with corruptions at least 10 years ago. And one guy was saying, "Well, you guys in New Jersey, you know, my state is more corrupt than your state." But it's [inaudible 02:00] throughout the country, in my opinion. The same song, but different key, so to speak.

Interview with New Jersey police whistleblower, Samuel Clark,

4. Kelly Patrick was a victim of domestic violence at the hands of her spouse. The case was dropped due to the perpetrator being the brother of prosecutor, Dan Kasaris.

Douglas, Brian "BZ". "The Skeletons in Ohio Assistant Attorney General Dan Kasaris' Closet." Nov 1, 2021. https://bzdouglas.substack.com/p/the-skeletons-in-ohio-assistant-attorney

5. Douglas, Brian "BZ". "Unreliable Witnesses, Suppressed Evidence, and a Dead Whistleblower: The Prosecution of Tony Viola." Unreliable witnesses, suppressed evidence, and a dead whistleblower: The Prosecution of Tony Viola, November 24, 2021. htttpps://bzdouglas.substack.com/p/unreliable-witnesses-suppressed-evidence.

6. Walking the Wire. ": S1E6 - 'The Wire' with Jason Goodrick, Exec. Dir. of Cleveland Community Police Commission ." Apple Podcasts, July 4, 2022. https://podcasts.apple.com/us/podcast/s1e6-the-wire-with-jason-goodrick-exec-dir/id1617149009?i=1000568724312.

7. The line representing the growth rate and amount of wealth from various income groups between 1980 and 2017 has been called the "elephant curve." It gets its name from the shape of the curve. The "forehead" of the elephant represents 50% of the population. The curve of the "trunk" curving upward represents the top 1% and higher.

Pistoria, *Code of Capital*, page 15

8. Collins, Chuck. "Updates: Billionaire Wealth, U.S. Job Losses and Pandemic Profiteers." Inequality.org, May 6, 2022. htttpps://inequality.org/great-divide/updates-billionaire-pandemic/.

9. Hanauer, Nick, David M. Rolf, and Pitchfork Economics. "America's 1% Has Taken $50 Trillion from the Bottom 90%." Time, September 14, 2020. https://time.com/5888024/50-trillion-income-inequality-america/.

10. Lucas, Brian. "Impacts of Covid-19 on Inclusive Economic Growth in Middle-Income Countries." GSDRC, May 18, 2020. htttpps://gsdrc.org/publications/impacts-of-covid-19-on-inclusive-economic-growth-in-middle-income-countries/.

11. Pistoria describes how capital is made from two basic ingredients: an asset, and the legal code. Manipulating financial instruments and ensuring that the assets not only are converted to capital but to "increase its propensity to create wealth for its holder(s)."

Pistoria, Katherine. *Code of Capital*

12. Bernard Rudden described a situation he referred to as "feudal calculus" that has

held throughout the history of the ruling class. The system may have moved beyond simply amassing land as capital, but apart from that the game is just as rigged against those without the money to afford equal treatment before the law.

Pistoria, Katherine. *Code of Capital*. p. 22

13.   Lambert Worldwide came to my attention when they asked me to pull some reporting I'd done (with the help of Alissa Fleck) related to the Houston ponzi ring. US-based law firm Lambert Worldwide, and Atkins Thomson sent legal letters to five Maltese news outlets trying to get stories pulled that alleged British-Azeri businessman Turab Musayev was involved in the murder of journalist Daphne Caruna Galizia.

Press-ECPMF. 2020. "Malta: Five Media Outlets Threatened by Lawyers of British-Azeri Business Owner." European Centre for Press and Media Freedom. July 12, 2020. https://www.ecpmf.eu/five-maltese-newspapers-threatened-by-lawyers-for-british-azeri-business-owner/.

14.   The first letter, titled, "courtesy request" was sent on 1 May 2020 to Malta Today by Lambert Worldwide in relation to an article published on its website mentioning Musayev. The letter demanded the media outlet remove the online article or undertake actions such as "de-indexing the article, or perhaps, removing our client's name from the article." The letter further stated that "they are not permitted to reveal any details at this time." According to the firm, "this letter does not constitute a notice of intent to take legal actions."

The Shift Team. 2020. "Mapping Media Freedom Registers Threat by Turab Musayev on Media." *The Shift*. July 12, 2020. httpps://theshiftnews.com/2020/07/12/mapping-media-freedom-registers-threat-by-turab-musayev-on-media/.

15.   Turab Musayev is still being mentioned in connection with the unsolved car bomb assassination of Galizia.

Agius, Matthew. 2022. "Senior Electrogas Consortium Players 'Not Being Investigated over Caruana Galizia Murder.'" *MaltaToday.com.mt*. January 12, 2022. https://www.maltatoday.com.mt/news/   court_and_police/114338/electrogas_consortium_players_not_   being_investigated_over_caruana_galizia_murder#.Y4ev2X3MK3A.

16.   London and New York are two of the major financial centers of the world. Taylor, Chloe. 2019. "New York Overtakes London as World's Financial Capital amid Brexit Chaos, Survey Claims." *CNBC*. May 28, 2019. httpps://www.cnbc.com/2019/05/28/new-york-replaces-london-as-global-financial-capital-amid-brexit-chaos.html.

17.   Max Weber argued that the state holds a monopoly over violent means of physical coercion.

Jachtenfuchs, Markus. "The Monopoly of Legitimate Force: Denationalization, or Business as Usual?" Chapter. In *Transformations of the State?*, edited by Stephan Leibfried and Michael Zürn, 37–52. Cambridge: Cambridge University Press, 2005. doi:10.1017/CBO9780511752193.002.

18.   The actual business of writing policy is often more in the hands of lobbyists than the

politicians themselves. K Street firms have long been pushing agendas in D.C.

Lillis, Mike. 2019. "Anti-Corruption Group Hits Congress for Ignoring K Street, Capitol Hill 'Revolving Door.'" The Hill. May 29, 2019. https://thehill.com/business-a-lobbying/business-a-lobbying/445888-anti-corruption-group-hits-congress-for-ignoring-k/.

Fuchs, Hailey. "American Influence Has a New Address on State Street." *POLITICO,* June 22, 2022. https://www.politico.com/news/2022/06/22/statehouse-lobbying-rise-k-street-00041217.

OpenSecrets. 2019. "Recent Ex-Members of Congress Head to K Street as 'Shadow Lobbying' Escalates." OpenSecrets News. May 30, 2019. httpps://www.opensecrets.org/news/2019/05/recent-ex-members-of-congress-head-to-k-street-as-shadow-lobbying-escalates/.

19. Pistoria, p. 220

20. An, Ran. *Lawyers as Corruption Brokers: the" Production" of a Corrupt Legal Profession and the Chinese State.* McGill University (Canada), 2019.

21. "Anti-camping" legislation (thinly veiled anti-homeless laws) has been popping up in several states, often with very similar language. Of the nine bills introduced in six states that Pew Trusts mentioned, many are strikingly similar to a model bill by the Cicero Institute. Cicero Institute was founded by the co-founder of Palantir a corporation which has been involved in migrant surveillance, predictive policing, and other controversial measures.

    Hernández, Kristian. 2022. "Homeless Camping Bans Are Spreading. This Group Shaped the Bills." Pew.org. April 8, 2022. httpps://www.pewtrusts.org/en/research-and-analysis/blogs/stateline/2022/04/08/homeless-camping-bans-are-spreading-this-group-shaped- the-bills.

22. Covid-19 and the ensuing global recession has put stress on homeless shelters and many have buckled under the stress.

    "Shelter Closings." 2020. National Low Income Housing Coalition. May 3, 2020. https://nlihc.org/coronavirus-and-housing-homelessness/shelter-closings.

23. The Covid-19 pandemic hit the working class and poor hardest, but despite that billionaires had record profits. Trillions were shaved off the holdings of those who have little while extra trillions went to companies like Amazon. US billionaire wealth surged over 35% between January 2020 and April 28, 2021.

    Daniel, Will. 2022. "U.S. Companies Posted Record Profits in 2021, Jacking up Prices as Inflation Surged." *Fortune.* March 31, 2022. httpps://fortune.com/2022/03/31/us-companies-record-profits-2021-price-hikes-inflation/.

Peterson-Withorn, Chase. 2022. "How Much Money America's Billionaires Have Made during the Covid-19 Pandemic." *Forbes.* April 28, 2022. httpps://www.forbes.com/sites/chasewithorn/2021/04/30/american-billionaires-have-gotten-12-trillion-richer-during-the-pandemic/?sh=236bcb8af557.

24. The war in Afghanistan cost taxpayers over $2.3 Trillion.

    Brown University. 2021. "Human and Budgetary Costs to Date of the U.S. War in Afghanistan, 2001-2022 | Figures | Costs of War." The Costs of War. August 2021.

httpps://watson.brown.edu/costsofwar/figures/ 2021/human-and-budgetary-costs-date-us-war-afghanistan-2001-2022.

25. Mari, Francesca. 2020. "A $60 Billion Housing Grab by Wall Street." *The New York Times*, March 5, 2020, sec. Magazine. httpps://www.nytimes.com/2020/03/04/magazine/wall-street-landlords.html.

26. "Laws regulating the movement, residence, employment, and labor of the poor, and especially of poor African Americans in states with burgeoning free populations, demonstrate how mobility, when enacted by the poor and by non-whites, was classified as a criminal action in the eighteenth- and nineteenth-century United States. In the Upper South especially, these laws had the express goal of attaching to all people of color the potential consequences of enslavement. This essay will link these ideas by tracing mobility and its construction as a classed and raced activity, as threats to existing labor regimes and social systems. This was most commonly and notoriously done through the policing of vagrancy, which allowed authorities to punish the poor, most punitively, in the South, African Americans, for unemployment or a reluctance to enter into a particular labor contract. This essay argues that the power dynamics of the South can be read clearly in the classed and raced regulation of vagrancy and geographical mobility in the antebellum era."

   O'Brassill-Kulfan, Kristin, Matthew Hild and Keri Leigh. "Vagrant Negroes": The Policing of Labor and Mobility in the Upper South in the Early Republic Reconsidering Southern Labor History: Race, Class, and Power. University Press of Florida, 2018

27. Reiman, Jeffrey, and Paul Leighton. *Rich get richer and the poor get prison, the: Ideology, class, and criminal justice.* Routledge, 2015.

28. CBSNews. "Meat Scandal at Sara Lee." *CBS News*, August 30, 2001. httpps://www.cbsnews.com/news/meat-scandal-at-sara-lee/.

29. Hoskins, Peter. "Johnson & Johnson to Replace Talc-Based Powder with Cornstarch." *BBC News,* August 12, 2022. httpps://www.bbc.com/news/business-62514263.

30. MacMillan, Carrie. "Is My Sunscreen Safe?" Yale Medicine, August 1, 2022. https://www.yalemedicine.org/news/is-sunscreen-safe.

31. Edney, Anna. "A Threat of Contaminated Drugs Persists Four Years Later." *Bloomberg.com*, August 17, 2022. httpps://www.bloomberg.com/news/newsletters/2022-08-17/a-threat-of-contaminated-drugs-persists-four-years-later.

32. The Holder Memorandum brings up "collateral consequences" as an issue to take into account when considering prosecuting a large corporation. On page 4, Foster notes: "A critical problem with this collateral consequences policy is that it has created a public perception that the legal system is unfair, with real and perceived prosecutorial preferences for corporations with many employees and shareholders and great economic impact."

   Foster goes on to point out how corporations are given a favorable position in the legal process. This issue, she argues, threatens faith and trust in the legal process.

   "Section II of this Article provides some historical context for the term "collateral consequences" and its policies. As explained in detail below, the term collateral consequences has been used to describe the consequences individuals and corporations face if charged with and/or found guilty of a crime. Most people think of criminal con- sequences in terms of incarceration and/or fines, but the consequences are much more extensive. There are statutory consequences, such as loss of voting privileges, and de facto consequences, such as reputa- tional and emotional harm.17 The policy of collateral consequences, as implemented by the DOJ, takes such statutory and non-statutory consequences into consideration when exercising prosecutorial discre- tion to determine whether to prosecute systemic institutions or pursue an alternative course of action such as DPAs. But collateral conse- quences are not taken into consideration for individuals or non- systemic institutions."

Foster, Sharon E. Too Big to Prosecute: Collateral Consequences, Systemic Institutions and the Rule of Law

33. Berman, Jillian. "Eric Holder's 1999 Memo Helped Set the Stage for 'Too Big to Jail.'" *Huffington Post,* June 4, 2013

34. Douglas, Danielle. "Holder Concerned Megabanks Too Big to Jail." *The Washington Post,* March 6, 2013. https://www.washingtonpost.com/ business/economy/holder-concerned-megabanks-too-big-to-jail/ 2013/03/06/6fa2b07a-869e-11e2-999e-5f8e0410cb9d_story.html.

35. Barnett, Cynthia. "Measurement of White-Collar Crime Using Uniform Crime Reporting (UCR) Data." Measurement of White-Collar Crime Using Uniform Crime Reporting (UCR) Data | Office of Justice Programs, 2000. https://www.ojp.gov/ncjrs/virtual-library/ abstracts/measurement-white-collar-crime-using-uniform-crime-reporting-ucr.

36. Sivin, Miller & Roche LLP. "Some Stats on White Collar Crime: ." Sivin, Miller & Roche LLP Attorneys at Law, March 14, 2022. httpps://www.sivinandmiller.com/ blog/2022/03/some-stats-on-white-collar-crime/.

37. White, Lawrence. "HSBC Draws Line under Mexican Cartel Case after Five-Years on Probation." *Reuters,* December 11, 2017. httpps://www.reuters.com/article/us-hsbc-usa-idUSKBN1E50YA.

38. Woodman, Spencer. "HSBC Moved Vast Sums of Dirty Money after Paying Record Laundering Fine." *ICIJ,* March 21, 2020. httpps://www.icij.org/ investigations/fincen-files/hsbc-moved-vast-sums-of-dirty-money-after-paying-record-laundering-fine/.

39. Boulder Criminal Defense Lawyer. "Boulder Marijuana Charge Defense Lawyer: Colorado Criminal Defense Attorney." Boulder Criminal Defense Lawyer, October 5, 2018. httpps://www.boulderdefenseattorney.com/top-10-non-violent-marijuana-lifelong-sentencing-cases/.

40. Loudis, Jessica. "In Mexico, 'the Cartels Do Not Exist': A Q&A with Oswaldo Zavala." *The Nation,* April 22, 2019. httpps://www.thenation.com/article/archive/ oswaldo-zavala-interview-mexico-cartels/.

41. In Tolka's book, he cites a case that occurred during the New Orleans consent decree. Federal investigators had uncovered evidence that a police officer hired a drug-dealer to kill someone. In this case, the officer was actually prosecuted. A

similar case in Youngstown, Ohio, however "involved cops hiring a hitman to kill a government witness for a jailed coke-dealer was ignored and the cops stayed in their positions while their department was under DOJ insight."

Tolka, Tim. *Blue Mafia: Police Brutality and Consent Decrees in Ohio*. April 27, 2018. page 153

42.   Dyer, Joel. T*he Perpetual Prisoner Machine*. 2000

43.   "Some big high-roller once said: 'The business of America is business.' And I'm happy to report the criminal justice business is booming. With heavy industry headed south, small towns are battling for state contracts to build correctional facilities. Who'd have thunk it? Nice, upstanding citizens begging to have rapists, drug dealers and murderers right in their own backyard."

So begins the episode "Town Without Pity" in the fourth season of *Oz*. The narration goes on to explain that (at the time, in the late 90s) seven out of ten inmates came from cities, but most prisons were in rural areas. It's pointed out that census numbers are used to count the inmates (often people of color) for the census meaning tax dollars are allocated away from struggling communities that result in high crime.

Oz. "A Town Without Pity," Season 4, Episode 7.

44.   The 13th Amendment promises that "[n]either slavery nor involuntary servitude, except as a punishment for crime whereof the party shall have been duly convicted, shall exist within the United States, or any place subject to their jurisdiction." In essence, far from making slavery unconstitutional it guarantees the legitimacy and legality of slavery "as a punishment."

13th Amendment of the Constitution

45.   Billionaire Mike Bloomberg's news outlet feigned outrage at Russia's plan to put prisoners to work. Apparently, when Russia does it, it's more like a gulag than when Bloomberg (who used unpaid prison labor for his presidential campaign) does.

Quinn, Aine. 2021. "It's Not a Gulag, Russia Says of Plan to Put Prisoners to Work." *Bloomberg.com*, June 9, 2021. https://www.bloomberg.com/news/articles/2021-06-09/it-s-not-a-gulag-russia-says-of-plan-to-put-prisoners-to-work.

Washington, John. 2019. "Mike Bloomberg Exploited Prison Labor to Make 2020 Presidential Campaign Phone Calls." *The Intercept*. December 24, 2019. https://theintercept.com/2019/12/24/mike-bloomberg-2020-prison-labor/.

46.   Semler, Stephen. How much did the US spend on police, prisons in FY2021?, January 20, 2022. htttps://stephensemler.substack.com/p/how-much-did-the-us-spend-on-police.

47.   Iritani, Evelyn. "Do Private Prisons Lead to Higher Incarceration Rates?" UCLA Anderson Review, March 13, 2019. https://anderson-review.ucla.edu/private-prisons/.

48.   *Class, Race, Gender and Crime*, p. 57

49.   In addition to *Forbes*, *The National Review*, and *HuffingtonPost* also placed puff pieces for Epstein after his initial conviction for trafficking minors.

Hsu, Tiffany. 2019. "Jeffrey Epstein Pitched a New Narrative. These Sites Published It." *The New York Times*, July 21, 2019, sec. Business. httpps://www.nytimes.com/2019/07/21/business/media/jeffrey-epstein-media.html.

50.   Perper, Rosie. "The Former Editor-in-Chief of Vanity Fair Is Said to Have Found a Dead Cat's Head Outside His Home after the Magazine Began Pursuing a Story about Jeffrey Epstein." Business Insider, August 23, 2019. https://www.businessinsider.com/npr-vanity-fair-editor-in-chief-cat-head-jeffrey-epstein-2019-8.

51.   Longreads. "How the Cosby Story Finally Went Viral — and Why It Took so Long," June 6, 2019. https://flipboard.com/article/how-the-cosby-story-finally-went-viral-and-why-it-took-so-long/f-5f6f262866%2Flongreads.com.

52.   Molloy, Tim. "Disney Suspends Music Exec Jon Heely after Felony Child Sex Abuse Charges." *TheWrap*, December 9, 2017. httpps://www.thewrap.com/jon-heely-disney-music-child-sex/.

INDEX

Symbols 0-9

A

B

M

Y

Z

www.ingramcontent.com/pod-product-compliance
Lightning Source LLC
Chambersburg PA
CBHW020752300326
41914CB00050B/166